The Pashtun Tribes in
AFGHANISTAN

The Pashtun Tribes in
AFGHANISTAN

BEN ACHESON

Pen & Sword
MILITARY

AN IMPRINT OF PEN & SWORD BOOKS LTD.
YORKSHIRE - PHILADELPHIA

First published in Great Britain in 2023 by
PEN AND SWORD MILITARY
An imprint of
Pen & Sword Books Limited
Yorkshire – Philadelphia

ISBN 978 1 39906 920 5

A CIP catalogue record for this book is available from the British Library.

Typeset in Times New Roman 10/13 by
SJmagic DESIGN SERVICES, India.
Printed and bound in the UK by CPI Group (UK) Ltd.

Pen & Sword Books Limited incorporates the imprints of Atlas, Archaeology,
Aviation, Discovery, Family History, Fiction, History, Maritime, Military, Military
Classics, Politics, Select, Transport, True Crime, Air World, Frontline Publishing,
Leo Cooper, Remember When, Seaforth Publishing, The Praetorian Press,
Wharncliffe Local History, Wharncliffe Transport, Wharncliffe True Crime and
White Owl.

For a complete list of Pen & Sword titles please contact
PEN & SWORD BOOKS LIMITED
47 Church Street, Barnsley, South Yorkshire S70 2AS, United Kingdom
E-mail: enquiries@pen-and-sword.co.uk
Website: www.pen-and-sword.co.uk

Or

PEN AND SWORD BOOKS
1950 Lawrence Rd, Havertown, PA 19083, USA
E-mail: Uspen-and-sword@casematepublishers.com
Website: www.penandswordbooks.com

Contents

Acknowledgements

If there is one lesson I learned from writing a book, it is that it is an act of perseverance and an almost daily battle against self-doubt. It takes constant effort to quieten internal and external voices that question why you would be so arrogant as to write one.

To be victorious, you need allies. My main allies, without whom this book would not have been possible, were my parents. They put up with my living with them for many months, giving me the space to write at my own pace, with only occasional questions about when I would get a job and an apartment of my own! My father deserves special mention as he didn't envision spending his retirement being my sounding board, editor, proofreader, counsellor and friend.

I am grateful to Conor McCracken for reading each section as I finished it and for providing critical comments that were encouraging rather than deflating. Thanks also to Megan Gooch, Chris Smyth, Michael Woolslayer, Emma Williamson, Marika Theros, Dan Tomlinson, Sarah De Mol and Natalia Leigh for their constant support and encouragement. Marika and Natalia merit particular praise for their valuable suggestions and expert feedback on various drafts.

Multiple mentors also deserve a mention. Sir Nicholas Kay and Franz-Michael Mellbin constantly coached me through difficult times in Afghanistan and never ceased to provide me with opportunities – the hallmark of great leaders. I am also grateful to Struan Stevenson, who gave me my first opportunity to go to Afghanistan as well as helping to hone my writing ability.

Thanks also to Generals Scott Miller, Steve Marks and Miles Brown, Rear-Admiral Nicholas Homan, Kim Field, James Glancy, Aemal Karukhale, Megan Minnion, Ejaz Malikzada, John Alexander and Ken Handelman for the encouragement that they did not know they gave me. Each made throwaway comments that reminded me to persevere when self-doubt took hold.

A number of professionals helped me get this book over the line. I am grateful to Sarah Moloney for her brilliant illustrations, Alex Kirby for his thoughtful approach to the jacket and all the team associated with Pen & Sword Books – Tara Moran, Harriet Fielding, Olivia Camozzi-Jones and George Chamier. Tara, in particular, took the time to understand my vision when many others didn't. I am also indebted to Maren Meinhardt, my freelance editor who worked towards my unconventional vision rather derailing me from it. Book writing is a solitary, lonely journey, but Maren became the teammate I needed to direct me to the finish-line.

Most of all, thanks to my former colleagues but forever friends Wali Ahmadzai and Khalid Hamdard. They are constant reminders of the good that exists in Afghanistan. If I have any grasp of Afghan nuance, it is because of Wali. Years spent sharing an office with him were an honour, a privilege and an education – particularly when it came to the Pashtun tribes. Khalid is the person I trust most for feedback on my own understanding of Afghanistan. He is unfailing in his ability to provide the cold, hard, unvarnished truth, but to deliver it with a mischievous glint in his eye that provokes a smile no matter how painful it may be to hear. His meticulous editing of the final draft helped me identify – and navigate – some of the more controversial topics. I am grateful that they were both willing to let me immerse myself in their stories and be patient with my questions. This book is a tribute to them more than anyone.

Foreword

Sir Nicholas Kay

I knew Ben Acheson in Kabul in the years leading up to the chaotic withdrawal of NATO forces in August 2021. He was for a while my chief political adviser – my eyes, ears, mouthpiece and oftentimes my brain. I knew he knew a lot about Afghanistan. But I never imagined he knew quite this much!

The Pashtun Tribes of Afghanistan is a tour de force – combining erudite analysis, historical research, atmospheric story-telling, page-turning prose and above all, profound passion. Ben draws the reader in, and we, like him, run the risk of becoming intoxicated by the romance of the tribes, bewildered by the complexities and ambiguities of history and unsure how to make sense of it now and in the future.

I used to drive Ben mad when we worked in NATO by always asking, 'So what?' and warning of the risk of 'paralysis by analysis'. I was too often suffering from what Ben describes here as 'strategic conceit' – the exaggerated belief that UK or NATO policy and actions could determine the course of Afghan history. His book is a powerful corrective and sets out clearly how Afghanistan's past and present have been shaped decisively by deep-seated dynamics within Pashtun tribes, between tribes, and between those tribes and the central state.

Like so many ambassadors, generals and foreign advisers, I felt I had neither the luxury of time nor access to sufficiently reliable information. Policy judgements and interventions were often improvised and instinctive. Of course, we tried to build personal relationships with as wide a range of Afghans as possible – and in as many places as we could reach. Often, with Ben, I have spent hours in meetings sat on the ground, sometimes in the open air, listening to Pashtun tribal elders. My respect for them and empathy only got me so far. To borrow from T. S. Eliot, I often came away from these 'shuras' feeling that I had had the experience but missed the meaning.

Ben says this is the book he needed when he began working in Afghanistan and that he hopes it will serve as a toolkit for those who will engage in the future with Afghanistan. I am sure he is right, although to his credit Ben is also quick to acknowledge its inevitable limitations. As he says, 'With so many cultural complexities and subtleties, the reality is that an outsider, no matter how well briefed or how attuned to Afghan atmospherics, can only ever have a partial understanding of the Pashtun tribes.'

Ben also rightly points to the need not to overlook Afghanistan's diverse population. Its Tajik, Uzbek, Hazara, Turkmen, Baluch and Nuristani peoples have also been protagonists in Afghanistan's story.

Some may say the UK and the 'West' can now turn the page on Afghanistan. We left in August 2021. We are not going back. The Taliban are in charge, and Afghans will need to chart their own future. So Ben's scholarship and practical toolkit will gather dust on a shelf.

I beg to differ. I have been in and out of Afghanistan since 1976. In less than five decades I have witnessed multiple seismic upheavals there. Nothing has stayed the same for long – regimes and leaders have come and gone, foreign powers have invaded and fled, millions of Afghans have moved across the globe, millions of lives have been blighted by Afghan drugs, regional and international terror groups have burgeoned. I doubt the next years will be so different. Tumultuous change will happen again. We ignore Afghanistan at our peril. *The Pashtun Tribes* should be required reading for all who engage with Afghans as we and they start one more chapter in an epic that spans the ages.

Figures

Note on figures and spellings of tribal names

Most figures in this book outline various family trees or lineages within the Pashtun tribal structure. These trees have been simplified to focus only on the most prominent tribes or key individuals. They could be expanded, but doing so would over-complicate them and undermine their meaning by flooding them with too many names, tribal affiliations and locations. For example, Figure 7 shows a man named Painda Khan, whose three sons shaped Afghan history. Painda Khan, in fact, had between twenty-two and twenty-four known sons, by multiple wives. But to depict them all would unnecessarily over-crowd the diagram without adding any value.

Throughout the book, tribal names are given in the most common spellings used today. But different spellings may be encountered in other sources. They can vary by locality or speaker. Some have also changed over the years. For example, the tribe now known as 'Durrani' will be found as 'Dooraunee' in nineteenth-century texts. Tribes like 'Alikozai' can also be spelled as 'Alokozai' or 'Alokozay'. Terms such as 'Wazir' or 'Tiga' can also be spelled 'Wazeer' or 'Teega'. For consistency, 'Emir' has generally been used throughout this book rather than 'Amir'. Such variations and interchangeability simply have to be accepted as inevitable when dealing with Afghanistan.

Maps

Note on maps

The maps showing the spread of the Pashtun tribes are approximations only. The tribes defy neat mapping, especially since Afghanistan's recent conflicts prevent comprehensive collection of ethnic geospatial data, as well as having induced mass migrations and displacements. Endless Afghan turmoil since the 1980s has led to so much mixing of tribes that no clean-cut, easy-to-read tribal map will ever be entirely accurate. There will also be variations – even among Pashtuns – in how various regions are defined. The maps in this book should be approached with this in mind.

For example, there are varying views on the three Pashtun regions in Map 3. Herat Province is sometimes included in the region known as 'Loy Kandahar'. The extent of the 'Loya Paktia' region varies among observers. This book includes Logar Province on the advice of a Pashtun expert, although some purists would dispute this. Other more liberal observers would also argue that parts of Ghazni and even Wardak provinces should be included. Different names will also be encountered. The 'Loy Nangarhar' region is often colloquially known as 'Loy Mashriqi' (Mashriqi means 'Eastern').

Map 5 outlines the approximate spread of individual tribes within the Pashtun Belt. For readability, only the larger tribes or those prominent in this book are named. The names in bold represent tribes that are spread across a larger swathe of territory, while the other names signify a more specific area that the tribe is traditionally associated with or has an attachment to.

Map 6 is based on first-hand engagement with local contacts in each province, but must also be considered as an approximation. The size and spread of the shaded areas are rough and are used only to illustrate the general area of small Pashtun pockets outside the Pashtun Belt whose presence is explained in this book.

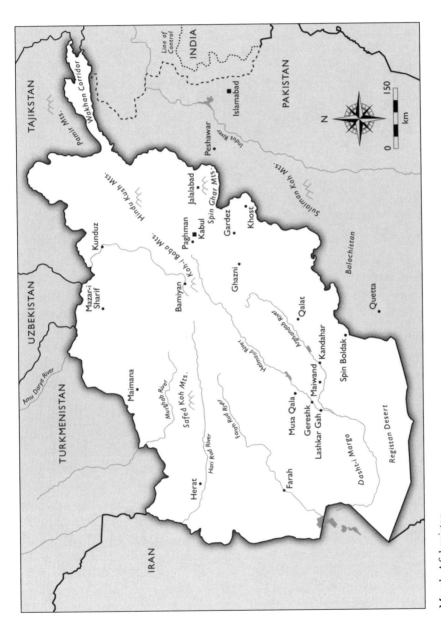

Map 1: Afghanistan

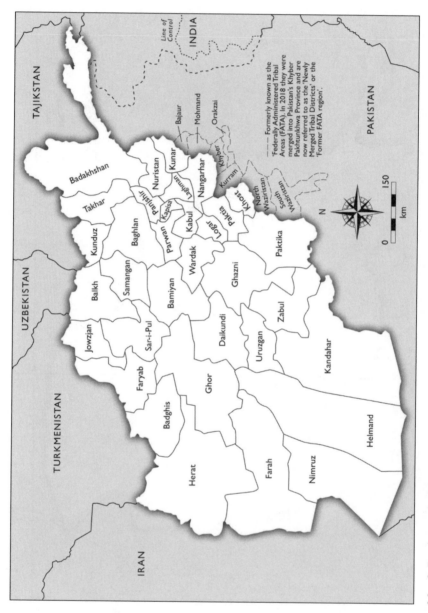

Map 2: Provinces of Afghanistan

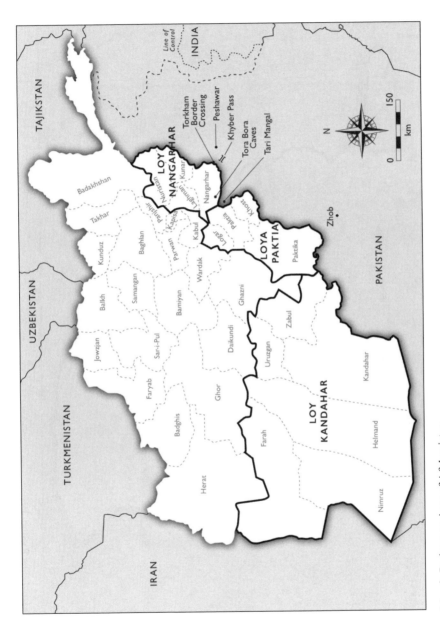

Map 3: Pashtun regions of Afghanistan

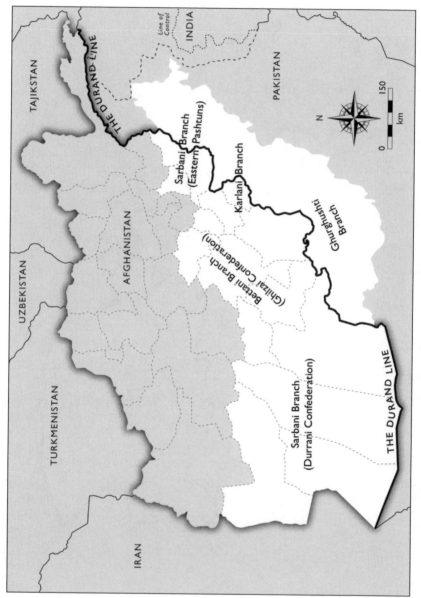

Map 4: The Pashtun Belt

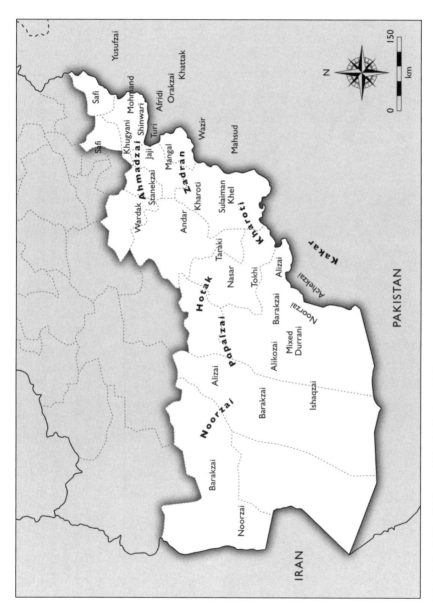

Map 5: Individual Tribes within the Pashtun Belt

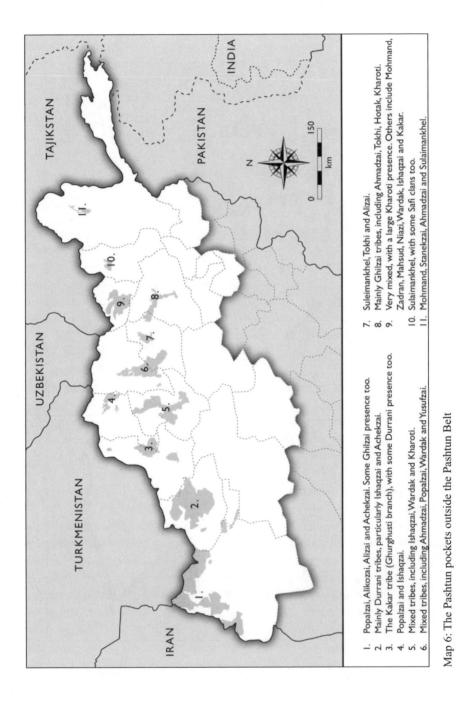

1. Popalzai, Alikozai, Alizai and Achekzai. Some Ghilzai presence too.
2. Mainly Durrani tribes, particularly Ishaqzai and Achekzai.
3. The Kakar tribe (Ghurghusti branch), with some Durrani presence too.
4. Popalzai and Ishaqzai.
5. Mixed tribes, including Ishaqzai, Wardak and Kharoti.
6. Mixed tribes, including Ahmadzai, Popalzai, Wardak and Yusufzai.
7. Suleimankhel, Tokhi and Alizai.
8. Mainly Ghilzai tribes, including Ahmadzai, Tokhi, Hotak, Kharoti.
9. Very mixed, with a large Kharoti presence. Others include Mohmand, Zadran, Mahsud, Niazi, Wardak, Ishaqzai and Kakar.
10. Sulaimankhel, with some Safi clans too.
11. Mohmand, Stanekzai, Ahmadzai and Sulaimankhel.

Map 6: The Pashtun pockets outside the Pashtun Belt

Preface

This is the book that I needed. It is the book that I wanted. But it is the book I could never find.

It contains insights I wish I had had when I first stepped onto Afghan soil in June 2012, crossing the hazy Amu Darya River from Tajikistan into Afghanistan's bakingly hot Kunduz Province. I was supporting a high-level delegation of European politicians on a fact-finding mission to learn about heroin flows coming to Europe from Afghanistan via Russia. As the delegates exchanged pleasantries and sipped green tea with Afghan Border Police in a stuffy meeting room, word came that the Taliban were approaching the checkpoint. Panic ensued.

The delegates were bundled into armoured Land Cruisers and sped across the bridge back to Tajikistan, where the Tajik President's personal helicopter was waiting to whisk them to the capital, Dushanbe. During their chaotic escape, one worried politician shouted to me that their passports had been given to the border guards to get an Afghan stamp as proof of their visit to the world's most dangerous warzone. After a frantic search I located them and raced to the helicopter just as its blades started spinning. That was my first experience inside Afghanistan. My last was similar. It involved another helicopter, this time flying across Kabul in March 2020 to reach one of the last planes back to Europe before COVID locked down the world.

This book reflects much of what I learned during my time working as a Political Adviser for NATO and other institutions in Afghanistan, having been responsible for building relationships with Afghans in Kabul and across the country. It contains what I would tell others who will work in, or on, the Afghan context in the future, as well as the things that I constantly had to re-explain to Ambassadors, Generals and other decision-makers in the international coalition. It is written as a 'Things We Needed to Know' rather than a diary of personal experiences or complaints about any international failures since 2001 – both of which subjects have been covered by many, many other authors. My own positionality is important to underline here, because the 'We' refers to Westerners rather than Afghans, and strategists or policymakers rather than tactical troops or village-level aid workers. It is not an operational field guide to advise deploying personnel on how to respect personal space or avoid breaking cultural taboos. Those exist already.

That said, this book is shaped by my own experience of witnessing the astounding lack of cultural understanding among highly paid foreign 'experts' sent to find solutions to Afghan problems. I think of the time when an international colleague confidently lauded her ability to analyse Afghan dynamics while being unable to point to Afghanistan on a map; or when I watched a senior Western official, in a highly classified meeting, be reminded that Islamabad is not in Afghanistan but is actually the capital of Pakistan.

These examples reflect the strategic narcissism and over-optimism about our own grasp of Afghan dynamics that consistently damaged post-2001 Western efforts in Afghanistan. It was evident right up until the end of the twenty-year international military presence that we failed to appreciate why certain actors think and act as they do. No outsider can ever acquire the instinctive contextual understanding of someone who has lived it – and it is an insult to think otherwise – but not enough effort was made to read the subtext of what interlocutors were telling us. Afghans, including the Taliban, were always one step ahead of us as we tried to figure out what happened but rarely grasped why it happened or what was likely to happen next. This strategic narcissism poisoned our relationships – and will continue to do so unless it is challenged. Afghans grew tired of it and increasingly interacted with Westerners only superficially, while they worked in the deeper layers of Afghan dynamics. At best, they hid their frustrations, symbolically patted us on the head and engaged nicely until we left. At worst, some simply started telling us what we wanted to hear, or even used our own ignorance to manipulate us. Even when knowledgeable Afghans were hired to help navigate the cultural minefield, we tended to treat them as little more than translators rather than listening to and learning from their lived experience. We assumed that we knew better, or that every Afghan was biased.

Dedicated reading around Afghan issues, prior to and during deployments, did help. But this was not without problems. Bookshelves are buckling with Afghan-related literature, but most is either 'dry' academic material that is a turn-off to practitioners, or first-person memoirs and other texts that focus too heavily on 'juicy' subjects such as war, insurgency or international terrorism. There are countless chronological histories of Afghanistan, dozens of books on Taliban tactics and innumerable stories about the Soviet-era superpower rivalries. But there is comparatively little available to help understand the people behind the politics – particularly the Pashtun tribes.

As Afghanistan's majority and the world's largest tribal society, the Pashtuns are pivotal to how – and why – events play out as they do. Yet international understanding of them is limited. Well-read observers may know the general regions where Pashtuns live or the names of some prominent figures. But knowledge rarely extends beyond that. This leads to three recurring mistakes in how we approach the tribes. First, we wrongly treat them as 'one' and engage them with a blanket approach that ignores their internal divisions and rivalries. Second, we look at them through a Western lens and fail to understand them as they understand themselves. Third, we overlook their positive qualities and fall back on the unbalanced stereotype of rough, turbaned warriors who are landlords of the crucible of international terror. Policy failures inevitably follow this flawed approach, as opposed to the constructive partnerships that are needed.

Throughout my time in Afghanistan, I witnessed relationships between foreigners and Afghans deteriorate. They gradually became more perfunctory and transactional. One way I tried to avoid this trend was by better understanding the Pashtun brand of tribalism. I soon became gripped by its paradoxes, its shifting allegiances, subtle layers and complex power dynamics. My own background, growing up amid the Troubles and the peace process in Northern Ireland, influenced my fascination with it. I could appreciate how deep history and long-running grievances shape modern mindsets, especially during conflict. I could see the fallacy in analysing Afghan affairs at face value. I could sense the unspoken rivalries and meaningful insinuations being picked up by Afghans but missed by most foreigners. I knew that there was always much more driving decision-making than just the events of the day – and I was itching to understand what.

I was lucky to have Pashtun friends to teach me, because finding other resources is difficult. The majority of existing literature on the tribes tends to be skewed towards Pakistani tribal areas, treating tribes in Afghanistan as a relative afterthought. In Afghanistan's traditionally word-of-mouth society there are few Pashto texts available – and even fewer that have been translated. In the English language, most available Pashtun-specific books were written by nineteenth-century British orientalists and are filled with the language and prejudices of that era. They are difficult to decipher and do not reflect current realities on the ground. They are a tough read for those starting from a low base of knowledge about Afghanistan. Accessible, detailed and up-to-date sources on the Pashtun tribes are absent.

That's why I decided to write one myself.

It wasn't easy. I was more nervous writing this book than I ever was working in Afghanistan. I worried about the presumption of describing an entire ethnic group in a single book. I worried about reducing millions of people to a few prominent characteristics, or perpetuating inaccurate stereotypes by choosing the most readable anecdotes. I worried that my commitment to accessible writing might be misinterpreted as superficiality, or an unfair oversimplification of a complex culture. I worried about being biased in conveying the harsher realities of tribal life – especially for women. I worried most about what my Afghan friends would think. What if they were to write about the idiosyncrasies of my country? I'm sure I would pick holes in their analysis, no matter what.

But I would also appreciate their effort. In Afghanistan, that effort alone tends to start relationships off on the right foot – which is the main reason for writing this book. It aims to provide 'need to know' contextual awareness that will help future strategic-level officials build better relationships in a fundamentally relationship-based society. At a minimum, its information and anecdotes are cultural icebreakers. If deployed in the right way, at the right time, they will signal at least an attempt to understand Pashtun culture – which is what international actors often failed to do in the post-2001 era. I know because I was one of them.

It is not too late to build better relationships with Pashtuns or other Afghans. In fact, it is more important than ever. As this book was being finalized in late 2021, US and NATO forces withdrew from Afghanistan. That precipitated the collapse of the Afghan Republic, which allowed the Taliban to walk – largely unchallenged – into Kabul's Presidential Palace. Such was the magnitude of those developments that many readers may approach this book seeking insight into these events. While the following chapters will open eyes to some of the drivers, this book should not be misconstrued as an analysis of the Taliban takeover or its ramifications. The intention is, in fact, to step back from political commentary about Afghanistan today. This book aims to shed light on longer-term trends and deeper undercurrents of a still-opaque part of Afghan society, rather than offering a contemporary analysis that will be overtaken by events in a matter of months.

That said, the Taliban takeover does make this book even more important. It underlines the fact that foreign military might is no longer the answer – or even much of an option – in Afghanistan. International influence will now depend solely on building constructive relationships with Afghans – particularly Pashtuns. Talking will be the key task from now on. After years of talking *at* our Afghan friends and foes, now we need to talk *to* them and talk *with* them. A new era of international engagement has dawned in Afghanistan.

This book is the toolkit for getting that engagement right.

PART I

The Origins of the Pashtun Tribes

Chapter 1

A Wolf among Men?

His presence is as menacing as it is mysterious. It infects the atmosphere with anxiety wherever he goes, putting everyone else on edge and creating an eerie silence, only broken by apprehensive murmuring as people warn each other of his arrival. Their fear is palpable. The tension can be tasted. Their every artery becomes saturated with stress, because he is built to intimidate.

Heavy-set and imposing, he towers over all others. He wears a traditional off-white *shalwar kameez* and a black waistcoat that hangs off his broad, granite-like shoulders. A well-worn leather bullet-belt is an intimidating accessory, wrapped around his chest like a sash.

A black turban snakes around his head, somehow making his dark features more threatening and his stature even more daunting. It rests above a weather-beaten forehead, cheeks stamped with deep creases and a strong jawline that projects power in a way reminiscent of a chiselled Easter Island statue. An unkempt jet-black beard matches thick, slug-like eyebrows that almost meet above his nose. Deep-set, mysterious eyes betray a life spent living in perpetual war. They prowl his surroundings, looking for prey.

This hardened exterior conveys little emotion. He is unanimated and unflinching, like a resting predator conserving energy until the hunt. The only perceptible sound is the air growling quietly through his nose and an occasional grunt as he clears his throat and swallows loudly. Anyone daring to talk to him receives a silent, emotionless stare until they capitulate into quietness. All of this body language is a warning: be wary of him; be cautious around him; he is the personification of the wolf, and he is ready to bite.

He is the Pashtun tribesman.

This is the hyperbolic image constructed over centuries by those who bravely – or misguidedly – dared to enter Pashtun tribal territory. They have painted a picture of rough warriors who live in wild, remote landscapes where birds of prey circle ominously above and where even the boldest smugglers and thieves are scared of the shadows that lurk among the arid, sun-blasted valleys.

Those who have engaged the Pashtuns – whether adventurers or naïfs – have built a narrative of bloodthirsty fanatics and militant sympathizers still living life as it was in biblical times. These tribesmen are painted as defiant, ruthless marauders who deliberately shun the pen to live by the sword. They battle against modernity, preferring to bathe in a daily orgy of barbarity, betrayal and blood feuds.

This is not a new narrative. As far back as the fourth century BC, Alexander the Great stepped onto Pashtun soil in his quest to conquer Asia. After swiftly slicing through the Persian armies, he stumbled into the tribal quagmire. Lost in tribal territory, he suffered physically, taking an arrow in the leg. But the psychological torment was more debilitating. The young general is supposed to have uttered the warning, 'May God keep you away from the venom of the cobra, the teeth of the tiger and the revenge of the Afghans.'

When Alexander's own mother taunted him for his trepidation in the face of the tribes, he retorted that, in Pashtun territories, 'Every foot of the ground is like a wall of steel, confronting my soldiers. You have brought only one Alexander into the world but every mother in this land has brought an Alexander into the world.'

He then sent her a sack of soil, instructing her to spread it around her Palace. She did so and, according to legend, infighting erupted among the Macedonian elites as soon as they stepped on it.[1]

Alexander is not solely responsible for creating the Pashtuns' reputation. Over the two millennia since his armies roamed the high Hindu Kush and Afghanistan's unforgiving southern plains, many other invaders have added to it. Various Arab armies regretted encroaching into Pashtun territories in the 700s. Texts dating from around 1000 AD describe Pashtuns as men the size of elephants who are 'daring, intrepid and valiant soldiers, each one of whom, either on mountain or in forest, would take a hundred Hindus in his grip and, in a dark night, would reduce a demon to utter helplessness'.[2]

The Mughals tried to conquer the Pashtun tribes in the fifteenth and sixteenth centuries. The Mughal Emperor Babur suffered a similar fate to Alexander. Constantly frustrated by the independent-minded tribesmen, he described them as unmanageable and naturally insubordinate.[3] Many of these ancient accounts are mirrored by modern-day examples. The Soviet experience in the 1980s is well known, with President Gorbachev famously calling Afghanistan a 'bleeding wound', thanks in part to the prowess of the Pashtuns on the battlefield.

Osama bin Laden was equally wary of Pashtun wrath. He was hosted in Pashtun strongholds in the 1980s, and letters found after he was killed show clear reluctance to trigger the 'vengeful attitudes' of 'intense and uncontrollable' tribes. He cautioned al Qaeda militants to 'be extremely careful about initiating operations to which they know little about the consequences', warning that many governments 'made big mistakes when they ignored tribal attitudes'.[4]

Bin Laden's experiences largely mirror those of Babur, Alexander and many others before him. But of all the outsiders who have incurred the Pashtuns' wrath, it was officials of British India in the nineteenth and early twentieth centuries who did most to shape the stereotype of Pashtun tribesmen as fierce, predatory warriors with an inborn desire to repel invaders.

Tales of the Raj conjure the clichéd images of harsh mountains and remote deserts, where life is cheap and men are constantly embroiled in violent conflict. They portray the Pashtuns as simple, violent and ruthless tribesmen who willingly sacrifice their wealth for perceived 'freedom'. Rudyard Kipling is the most famous British writer to have described the Pashtun penchant for rebellion against authority. He wrote that 'to the Afghan neither life, property, law nor kingship are sacred when his own lusts prompt him to rebel'.[5] He characterized the Pashtun tribesman as 'a thief by instinct' and 'a murderer by hereditarian training', although he admitted that 'he has his own crooked notions of honour and his character is fascinating to study'.[6]

Before Kipling, the first British envoy sent to Kabul in 1809, Mountstuart Elphinstone, also evoked images of feuding barbarians who find pleasure in slaughtering unwelcome outsiders. His seminal book, *An Account of the Kingdom of Caubul* (1815), set the tone for future generations of British adventurers and administrators. It became the main reference for study of the the Pashtuns – and was still used even after the US invasion in 2001. It has been the cornerstone of the negative stereotypes, with Elphinstone characterizing Pashtuns as 'brave but quarrelsome', 'industrious but selfish' and 'contentious and dishonest'. He wrote that they are 'more bigoted and intolerant than other Afghans' and 'more under the influence of mullahs'. Twisting the knife, he concluded that they are 'vicious and debauched' and 'the worst of the Afghans'.[7]

The academics, anthropologists and army officers who came after Elphinstone usually echoed his views. Diplomats wrote of Pashtuns being 'perhaps the most barbaric of all the races' and 'bloodthirsty, cruel and vindictive in the highest degree'.[8] One soldier's account described Pashtuns as brave and independent 'but of a turbulant [sic] vindictive character, their very existence seemed to depend upon a constant succession of internal feuds'.[9] The nineteenth-century geographer Thomas Holdich added that a true Pashtun will 'shoot his own relations just as soon as the relations of his enemy – possibly sooner – and he will shoot them from behind'.[10]

Even those who tried to write more balanced appraisals tended to belittle Pashtuns as simple but entertaining curiosities rather than focus on any positive qualities. One influential British text of the early twentieth century admitted that the tribesman is 'not so black as he is painted' and there was 'a good deal to like', before going on to point out:

> Their habits are not really much worse than were those of the various English tribes during the first few centuries after their final settlement. The conditions of a feudal system, under which each baron lived in

4

his own castle, and waged constant war with his neighbours over disputes relating to land and women, are simply being repeated again across our border . . . In fact, it seems quite unfair to judge the Pathan according to twentieth century standards. For him it is still the tenth century.[11]

Most accounts written by officials of the British Empire were much more derisive. A former British Viceroy of India likened the Pashtun tribesman to 'a child-like species of cat'.[12] A young Winston Churchill also described Pashtuns as 'animal-like'. Writing dispatches to the *Daily Telegraph* in 1897, he said that the tribesmen are

among the most miserable and brutal creatures of the earth . . . intelligence only enables them to be more cruel, more dangerous, more destructible than wild beasts. Their religion – fanatic though they are – is only respected when it incites to bloodshed and murder. [As soon as] these valleys are purged from the pernicious vermin that infest them, so will the happiness of humanity be increased, and the progress of mankind accelerated.[13]

This type of imperialist attitude was reinforced by successive British expeditions against tribesmen who resisted foreign incursion. British defeats at the hands of Pashtuns during the Anglo-Afghan Wars in the 1800s were particularly influential in creating a footing of mutual antagonism. Foreign writers tended to overlook any redeeming qualities or rationale for fighting, instead sticking to stereotypical descriptions of Pashtuns as 'subhuman savages, uncivilized brutes, and treacherous murderers'.[14] The problem is that those ancient narratives still shape modern perceptions of Pashtuns. They have survived the centuries and still inform opinion to this day. But why?

A lack of prominent counter-narratives is often the explanation. Whereas British envoys described their experiences in detail, there is an absence of high-profile Pashtun (or other foreign) voices in the English-language literature.[15] Afghan record-keeping has also faced obliteration in successive conflicts, and the fact that the Pashtun tradition is oral rather than written doesn't help. One of the most authoritative English-language texts notes that the Pashtuns 'left themselves no early contemporary literature, they built no monuments', and that to understand them, 'we must at least start by looking elsewhere'.[16]

This is not to say that British works on the subject are fictional or that the narrative of barbarity was created from thin air. Violence has been a common feature of Pashtun life, and it is no accident that blood feuds, banditry and vengeance have secured a place at the forefront of Pashtun folklore. History is littered with reasons why Pashtuns might be described in a negative light. There is even an argument that Pashtuns, on occasion, encouraged narratives about barbarous behaviour as a means of deterring invaders. Nor should it be overlooked that British imperialist expeditions, so-called 'butcher and bolt' operations, were specifically designed to be a savage application of punitive brutality against the tribes. Is it any wonder that Pashtuns resisted ferociously?

But this type of narrative tells only half the story. It is unbalanced. Depicting Pashtun tribes as wild, treacherous or savage is romanticism rather than reality. It is mischaracterization of a culture more complex than most outsiders comprehend. An over-reliance on stereotype-fuelled historical literature also means that positive Pashtun qualities and legitimate reasons for their violent behaviour get overlooked in favour of legend, mystery and intrigue.

The layer of legend needs to be penetrated. A closer examination can show why there is a focus on such negative stereotypes and expose the Pashtuns' more positive traits: a deep-seated rejection of injustice, a constant struggle for equality (among men) and a dedicated pursuit of peace, often by methods which might be more democratic than anything foisted upon them by foreigners.

Pashtuns may appear rough around the edges, but not every aspect of their culture is authoritative, archaic or abusive. Pashtuns and other Afghans are known for their hospitality. An inborn need to fight invaders is matched by the imperative to be a good host, even to enemies. Kindness is at the core of the Pashtun nature, albeit often hidden in case it is seen as a sign of weakness. Politeness, generosity and friendship are measures of Pashtun honour more than raiding and revenge. Such 'soft' attributes are antithetical to the traditional stereotypes. But to overlook them is to dismiss a key part of the Pashtun character. Pashtuns themselves say that it is these qualities, and not barbarity, that make 'even the poorest tribesman walk like a King'.[17] These seemingly paradoxical characteristics hint at why the Pashtun tribes are so difficult to understand and even harder to navigate. They also raise questions about past assessments of the Pashtuns and the persistence of one-dimensional Churchillian stereotypes.

Have they been consistently mischaracterized? Or were men like Kipling right to conclude that the Pashtun tribesman is 'bestially immoral' and 'as unaccountable as the grey Wolf, who is his blood brother'?[18]

Chapter 2

Who are the Pashtun Tribes?

Reference to Kipling's wolf comparison risks insulting Pashtuns, given that they and other Afghans usually associate wolves with rapacious, corrupt government officials – as well as dogs, which can be considered ritually impure in Islam.[1] It is provocative but it typifies the often ill-judged descriptions that have long fuelled negative stereotypes of the Pashtun tribes.

Dissecting these stereotypes is a central theme of this book – although 'dissect' should not be misinterpreted as 'debunk'. The following chapters explore the stereotypes and examine how they were shaped, rather than deliberately setting out to refute or invalidate them. This needs to be underlined early, as it illuminates the book's intended audience, style and objectives.

This book approaches Afghanistan by trying to understand Afghans (Pashtuns in particular); it is not another exposé of American exceptionalism, international failures or the personal adventures of foreigners. It uses stories, anecdotes and historical vignettes to unveil the extra layers of Pashtun culture, social dynamics and ethnic intricacies. It highlights what drives tribal behaviour, as opposed to criticising it or pontificating about how it could be improved, which has often been the Western way of writing about Afghanistan. This approach suits those who need it most – the Ambassadors, Generals, civil servants, soldiers, spies and even the businesspeople and charity workers who operate in, or work on, Afghanistan.

This primary audience underlines the fact that the book is aimed at practitioners rather than academics. It is not a study in methodological ethnography, or a PhD thesis turned into a book. While still of value to scholarly researchers, given that the Pashtun tribes in Afghanistan remain so opaque, the book is purposely designed to be accessible and appealing to senior decision-makers and strategic policymakers. Many of these flooded into Afghanistan after 9/11, whether they were diplomats, door-kickers or development experts, and were genuinely driven to help Afghans. Most were impressively well-educated and skilled in warfighting, diplomacy and strategy. But the vast majority arrived 'green' in terms of understanding the country, while some equally lacked professional experience. Many young diplomats were (and continue to be) put on the Afghanistan desk or deployed to Kabul for their first posting, to get experience under their belt or to fill a 'hardship' position that more seasoned veterans declined. They were by no means incapable, but they were expected to influence positive change in a country as dynamic as Afghanistan, with little more than a rudimentary understanding of its politics or people. They needed help.

They still need help. The end of the US/NATO military presence in Afghanistan does not halt the need for foreign engagement with Afghans. If anything, building constructive relationships, including with the Pashtun-dominated Taliban, will be even more imperative in the coming years. Those tasked with building them still need help to understand what makes Afghans tick and what drives Afghan decision-makers. They need help in grasping the nuances, subtleties and cultural subtext. Without doing so, few foreigners will succeed in advancing beyond the platitude-laden introductory conversations that Afghans conduct with those who show only elementary knowledge of their country.

That is where this book can contribute. Whether it is a more holistic understanding of Pashtun stereotypes, an appreciation of macro-level tribal dynamics or simply learning to place where a person is from upon hearing their tribal name, it provides the insight needed to better contextualize comments, read the subtext and know when – and why – Afghans frame arguments in a certain way. The book will be of most benefit to those with some lived experience in Afghanistan, as it will help piece together the patterns of a uniquely complicated context. For those who spent time in Afghanistan in the post-2001 decades, it will help connect the dots and make sense of dynamics that eroded the Republic from within. For those working on or even going to Afghanistan, it provides a backdrop for building more constructive relationships and making better decisions in a uniquely complicated context. It will help avoid the pattern of the post-9/11 era, when an entire posting is spent learning little more than the basics, and just as a grasp is within reach, a return home beckons.

Given this aim and audience, the book's layout has two elements. First, it is arranged around the Pashtun tribal structure – a basic awareness of which is a prerequisite for understanding the tribes, their rivalries, allegiances and outlook. The four main branches of the tribal structure are used throughout as a way to disentangle and present complicated information as cleanly as possible. This is a uniquely useful way of explaining the complex tribal system – and valuable, given that digestible descriptions are glaringly absent in existing literature. Few foreigners, even so-called experts, have more than a rudimentary grasp of how the tribes organize themselves. This book will change that.

Second, the book is sequenced as an 'inverted pyramid'. It starts at the macro-level, first explaining the largest confederations of tribes. As the book progresses, it moves on to specific tribes, sub-tribes and eventually the stories of some individual Pashtuns who exemplify tribal traits. This approach enables incremental knowledge-building, gradually adding more detailed layers onto a simple starting framework. Critics might complain that this makes the early chapters superficial or skin-deep, but the benefit is that it avoids becoming too detailed too quickly, and overwhelming the reader with a disorderly barrage of unfamiliar names, tribal affiliations and other complex dynamics. More importantly, this reflects how Pashtuns think about themselves and their place in the world – as individuals, but individuals who belong to a series of progressively larger communities under the overarching Pashtun identity.

Structuring the book this way means eschewing a chronological approach, which would be the conventional choice. This is deliberate. The intention is not to be a 'History of Pashtuns' but a book that facilitates engagement with them. Historical events inevitably feature heavily, but they are used as illustrative examples and eye-openers, rather than being part of an encyclopaedia that chronicles every event that has ever involved the tribes. The chosen style and structure also align with one of the book's main aims – to understand the Pashtuns as they understand themselves. A chronological structure does not suit the Afghan context, where time is considered differently than in the West. The Western world is organized around the clock and the calendar, but Afghan – and Pashtun – life is not. The Taliban put it best when explaining how they would simply wait out the Western military presence: 'You have the clocks, but we have the time.'

Pashtun Tribes: the basics

Before embarking on a journey into tribal life, there are some basics to explain so that all readers begin on an equal footing. The first clarification is that this book's sole focus on Pashtuns is not a dismissal of the importance of other Afghan ethnicities, such as the Tajiks, Hazaras, Uzbeks or others. Likewise, a focus on Pashtuns only in Afghanistan is not to dismiss the larger tribal population in Pakistan. This book seeks to counter the tendency of existing literature to be skewed towards Pakistani tribal areas, leaving tribes in Afghanistan as a relative afterthought.[2]

'The world's largest tribal society' is the classic description used to introduce the Pashtuns. It is usually followed by a claim that they are the largest ethnic group in Afghanistan, constituting between 40 and 50 per cent of the population. They are also spoken of as predominantly Sunni Muslims who speak Pashto – one of Afghanistan's two national languages (the other being Dari). While all of these assertions are true, they are clichéd. If they are the only characteristics ascribed to the tribes, they risk oversimplifying a hugely complex social structure and glossing over a very deep history.

Believed to be the oldest continuous inhabitants of the region where they live today, the Pashtun homeland stretches across Afghanistan and Pakistan. This area is often called the 'Pashtun Belt'. It runs along both sides of today's border in a crescent-like shape (see Map 4). This frontier is famed for being of strategic interest to successive superpowers, with some of history's most glamorous figures being made or broken there – from Alexander, Timur and Babur to Kipling and Churchill. Contemporary names like Blair, Bush and Biden might soon be added to that list.

There are generally assumed to be around 60 tribes and 400 sub-tribes in the Pashtun tribal structure, with some growing and splitting over time while others shrink and die out. On paper, this structure looks like a family tree with genealogical lines resembling branches that flow out from a main trunk. Each tribe is further divided into smaller branches (or sub-tribes). Affiliation to one or more of these segments is integral to Pashtun identity. Most Pashtuns can recite multiple generations of their genealogy based on patrilineal descent – that is, descent traced exclusively through male ancestors; if you have a Pashtun father, you are a Pashtun.

Confusion sometimes arises from the interchangeable use of the terms 'Pashtun', 'Pukhtun' and 'Pathan'. These all mean the same thing. 'Pathan' is a Hindustani word used by British administrators in the nineteenth century and is said to stem from some tribes who settled at Patna in India. It is not widely used in Afghanistan today. In fact, James Spain, in *The Way of the Pathans* (1962), wrote that it is the last thing a tribesman would call himself, as it is a term used by Hindus and adopted by the British (both traditional enemies of the tribes).[3] The term 'Pukhtun' is still used in certain regions, particularly eastern areas and Pakistan, but 'Pashtun' is now the predominant designation used in Afghanistan.

Afghanistan itself is a name that is synonymous with Pashtuns. Historically, 'Afghan' was used to refer to Pashtuns alone, rather than the collection of varied ethnicities that make up Afghanistan today. It was only in the nineteenth century that Afghanistan became talked of in national terms. One suggestion is that the term 'Afghan' stems from the Persian word for 'lamentation'. Another theory is that it comes from the Greek term *epigoni*, which refers to youths in Pashtun areas recruited by Alexander the Great.[4] A third claim is that the term is taken from the name of a common ancestor – something that will be explored in following chapters.

Pashtunwali is the most intriguing aspect of Pashtun life for foreigners. It is the honour code that Pashtuns live by. It governs tribal behaviour and relations with others. It dictates when to seek revenge, when to forgive and when to offer hospitality – even to enemies. It is among the most prominent influences on Pashtun psychology although, like many aspects of Pashtun life, it is often mystified, romanticized and idealized by Afghans and foreigners alike. It is flexible and dynamic, often subject to personal interpretation and may even be circumvented if necessary. What is important to keep in mind is that its principles are normally written about in their most traditional or idealized forms and may not always be so absolute in reality.

WHO ARE THE PASHTUN TRIBES?

The oft-cited population figures are another source of confusion about the Pashtun tribes. Nobody really knows how many Pashtuns there are, since there has been no Afghan census since 1979 (and even that was halted due to security) and – as this book shows – a Pashtun guards his household so closely that any statistics should come with a healthy dose of scepticism. Pashtuns say, when asked about population statistics, 'God knows. I don't.'

If the figure of Pashtuns making up 40 to 50 per cent of the Afghan population is to be believed, then roughly 15– 20 million Pashtuns live in Afghanistan. Figures from Pakistan can be equally uncertain, ranging between 15 and 30 million. This does not include the sizeable Pashtun diaspora in other countries – the legacy of decades of conflict and internal strife encouraging emigration. Figures aside, what matters is that Afghanistan's Pashtun population is unlike tribal groups elsewhere in the world. They are not a small minority in a modern state which has grown around them. Pashtuns are the ethnic majority that built the modern Afghan state. Even if they may not be an absolute majority, their numbers are large enough to dictate the direction of the state and shape the culture of the country – which they have done since the beginning of recorded history.

Also important to understand when talking about Pashtun tribes is what 'tribe' actually means. For westerners, the term comes with crude, derogatory connotations, evoking images of primitive early humans. Westerners tend to look down on tribes as uncivilized savages or backward hunter-gatherers. This is not the case in Afghanistan, where there is no stigma attached to being a tribesman, whether a rural traditionalist or a modern, iPhone-addicted teenager. Being part of a tribe is actually a source of pride. It is a primary marker of Pashtun identity.

Still, there is no clear consensus on what 'tribalism' means in the Pashtun context. Some deem a tribe to be a sub-sect of a wider ethnic group that organizes itself based on kinship and locality.[5] Other accounts describe the Pashtun tribes as social and political units formed around specific rules, as well as a common genealogical origin. A tribe has also been defined as a collective defence measure or a mechanism for the maintenance of law and order.[6]

Delving too deeply into definitions risks becoming bogged down in an academic quagmire. The key concept for now is 'kinship'. A tribe is a kinship group made up of those who share a common ancestry and culture and who are often linked by geographical locality. The Pashtun tribe is more of a social than a political unit, even though it is often the blueprint for a political alliance based on kinship ties.[7]

These are some of the basics that will be explored more deeply over the course of this book. The following chapters will help break down the complexities and the paradoxes of the Pashtun tribes into something more manageable.

That journey begins at the very start, with the hotly contested origins of the Pashtun tribes.

11

Chapter 3

Contested Origins of the Pashtun Tribes

How did Pashtuns arrive in Afghanistan? This question has gripped anthropologists for two centuries – and tribesmen for much longer. Sir Olaf Caroe, a British administrator in the region, wrote in the 1950s that the 'question of the origin of the Pashtun is left partially addressed'.[1] Half a century on, his statement is still correct. Still nobody knows for sure. Their exact origins remain shrouded in myth.

The uncertainty is sometimes blamed on tribal territory generally having been at the margins of historical empires and suffering a lack of attention as a result. Some blame the Pashtun tendency towards oral rather than written record, with Pashtuns sometimes preferring proverbs over precision and folklore over facts. Those who dig into the ambiguity of pre-modern Pashtun history usually retreat back to the timid position that Pashtun genes are a mix of many different types of DNA, from the many different peoples who traversed tribal territory over the centuries.

Some of the most eminent historians, including former Kabul University academic and so-called 'grandmother of Afghanistan' Nancy Dupree, posit that Pashtuns have been present around the Hindu Kush and other Afghan mountain ranges since the beginning of the region's recorded history – around 2000 BC.[2] One theory is that they originate from prehistoric settlers who belonged to the Indo-Aryan sub-sect of Indo-Iranian language speakers. The term 'Aryan' was originally used to describe these settlers, before Europeans transformed it into a racial epithet in the mid-nineteenth century. This is why many Afghans – not just Pashtuns – still openly cite possible Aryan roots, not realizing the sinister connotations that the term now carries in the West. 'Aryan', sometimes spelled 'Arian', is a common first name in Afghanistan, translating as 'noble' or 'high-born'.

Proponents of the Indo-Iranian theory cite terms resembling 'Pashtoon' and 'Pashto' found in the *Rig Veda* – the ancient collection of Vedic Sanskrit hymns and other religious texts written between 1100 and 1500 BC. The *Rig Veda* is often regarded as the first historical documentation of the Pashtuns as a single distinct group. It talks of 'Phaktheen' living near modern-day Balkh province in northern Afghanistan. Some *Rig Veda* passages are still used today in Hindu ceremonies.[3]

The Ancient Greeks also appear routinely in debates about Pashtun origins. A common claim is that there are Sanskrit references in Greek texts that talk of 'Paktha' people residing in areas between the Hindu Kush and the Indus River. The Greek historian Herodotus talked of the 'Pactyan' people who were part of the First Persian Empire in the fifth century BC.[4]

Alexander the Great's exploits in the late fourth century BC are still talked of by Pashtuns today. He is supposed to have made it to Afghanistan around 330 BC, having conquered Persia. His armies filtered into the region, spreading as far north as the Amu Darya River (today's border between Afghanistan and Central Asia) and throughout the so-called 'Pashtun Belt' to the south (see Map 4).

Alexander made the now-familiar mistake of seeking to subdue and subjugate the Pashtun tribes. An early history of his conquests explains how he addressed his troops before entering Afghanistan:

> It is by your arms alone that they are restrained, not by their dispositions, and those who fear us when we are present, in our absence will be enemies. We are dealing with savage beasts, which lapse of time only can tame, when they are caught and caged, because their own nature cannot tame them . . . Accordingly, we must either give up what we have taken, or we must seize what we do not yet hold.[5]

But rather than catching and caging the Pashtuns, Alexander's armies encountered stiff resistance in tribal territory, prompting another of his infamous observations, that Afghanistan was a land 'easy to march into and hard to march out of'. That is when he wrote the letters to his mother comparing Afghan ground to a wall of steel and talking of brave and 'leonine' people.[6] After two years of hard fighting, Alexander pushed his armies further east, through the Khyber Pass and into what is now Pakistan. But his men were so battered by their experiences that they refused to continue and allegedly forced a return to their homeland. Alexander died not long afterwards, and his empire was carved up by his generals.

It is common knowledge that Alexander helped build older parts of Kandahar city, calling it 'Alexandria in Arachosia'. Both historians and locals claim that the name 'Kandahar' evolved from 'Iskandar', which was how locals pronounced 'Alexander', although this has been disputed by some who suggest that 'there is no local written record, Indian or Achamenian, inscriptional or other, of Alexander's passage through the country; indeed there is no contemporary or even near contemporary reference to his Indian expedition at all.'[7]

Disputes aside, most published works on Pashtuns still talk of the links between Alexander's armies and the local people, leading to claims that today's Pashtuns are infused with Hellenic blood inherited from Alexander's troops.[8] The Afridi tribe – a large Pashtun tribe – usually receives mention as descendants of deserters from Alexander's army. This is due to their supposedly Hellenic features.

There is also speculation that the Scythians, who lived around the time of Alexander, may be the ancestors of the Pashtuns. They were nomads who roamed the steppe around modern-day Bulgaria, Romania and Ukraine, stretching into Russia, Kazakhstan and other parts of Central Asia too. The theory is that they were pushed off the steppe sometime around 100–130 BC and took refuge in parts of Ghor, the Hindu Kush and around the Peshawar Valley – where Pashtuns live today.

'Ghor' is a term constantly tied to any debate on Pashtun origins. Today, Ghor is one of Afghanistan's thirty-four provinces but is largely forgotten, neglected and unknown to anyone but its own residents, because it is in the remote highlands of central Afghanistan and, in recent decades, was never a Taliban hotspot. But it might be the most prominent province in Pashtun history. Many Pashtun origin theories centre on the idea that the tribes are descended from migrants who left ancient Persia and settled in the mountains of Ghor, before moving further south and east to where Pashtuns reside today.

A different school of thought claims that Pashtuns have Turkic origins and are related to the 'White Huns', also known as Hephthalites. These people lived in Central Asia between the fifth and eighth century AD. Like the Pashtuns, some were nomads while others were settled. All were renowned for their fighting abilities. The theory is that they travelled south at some point and mixed with people present in the Pashtun Belt. Pashtuns themselves point to physical commonalities with Central Asians, with their 'fine, aquiline features, high cheekbones and light skin'.[9]

Given the range of raiders and residents that the area has seen over the centuries, it is easy to see why today's Pashtuns could be descended from Persians, Greeks, Turks, Bactrians, Scythians, Tartars, Huns, Mongols, Moghuls or anyone else who has crossed the region over the years.

More unexpected are the alleged Pashtun ties to Israel.

Chapter 4

Descendants of Jewish Kings?

Is it possible that the Pashtun tribesman, who is so often sweepingly branded as an Islamic fundamentalist, is in fact from Jewish stock? Is he a direct descendant of ancient Jewish Kings?

This is the 'Bani Israel' (Children of Israel) theory, which has never been proved (or disproved) and could even be described as 'fringe science'. But it merits attention because it has continually aroused the interest of Afghanistan-watchers, and Pashtuns themselves still speculate about it today.

The theory suggests that Pashtuns are descendants of King Saul, the first King of Israel and Judah, who ruled between 1047 and 1010 BC. There are differing versions of Saul's family tree, but for Pashtuns the key individuals are King Saul and King David (of David and Goliath fame). David was the second King of Israel, taking over from one of Saul's sons. David was not related to Saul but was a shepherd who rose to fame by killing Goliath. He then became a close friend of Saul's son, Jonathan. David was made King after Saul and Jonathan died in battle. Legend also has it that David took in and raised one of Saul's grandsons who had been orphaned. That child was called Afghana.

Afghana (sometimes 'Malik Afghana') grew up with King David's son, Solomon. When Solomon became King of Israel in 970 BC, he made Afghana a courtier and Commander-in-Chief of the Army. Some histories, such as William Sherman's *The Lost Tribes of the Afghans* (2020), posit that Afghana played a prominent advisory role in the construction of Jerusalem's First Temple, also known as Solomon's Temple, which was completed in 957 BC. But Afghana is more famous in Afghanistan for supposedly being an early ancestor of today's Pashtuns. The phrase 'Bani Israel' is sometimes used interchangeably with 'Bani Afghana'.

As to how the ancestors of the Pashtun tribes may have moved from Israel and ended up in Afghanistan, that story also varies depending on the narrator. The most common thesis is that there were twelve tribes of Israel divided into two kingdoms. The northern kingdom consisted of ten tribes and the southern kingdom of two. Both kingdoms were conquered by the Assyrians around 730 BC. The two tribes of the southern kingdom – Benjamin and Judah – remained intact and are the ancestors of today's Jewish communities. The ten other tribes, formerly of the northern kingdom, were exiled. They became 'lost' and are still called 'the Lost Tribes of Israel' today.

Those lost tribes have never been found, despite searches, studies and fantastical theories claiming evidence of them in areas ranging from China to Nigeria. The Bani Israel theory posits that today's Pashtuns living in Afghanistan can be traced to one of the Lost Tribes of Israel.

One claim is that King Solomon posted Afghana and one of the tribes to the Sulaiman Mountains in Pakistan, on the border with south-east Afghanistan.[1] Another suggestion is that the lost tribes were resettled by the victorious Assyrians near the River Gozan,[2] which is known today as the Amu Darya River in northern Afghanistan. Yet another theory is that the Lost Tribes were exiled to the area now known as Kurdistan in Iraq. From there, some went on to Arabia and others moved north to Afghanistan, initially settling around Ghor but eventually moving further east to where the Pashtun tribes are today, supposedly arriving around 700 BC.[3]

While never proved (or disproved), the Bani Israel theory has persisted for centuries. Those who have written about it usually reference (or plagiarize) the *Makhzan-e-Afghani* text, written by Niamatullah Harawi in 1612 AD. Niamatullah was a scribe in the court of the Mughal Emperor Jahangir and was commissioned to write a comprehensive history of the Pashtun tribes. His research came to the conclusion that Pashtuns were originally Israelites.[4]

Another early work on the Israelite link is *Tarikh-i-Hafiz Rahmatkhani* by Muhammad Zadeek, written in 1770. Half a century later, Sir Alexander Burnes in *Travels into Bokhara* (1835) wrote that 'Afghans call themselves Bani Israel, or the children of Israel'[5] and claimed that the Babylonian King Nebuchadnezzar transplanted them in the sixth century BC to Ghor, where they lived as Israelites until the seventh century AD. Other sources talk of 'Yahoodin' communities living in the Jam area of Ghor and in the Maimana area of Faryab Province until the thirteenth century.[6] Burnes cites supposed similarities in physical features and customs as evidence of the links between Pashtuns and Jews, although he warned that while many Pashtuns believe the Bani Israel theory, they consider the term 'Yahoodi' (Jew) insulting.[7]

As studies of Afghanistan flourished during the nineteenth century, many other authors made similar claims about Pashtuns believing themselves to be descended from Israelites.[8] There are also modern texts, such as the 1957 book *The Exiled and the Redeemed* by the former president of Israel, Itzhak Ben-Zvi, claiming that Hebrew migrations to Afghanistan started in 719 BC.[9] The post-9/11 invasion of Afghanistan also led to hordes of analysts and researchers reinforcing the theory – by repeating interesting but unscientific hearsay – as they tried to understand the Taliban and its tribal links.

But hard evidence on the Bani Israel theory remains limited, no matter how much is written about it or how often Pashtuns subscribe to it. Most of the support for it is based on similarities between Israelite and Pashtun names and cultural traits. Proponents are quick to point to names of prominent Pashtun tribes that supposedly descend from Hebrew names, including Ibrahimkhel (Abraham), Isakhel (Jesus), Musakhel (Moses), Yahyakhel (John), Yaqubzai (Jacob), Yusufzai (Joseph) and Ishaqzai (Isaac). The '-khel' and the '-zai' on Pashtun tribal names are suffixes meaning 'son of'. Similarities of name have also been pointed out between the Barakzai tribe and the prominent Israeli name 'Barak', as borne by former Israeli Prime Minister Ehud Barak. The Afridi tribe – one of the most famous Pashtun tribes – has been claimed to originate from the Biblical figure 'Ephraim', while the Shinwari tribe is alleged to stem from the name 'Shimon'.[10]

Place names are also frequently presented as evidence of Israelite ancestry. Afghanistan's Zabul province has been claimed to be named after Zebulun, a son of Jacob (an Israelite patriarch). The *Dasht-i-Yahoodi* (Jewish Desert) is a term historically used by Persians and Mughals to refer to a stretch of territory within the Pashtun tribal belt.[11] The town of Kohat in Pakistan's tribal areas shares its name with the Hebrew term for 'assembly'. The Kohathites were a group of Israelites descended from Kohath, a son of Levi (a character in the Book of Genesis).

The Bani Israel theory is also built on dubious correlations between Pashtun and Jewish customs. Similar practices ranging from circumcision of boys eight days after birth to prayer shawls that double up as prayer mats are cited as supposed evidence of shared history.[12] Both Pashtuns and Jews practise levirate marriage, by which the brother of a deceased man will marry his widow. The Pashtun use of the Star of David, as well as parallels between the Torah (Book of Moses) and Pashtunwali, are also alleged to be proof of Pashtun links to the ancient Israelites.

Physical similarities are also frequently mentioned. Having lighter skin than most South Asians and being taller than other ethnic groups in the region (a tenuous purported similarity to King Saul) have been put forward to explain the Bani Israel theory.[13] Other observers, including Sir Percy Sykes in *A History of Afghanistan* (1940), point to Pashtuns having curved noses that conform to the Semitic stereotype. Recent scientific research has tried to find a more substantial basis for the Bani Israel theory. In 2010 Indian academics sampled the DNA of 1,500 Pashtuns living in northern India, finding that 650 had similar DNA to Jewish communities in Iran and Iraq. The claim was that the presence of a rare genetic disease called inclusion body myopathy (muscle breakdown) in both Pashtuns and Jewish communities potentially indicates a common origin.[14]

While scientific proof is scant, critics of the Bani Israel theory also struggle to provide hard evidence to disprove it. Most point out historical inaccuracies and scepticism about Niamatullah's *Makhzan-e-Afghani* text, which is regarded as the foundation of the theory. Physical resemblances have been refuted for being unscientific and anecdotal, as well as somewhat disquieting examples of racial or ethnic profiling.[15] Dissenters put the physical differences between Pashtuns and other South Asians down to Pashtuns mingling 'with races who passed through their territory to conquer Hindustan' or Silk Road merchants.[16] The Pashto language has also been pinpointed as having little, if any, resemblance to Hebrew or ancient Aramaic languages.[17]

James W. Spain, a former US Ambassador in the region in the 1950s and 60s who wrote extensively on the Pashtun tribes, was clear in his scepticism about the Bani Israel theory:

> The idea that the Pathans were descended from the nation of Israel was encouraged by their tight tribal structure, their stark code of behaviour, their strikingly Semitic features, their bearded patriarchal appearances, and their predilection for biblical names ... It was a favourite subject of speculation by British soldiers, administrators, and missionaries, and persisted in memoirs and travel books well into the twentieth century. The only trouble is that it was not true. I feel something of a coward saying this here in a book written half a world away from the Frontier, when I know that I would never have the courage to say it to a Pathan. Nevertheless, we must face the facts, although, happily, the facts about the Pathans are anything but prosaic.[18]

'Anything but prosaic' is an appropriate description of the Bani Israel and other origin theories. They are seductive stories, laden with intrigue and legend. Their romantic allure means they will continue to be a favourite subject of speculation, even if more scientific research eventually disproves the alleged links.

One question that will continue to be asked is how, if they are of Jewish ancestry, Pashtuns were converted into the ardent followers of Islam that they are known as today. The answer to that question revolves around one man, the common ancestor of all Pashtuns: Qais Abdur Rashid.

Chapter 5

The Founding Father of the Tribal Structure

Qais Abdur Rashid is a pivotal figure in the Pashtun story. While elements of his history probably stray more towards folklore than fact, his name will appear in almost every discussion of Pashtun genealogy and background. As the supposed common ancestor of all Pashtuns, it is not uncommon to hear him described as the 'founding father'.

But such a designation is controversial and misleading. It could be misinterpreted as a suggestion that Qais was the originator or initial creator of the Pashtun tribes. This is not true. There are multiple theories to suggest that Pashtun tribalism has existed far beyond Qais' era in the sixth century AD – as previous chapters outlined. Today's Pashtuns are adamant that their language, traditions and existence pre-date Qais. The crucial caveat is that Qais is an agreed starting point in terms of the formalized tribal structure and the Pashtun adoption of Islam, but not in terms of their existence. This is important to clarify, otherwise there is a risk of wrongly suggesting that Pashtun history does not extend much beyond 1,400 years – an insinuation that stokes resentment.

Most accounts say that Qais was born around 575 AD and lived in the Ghor area, which is now part of the central highlands of modern-day Afghanistan. Biographical information beyond this is scant. Those who buy into the Bani Israel theory claim that Qais was a descendant of King Saul (albeit in the 37th generation after him) and Saul's grandson Afghana. Other accounts of Pashtun history see it as futile to try to determine where Qais came from, and some authors point to the near-absence of historical and biographical documentation to suggest that he might not have existed at all.[1] Sceptics have written that it 'is far more likely that this is a further example of how the Pashtuns have compiled an oral history from the cultures and traditions surrounding the historical Afghan borderland.'[2]

What matters more than where Qais came from is what he achieved during his lifetime. He has a lasting legacy because he did two things – he travelled and he had children. The legend goes that Qais heard about the advent of Islam and was sent by his people to Medina (in modern-day Saudi Arabia). It was there that he met the Prophet Muhammad, who allegedly added 'Abdur Rashid' to Qais' name. Another common – but unverified – anecdote is that the Prophet also gave Qais the name 'P'thun'. This is supposedly because it was a term commonly used for the rudder or a keel on a ship – the meaning being that Qais' faith would be as strong as the wood used in making a keel.[3]

The keel-related story contradicts the claim that the term 'Pathan' comes from the place in India called 'Patna', highlighting the difficulty of pinning down the history of the Pashtun tribes. Many aspects of their origins and culture have wildly differing theories and narratives underpinning them, often based on similarities rather than science. The more they are repeated the less they are verified but the more they become seen as reality. The internet hasn't helped the trend towards repeating unverified 'facts'. It makes disentangling fact from fiction increasingly difficult.

Another variation of Qais' story suggests that, instead of his travelling south to Medina, the Prophet sent emissaries far and wide to invite people to convert to Islam – and one of them reached Afghanistan. Some versions suggest that it was Khalid bin Walid, a famed general of the early Islamic army, who either wrote to or visited Qais to invite him and his companions to Medina, where they converted to Islam. Khalid is generally considered to be an ethnic Arab, but some claims have been made that he, too, can be traced back to Afghana, thus making him a distant relation of Qais. Regardless of how Qais came to Medina, there is agreement that he spent time there, was converted to Islam and eventually returned to Ghor to spread his new faith. Pashtuns have been Muslims ever since, with tribesmen still claiming emphatically that their conversion to Islam came thanks to Qais.[4]

Qais supposedly lived into his eighties and was buried in the Sulaiman Mountains, which surround what is now the south-eastern border between Afghanistan and Pakistan. This is also the place where his alleged ancestor Afghana is said to be buried. Qais' burial site is atop of Takht-e-Sulaiman (Throne of Solomon) Mountain in Zhob district in modern-day Pakistan. There is still a shrine there today which locals call Da Kasi Ghar (Mount of Qais).

At some point after his return from the Gulf, Qais allegedly married a daughter of General Khalid bin Walid called Sara Bibi. With Sara he fathered a number of sons. These sons, four of them in particular, are less well known than Qais, but they are of equally critical importance to the Pashtun tribal structure.

Whether or not he is a folkloric rather than a historical figure, modern explanations of the tribal structure – often if talking to Pashtuns themselves – will start with Qais and his four sons. This is because the structure is split primarily into four broad branches. Within each of these four branches there are many complex networks of individual tribes and sprawling webs of sub-tribes, clans and other smaller units. But all of the tribes and various segments within a given branch trace their patrilineal descent back to one of the four sons of Qais. Each of the four branches of the tribal structure takes its name from one of the four sons, and these names are the starting point for understanding the tribal structure. They will constantly reappear throughout this book. They are Sarban, Bettan, Ghurghusht and Karlan.

PART II
The Pashtun Tribal Structure

Chapter 6

The Segments of the Pashtun Tribal Structure

The four branches, each named after one of the sons of Qais Abdur Rashid – the supposed common Pashtun ancestor – constitute the most fundamental organizing principle of the Pashtun tribal structure. Each branch is further sub-divided into collections of individual tribes, which are themselves broken down into sub-tribes. The result is a sprawling network of segments that is continually growing. As new generations of children are added to each tribe or sub-tribe, they split into further sub-divisions. This dynamism is what makes the tribal structure so intricate and difficult to follow, including for Pashtuns born into it.

The complexity often leads Westerners to avoid or brush over learning about the tribal structure. It takes a back seat to other, seemingly more pressing issues like insurgency, extremism or day-to-day politics. Interest in family trees in Western societies also tends to be regarded as little more than a hobby or a curiosity for retirees to study. But this is not the case for Pashtuns. Tribal affiliation matters, and every Pashtun knows their place in the tribal structure. It shapes worldviews, prospects, friends and foes. Most Pashtuns can recite at least seven or eight generations of their direct ancestors. Tribal elders, or 'whitebeards', can rhyme off even more.[1]

For Pashtuns, genealogy and tribal affiliation are more than a source of identity and pride. They influence social, political and economic connections, as well as relations with outsiders. A Pashtun's place in the tribal structure can dictate his culture and values. It is often the basis for mobilizing political and economic resources. In post-2001 Afghanistan, the tribe is just one network in a country of many networks, and the importance of each network waxes and wanes over time. But tribal affiliation is always important, and in recent years it has routinely been employed to advantage by election candidates or leveraged by individuals seeking jobs in state institutions. No Pashtun ignores their heritage or forgets their tribal ties. Kinship is key, which makes a grasp of this segmentary system an essential part of understanding the Pashtun tribes.

The basics of the tribal structure

Existing explanations of the tribal structure tend to take the form of heavy doses of academic language or social anthropologies bloated with obscure terminology. The simplest explanation is that Pashtuns have a patrilineal system (organized around the male ancestors). It is also based on segmentary lineage, meaning that there are lots of different layers, each of which is made up of different segments.[2] But all segments share some form of connection – for Pashtuns, it is genealogy. The main segments of the Pashtun tribal structure, in ascending order of size, are:

1) *Kor* – a household or a nuclear family
2) *Koranay* – a collection of *kor* that equates to an extended family
3) *Khel* – a sub-tribe or a group of *koranay*
4) Tribe – a group of multiple *khels*, often referred to as a *qawm*
5) Confederation – a 'super-tribe' made up of numerous individual tribes

Figure 1 is a simplified sequence of the basic segments of the Pashtun tribal structure and their connection back to the supposed common ancestor. The numbers beside each segment are broad approximations to show how the structure expands considerably as the segments get smaller in size. They are not exact or agreed. Like many elements of Pashtun life, the tribal structure has many inconsistencies, caveats and variations. For example, one branch may have two confederations, while another has four. One confederation may consist of ten main tribes, while another has half that number. Some tribes consist of dozens of *khels* while others have only a handful. The tribal structure is anything but neat and linear. This, along with its sheer size, is why it is rarely comprehensively mapped. With this maze-like structure, it is imperative to understand the individual segments in general terms. They include:

1) ***Kor***: The smallest sub-group. *Kor* translates as 'home' or 'household'. It is equivalent to the nuclear family in Western countries and generally includes three generations of men (and their wives). It is the most basic building block in the tribal structure (other than the individual Pashtun man) and is among the most important, given that the family remains the primary social institution for Pashtuns – more so than the tribe, ethnicity or nation.

2) ***Koranay***: The plural of *kor*. A *koranay* is an extended family. It is a small collection of *kor* and often represents a multi-generational network of relatives or those living in a common area. It is often said that the common ancestor of a *koranay* lived seven or eight generations ago.[3] The leader of each *koranay* or village tends to be called a *Malik*, who acts as a first among equals.[4]

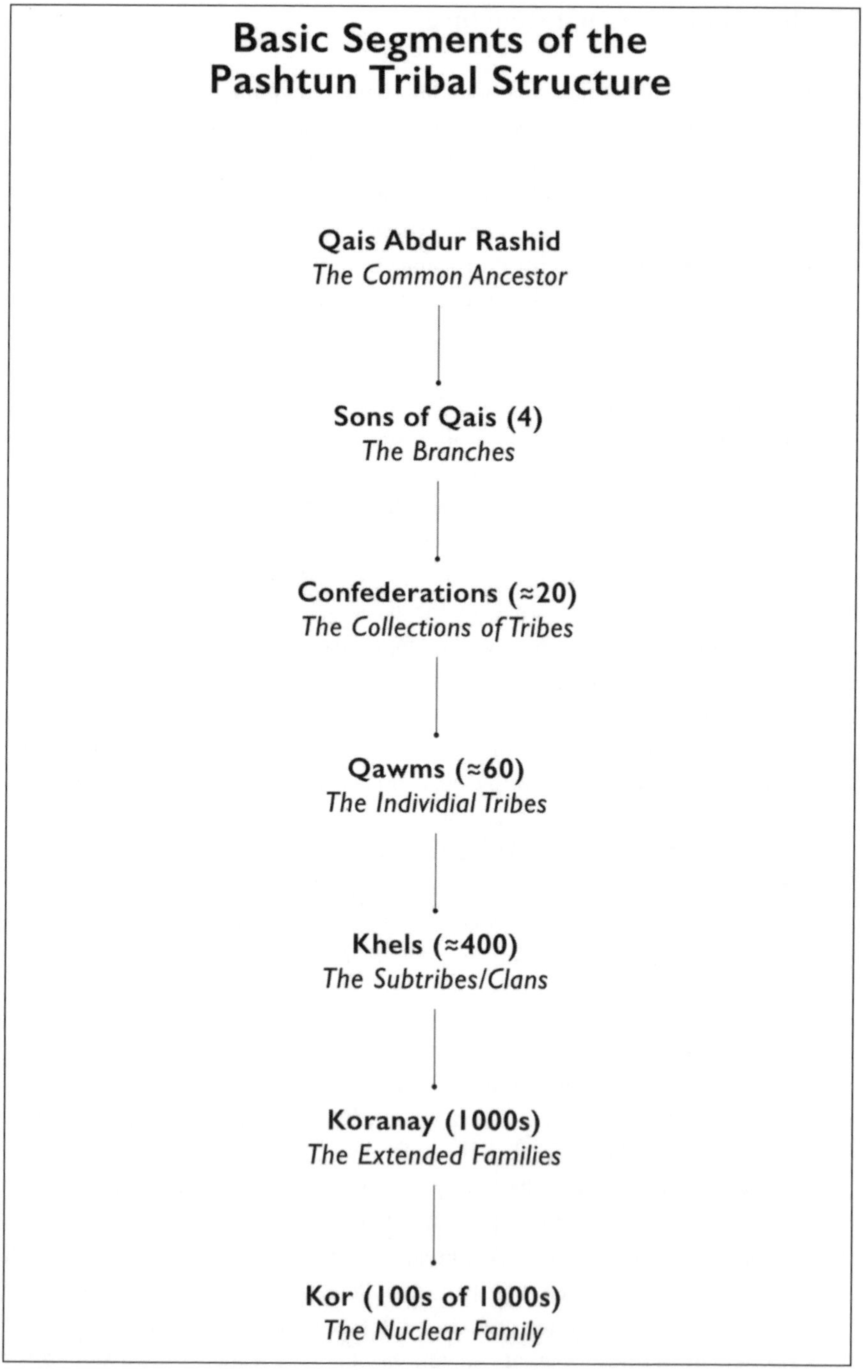

Basic Segments of the Pashtun Tribal Structure

Qais Abdur Rashid
The Common Ancestor

Sons of Qais (4)
The Branches

Confederations (≈20)
The Collections of Tribes

Qawms (≈60)
The Individial Tribes

Khels (≈400)
The Subtribes/Clans

Koranay (1000s)
The Extended Families

Kor (100s of 1000s)
The Nuclear Family

Figure 1: Basic Segments of the Pashtun Tribal Structure.

3) **Khel**: Many *koranay* that share a genealogical link make up a *khel*, often described as a sub-tribe or a clan. The term is said to come from the Arabic for 'association' or 'company' and describes a collection of related families, traditionally from a similar area, who trace their lineage back to one man. Both *-khel* and *-zai* (meaning 'son of') are commonly used suffixes on a surname to denote the common ancestor; i.e. Ibrahimkhel members trace their lineage back to Ibrahim, just as Ahmadzais descend from Ahmad.[5] Pashtuns are often judged by outsiders on their *-khel* or *-zai* affiliation, with assumptions about their personality traits and tribal stereotypes being based on it.

4) **Tribe/Qawm**: A collection of *khels*, sometimes up to a dozen, make up a *qawm*. A *qawm* is traditionally led by a *Khan* who comes from the *Khan Khel*, which is the *khel* within the tribe that has the most social prestige or power, i.e. the ruling family. But context is needed when using the *qawm* designation. It is fluid and expandable. The direct translation is 'solidarity group' or 'kinship group', meaning that it is used to describe various segments of the structure, from the smallest family unit to an entire ethnic group. Some non-Pashtuns also use the term, although they use it to denote groups that share territory, occupation or ethnicity rather than genealogy. To avoid confusion, this book uses the term 'tribe' instead of *qawm*.

5) **Confederation:** A collection of individual tribes belonging to the same lineage form a larger super-tribe or conglomerate called a confederation (which can be referred to as *Leg* or *Pasha* in Pashto). This is the highest common denominator of the Pashtun identity, other than the Pashtun ethnicity itself. But size does not always confer importance. Rarely does a tribesman use the confederation as a marker of identity. He owes allegiance first to the family, then to the clan, followed by the tribe and finally the confederation.

Understanding these five segments is the easiest way to introduce the Pashtun tribal structure and make it digestible – as long as some fluidity and some interchangeable terminology are accepted. Any neat linear sequences from *kor* to confederation that may have existed long ago have been corrupted by evolution over intervening centuries. Some tribes have grown so large that they have split into two parts that are now both seen as full tribes. Some clans have grown so large that they are now considered tribes in their own right and now have the same stature as other segments that would have once been superior. Some tribes have lost prominence to the point where they still appear on diagrams of the tribal structure but are effectively absent.

There are many more complications, phrases and nuances.[6] But at this point it is enough to understand three things: first, that the Pashtun tribal structure is made up of various different segments, from the confederation down to the *kor*. Second, the tribal structure is dynamic in nature. It is constantly evolving. The smallest units do not stay the smallest. They increase in number with every new generation and progressively transform into clans, *khels* and tribes.[7] Thirdly, whether it is a single tribesman or millions who are part of a large confederation, all Pashtuns trace their ancestry back through the male line to a common ancestor – Qais Abdur Rashid. While Pashtun history extends far beyond Qais, it is from him and his four sons that the known tribal structure flows. Every segment of this structure, from confederations down to *kors*, belongs to one of these four branches – each of which is named after one of his four sons. They are:

1) the Sarbani branch, named after Sarban
2) the Bettani branch, named after Bettan
3) the Ghurghushti branch, named after Ghurghusht
4) the Karlani branch, named after Karlan

Chapter 7

The Four Branches of the Tribal Structure

The most commonly cited story is that Qais' first three sons – Sarban, Bettan and Ghurghusht[1] – were his own flesh and blood, while the fourth son, Karlan, was not. He was supposedly adopted, which fuels an aura of the outcast that still surrounds the tribes of the Karlani branch. It also highlights how each branch, and the tribes within it, have their own histories, heroes and character traits.

Sarban and the Sarbani branch

Sarban was the eldest son of Qais. He had two sons of his own, Sharkhbun and Kharshbun (sometimes Islamified into 'Sharfuddin' and 'Khairuddin'). These are important figures for understanding the tribal structure, but they are not well-known names, even among Pashtuns. They are unlikely to be dropped into conversation today because they are too high up in the organizational structure to be a common marker of identity for any Pashtun. Most tribesmen will recite the name of their tribe or *khel* rather than identify with a confederation or any ancient ancestor.

As Figure 2 shows, the main tribes that descend from Sharkhbun are collectively grouped together into the Durrani Confederation. This grouping was originally called the Abdali Confederation until a name change in the 1700s (which will be explained in later chapters).[2] Today, Durrani is a name to remember. This confederation is renowned as one of the two largest and most politically prominent confederations in Afghanistan. It is so high-profile that it is often (wrongly) deemed to be one of the four main branches of the tribal structure.

The tribes within the Durrani Confederation are synonymous with Afghanistan. They reside in southern parts of the country (see Map 4) and have been at the heart of most historic events. They continue to have a pronounced influence on the direction of the state today. These tribes – including the prominent Popalzai,

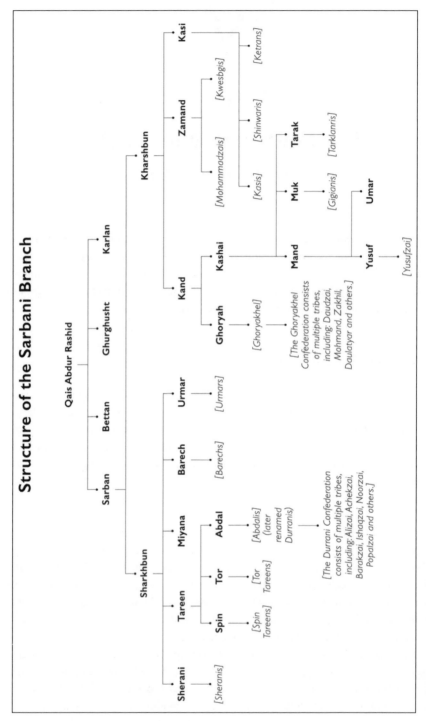

Figure 2: Structure of the Sarbani Branch.

Barakzai and Alikozai tribes – consider themselves to be 'Afghans proper' and the embodiment of Pashtun ideals like bravery in war and dignity in ruling. They see themselves as leaders among Pashtuns due to their long-held grip on state institutions. Their ancestors are the men who created the modern Afghan state in 1747 and who have dominated central government positions ever since. Whether as emirs, kings or presidents, the Kabul elite have generally come from Durrani tribes. The most recent Durrani tribesman to hold the Afghan Presidency was Hamid Karzai, who was installed after 2001 and presided until 2014.

The other tribes of the Sarbani branch – those who descend from Sarban's second son, Kharshbun – are also famed, but for different reasons. They reside further towards the east of Afghanistan (see Map 4) rather than in the Durrani-dominated southern areas of the country. This is why they tend to be called 'Eastern Pashtuns', to differentiate them from the Durrani. Prominent tribes on this side of the Sarbani branch include the Mohmand, Yusufzai and Shinwaris. While their cousins in the Durrani Confederation reside almost exclusively in Afghanistan, the Eastern Pashtun tribes also stretch over the border into Pakistan. They were some of the tribes most affected when the frontier – the Durand Line – was drawn up by officials of British India and signed with the Afghan government in 1893.

The creation of the Durand Line meant that territories held by tribes from the Eastern Pashtuns were split right down the middle, often with entire villages severed in half. This left an indelible imprint on these tribes, and not only physically – in fact, it permanently scarred their psyche, creating grievances that still shape their approach to life, and their engagements with foreigners, to this day.

Figure 2 illustrates the main ancestors and prominent tribes of the Sarbani branch.[3] The ancestors are depicted in **bold** while the tribes are depicted using [*brackets*].

Bettan and the Bettani branch

Bettan was Qais' second son. He was also known as Sheikh Beyt, having been given the honorific title 'Sheikh' on account of his reputation as a devout follower of the new faith of Islam that his father had brought back from Medina.[4]

While Pashtun ancestry usually is traced through male family members, the Bettani branch is particularly noteworthy for having an important *matrilineal* link. In addition to multiple sons, Bettan also had a daughter called Bibi Mato. The story goes that Bibi Mato married a Persian Prince called Shah Hussain. He had fled from his family and took refuge with Bettan, who at the time lived in the mountainous region of Ghor – now a province of central Afghanistan. As time passed, the Persian

Prince, Shah Hussain, grew close to Bettan and even came to see him as something of a father figure.

But he also grew friendly with Bettan's daughter, Bibi Mato. Soon enough, 'matters gradually went so far, that they, by mutual consent, but without the sanction of either father or mother, proceeded into intimacy'.[5] Bibi Mato became pregnant via this illicit affair. Her mother found out and urged Bettan to arrange a marriage between his daughter and Shah Hussain in order to avoid the shame of conceiving out of wedlock. But Bettan was apparently unconvinced of the Persian Prince's royal credentials and worried that it would bring more shame to marry his daughter to a man without honour. Bettan dispatched an aide to Persia to obtain proof of his would-be son-in-law's nobility. Only when this was obtained did he agree to the marriage.

Soon after the wedding, Bibi Mato gave birth to a boy who, 'being the fruit of a clandestine amour', was named Ghalzoe because *Ghal* means 'thief' and *-zoe* means 'born of.[6] Bibi Mato and Shah Hussain later had another son, Lodi, who is the ancestor of another important network of Pashtun tribes mostly living in Pakistan today. But it is Ghalzoe that is more important in the Afghan context.

It is from Ghalzoe that the tribes of the Ghilzai Confederation supposedly descend. Well-known tribes within this confederation include the Sulaimankhel, the Ahmadzai and the Hotak – the latter being the tribe of Taliban founder Mullah Omar. Figure 3 illustrates the key personnel and the prominent tribes in the Bettani branch, including the Ghilzai Confederation.[7] The individual ancestors are depicted in **bold** while the tribes are depicted using [*brackets*].

The Ghilzai Confederation is often described as the most populous network of tribes in Afghanistan, being even larger than the Durrani Confederation of the Sarbani branch (although accurate population estimates are unobtainable). An equally important aspect of the Ghilzai Confederation is its long-running rivalry with the Durrani Confederation. As the two largest and most powerful collections of tribes in Afghanistan, they have been pitted against each other for centuries. Their enmity is often characterized as 'rulers vs warriors', with the Durrani controlling Kabul and the Ghilzai generally roaming rural areas in south-east Afghanistan, along the border with Pakistan (see Map 4).

This Durrani vs Ghilzai rivalry has been described as the 'best documented of the many fault lines running through Pashtun society'.[8] Their constant power struggle has been a primary factor in many of Afghanistan's various conflicts, and has even been described as 'one of the underlying reasons for the struggle between the Taliban and the government'. This is because the early post-2001 state, during Hamid Karzai's time as president, was generally regarded as Durrani-led, while many (but not all) Ghilzai veered towards the Taliban.[9] Even when it does not spark open violence, the antagonism between these two

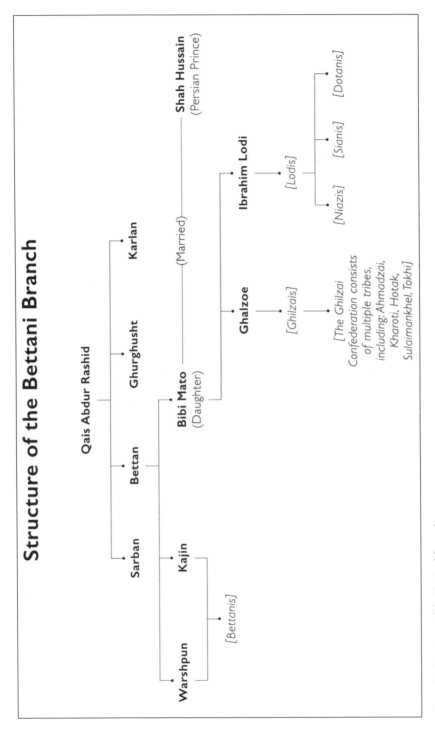

Figure 3: Structure of the Bettani Branch.

confederations is always present – subtle, sub-surface and unseen to outsiders. It will be looked at more closely in succeeding chapters because it is an unending feature of Afghan politics and tribal life. It is a central piece of the Pashtun puzzle.

Ghurghusht and the Ghurghushti branch

The Ghurghushti branch is smaller and less prominent in Afghanistan than the three other branches. Geographically, the majority of its tribes reside in modern-day Pakistan rather than Afghanistan, mostly in the Balochistan region and areas around Quetta (see Map 4). Being nestled among the Balochis means that foreign experts – and even Afghan Pashtuns – tend to have much less granularity to their knowledge about the Ghurghushti tribes compared to other branches. This has been the case for centuries, with the British envoy Mountstuart Elphinstone, in his seminal book *An Account of the Kingdom of Caubul* (1815), writing that the mountainous and remote Ghurghushti territory is 'nearly inaccessible to enquiry'. Like many others, he had to rely upon second-hand stories and 'vague relations from travellers', leading him to conclude that he 'must forgo the attempts . . . made at minute description'.[10]

But Ghurghushtis are not completely absent from Afghanistan. There are a few Ghurghushti tribes that have been prominent in Afghan history and remain relevant to this day – including names like the Kakars, Ludins and Safis.

The Kakars are remembered for some of their actions against the British during the Second Anglo-Afghan war in the late 1870s. Kakar tribesmen still talk of beating back British 'punitive expeditions' into their territories in the 1880s, when British-Indian forces ventured into then unknown areas to take control of strategic passes and bring order to what they saw as unruly tribal areas. The Taliban have also had some prominent Kakar members in the post-2001 era, one of whom, Mullah Dadullah, is often credited with using his links to al Qaeda to introduce suicide attacks to Afghanistan. His story is probed more deeply in later chapters.

The Safi tribe is another famous tribe of the Ghurghushti branch that has a reputation for rebellion, leading a famous anti-government uprising in the 1940s. They also have a reputation as staunch Islamists, despite being among the last of the Pashtun tribes to embrace Islam – as late as the seventeenth century. Both of these distinctions, and other Safi characteristics, are covered in Chapter 31.

Figure 4 illustrates the primary ancestors and well-known tribes of the Ghurghushti branch.[11] The individual ancestors are depicted in **bold**. The tribes are printed in [*brackets*].

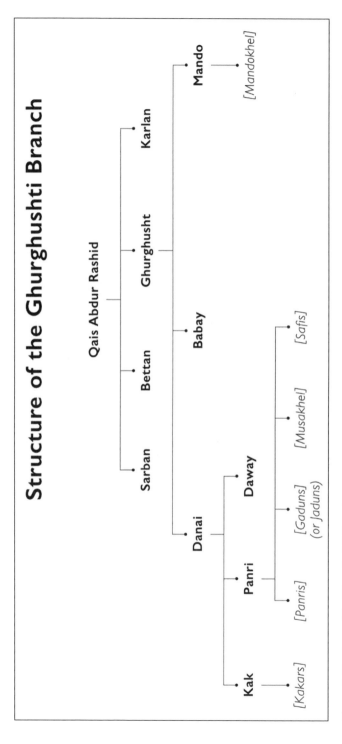

Figure 4: Structure of the Ghurghushti Branch.

Karlan and the Karlani branch

If any tribes evoke the stereotypes shaped by British imperialist narratives, it would probably be those in the Karlani branch. These are the 'hill' tribes who lurk in the shadows around the border between Afghanistan and Pakistan, or the area previously known as the Frontier (see Map 4). They control the high mountain passes between the two countries and are experienced in insurgency, from fighting nineteenth-century British Indian armies to frustrating modern-day foreign forces. They were the guerrillas in three Anglo-Afghan wars, mercenaries in many famous rebellions and key players in the anti-Soviet resistance of the 1980s.

Karlani tribesmen were also the bane of the Afghan Government and foreign forces in the post-2001 conflict, with the notorious Haqqani Network, a group which can be described as 'the teeth of the Taliban', being dominated by militants born into Karlani tribes. Befitting their cross-border presence, Karlani men have also led anti-state networks in Pakistan. This includes the Tehrik-i-Taliban group (known as the TTP or Pakistani Taliban), which was blamed for assassinating Benazir Bhutto and targeting the activist Malala Yousafzai, among other high-profile attacks.

While sweeping and hyperbolic, all of this feeds the Karlani reputation as ferocious fighters who are almost hell-bent on repelling unwanted outsiders and international invaders. Their freedom is fiercely defended, and independence is a cause they are willing to die for. Their loyalties are supposedly to the tribe rather than the state and, to this day, they take pride in never being 'tamed' by any invading force or domestic army.

The mystique associated with the tribes of the Karlani branch may be traceable to their being the black sheep of the Pashtun family – although it would be unwise to risk their wrath by saying this directly to them. Confusion about where they come from adds to their edge, with one expert noting that the Karlani tribesman's uncertain genealogy makes it seem 'as if he had a bar sinister in his pedigree.'[12] The predominant school of thought is that Karlan was adopted by Qais, thus becoming his fourth son. But there are variations of this theory – one being that Karlan was the first son of Qais' grandson, Sharkhbun (the son of Sarban).[13]

The most common Pashtun tale tells of an infant Karlan being adopted in exchange for a cooking pot. He was supposedly found in an empty field where an army had camped the previous night. Two brothers who found him were scouring the camp for leftovers. One found a cooking pot and the other found a newborn baby. The brother who found the cooking pot was childless, so they swapped their newfound treasure – this was how Karlan came to be adopted.[14] As always in Pashtun folkore, there are multiple variations of this story, including one in which the cooking pot was actually an axe. There is also dispute over which tribe the brothers belonged to, all of which adds confusion to the exact origins of the tribes within the Karlani branch.

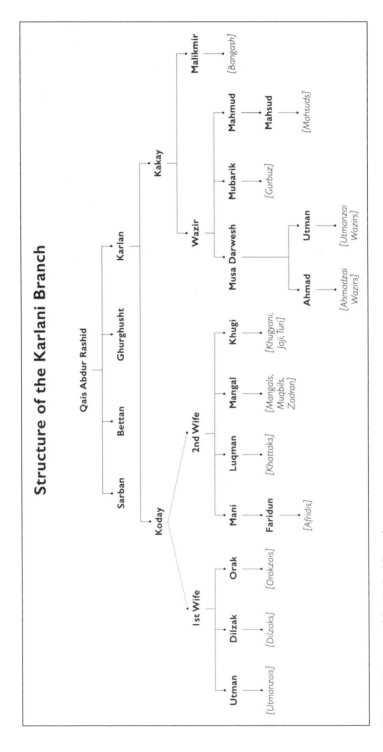

Figure 5: Structure of the Karlani Branch

Whatever his origins, everybody seems to agree that Karlan grew up, got married and had children. They are the ancestors of the tribes that make up the Karlani branch today, which include some famous names such as the Wazir, Afridi, Mangal and Zadran. Figure 5 illustrates the main individuals and prominent tribes of the Karlani branch, with the individuals depicted in **bold** and the tribes printed in [*brackets*].[15]

It is common for detractors to denigrate the Karlanis' genealogy and point to their not being 'true' Pashtuns. But the criticism rarely carries weight. Men from these tribes have been at the forefront of key historical events, including the Taliban's return to power in August 2021. Despite their alleged lack of patrilineal links to Qais, their exploits and attitude have earned them a reputation as quintessential Pashtuns who have kept traditional tribal ways of life intact at a time when other segments of the tribal structure have seen their systems crumble. This puts their importance almost, if not quite, on a par with the two most prominent parts of the Pashtun tribal structure in Afghanistan – the Durrani and Ghilzai Confederations.

PART III

The Durrani Confederation

Chapter 8

The Deadly Durrani Division

If only one thing is remembered about the Durrani Confederation, it is that its tribesmen have been the ruling elite in Afghanistan for most of the past 300 years. They have held power almost consistently in Kabul since the creation of the modern Afghan state in 1747.[1]

Their status as Afghanistan's aristocracy is part of the Durrani identity. The greater Kandahar area, known as Loy Kandahar, is equally important to these descendants of Sarban, the first son of Qais. Their traditional tribal homeland, it spans today's provinces of Kandahar, Zabul, Uruzgan, Helmand, Nimroz and Farah (see Map 3). It was referred to as 'Arachosia' when Alexander the Great invaded in the fourth century BC. As the 'seat' of the powerful Durranis, it is often said that what happens in Loy Kandahar ultimately determines the destiny of Afghanistan. Yet it should be no surprise that the story of how the Durranis came to Kandahar is unclear – inconclusive history is a hallmark of the Pashtun tribes.

The Durranis are not mentioned in recorded history until the sixteenth century. They first appear in 1587, when a man called Sado was chosen as their leader. His descendants formed the Sadozai clan, which is a sub-tribe within the Popalzai tribe (one of the prominent tribes in the Durrani Confederation). Sado's clan subsequently produced many of Afghanistan's state leaders.[2]

Early foreign accounts do not add much to our knowledge of Durrani origins. In 1815, the first British envoy to Afghanistan wrote that 'little is known of the early history of the Dooraunees' and that 'more numerous traditions present them as having descended into the Plains of Khorasan, from the mountains of Ghor, but leave it uncertain whether that tract was their original seat, and by what causes their immigration was occasioned.'[3] Regardless of how they came to Kandahar, these ruling elites have acquired a reputation for showing an air of superiority, which often rankles with rival tribes. One nineteenth-century British official expressed his astonishment at how the Durranis were able to 'so successfully embitter and stir up the hatred of the other races towards us, for [they themselves are] detested and feared by all classes of the people'.[4]

While the Durrani Confederation is often talked of as a single entity, not all Durrani tribes have a reputation as rulers. The Durrani Confederation in fact is deeply divided, with its main tribes separated into two groups. The tribes on one side of the divide have historically dominated the state apparatus and enjoyed the spoils of political prominence. Those on the other side have largely been left outside the circles of power, and their long-standing marginalization is said to still fuel resentment today. This dynamic has prompted intra-tribal conflict throughout history. In its post-2001 manifestation, the tribes on one side of the divide tended to support the Afghan Government, while the others often turned to the Taliban. The names of these two divisions are the Zirak and the Panjpai.

The two sides of the Durrani division

The intra-Durrani division influences Afghanistan's national power dynamics and can determine which side a tribesman takes in various conflicts. But it is often overlooked – at least by Westerners – because the terms Zirak and Panjpai are rarely used in daily life. They are not primary markers of Pashtun identity. Few, if any, tribesmen belonging to any tribe within each division would introduce themselves by saying 'I am Zirak' or 'I am Panjpai'. The early nineteenth-century British administrator Mountstuart Elphinstone aptly wrote that 'those divisions are of no use whatsoever, except to distinguish the dissent of the different clans'.[5] This is yet another reminder that it is the smaller units of tribal membership – usually the tribe or *khel* level – that Pashtuns affiliate with first. In other words, they would introduce themselves as 'from the Popalzai tribe'.

Traditionally, there are eight main tribes in the Durrani Confederation – three Zirak and five Panjpai (which translates as 'five feet'). They are:

Panjpai	*Zirak*
Alizai	Popalzai
Ishaqzai	Alikozai
Noorzai	Barakzai
Maku	[Achekzai]
Khogiani	

Figure 6 illustrates the important ancestors and main tribes in the Durrani Confederation. It includes the Sadozai and Mohammadzai clans, given the importance of these sub-tribes to the Durrani story and their mention in later chapters.[6]

An updated Pashtun tribal structure, if drawn today, would likely see additions to the Zirak side and changes to the Panjpai. The Achekzai would be added to the

Zirak tribes rather than being depicted as a Barakzai sub-tribe (hence the dotted line in Figure 6 and the bracketed addition in the list above). The Achekzai are today regarded as a tribe in their own right, having been deliberately split from the Barakzai in the 1700s by a Durrani monarch who worried that the Barakzai would become too powerful and challenge his control of Kabul. The Achekzai have operated independently ever since.[7] They have been said to possess a 'predatory spirit' and to attract animosity from almost all other tribes, even their own Durrani brethren.[8]

The Zirak side of the division takes its name from their ancestor Sulaiman Zirak. Tradition says that he had four sons. One day, so the story goes, the family was breaking camp near Kandahar. The elderly Zirak was too old to move, let alone saddle his horse. He asked his oldest son Barak for help, but Barak refused, mocking his father for his weakness. The second son, Alik, did the same. The third son, Musa, berated his father too, telling him to hurry up and get on a horse. When old Zirak was unable to do so, Musa kicked him and told him to remain behind until wild beasts devoured him.

Popal, the youngest son, then offered to carry his father on his back. Old Zirak never forgot the gesture, and before he died he designated Popal as his successor.[9] This increased the Popalzai tribe's power and prestige, giving them a claim to the tribal leadership that they still see as theirs today. It also set the scene for a centuries-long inter-tribal power struggle between the Popalzai and the Barakzai tribes, despite their genealogical affiliation. Popal's story is still recited by Popalzai tribesmen. Former Afghan president Hamid Karzai, himself a Popalzai, is known for taking delight in this tale.[10]

Hamid Karzai is the latest Afghan ruler with Zirak heritage, with multiple other ancestors having held state power, and all the patronage opportunities it entails, for most of modern Afghan history. But their privilege was often built on the backs of others. It was the less-favoured tribes of the Panjpai division who worked their land. Those Panjpai tribes were deliberately ostracized, weakened and even forcibly displaced, so that the Zirak tribes could maintain the upper hand. A perceptible sense of anti-state resentment among Panjpais still hangs in the Kandahari air today. It is no coincidence that Panjpai tribes – particularly the Noorzai, Ishaqzai and Alizai – have held prominent roles in anti-state movements and insurgencies (including the Taliban), while their cousins in the Zirak division have often held power in Kabul.

Within the Panjpai division, the Alizai, Ishaqzai and Noorzai tribes are not without influence. They have prominent pasts and will likely be at the heart of future Afghan developments. But the influence of the two other Panjpai tribes – the Maku and Khogiani – has waned. They are still presented on written depictions of the tribal structure, but even as long ago as the early nineteenth century they were described as 'small clans, who have no distinct lands' and who 'are likely soon to be extinguished'.[11]

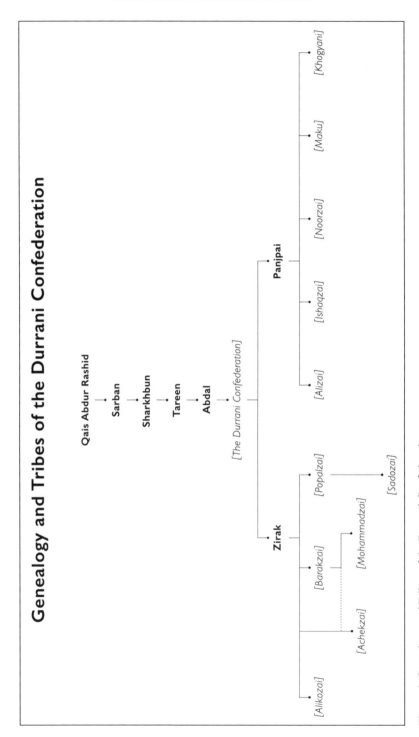

Figure 6: Genealogy and Tribes of the Durrani Confederation.

The Panjpai tribes are sometimes rumoured to have been members of the Ghilzai Confederation (of the Bettani branch) in the past, i.e. not 'true' Durranis. But this claim is usually levelled by their competitors to try to portray them as second-class Durranis. The suggestion is that they originally belonged to the Ghilzai Confederation and only joined the Durranis in the early 1700s after Ghilzai lands were given to Durrani tribes by Persian officials as a reward for their service in the Persian armies.[12]

This unending divisional competition highlights how intra-tribal rivalries constantly perpetuate in Pashtun life. One tribe tends to gain prominence at the expense of another, inevitably stirring resentment. This dynamic has been an observable feature of Afghanistan since the state was created in 1747 by the most famous member of the Durrani confederation, who is still known as 'the Father of the Nation' – Ahmad Shah Durrani.

۹

Chapter 9

Ahmad Shah Durrani:
Father of the Nation

Ahmad Shah Durrani's coronation was not just a pivotal point in Pashtun history; it was a defining moment for Afghanistan. It was, arguably, the de facto creation of the modern state (hence the appellation 'Father of the Nation'). Yet despite being so consequential, it remains shrouded in myth. The outcome was unambiguous, but the details of how events actually played out can only be imagined.

Picture a warm summer evening in 1747. Dusk is descending as the main men dismount. The dry Kandahari desert dust is unsettled by the men and their horses that have gathered at the shrine, creating a light haze that envelops the arena where they will sit. Some have travelled from far and wide, such is the importance of this ceremony. It is of once-in-a-lifetime magnitude.

The setting sun deepens the sky's reddish tint, bathing the gathering in a warm glow as if to provide an atmospheric backdrop to this important meeting. But the grandeur of the setting still does not match the gravity of what is about to happen.

The troupes of horses encircle the gathering, and there is a soft undertone of chatter as servants tend to their tack. Hooves thud on the dry dirt and there is an occasional whinny. The distinctive equine smell – and the sweaty scent of the riders – fills every nostril, complementing the earthy taste of the desert dust.

The tribal chiefs are easy to identify among the busy throng. All are big, burly and battle-hardened. These Khans ooze warrior wisdom. They walk with a natural charisma. Their aides scamper behind them, while everyone else moves out of their way. Their long traditional coats sway with every step they take. Their turbans sit perfectly, as if the better they are shaped, the more honour it affords. One or two are 'whitebeards', elevated in age and experience. Others have salt-and-pepper beards and are well on their way to elder status. Some still have beards as black as night; they are approaching their prime and are ready to take what they see as rightfully theirs. One of these chiefs is particularly young and more sprightly than the others. But he does not look out of place. He carries himself with quiet courage.

Each Khan moves towards the seating area, where well-worn carpets are laid out on the desert floor. He greets his counterparts in the classic Pashtun way: strong embraces, vice-like handshakes and forearm grasps. Head-nods greet inquiries about family. It is a competition to see who is most courteous, no matter what has gone on between them previously. It takes time. None disregard this ritual. Not when honour is at stake.

Each chief finally reaches the carpets. Their entourages gather in groups close behind, watching on from the shadows. The chiefs take their seats, sitting cross-legged in a circle, all facing one another as equals. With nobody needing to be told, a deathly silence falls. Not even the horses stir. The last glimmer of sun strains to see over the horizon, as if it does not want to miss what is about to happen.

The traditional tribal assembly – known as a *jirga* – has begun.

A prominent religious figure holds court. He is a Sufi Pir named Sabir Shah Kabuli, who acts as a spiritual guide to the tribal chiefs (sometimes referred to as 'Hazrat', or 'Sheikh' in Arabic). He starts with a haunting prayer. It rings out into the night sky like a warning to anyone or anything not to interrupt what comes next. When his voice reaches a crescendo, it is as if he could be heard as far away as Kabul. Each of the tribal chiefs is then invited to make his pitch. One by one, they present their argument on who should assume the tribal leadership. Inevitably, each one proposes himself.

The whole world feels as if it has paused to watch this spectacle. Nothing stirs. The only sound is the powerful oratory of each man. Voices start slow and deliberate but gradually rise in volume and intensity. There are no claps or congratulations when they finish. Nor do any heads nod. Nobody wants to give anything away. The Sufi Pir simply gestures to the next tribal chief, who starts speaking after a considered pause.

This process continues until all but one of the men has had his say. All give their best performances, as energetic as any tribal elder can be, their words infused with as much emotion as any hardened man is able to reveal. All give strong reasons why they alone should assume the leadership and become the Khan of the tribal confederation. After the soliloquies, there is an equally heated back-and-forth as they debate who is best placed to be chief.

Only when the arena is cloaked in almost complete darkness, illuminated by a few struggling lamps and some emerging stars, do heads turn toward the one man who has not yet spoken. Everything falls silent. No one in the entourages or any close adviser makes any movement. Even the horses seem apprehensive. The wrath of the warrior chiefs is not worth risking.

As every participant turns towards the last tribal chief, they gaze at him in a way that suggests he is an outsider; but every participant's right to be heard will be respected. He is a relative unknown, although stories circulate about his exploits leading his tribesmen in battle on behalf of the Persians. He is only in his twenties, and looks it. A jet-black beard betrays his youth, as does the absence of wrinkles around his almond-shaped eyes. He is tall and robust, wearing the traditional dress of a cavalry officer. But everyone knows that he is here to represent the Popalzai tribe.

His name is Ahmad Shah Abdali.

Those within earshot wait for his words. The Sufi Pir motions for him to start, but young Ahmad stays silent. It is a deliberate rather than a fearful silence. He is sitting cross-legged but bolt upright, his arms straightened to his knees. His striped turban is perfectly placed, and his pearl earring occasionally glints when the light of a lamp catches it. There is a pensive look on his face.

This is unusual. As more minutes pass, there is some fidgeting among the advisers and household troops who surround the assembly. Fidgeting soon turns to muffled murmuring. But Ahmad stays silent. Some of the other tribal chiefs now start to glance sideways or look towards the moderator, who himself is assessing what his next step should be.

Silence falls again when the Sufi Pir stands up. He strides over to Ahmad, clutching an ear of wheat between his finger and thumb. The other tribal chiefs sense what is coming but do not react. He stops in front of Ahmad, who is still sitting cross-legged and perfectly still. The wheat is gently placed on Ahmad's head. The symbolism is clear. History has been made. Ahmad Shah Abdali is the new chief, chosen because he was the only one who did not put himself forward.

From Ahmad Shah Abdali to Ahmad Shah Durrani

The sequence of events sketched above is how Ahmad Shah Durrani's coronation is most commonly portrayed by Pashtuns (and foreigners). Yet, with no eyewitness accounts of it available, anyone who paints a detailed picture will probably be guilty of adding their own colour or presenting their own interpretation. This book is no different. The atmospherics of the above story are imagined by the author, based on personal experience of similar gatherings and engagements with prominent Pashtuns.

But it is not only the atmosphere of the occasion which is unknown. Some widely agreed aspects of that day are also open to question, and we need to try to cut through the romanticized hearsay and identify the hard facts of it. While difficult, this is not wasted effort because, particularly in this case, inaccuracies are not always innocent mistakes. Ahmad Shah Durrani's coronation has been misrepresented, on occasion, to suit individual or tribal agendas.

There is general consensus that the *jirga*'s location was the Sher-i-Surkh shrine outside Kandahar.[1] There is also agreement that the other Khans jostled for position while young Ahmad stayed silent, before the wheat was bestowed on him and he became the leader.[2] Some accounts suggest that the gathering lasted for nine days as the tribal chiefs struggled to come to an agreement.[3] It also makes sense that the Barakzai chief, Haji Jamal Khan Barakzai, was aggrieved that his powerful and populous tribe was passed over.[4] This forced young Ahmad to make a range of concessions, involving tax and conscription benefits, to the other chiefs to prevent their loss of face, as well as giving Haji Jamal Khan day-to-day control over the state's political affairs. The Alizai tribal chief, Nur Muhammad Khan Alizai, was also given a senior military position.[5]

Some accounts relate that Ahmad's competitors only acquiesced to his leadership upon realizing that he was from the relatively weak Sadozai clan (of the Popalzai tribe). This meant that he could be easily removed if he did not accept counsel from the other elders.[6] To demonstrate consent, they supposedly placed pieces of grass in their mouths to show they were Ahmad's cattle.[7] Less credible is the suggestion that they also threw 'pieces of cloth around their necks as a sign of willingness to be led, submitted to his rule and gave him powers of life and death'. There is no clear consensus that this actually happened. There is an argument that it is a perversion of history and a narrative that later Afghan rulers fabricated in an attempt to subordinate potential rivals in the same way as Ahmad Shah Durrani supposedly did.[8]

Questions also exist about the Sufi Pir who oversaw the event. The Popalzai tribe's rivals suggest that Sabir Shah Kabuli was an oddball who professed an ability to interpret dreams, rather than a respected cleric. Another charge is that he may have had an 'unholy alliance' with Ahmad Shah, and therefore a bias towards him. The historian Jonathan Lee wrote that 'By 1747 the relationship between Ahmad Shah and Sabir Shah had grown into one of extreme intimacy, which for some went beyond the bounds of propriety. Shortly after his coronation, a courtier who was granted an audience with Ahmed Shah was shocked to see Sabir Shah, "naked from head to foot with his body covered in dust", lying in the lap of the King, and Ahmad Shah feeding him with his own hand from the Royal plate.'[9]

Whatever the exact details, none of this explains how Ahmad Shah *Abdali* became Ahmad Shah *Durrani*.

As always, there are varying accounts of how the Durrani name entered usage. The most common is that Ahmad Shah, who was born an Abdali as his father was head of the Abdali Confederation, was fond of wearing a pearl earring. In his early twenties Ahmad was employed as an aide-de-camp to the Persian military leader Nader Shah, whose own royal guard also wore pearls. Nader Shah was so fond of Ahmad that he gave him the nickname 'Durr-i-Durrani' (Pearl of Pearls). Young Ahmad continued to impress Nader Shah in battle and was eventually promoted to lead an elite unit of 3–4,000 cavalry – an important promotion, given that rulers of that era generally measured their military strength by the size of the cavalry they commanded. After Ahmad Shah's coronation at the 1747 *jirga*, he formally adopted the title 'Durr-i-Durrani', and the Abdali Confederation became known as the Durrani Confederation.[10]

Another jewellery-related tale links Ahmad Shah to the British crown jewels. Pashtuns generally believe that, around the time of the 1747 *jirga*, Ahmad came across a caravan loaded with treasure that the Persians had plundered from India. The loot contained the Koh-i-Noor diamond, one of the largest cut diamonds in the world, which Ahmad seized to pay for his coronation and his new state. A different theory, posited by Jonathan Lee, is that he pilfered the diamond from Nader Shah's dead body after his assassination. Afghan historians, unsurprisingly, prefer a more noble theory, that Ahmad, rather than being a thief, acquired it years earlier when he saved a Persian Queen from being assaulted. Whatever the truth, the Koh-i-Noor (Mountain of Light) eventually made its way into the British Queen Mother's Crown, which now sits in the Tower of London. It is still at the centre of an ongoing international dispute as Afghanistan, Pakistan, Iran and India all claim rightful ownership of it.

After his election as overall chief of the Abdali confederation, now known as the Durrani confederation, Ahmad Shah wasted little time in fanning out his armies in all directions to build his empire. He quickly took Ghazni city back from the rival Ghilzai Confederation, reducing them to subordinate status. He then moved on Kabul. Within two years he travelled east to modern-day Pakistan, where the Mughal Empire ceded territory to prevent him sweeping through their capital.

Buoyed by these victories, Ahmad moved west to Persian-controlled Herat, besieging the city and wresting parts of modern-day Iran from Persian control. He then advanced north to battle the Turkmen, Uzbeks, Tajiks and Hazaras, before sending troops back east to take Lahore and Kashmir. He attacked Delhi but allowed the Mughals to stay in nominal control, leaving a trusted adviser to oversee the Mughal Emperor and ensure payment of an annual tribute. Ahmad then returned to Kandahar.[11]

Ten years on from his accession, Ahmad's Afghan empire covered parts of Iran, Pakistan, Kashmir and northern India. But such an expanse required control. As ruler of many unstable territories, he was soon subject to attacks from restless and rebellious foes, including rival Pashtun tribes, and his empire began to unravel. He lost territory in some areas and made agreements to cede control in others. He agreed with the Amir of Bukhara that the Amu Darya River would mark the boundary between their lands.[12] It remains the border between Afghanistan and Central Asian states today.

In total, Ahmad Shah conducted fifteen major expeditions outside his own territory, including nine in India. In part this was just good politics – as the leader of a disparate group of restless tribes, waging war helped to maintain unity. It was also good business, given that plundering other empires was a primary source of income. But it also highlights that, although generally glorified as valiant, empire-building conquests, Ahmad Shah's campaigns can equally be seen as opportunistic raids that further helped shape the stereotype of Pashtuns as fanatical barbarian plunderers.

The patchwork empire that Ahmad created was never going to remain united for long, especially with its most populous and productive cities like Delhi, Lahore and Bukhara being on the periphery rather than in the Afghan heartland. But even though it started to collapse before his death, Ahmad's tenure is still romanticized as the golden era of Pashtun power. He is still seen, at least by Durranis, as the greatest Pashtun leader, a man who forged unity amongst warring tribes, halted the advance of the Sikhs and created an extensive empire. He gave Afghans an independent homeland and is regularly called the creator of the modern Afghan state – even if it was more a Kingdom of Kandahar.

Critics can pick holes in Ahmad's efforts. Some suggest that the pinnacle of Pashtun power came not because of any tribal heroics but was merely due to Persian collapse – with Ahmad Shah filling the vacuum. A similar charge is that Ahmad Shah only fostered some semblance of tribal unity because he learned aspects of imperial management from Persian rulers, i.e. that he was Persianized rather than being a true Pashtun. All of this is often airbrushed out of history as it undermines the Pashtun narrative of free-thinking warriors who shape their own destiny.[13]

Whichever version is believed, by the time that Ahmad Shah retired to Kandahar in 1772 he was known as Ahmad Shah Baba (*baba* means 'father'). He died not long afterwards, allegedly of nose cancer, although it may also have been leprosy. By then, his territory had shrunk to something resembling modern-day Afghanistan, and he was ready to hand over the First Durrani Dynasty to his chosen successor – an event that would divide the Durranis and spark decades of fratricidal conflict among the Pashtun tribes.

Chapter 10

The Three Durrani Dynasties

The First Durrani Dynasty – The Popalzai Era

Ahmad Shah Durrani's tenure as tribal chief marked the zenith of Durrani power. But when he died in 1772, the transition to his son, Timur, was so tempestuous that it began to weaken Durrani control. Ahmad had anointed Timur without consulting other tribal chiefs, who were worried by Timur's sub-par military performances against the Sikhs. Timur, known for wearing a jewel-adorned sash and diamond-studded brooch on his turban, was a *bon vivant* rather than a respected warrior. Being small of stature further damaged his reputation – especially as he used a bespoke, bejewelled step stool to mount his horse.[1]

Timur annoyed fellow tribesmen throughout his rule by relying on non-Pashtun royal guards to quell rebellions, while he spent time on pet projects such as renovating the ancient Bala Hissar fort in Kabul, after being inspired by his Mughal wife's stories about growing up in Delhi's famous Red Fort.[2] But Timur did make one deft political move, shifting his capital from the indefensible plains of Kandahar to the high mountain plateau of Kabul. This kept his seat of power out of the turbulent tribal heartlands and increased his revenue, given Kabul's position on the Bukhara–Delhi trade route. It also posed a dilemma to the other Durrani chiefs – either stay in Kandahar and be politically isolated from Kabul, or move to Kabul and be cut off from their tribal bases in Kandahar.

Yet Timur's strategic nous did not stop him losing huge swathes of the territory that he inherited from his father, particularly in Persia and India. When he died in 1793, aged forty-six, he had almost bankrupted the Durrani empire. On his deathbed he anointed his son Zaman as his successor, sparking a messy succession struggle even before his body was cold.

Zaman eventually secured the tribal leadership by imprisoning his two rival brothers – Shuja and Mahmud. But his rule was short-lived because he made the mistake of turning the powerful Barakzai tribe, who had supported his rise to the throne, against him. After a minor disagreement, Shah Zaman executed the Barakzai chief, Painda Khan. This started a blood feud between Shah Zaman's

Popalzai tribe and their Barakzai rivals – adding another layer to the long-running enmity between the two tribes (which is still perceptible today).

To defend their tribe's honour, Painda Khan's sons sought revenge. Within days they allied with Zaman's own brother Mahmud. They caught Zaman and lanced his eyes (in Afghan tradition, a blind man cannot rule). Mahmud then replaced Zaman as Shah, but ruled for just three years before his other brother, Shuja, led a tribal revolt in Kandahar and overthrew him.[3]

Despite Shuja's violent rise to power, he had the reputation of being a bookish, poetry-loving intellectual. He was about 5 feet 6 inches tall, with a well-groomed, jet-black beard, and those who met young Shuja considered him princely and dignified – although in later years he hardened into a power-hungry megalomaniac who became known for dismembering his servants. Shuja's first period in power lasted only from 1803 to 1809, but his actions still reverberate around Afghanistan today.[4] His name is still synonymous with shame. The historian Thomas Barfield pointed out that, by making alliances with the British Indian government, Shuja was the first monarch to invite infidels into Afghanistan. Ever since, 'Nothing [has] undermined the legitimacy of any Afghan government faster than the charge that it was beholden to foreign masters.'[5]

It was in 1809 that British officials undertook their first mission to Kabul, led by the diplomat Mountstuart Elphinstone. They arrived laden with lavish gifts for Shuja, one of which was Afghanistan's first organ. But it was not an exercise in friendship; Shuja was a pawn on the imperial chessboard. Britain was anxious about Napoleon's potential encroachment into the region and wanted Shuja's support to prevent it. Shuja himself received the British mission with open arms, hoping that new foreign friends would shore up his fragile grip on power. He also knew that Napoleon had promised Afghan lands to the Persians.

But signing a Treaty of Friendship with British officials led to Shuja becoming known as the instigator of foreign meddling and the man who made Afghanistan the centre of geostrategic rivalries.The treaty amounted to political suicide, and Shuja was quickly deposed by his brother Mahmud, who had escaped from prison and joined Shuja's rivals in the Barakzai tribe to take back power. Shuja fled into exile, taking the Koh-i-Noor diamond with him. He eventually lost it in India – another unforgiveable transgression that is remembered to this day.

Shah Mahmud's second reign lasted until 1818, at which point he made the same mistake that his brother Zaman had made more than twenty years earlier: he turned on the Barakzai tribe, who had supported him in taking the throne. The story goes that the Barakzai chief, Fateh Khan, raped some relatives of Shah Mahmud in 1817. He was then imprisoned and his eyes cauterised with a hot iron. After months locked in squalid conditions he was sent, in chains, to meet Shah Mahmud, who offered to spare him if Fateh Khan's brothers came and swore allegiance on behalf of the Barakzai tribe. But Fateh Khan smelled a trap and defiantly refused

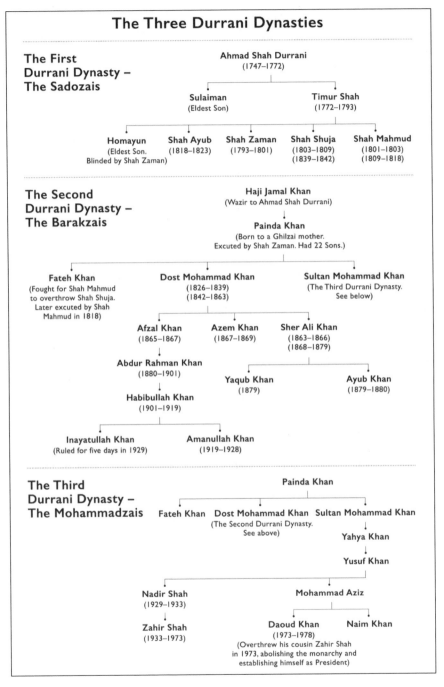

Figure 7: The Three Durrani Dynasties (The years of each man's period in power are depicted in brackets)[6]

Mahmud's offer. In anger, the Shah drew his sword and severed one of Fateh Khan's limbs. Mahmud's entourage then took turns in slicing off Fateh Khan's extremities, although it is alleged that he did not cry out in pain once.

Eventually, Mahmud beheaded Fateh, which was a politically disastrous move because it besmirched Barakzai honour.[7] Shah Mahmud had effectively kicked the hornet's nest. The Barakzais mobilized, ready to take the throne that they saw as rightfully theirs. Fateh Khan's brothers, backed by Persians of the Qizilbash minority, marched on Kabul. Shah Mahmud fled, and the First Durrani Dynasty – led by the Popalzai tribe – unravelled in 1818.[8] Tribal unrest continued for several years, with the country effectively splitting into smaller fiefdoms, each ruled by individual tribes. It took until 1826 for someone to foster any semblance of unity. His name was Dost Mohammad Khan, and with him arrived the Second Durrani Dynasty.

The Second Durrani Dynasty – the Barakzai take control

Dost Mohammad Khan represented a shift from the First Durrani Dynasty to the Second, and with this, a shift from Popalzai to Barakzai rule. He was a younger brother of Fateh Khan – the Barakzai chief who had been tortured, blinded and eventually beheaded by Shah Mahmud. He was also a descendant of Haji Jamal Khan Barakzai, the warrior-chief who attended the 1747 *jirga* and reluctantly accepted Ahmad Shah Durrani's accession after receiving concessions.

In the unrest during the dark years after Fateh's killing, between 1818 and 1826, Dost Mohammad had used his 'ruthlessness, efficiency and cunning' to cultivate popular support, finally taking Kabul in 1826 and ruling until 1838.[9] During his tenure, he declared himself to be Emir rather than Shah, as the latter title was traditionally held by his Popalzai rivals. Dost Mohammad's reign is also remembered for the intensification of the infamous 'Great Game' (or the 'Tournament of Shadows' as Russians call it). By the 1820s the Napoleonic threat had been neutralized, but now Russia was pushing southwards just as British India looked north. Superpower competition simmered throughout the 1830s, with growing British anxiety prompting increased espionage and counter-espionage in Central Asia.

Dost Mohammad Khan initially spurned the Russians in favour of the British. Yet while the British envoy in Kabul, Alexander Burnes, regarded him as 'high character',[10] the British Governor General in Delhi saw him as a threat to British interests and urged him to accept British foreign policy guidance. Feeling dishonoured by this challenge to his independence, Dost Mohammand wrote to the Russians in 1837, warning that Britain was trying to conquer the entire region and claiming that only he could stop them – if he was supplied with arms and assistance. Under the pretence of a trade mission, a Russian delegation travelled to Kabul in 1838 and was received by Dost Mohammad with full pomp and ceremony. This was the final straw for the British, who decided to overthrow him, sparking the First Anglo-Afghan war and Dost Mohammad's exile to India.

Shah Shuja, who since 1809 had enjoyed asylum in the arms of the British East India Company, now returned to Kabul with British backing. But this only reinforced his reputation as a puppet of foreign infidels. The manner in which he retook the throne was equally affronting to many Afghans.[11] The amusing story has it that the British force marched to Kabul with 260 camels for one general's luggage, 300 camels for the military's wine collection and two camels for their cigars. But the Afghans saw this 'Angreez' (Pashto corruption of 'English') force as an instrument of dishonour.

While passing Kandahar on the way to Kabul, a drunken British soldier assaulted a virgin from a noble Pashtun family, dragging her into a ditch and raping her. Local tribal leaders were outraged. They questioned Shah Shuja's association with the barbarous British, and when Shuja arrived in Kabul his reception was 'more like a funeral procession than the entry of a King into the capital of his restored dominions'.[12]

The Afghan sense of honour was further challenged when a British captain married a niece of Dost Mohammad, and when prostitution rings sprang up to service booze-fuelled British military parties. British soldiers even coined a popular couplet:

A Kabul wife under burqa cover
Was never known without a lover.[13]

But this narrative is controversial. While numerous English-language texts still flippantly refer to prostitution rings and British debauchery, treating these almost as expected by-products of an imperialist presence, the Afghan attitude is very different. To this day, Afghans argue that foreign writers fail to realize that most of the prostitutes, vagabonds, musicians or dancers were not Afghans but Indian or Central Asian immigrants, some being descended from soldiers and slaves that Ahmad Shah Durrani brought back from his conquests in the previous century.

Either way, British bad behaviour added to the simmering tribal unrest. This then started to boil over when Shah Shuja alienated powerful tribes by imprisoning rival chiefs. Even British advisers worried when he called fellow Afghans 'packs of dogs', and the inevitable uprising started in 1841. While often described as a protest by ordinary people that got out of hand, it may have been more coordinated than most think. One instigator was a tribal chief named Abdullah Khan Achekzai, and he had a personal score to settle. One of his own harem had escaped and taken refuge in the house of the British envoy, Alexander Burnes. Abdullah sent his men to retrieve her, but Burnes denied that she was there and beat Abdullah's envoy. Even when Burnes was found to be lying he still refused to hand her over. This directly challenged Abdullah Khan's honour, and the shame of her escape was only made worse by her being protected by foreign infidels.

Abdullah Khan set Burnes' house alight and caught him trying to escape in Afghan disguise. Burnes was swiftly murdered and dismembered, which sparked a wider public uprising. Once the tinder was lit, Shuja did not last long. Neither did the British, who were forced to retreat from Kabul in 1842, ending the First Anglo-Afghan War. It was a humiliating defeat at the hands of what were regarded as wild, medieval tribesmen. For Afghans, it was a historic victory that cemented the determination never to be subjugated by scheming, untrustworthy foreigners. It created a chasm of mistrust with modernizing Europeans, one that has never been completely bridged.

Shah Shuja was soon assassinated and replaced by a General (*Wazir*) who led the massacre of British forces on their withdrawal from Kabul. Wazir Akbar Khan was the 'most dashing of the resistance leaders in Kabul'[14] and a son of the exiled Emir Dost Mohammad Khan. He had personally killed a British diplomat who visited him to negotiate the British withdrawal in 1842, shooting him with a ceremonial pistol that had been gifted to him the day before. The British delegates were then hacked to pieces and their heads paraded through Kabul's streets. Akbar Khan did not survive long, allegedly poisoned in 1845 by his own father, Dost Mohammad Khan, who returned from exile. But Akbar Khan is still celebrated for his successes against the British, and the now wealthy district in central Kabul which houses foreign embassies is named after him.

Dost Mohammad's second reign lasted until he died in 1863. During this time, he devoted himself to developing state institutions and centralizing power in Kabul. Breaking with tradition, he appointed his sons as ministers and governors rather than relying on rebellious tribal chiefs. When he died, a bitter feud was sparked between three of his sons. It lasted nearly five years and effectively split the country into two rival states, until the eventual winner, Sher Ali, defeated his brothers.

Sher Ali became known as the first Afghan ruler to wear European dress – even a Russian military uniform at some official functions.[15] His reign took place against a backdrop of Russian expansion in Central Asia, including the annexation of Samarkand and Bukhara in 1868. This led to Anglo-Russian negotiations, starting in 1869, on their respective spheres of interest in Central Asia. Sher Ali was not part of the superpower discussion and focused his efforts on raising a professional army to help combat challenges from his own family. He is often referred to as the founder of the Afghan National Army.

By 1874 the British and the Russians had agreed that the Amu Darya River would mark the boundary between their two spheres of influence. Anything south of the river would be Afghan territory, and Russia agreed that Afghanistan was in the British sphere of influence. This made Afghanistan a buffer state between the two great powers.

Then came Sher Ali's big mistake. In July 1878 he received a Russian delegation in Kabul. The British were livid and demanded equivalent treatment. When he refused, British troops marched on Kabul and the Second Anglo-Afghan War began. Sher Ali sought asylum in Russia and was succeeded by his son, Yaqub Khan. The latter now stands alongside Shah Shuja in the pantheon of Pashtun villains for having signed the 1879 Treaty of Gandamak, which relinquished control of Afghan foreign affairs to the British. An inevitable tribal uprising led to his abdication within a year. His brother Ayub Khan took over but lasted only six months before he was routed by British forces and fled into exile.

Ayub's cousin, Abdur Rahman Khan, was next. The 'Iron Emir' was installed in Kabul, with British backing, at the end of the Second Anglo-Afghan War in 1880. He had early success in uniting the tribes and establishing Afghanistan's bureaucracy – which is why he, not Ahmad Shah Durrani, is sometimes called the founder of the modern state.

Yet, as many Afghan rulers have found over the centuries, the tribes interpreted Abdur Rahman's centralization of power as an attack on their independence. This led to rebellions, which he ruthlessly crushed. He also forcibly displaced some tribes and signed the infamous Durand Line Agreement in 1893, which ceded Pashtun territory to the British and created the current boundary line between Afghanistan and Pakistan – severing tribal territories and communities in doing so. These events make Abdur Rahman the most famous Durrani leader after Ahmad Shah Durrani and one who is revered and despised in equal measure. By his death in 1901, his efforts had embedded the 'state vs tribe' competition that has been a constant feature of Afghan life ever since.This competition, and Abdur Rahman himself, are so central to the Pashtun story that they are explored in greater detail in later chapters.

Abdur Rahman's son Habibullah took over in 1901 in one of Afghanistan's rare peaceful transfers of power, supposedly because Habibullah's brothers had become accustomed to the idea and the right marriage alliances had been made with powerful tribal leaders. Habibullah was also seen as less of a threat to traditionalists and tribes. At just twenty-nine, he was more interested in women and his hobbies than governing; he had particular penchants for photography, tennis and cooking (his speciality was turnip soup).[16] Habibullah did grow into the role and tried to implement some reforms, including dismantling repressive state institutions and bringing modern medicine to Afghans. He established Afghanistan's first secular secondary school but let state-funded madrassas be established at the same time. This sort of balance is one reason why Habibullah faced only a few tribal uprisings and why his rule is remembered as a period of relative calm.

But calm never lasts long in Afghanistan.

Habibullah kept Afghanistan neutral through the First World War, only to be murdered a year later on a hunting trip. A silent assassin slipped through his security and shot him at point blank range. Who pulled the trigger remains a mystery to this day, but it is alleged that the order was given by his son, Amanullah, to clear his own path to power.

Amanullah ruled as Emir from 1919 to 1926. Within a week of taking over he declared Afghanistan's independence and regained control of foreign policy from Britain. Despite his treacherous accession to power, he is remembered as a reform-minded modernizer who was well-liked in the West – partly due to his glamorous wife, Queen Soraya, who dazzled diplomats but incensed tribesmen with her efforts to promote gender equality.

In 1923, Amanullah presented his 'Nizamnama'. This self-written legal code was inspired by Turkey's reform movement, which itself had been influenced by Swiss, French and Italian reforms. It was a bold move given that Afghanistan's Islamists believed in divine law and its tribesmen followed customary law. The *Nizamnama* stipulated that all government employees be clean-shaven and wear Western clothes. Traditional Punjabi-style shoes, with curled toes, were banned. Conscription was reintroduced and a new national currency was announced, with bank notes issued for the first time. There were also moves towards secular education and liberalization for women. All of this angered illiterate clerics and tribal elders, who now had to abide by a code that was part Napoleonic and part Young Turk, with a sprinkling of Italian and French influence, but adapted to Afghanistan. Bitter hostility ensued, and tribal elders felt alienated. Uprisings were inevitable.

In 1926 Amanaullah scrapped the Emirate in favour of a monarchy. Then he became the first Afghan ruler to step onto European soil in 1927. His trips sparked outrage at home when photographs appeared of Queen Soraya, with bare shoulders and an unveiled face, shaking hands and mingling with European leaders. Afghans also resented Amanullah's shopping trips in London. On one of these visits he bought three Rolls-Royces and Soraya acquired ten lorry-loads of furniture.[17] Chinese whispers spread among rural tribesmen that Amanullah was buying German equipment to open a soap factory in Kabul, where Muslim corpses would be boiled down, shaped into bars and sold to Hindus and Europeans.[18]

By 1929, enough was enough. Tribesmen, clerics and traditionalists wanted to halt the erosion of their traditional ways. The central state, it was felt, had insulted their honour for too long. A coalition of dissenters formed, and Amanullah fled Kabul in a Rolls-Royce, chased on horseback by the rebel leader, a Tajik named Habibullah Kalakani.

Before Amanullah's escape he had handed his throne to his brother Inayatullah. But Inayatullah had no desire to rule. When Kalakani warned him of impending war, Inayatullah abdicated and went into exile in Iran, airlifted to safety by the RAF. His rule had lasted less than five days, and with his abdication, Habibullah

Kalakani, the first non-Pashtun, non-Durrani leader of modern Afghanistan, seized the throne.

Nicknamed *Bacha-e Saqaw* (son of a water carrier), Kalakani was an ethnic Tajik who had defected from the army and marched on Kabul at a time when the military was overstretched fighting Pashtun tribal rebellions in the east. Despite only clinging to power for nine months, Kalakani's tenure has become legendary. Before taking Kabul, he had already acquired the reputation of a swashbuckling, mischievous Robin Hood; finding himself cornered in a house by government forces, for example, he had set fire to it and escaped in the smoke. Immediately after he seized power in Kabul, by storming the Palace, his men gathered government officials in the courtyard so they could watch him eat his first meal as ruler. Kalakani's men tried to throw the left-over chicken bones at the assembled officials, but were confused when they kept bouncing back. These bandits had never been in a building with windows. They were also dismayed by the tiny, delicate clothes they found in the Palace. They could not understand why they were so tight. Little did they know that they were trying to wear things left behind by Queen Soraya.[19]

Kalakani's tenure wasn't all comical. His followers raped, pillaged and murdered at will. Teachers were arrested for teaching anything deemed to be un-Islamic. State revenues dried up and metal coinage ran out, so Kalakani resorted to using leather money. The Pashtun tribes quickly grew sick of the 'Bandit-King', even though some had initially supported him. They chafed under rule by a non-Pashtun. They wanted their seat of power back.

In late 1929, five brothers from the Mohammadzai clan of the Barakzai tribe marched on Kabul and ousted Kalakani. They were led by Nadir Shah, who had been Amanullah's Minister of War and a General before that. He executed Kalakani by firing squad inside the Presidential Palace. The memory of these events can still be a sensitive subject today. In 2016 violence erupted when Kalakani's remains were reburied in Kabul. Days of political and sectarian stand-off led to one death and several injuries.

The Third Durrani Dynasty – the Mohammadzai and the modern era

Nadir Shah restored the Durranis to the throne but was more cautious in reform than his predecessors, declaring that 'Amanullah tried to change the minds of people by changing their hats'.[20] Nadir used his early public statements to underline his commitment to Islam and Pashtun traditions – including compulsory veiling and banning Queen Soraya's newspaper for women.

But his tenure was still pockmarked by tribal uprisings and even incursions by Soviet forces – an early warning of what was to come. Under Nadir, Afghanistan became a constitutional monarchy in 1931, two years before he was assassinated at a school graduation ceremony.[21] Nadir's son, Zahir, then succeeded him. Zahir had been educated in France but had returned to serve in his father's government. This shy introvert became King at the age of nineteen, so his paternal uncles served as Prime Ministers and did much of the initial governing.

Zahir reigned from 1933 until 1973, keeping Afghanistan neutral in the Second World War and introducing elections and a Parliament with a new constitution in 1964.[22] His reign is regarded as another period of relative calm and even the model which a modern peace process should try to aim at. But the word 'relative' must be stressed. Many observers are guilty of looking upon Zahir's reign through the rose-coloured spectacles of nostalgia. The lack of foreign invasion means that his tenure is held up as an era of peace. It is often forgotten that he still faced a series of tribal rebellions and internal challenges.

Zahir's reign was ended by the familiar fratricidal dynamics that had dismantled previous Durrani dynasties. The Third Durrani Dynasty collapsed in 1973, when Zahir's cousin Daoud Khan staged a coup while Zahir was in Europe for eye surgery. Zahir went into exile rather than risk civil war, but Afghanistan still descended into chaos, anarchy and economic meltdown. The Soviets invaded a few years later, marking the end of centuries of Durrani rule.

What all of these eras show is that, while battles against invaders are a well-documented part of Pashtun history, internal rivalries clearly permeate Pashtun life too. Fratricide, subversion and subterfuge have been a persistent plague among leaders. Even close family members are fair game in the quest for honour, independence and power. The Durrani history also demonstrates that attempts by the central government to control the Pashtun tribes rarely end well. If tribesmen perceive anything as an attack on their independence or honour, a coup d'état is not just a risk, it is an inevitability.

But the eventual downfall of the Durrani dynasties was not the end of the Pashtun grip on power. Instead, it finally cleared a path for the tribes who had been deliberately kept out of Kabul, marginalized and ostracized by the Durranis for the past two centuries – the men of the Ghilzai Confederation.

PART IV

The Ghilzai Confederation

Chapter 11

Ghilzai Genealogy and Geography

If the Durrani tribes are typecast as the 'royals', then their counterparts in the Ghilzai Confederation are the 'rogues'. While central government has been the Durrani domain, the historical stereotype of Afghanistan's other main tribal confederation is that of mountain-men who inhabit the more remote rural regions.

Belonging to the Bettani branch of the Pashtun tribal structure, the Ghilzai are often said to be the most populous confederation in Afghanistan, larger even than the Durrani.[1] But such a statistic is difficult to verify. Even after years of international presence in Afghanistan, copious academic studies and endless reams of research, much about the Ghilzais is still shrouded in myth – or simply misunderstood.[2]

While their record as state rulers is less lengthy than that of their Durrani rivals, the Ghilzai tribes have not been absent from historical events. Whenever there has been a tribal uprising, Ghilzai have not been far away. This has earned them a reputation as fearless, independent warriors but also a constant source of instability in the region. In modern history alone they have been belligerents in three Anglo-Afghan Wars and in many revolts against the Durrani dynasties. This is why foreign descriptions of Ghilzai tribesmen are frequently pejorative. In the 1880s, after the Second Anglo-Afghan War, one British soldier wrote:

> Physically they are a remarkably fine race, and in stature, courage and strength of body they are second to none in Afghanistan, but they are a very barbarous people, the pastoral clans especially, and in their wars excessively savage and vindictive.[3]

The same author, Surgeon-Major Bellew, then doubled down on his criticisms, claiming that any contact with the Ghilzai 'has been that of unmitigated hostility and the deepest treachery', as they are 'notoriously predatory in their habits and feud amongst themselves and with their neighbours'.[4]

Such withering criticism is not reserved for Bellew's era. It still infuses modern texts, partly because descriptions from British imperialist accounts have often been cherry-picked by later writers. The stories that tend to be regurgitated are those laden with the most intrigue, meaning that the negative qualities of the Pashtun tribes – particularly the Ghilzais – are perpetuated, while positive traits are less commonly referenced or ignored altogether. This is despite the fact that even the most scathing accounts by nineteenth-century British orientalists actually convey a grudging respect for Ghilzai courage and fighting abilities. The first British envoy to engage the Pashtuns, Mountstuart Elphinstone, admitted that Ghilzais are

> more turbulent and less civilised than any Durranis but they are brave and respectable people . . . they are probably the largest, handsomest and fairest of all the Afghans.[5]

Some texts, including Surgeon-Major Bellew's, recognize the Ghilzais' independent spirit and their tendency to be much stricter than the Durrani in following the *Pashtunwali* honour code. They also concede that the Ghilzai display many 'softer' attributes which seemingly run counter to the negative stereotype, including an insistence on providing hospitality, shelter and forgiveness to anyone needing it – including sworn enemies. This is why centuries-old texts like Bellew's are still useful. Despite their difficult language and outdated attitudes, they were written as ethnographic studies which cover culture, customs and habits – including some of these gentler qualities. More recent research tends instead to frame tribal characteristics in terms of modern-era militant jihadism or Taliban-related terrorism, which risks reducing the tribes to their most aggressive tendencies, overlooking their softer qualities and perpetuating their demonization as violence-prone barbarians.

Ghilzai origins

Whether his portrayal is accurate or not, Surgeon-Major Bellew's writings about the Ghilzai – dating from 1880 – remain among the most comprehensive accounts of their origins and etymology. In his book, *Races of Afghanistan*, he details some of the disputed claims around the origin of the Ghilzai name, mentioning supposed links to today's Central Asian states and potential Turkic origins. Bellew suggests that 'Ghilzai' stems from the Turkic word *Khilich*, meaning 'sword' (and *Khilici*, 'swordsman').[6] He adds that this could be another example of the Turkic trend of naming peoples after a specific peculiarity. Other examples are 'Kazakh', which comes from 'cossack' (robber), or 'Kyrgyz' coming from *cirghiz* (wanderer).[7] Bellew is not the only source to mention possible Turkic ancestry. Other anthropologists tie the Ghilzais to Hepthalite Turk nomads, who roamed a region from the Indus River to Persia and Central Asia between the fifth and seventh centuries.[8]

Bellew also wrote that the Khilici were a 'mixed population of Jews, Israelites, Afghans, Indians and Persians' who lived around Ghor, and that 'likely due to Arab incusions they moved and settled south of Ghazni'. From there, he suggests, they spread further south and east into the Sulaiman Mountains and border areas where their homeland is today.[9]

More recent accounts expand on the Turkic theory, claiming that the Ghilzai may descend from the Khalaj people – commonly known as Attila's Huns – who originally lived along the Syr Darya River which runs through Kyrgyzstan and Kazakhstan.[10] The historian Jonathan Lee is one proponent of this hypothesis. In *Afghanistan: A History from 1260 to the Present* (2018), he traces the Khalaj-Ghilzai connection back to tenth century sources and also points out that the Khalaj were semi-nomadic pastoralists – a way of life that many Ghilzai tribes continue to follow today. The theory is that some Khalaj communities were brought to Afghanistan between the tenth and fourteenth centuries to fight as mercenaries for successive empires that ruled the region – being called *Ghulams* (slave troops). Some of these mercenaries stayed, settled and intermarried with locals, eventually becoming Pashtunized. The name 'Khalaj' gradually morphed into 'Khalji', then 'Ghilji' and then 'Ghilzai'.[11]

Other common – but suspect – claims which tend to circulate in casual conversation are that 'Ghil' means 'third' and 'zai' means 'born a son', or that the Ghilzai name derives from 'ghar-zai', which means 'born of a mountain' and refers to the Ghilzai tribes generally living in the mountainous regions of the east, as opposed to the Durranis who dominate the southern flatlands.

As with much of Pashtun history, there is no conclusive scientific or definitive answer. The theory generally accepted by Ghilzais themselves is that they descend from Ghalzoe, the son of Qais Abdur Rashid's granddaughter Bibi Mato and her husband, the Persian Prince Shah Hussain. There is broad Ghilzai consensus on this, even if it bolsters their rivals' claims that the Ghilzai are not of true Pashtun stock because their supposed progenitor was a foreigner who seduced an Afghan maiden and fathered an illegitimate child – all sources of shame which run counter to the principles of *Pashtunwali*.

Ghilzai geography

What is more conclusive than any origin theory or etymology is geography. Unlike other Pashtun tribes that spread across the international boundary, the vast majority of Ghilzai tribesmen reside in Afghanistan, not Pakistan. The tribes of this confederation cover a wide area colloquially known as the Ghilzai belt (see Map 4). At the northern end of the Ghilzai belt, Kabul is the buffer between the Ghilzai tribes and the other non-Pashtun ethnic groups who dominate Afghanistan's northern provinces. At the southern end, Zabul is a province that forms the last bastion of the Ghilzai tribes before the Durrani-dominated southern provinces (known as Loy Kandahar). The capital of Zabul, now known as Qalat, was historically called Qalat-i-Ghilzai. Given that the area around it is the faultline between the Ghilzai and the Durrani homelands, it has been called the crucible where 'present day mutual antipathy between the Durrani and Ghilzai was forged'.[12]

In addition to Zabul Province, Ghilzai tribes dominate Afghanistan's southeastern area, known as Loya (Greater) Paktia (see Map 3). While Pashtun purists would argue that it consists of Khost, Paktia and Paktika alone, others often include parts or all of Logar, Ghazni and Wardak provinces (and even Waziristan in Pakistan). The foothills of the Sulaiman mountain range, allegedly named after the Israelite King Solomon, stretch across this area and stitch Ghilzai lands together, providing hideaways and natural defences against invaders.[13]

The western edge of Loya Paktia and the Ghilzai belt, areas which border Daikundi and western Ghazni provinces, are where Ghilzai tribes' territory rubs up against the lands of the Hazaras in Afghanistan's central highlands. These interethnic faultlines are long-running sources of animosity and inter-ethnic feuding. Violence frequently flares when Ghilzai tribes stray into areas 'belonging' to other ethnic groups. This happens because some Ghilzai tribes have historically been – and still are – practising nomadism.

Chapter 12

The Kuchi Nomads and Other Ghilzai Tribes

Nomadism is central to the Ghilzai identity, even if not all Ghilzai tribes are nomadic. Those who are known as *Kuchis* (or *Powindah* in Pakistan). The term is said to stem from the Persian word for migrations (*koch*)[1] and refers to those who 'from time immemorial . . . have spent the winter months in the plains of what is now Pakistan and indeed beyond that in India too, as far as Calcutta and even to Australia'.[2]

Traditionally, the Kuchi migratory lifestyle was based around livestock, meaning they would follow their herds of sheep or goats around the region. It would be a mass movement in that all Kuchis moved at the same time of year, but not as one unit or on the same migratory path. In early spring, communities would pack up their famous black tents into caravans consisting of eleven households and move towards Afghanistan's central highlands to find fresh grazing.[3] As summer ended, they returned to warmer lowland pastures in the Indus Valley of Pakistan or areas with similar climates. While climatic reasons were the main motive for migration, the movement also had economic benefits, since it enabled money to be made from trading along the migratory routes. The Kuchis transported products from Afghanistan and Central Asia to be sold in Indian markets – and vice versa. Some Kuchi men also took winter jobs in Pakistan and India, contributing to their reputation as the most industrious, adventurous and enterprising of all Pashtuns.[4]

Some Kuchis famously made it as far as Australia, where British officials once took them and their camels to open up the West Australian desert.[5] Between 1870 and 1920, up to 20,000 camels were shipped to Australia from the Gulf States, India and Afghanistan, together with around 2,000 cameleers.[6] The animals were suited to the harsh climate, having the resilience to carry riders and cargo across the unforgiving Australian interior.

Some Kuchi communities still practise nomadism today, albeit fewer than in the past. Estimates of the total Kuchi population range from 300,000 up to 3 million[7] – a 2005 Afghan government survey is most often quoted, putting the Kuchi population at about 2.5 million – and around 1.5 million are fully nomadic.[8] Yet even many of those who have settled, or have at least become semi-nomadic, still identify proudly as nomads and have a longing to travel.

Any Kuchi discussion of land or migrations will inevitably feature the heated issue of the Durand Line. One incident that is still sensitive in Kuchi minds occurred in September 1961 and was fuelled by a break in diplomatic relations between Afghanistan and Pakistan. Within weeks of Pakistan accusing Kabul of harassing Pakistani diplomats, the Afghan authorities unilaterally closed the border. This was a largely symbolic move given the border's porosity, and would not have prevented the Kuchi seasonal migration. But the Kuchis were then stopped from crossing by Pakistani authorities, who accused Afghanistan of sending subversive elements along with the nomads. Pakistan is also said to have resented the burden that the migrating Kuchis placed on the Pakistani economy and 'the damage they did to crops, the diseases they brought, the complaints they provoked from resident tribesmen'. Pakistani officials claimed that extra wheat had to be imported to feed them and that public health teams had to be diverted from other areas to inoculate and treat the nomads.[9] This halting of the seasonal migration – which lasted for two years – ignited what a classified CIA report called a 'period of stress' between Afghanistan and Pakistan. Even travellers who had visas were denied entry, and it was only in 1963 that both countries started to permit the border to be crossed again.[10] For Kuchis, being caught in the middle of this politicking raised the prospect of starvation, so many chose to settle or were encouraged to do so by the Afghan government (with Soviet aid).[11]

Problems with Pakistan are not the only long-running feud involving the Kuchis. They are also known for the tensions that their migrations stoke with other ethnic groups, usually over access to land. One longstanding conflict is between the Kuchis and the Hazaras of Afghanistan's central highlands, where Kuchis migrate as spring begins. Modern Kuchi leaders protest that they are being forcibly excluded from the lands they have used for hundred of years by Hazaras who want to create an Iranian-backed Shia ministate in the central highlands.[12] Hazaras contend that the predatory nomads are in cahoots with the Taliban, who forced the Hazaras into famine in the 1990s and who now want to manipulate inter-ethnic and sectarian tensions to take control of Hazara territory.

These feuds have damaged the Kuchis' reputation. Even fellow Pashtuns will disparage the Kuchis, especially when migrants take winter jobs in Pakistani cities as moneylenders – which some say contradicts the principles of Islam. Religious fundamentalists also criticize the Kuchis for allowing women go unveiled. Kuchi women are renowned for their colourful long dresses and, rather than wearing veils, simply turn their faces away from strange men to maintain their dignity.[13] Kuchis have also been derided for having to rely on others, for example to obtain permission to pass through their land.[14] To Pashtun traditionalists, this represents being at someone else's mercy, although Kuchis argue that despite living a hard life and being constantly on the move, no nomad will ever be caught begging.[15] Like all other Pashtuns, they value independence and honour above all else.

The tribes of the Ghilzai Confederation

None of the individual tribes within the Ghilzai Confederation are completely nomadic, although the majority have at least some Kuchi clans. There are also small Kuchi clans in other tribes, including the Zadran, Mangal and Khostwal tribes (of the Karlani branch), as well as small clans in the Durrani Confederation and parts of the Baloch and Tajik ethnicities.[16]

But there is another divide within the Ghilzai Confederation that is more important than any Kuchi vs non-Kuchi split. Just as the Durrani Confederation has the Zirak and Panjpai divisions, the Ghilzai Confederation is also divided in two. Its divisions are known as 'Turan' and 'Burhan'. Figure 8 depicts these divisions, along with other Ghilzai forebears and tribes.[17]

Within the Turan division, the Hotak, Tokhi and Kharoti tribes are the most prominent. The Hotak and Tokhi see themselves as 'true' Ghilzais and sometimes push a narrative that their Kharoti cousins are *hamsaya* – a term used to describe a group shunned by its own kin and given refuge by another tribe, eventually becoming part of the latter's lineage.

In earlier history, two tribes in the Turan division – the Hotak and Tokhi – formed the power base of the Ghilzai Confederation. They led the Hotak dynasty, which ruled Afghanistan and parts of Persia in the early eighteenth century, before Ahmad Shah Durrani emerged and the Durrani Dynasties took over. After the downfall of the Hotak dynasty, the Burhan tribes gradually rose to superiority within the Ghilzai Confederation. They are among the most prominent in Afghanistan today. In that division, the Sulaimankhel and Ahmadzai are the best-known names.

There is longstanding competition between the Turan and Burhan divisions, but it is less intense – or at least less famous – than the competition between the two divisions in the Durrani Confederation. One of the more commonly cited intra-Ghilzai rivalries is that between the Sulaimankhel tribe (Burhan) and the Kharoti tribes (Turan), which is usually put down to each tribe vying for influence in Paktika province (where both have a large presence).[18]

The Ahmadzai tribe deserve special mention as they have been particularly prominent in recent history. Originally a sub-tribe of the Sulaimankhel, the Ahmadzai grew so large and influential that they are now treated as an individual tribe. They have often been the Ghilzai tribe most closely associated with the Durrani rulers in Kabul (and have obtained government/military positions as a result).[19] Two of Afghanistan's recent leaders were Ahmadzais. One was President Mohammad

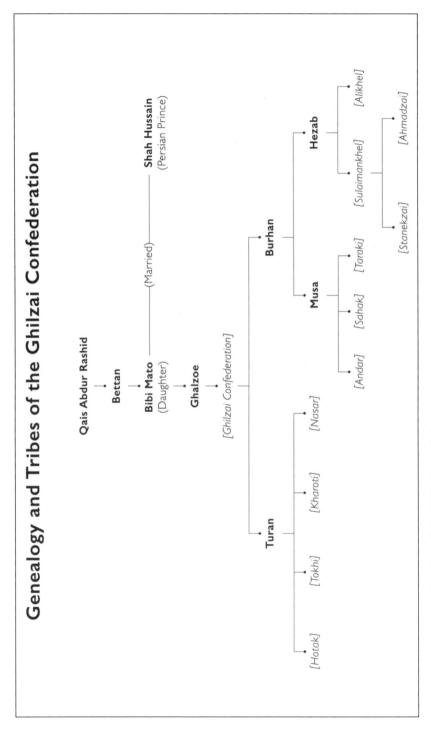

Figure 8: Genealogy and Tribes of the Ghilzai Confederation

Najibullah, who was in office from 1987 to 1992, overseeing the Soviet withdrawal and the period leading to the Afghan civil war. Hindsight increasingly paints him as a president who wanted to make peace with all of Afghanistan's factions, and who did not deserve his ignominious end in 1996, when he was castrated by the Taliban and hanged from a lamp post after years stuck in asylum in the UN compound in Kabul.

The other notable Ahmadzai president was Ashraf Ghani, although he symbolically dropped his tribal name upon being elected in 2014 as the second president of post-2001 Afghanistan. Ghani led Afghanistan through the NATO coalition's draw-down and into a fragile peace process with the Taliban. But he will be forever denigrated as a villain rather than recalled as a hero. As the Taliban advanced towards Kabul in August 2021, Ghani fled the Presidential Palace, first taking a helicopter to Uzbekistan and then flying on to Dubai. His escape was the final straw for the Afghan Republic. Rather than stand by his repeated vows to fight to the death, he essentially handed the keys of Kabul to the Taliban.

While both these presidents pursued national peace efforts with some vigour, the tribes of the Ghilzai confederation are more commonly seen as having a strained relationship with central government, even when they are part of it. Justifiably or not, the Ghilzais are generally typecast as tribes whose constant resistance to the central state, and any modernization or reforms it attempts to achieve, is at the root of many of Afghanistan's most difficult political power struggles – including those that have turned bloody.

Chapter 13

Recent Ghilzai Rule: Ideology over Genealogy?

While the Durranis are known for their long-term control of state institutions, the Ghilzai have not been completely absent from Kabul (as Presidents Ghani and Najibullah exemplify). But 'frenzied and fleeting' may be the best way to summarize the Ghilzai periods in power so far.

The presence of Ghilzai presidents in Kabul came after the downfall of the Third Durrani Dynasty. It coincided with the Soviet invasion, the communist years and the increasing intrusion of political ideologies into Afghanistan. Beginning in the late 1970s, a string of Afghan presidents had Ghilzai backgrounds. But unlike their Durrani predecessors, their rise to power was not based on ethnic or tribal affiliation alone. They identified as communists more than tribesmen. Complicating the tribal dynamics of that era is the fact that while Ghilzai presidents sat in Kabul, equally prominent Ghilzai men led the anti-state and anti-Soviet mujahideen. They, too, rose to prominence on ideology rather than ethnic or tribal affiliation – theirs being an Islamist rather than a communist agenda.

These dynamics highlight the late twentieth-century trend for political and religious ideology to take precedence over Pashtun genealogy – a trend which has hastened the crumbling of traditional tribal structures and threatens the future of the Pashtun tribal way of life.[1]

The Ghilzai during and after the Durrani Dynasties

The Ghilzai Confederation never faded into irrelevance during the Durrani Dynasties. Its tribes were said to be 'generally quiet under [Durrani] rule, but never very obedient'.[2] The Ghilzais led numerous uprisings, rarely threatening to undermine the state but forcing Durrani elites to devote attention to placating their Ghilzai rivals. This position is encapsulated in the saying, 'He who would rule at Kabul must make peace with the Ghilzai and make it to a great extent on their terms.'[3]

One example is a Ghilzai-led rebellion in 1885, which was crushed quickly by the Emir Abdur Rahman Khan. To reprimand the Ghilzai rebels, he forcibly resettled the culprits in the north of Afghanistan, creating Pashtun pockets in traditionally non-Pashtun areas (see Map 6). This did reduce Ghilzai troublemaking initially, and established a Pashtun buffer against Russian aggression, but in hindsight it was a historic mistake: it gave rise to grievances among the resettled tribes which the Taliban have successfully manipulated for their own gain in recent years (as later chapters will explain).

There are multiple other examples of Ghilzai-led uprisings throughout the period of the Durrani Dynasties. They demonstrate a distinct pattern of Ghilzai revulsion at perceived state interference in their affairs or challenges to their independence. Intermittent Ghilzai rebellions continued right up until the 1970s, when the Third Durrani Dynasty finally collapsed. It was only then – after 230 years of Durrani rule – that anyone of the Ghilzai Confederation returned to power in Kabul.

The first man to do so was Noor Mohammad Taraki. He was an initiator of the Soviet-backed coup in 1978 that became known as the Saur Revolution. From then until the collapse of communism and the civil war in 1992, almost all Afghan presidents were from a Ghilzai background.[4] The last was Mohammad Najibullah. In spite of his attempts to broker peace, his personality had some less palatable traits: his own brother described him as a vain and violent man who 'delighted in striking fear into his family, and whose private life departed sharply from Afghan moral codes'.[5] He was nicknamed 'Najib the Bull' on account of his physically imposing bulk and his 'better to be feared than loved' approach to governing. Najibullah was a long-time Soviet asset who had risen to become head of Afghanistan's vicious intelligence agency during the communist era. All of this fuelled the mujahideen's hatred of him and explains the barbarity of his eventual execution.

The Durrani Dynasties and the tenures of Ghilzai presidents were similar in that the pattern of assassinations, tribal strife and violent uprisings remained constant. While the Durrani Dynasties had seen frequent changes of leadership, Najibullah and most Ghilzai presidents enjoyed even shorter tenures, some counted in days rather than years. Another notable difference between Durrani and Ghilzai rule was that the Ghilzai period in power saw political ideology become more influential than tribal affiliation. The late twentieth century was marked by the repeated emergence of new and opposing ideologies, leading to increasingly violent cycles of conflict, each crippling the state even more than the last and leading Afghanistan deeper into the abyss in which it found itself in the early 1990s.

But the communist years are rarely described as 'a Ghilzai era' in the way that past centuries are identified by Durrani rule. The presidency may have been held by successive men who had grown up as Ghilzai, but not all Ghilzai tribes backed the communist regimes. As mentioned earlier, some of the most prominent anti-state leaders and Islamists in the mujahideen were also from Ghilzai tribes –

another reminder that the late twentieth century was an era where 'communist' or 'Islamist' were the primary markers of identity, rather than tribal affiliation or ethnicity.

The Durrani did not immediately regain Kabul when communism collapsed in the early 1990s. After President Najibullah's regime was overturned in 1992, Afghanistan descended into civil war. This period has been well covered in other books, and their analysis does not need to be reiterated here in detail. The broad trend was that the country split (again) into smaller fiefdoms, each ruled by a regional strongman – many of whom adopted a veneer of tribal affiliation, as well as manipulating concepts of honour and revenge to try to gain tribal legitimacy. As this situation spread, it set the conditions for the emergence of the Taliban in 1994, a movement initially welcomed by Afghans as a counterweight to havoc-wreaking warlords.

The Taliban was made up of students of Islam (*talibs*) and others from the mujahideen who had fought the Soviets. Its members were overwhelmingly Pashtun, but it was Islamist rather than tribal in outlook. They rolled into Kabul in 1996, establishing an Emirate and making their leader, Mullah Omar of the Hotak tribe, the de facto Head of State. This put a tribesman from the Ghilzai Confederation back in control of Kabul and the Afghan state, even if the Taliban was far from a Ghilzai-only organization. It also meant that, once again, a movement which seized power through rebellion and revolution would quickly have to try to transform itself into a legitimate government. It would have to learn how to rule the masses.

For Mullah Omar, it would be a tricky transition from leading a local insurgent group to governing a multi-ethnic nation. But this was a challenge not unfamiliar to the Ghilzai Confederation. It is one that they had faced nearly 300 years earlier, when the last Ghilzai tribesman ruled the area – just before the start of the Durrani Dynasties. Like Mullah Omar, he was also from the Hotak tribe.

His name was Mirwais Hotak.

Chapter 14

Mirwais Hotak and the Ghilzai Golden Era

The infusion of political ideologies into Afghan's already mixed melting pot of ethnic and tribal issues makes the events of the late twentieth century difficult to decipher. What can help illuminate the characteristics of Ghilzai rule is a look at a *pre*-modern example, when at the turn of the eighteenth century this confederation created an empire that ruled most of Afghanistan and parts of Persia.

Known as the Hotak Dynasty, it exhibited many familiar features of Pashtun politics, including fratricide and an inability to consolidate control over other tribes. In hindsight, this Ghilzai-led dynasty arguably created the conditions for Ahmad Shah Durrani's rise to power in 1747, and subsequent centuries of Durrani rule. But at the time it was a golden era for the Ghilzai Confederation.

The Hotak Dynasty: the Ghilzai golden era

Pre-modern Ghilzai history is poorly documented. Stories circulate of association with the Ghaznavid Empire that ruled much of South Asia from 977 to 1186 and whose leaders allegedly employed Ghilzais to help invade India and spread Islam.[1] But in general, little has been written about the Ghilzais until the early 1700s, when they instigated a tribal uprising against the Persian Governor in Kandahar.[2]

At that time, Loy Kandahar (Greater Kandahar) was the eastern limit of the Persian Safavid Empire. Sandwiched between the Sunni Mughal Empire that ruled India and the Shi'a Safavids in Persia, Kandahar became a battleground where powerful empires frequently clashed. As the seventeenth century ended, the Safavid Empire was in decline. Its Persian leaders faced a triple challenge of corruption, sectarian strife and foreign meddling.[3] By 1704 tribal unrest was also stirring, and Safavid representatives in Kandahar, led by a fearsome Georgian Prince named Gurgin Khan, were ordered to quell the bothersome Pashtuns using internment, execution and any other means necessary.

One Pashtun tribesman caught up in Safavid attempts to crush the dissent was Mirwais Hotak of the local Hotak tribe. Gurgin Khan had him arrested and sent to stand trial in the Safavid capital, Isfahan, approximately 400 miles south of Tehran. Worse still, Gurgin demanded to marry Mirwais' eldest daughter. A marriage alliance like this with a foreigner – and such a treacherous one – would stain the Hotak tribe's honour, so Mirwais sent a slave girl instead, to remind Gurgin that Mirwais saw him as nothing more than a Safavid stooge.

Once in Isfahan, Mirwais mustered all of his Pashtun charm and befriended the Safavid leader, Sultan Hussain. He convinced the Sultan that Gurgin Khan was plotting to overthrow him, so Sultan Hussain released Mirwais without charge and sent him back home to Kandahar. But before returning home Mirwais travelled on pilgrimage to Mecca, where he woke from a dream to find his sword unsheathed, a signal from Allah that he now had one task and one task only – to seek revenge.

Mirwais had seen that the Safavid Empire was crumbling. He had learned that Shah Hussain was more of a *bon vivant* than a warrior. He sensed opportunity. Back in Kandahar, his Sunni tribesmen were also ripe for rebellion, angered by Persian pressure to convert to Shi'a Islam.[4] In April 1709 Mirwais set out to woo Gurgin Khan, organizing a gathering in his honour. But the feast was a façade. Mirwais' men ambushed the Safavid attendees, slaughtering every single one of them, including Gurgin Khan himself. They then swiftly scythed through any remaining Persian military officials in the area. The rebellion was under way.

When news reached the Safavid leadership in Isfahan, they dispatched a large force – up to 30,000 troops – with orders to restore order and hunt down Mirwais. This army, led by Gurgin's brother, had some initial successes, even inducing the Afghans to agree terms of surrender. But the Safavids dismissed the Afghan offer because a superior Safavid fighting force would be shamed if it allowed an irritant bunch of tribesmen to negotiate terms. Such Safavid arrogance was misplaced. The Pashtun tribesmen withdrew their offer of surrender and fought even harder, soon turning the tide of the war. One historian wrote that the Safavids' 'uncompromising attitude impelled them to make a fresh desperate effort, resulting in the complete defeat of the Persian army (of whom only some 700 escaped) and the death of their General'.[5]

The slaughter of the Safavids only added to Afghanistan's growing reputation as the graveyard of Empires, a place where foreign armies missed opportunities and misjudged the Afghans' fighting abilities. For Mirwais, it meant power. It allowed him to establish the Hotak Dynasty in 1709, although he refused to call himself a King or Emir. To his people he was the Prince of Kandahar. To his men he was 'General'.

Mirwais died of natural causes just six years later, in 1715. But his family carried on building a dynasty that encompassed most of Afghanistan, Iran, western Pakistan and parts of Tajikistan and Turkmenistan. Yet not all Hotak rulers acted with the honour that Pashtuns associate with Mirwais. His son Mahmud, who had killed his own uncle in a quest to succeed Mirwais, started leading Ghilzai armies on raids into Safavid territory. Encouraged by a weak response from the already-disintegrating Safavid Empire, he pushed deeper. By March 1722 Mahmud's tribal forces had routed a much larger Safavid army at the so-called Battle of Gulnabad, on the outskirts of Isfahan. With the Safavids in disarray, Mahmud then encircled the city and blockaded it until starvation and disease forced it to surrender, with the Safavid Shah abdicating in his favour. The Ghilzais of the Hotak Dynasty had finally ended the Safavid Empire after 221 years.

But peace was fleeting. Mahmud was so gripped by paranoia about the vanquished Persian elites plotting against him that he invited them all to a meeting, locked them in and had his troops cut them to pieces.[6] This kind of approach had consequences – and the Ghilzai golden era was not to last. Persian communities rejected Hotak rule, aggrieved at the defeat of their empire and resentful of Sunni Islam seeping into Shi'a areas. The Hotaks had often mistreated their Safavid subjects, who never forgot the terrible sieges of Isfahan which had left its inhabitants 'reduced to eating rats and dogs'.[7] The Hotaks, inexperienced in multi-ethnic governing, also struggled to secure the large territory they had seized so quickly.[8] A series of bloody successions added to the turmoil, and continued challenges from a rival Pashtun tribe – then called the Abdali Confederation but now known as the Durranis – did not make life any easier. The Hotak Dynasty began to unravel as quickly as it had been created.

Ashraf Hotak, a nephew of Mirwais, took over in 1725 but was defeated in 1729 by a Persian military commander named Nader Shah, who reorganized and rallied the remnants of defeated Persian forces. Nader Shah also enlisted some tribesmen from the Abdali Confederation to help counter the Ghilzai tribes of the Hotak Dynasty. One tribe enlisted was led by a young cavalryman known as Ahmad Shah Abdali, who would later be known as Ahmad Shah Durrani.

By 1738 Nader Shah had conquered Kandahar and ended the Hotak Dynasty. As a reward for fighting alongside him, he restored the Abdali Confederation to power in Kandahar, while the tribes of the Ghilzai Confederation retreated north into what is known today as Zabul Province (now the southern extent of the Ghilzai belt).

This story of Mirwais and the Hotak Dynasty holds more than just historical interest. The chain of events that Mirwais set in motion shaped the conditions in which the Afghan state was eventually created in 1747. They also shaped the geographical spread of Afghanistan's two big Pashtun confederations, allowing the Durrani to dominate the southern flatlands of Loy Kandahar, while the Ghilzai stretched northwards from Zabul – an alignment that still exists today.

Mirwais' story shows that tribal strife is not only a contemporary affliction in Afghanistan. Fratricide, inter-tribal conflict and bloody successions form a longstanding Pashtun pattern. His story also introduces the idea – seen throughout Afghan history – that no matter how successful an insurgency is on the battlefield, moving into governing is not an easy transition. The Taliban are the latest testament to this.

But if there is one conclusion to be drawn from Mirwais' story, it is that those events of the early eighteenth century are part of the reason for an intra-Pashtun rivalry that still poisons Pashtun – and Afghan – politics today. They were the seeds of the deep-seated mistrust between the two most powerful tribal confederations in Afghanistan and the intense competition it engenders – the Durrani vs Ghilzai rivalry.

Chapter 15

The Durrani vs Ghilzai Rivalry

Foreign encroachment into tribal lands understandably grabs headlines – the 'Graveyard of Empires' epithet did not emerge from thin air. But Pashtuns don't spend every day driving off infidels and invaders. Internal power struggles are more of a constant. For all the talk of outsider incursions, a more pressing question for Pashtuns is, 'Who is our opponent *at home*?'

Afghanistan's most important internal power struggle is between its two largest tribal confederations, the Durrani and the Ghilzai. Although this rivalry does come with a caveat, being just one layer in a country gripped by multiple distinct conflicts. Outside of any fights with foreign invaders, they include struggles:

1) Between ethnicities
2) Between rural and urban societies
3) Between regional states, especially India and Pakistan
4) Between Pashtun tribes (i.e. the Durrani-Ghilzai rivalry)[1]

The conflict between the Durrani and the Ghilzai confederations has always shaped Afghan political developments, because these confederations represent the majority of the Pashtun and wider Afghan populations. It is a long-running conflict, but it may be better described as a rivalry, given that it is not always explosive or even visible to the international eye. It is often subtle and sub-surface, with passions only igniting periodically. It is often more a constant state of dull enmity than a casualty-inflicting conflict. Either way, how this political power struggle plays out has altered Afghanistan's past and will influence its future.

Animosity rooted in history

The Durrani-Ghilzai dynamic is not new. It has roots in the seventeenth-century battles between the Safavid and Mughal Empires, when the Durrani tribes sided with the Safavids and the Ghilzai joined the Mughals.[2] More has been written about this rivalry in the context of the events of the early eighteenth century, starting with Mirwais Hotak and his ruthless suppression of a 1707 uprising led by the Durrani tribes (then known as Abdalis).[3]

A century later, British orientalists alluded to the rivalry. In 1815, the first British envoy to Afghanistan wrote that 'There is not an inhabitant of the Caubul dominions who would hesitate between the Dooraunees and Ghiljies, or who does not look with dread to the chance of the ascendancy of the latter tribe.'[4] Other historical accounts identify a consistent divide-and-rule dynamic, with deliberate Durrani attempts to subordinate the Ghilzai by excluding them from power and expelling them from certain areas. Successive Durrani rulers tried to buy off certain Ghilzai tribes, while concurrently stoking infighting among others in order to weaken rival leaders and undermine revolts.[5] This kind of manoeuvring can be traced as far back as the first Durrani leader, Ahmad Shah Durrani, who allegedly gave powerful positions to his own kin ahead of an equal share with Ghilzai tribes – a tactic that many Afghans would say is not confined to the past.

Tension continued

Durrani vs Ghilzai antipathy is not a relic of yesteryear. It has survived the centuries. One trend seen in the early 1970s was the increasingly detribalized, urbanized Durrani elite building alliances with educated Tajiks and Uzbeks and recruiting other minorities into the emerging national army. This was easier than having to collect taxes from, conscript or subdue belligerent Pashtun rivals, but it fuelled intra-Pashtun fractures as it gave political prominence to non-Pashtun minorities, much to the chagrin of the Ghilzai tribesmen.

After the 1978 Saur Revolution and Soviet occupation, Durrani-Ghilzai tension was further heightened. While a string of Ghilzai presidents were installed or backed by the Soviets, the Afghan military became dominated by officers from the 'Khalq' faction of the Communist Party, many of whom were rurally-based Ghilzai. Their dominance of the security forces, complemented by Soviet-backed Ghilzai presidents, left the Durrani underrepresented in Kabul (at least when compared to historical trends). Similar dynamics were seen on the other side of the conflict. Of the seven mujahideen factions, the three Ghilzai-led groups received most support from Pakistan, leading to suggestions that this was Pakistan's response to Soviet backing of Ghilzai presidents.

Either way, the communist era led to a new phase in the long-running Durrani vs Ghilzai rivalry. A hangover from this time lingers on today. Not only is there residual animosity between men who were involved with various factions, but the communist drive for social revolution, land reform and reduced influence of Islam is often blamed for a perceived breakdown in traditional Pashtun values and structures.[6] Even in September 2020, as peace negotiations started between the Taliban and the Afghan government in Qatar, these attitudes emerged again. When government negotiators arrived at the first formal meeting, their chief (a Ghilzai former communist) suggested that participants start introductions from the left. His Taliban counterpart, a Ghilzai former mujahid, quickly quipped, 'You always do things from the left. We mujahideen start from the right always.'[7] To further underline how recent decades have seen ideology often take precedence over genealogy, both these opponents were born in the same province and belong to the same tribe.

The Durrani-Ghilzai rivalry today

The Durrani vs Ghilzai dynamic continued to shape Afghanistan in the post-Soviet years, although it became less clear-cut as tribal dynamics were interwoven with warlordism and other drivers of conflict. When civil war erupted in the 1990s and the armed forces collapsed, the Ghilzais who dominated the military generally gravitated towards Ghilzai warlords and in the later 1990s to the Taliban, providing technical military skills early in the movement's development.[8] Durranis and non-Pashtuns went into exile with King Zahir Shah or resisted the Taliban by joining the so-called Northern Alliance.

After the US invasion in 2001, the Durrani-Ghilzai rivalry evolved again. While it risks oversimplifying complex conflict dynamics to describe it as such, the confrontation between the government led by President Hamid Karzai (a Durrani) and the Taliban led by Mullah Omar (a Ghilzai) was sometimes characterized as another incarnation of tribal rivalry – one which makes it easy to explain why peace eluded the Karzai era. Even if political and ideological differences could be negotiated, why would Karzai, a Durrani who had finally reclaimed the 'throne' for his confederation, make peace – and share power – with a Ghilzai-led Taliban?

When Karzai's tenure ended in 2014, the Durrani-Ghilzai dynamic evolved once more. In the 2014 and 2019 presidential elections, the lead Pashtun candidate was Ashraf Ghani, who belonged to the Ahmadzai tribe of the Ghilzai Confederation. On both occasions his challenger was Dr Abdullah Abdullah, who drew support from Tajik and other non-Pashtun constituencies.[9] Ghani won both times, in very contested circumstances. The common perception is that Abdullah could never win, as the numerically superior Pashtuns would eventually put inter-tribal differences aside and unite for the greater Pashtun good and to avoid non-Pashtun control in Kabul. Whether Durrani, Ghilzai or any other branch, every Pashtun would prefer a Pashtun in Kabul over a non-Pashtun – a lesson learned after the Tajik upstart Habibullah Kalakani briefly took the throne in 1929.

President Ghani dropped his tribal name on being elected in 2014, to market himself as a more inclusive leader. But his tenure saw familiar tribal and ethnic issues, albeit in a more subtle form than in previous centuries. He was routinely accused of Pashtun nationalism and of giving positions only to his Pashtun allies in order to cement Pashtun power and marginalize others. Non-Pashtuns alleged that the important ministries were stocked with Pashtuns. Durranis claimed that the government was stocked with Ghilzais.

Communities like the Tajiks, Hazaras and Uzbeks, who gained unprecedented access to government positions when the Taliban fled in 2001, started to perceive Ghilzai gain and non-Ghilzai loss. President Ghani's sloganeering about 'reform' and 'anti-corruption' looked, in the eyes of minorities, like pro-Pashtun policy-making. Moves to ethnically balance the security forces were branded by Tajiks as 'Pashtunization'. Other initiatives to retire ageing generals were seen as deliberate efforts to reduce Tajik control. Disenfranchised Durranis also used these initiatives to shape a narrative of Ghilzai dominance.[10]

As in the Soviet years, the Durrani-Ghilzai dynamic also played out on the other side. As the Afghan Presidential Palace changed from Karzai to Ghani (i.e. Durrani to Ghilzai), the Taliban went the other way. The movement founded and led by Mullah Omar, a Ghilzai from the Hotak tribe, reeled when news of his death emerged in 2015. The ensuing leadership struggle was won by Mullah Mansour of the Ishaqzai tribe (of the Panjpai division of the Durrani Confederation). Mansour was killed in a US drone strike in 2016, but the Durranis retained the Taliban leadership, with a religious scholar named Mullah Haibatullah taking over (a Noorzai tribesman and also a Panjpai Durrani).

How seismic were these shifting tribal dynamics? Not very, if judged by media coverage or the conclusions of analysts. But this is because basic tribal dynamics are not widely understood by outsiders, and because plenty of other hot topics absorb their attention. Trends like the Durrani-Ghilzai dynamic are usually slow burners, explicable in hindsight rather than in the moment.

The next evolutions in this long-running rivalry, or how it will be impacted by the Taliban's return to power in 2021, are not yet clear. But whatever way events play out, the rivalry is almost certain to be once again overshadowed by headline-grabbing political developments and not appreciated – at least by Westerners – as the influential clash of competing confederations that it is.

Same ethnicity, different outlook

The broad generalization is that the Durrani have been – and still see themselves as – the political rulers and the Afghan 'royalty' who have rightfully controlled the state's institutions since Ahmad Shah Durrani created it in 1747. Their grip on central government has often been at the expense of their Ghilzai rivals, with Ghilzais resenting what they see as deliberate and often devious Durrani efforts to disempower and subdue them. One historian, writing in 1934, explained:

> The invariable object of Durrani policy has been to weaken the Ghilzai by widening the breaches which exist between their clans and depriving them of any chiefs of power and influence who might be tempted to lead revolt; And at the same time, to reward and placate them. And so far, this policy has found success, for the Ghilzais, like the Jews, have turned from politics to trade; And their tribes have become rather collections of individuals than combined political bodies.[11]

The general view of the Ghilzai is that its tribes are more traditionally-minded than the Durrani. They have been prominent in fighting foreigners but tend to be under-represented in national decision-making, preferring egalitarianism, independence and ruralism over central government. This has hindered Ghilzai ability to build empires or challenge the Durrani dynasties. They have been consistently less capable than the Durranis at 'organizing into larger social groupings, . . . raising large military forces, and . . . establishing lasting governments'.[12] It also leads to the Durranis disparaging Ghilzais as 'mountain men' or 'nomads' – although Ghilzais proudly use the same terms to describe themselves. Leon Poullada, a former US Ambassador in the Kennedy adminstration, summed it up by saying that while the Durrani rulers sat in Kabul,

> most of the time the Ghilzai loomed ominously in the background ready to pounce whenever outside intervention stirred up its latent aggressiveness or internal weakness made the central government an easy prey. Thus, for the most part the Ghilzai have remained an indigestible lump in the Afghan national stomach.[13]

The overarching point is that the Pashtun tribes in Afghanistan cannot be understood without appreciating the enduring rivalry between the two largest tribal confederations. The mutual Durrani vs Ghilzai antipathy is at the root of centuries of conflict and continues to shape Afghanistan today. It will continue to impact Afghanistan's future. It may be surface-level, subtle or overshadowed by more pressing issues, but it is always there – no matter which political grouping or ethnic faction controls the state at any given time. Foreign invasions dominate the headlines, but the Durrani vs Ghilzai rivalry remains the most important power struggle for Pashtuns. This again underlines the fact that it is a grave mistake to treat the tribes as a single group or a homogeneous entity. Despite their shared ethnicity, there are clear differences, even seemingly insurmountable divisions, at all levels of the Pashtun tribal structure.

They are not 'one'.

PART V
Pashtunwali

Chapter 16

The Tribal Honour Code

Pashtunwali is called the 'honour code' for good reason. Honour, known as *nang*, is such a central part of it that tribesmen often call it *Nang-e-Pashto*.

Although something of a simplification, Pashtun honour is often said to revolve around the three 'Zs': *zan*, *zar*, *zamin* (women, gold, land). They are the traditional sources of power and pride in male-dominated Pashtun society. They are the core tenets of Pashtun culture. Take land as an example. It has always been of existential importance, because owning land provided an income and enabled a tribesman to build allegiances, wield influence and raise his social status. Being a Pashtun was essentially synonymous with being a landowner.

The burning desire to acquire land was noted by a young British cavalry officer-turned-war correspondent at the turn of the twentieth century. Winston Churchill wrote:

> In any dispute about a field boundary, it is customary for both claimants to walk around the boundary he claims, with the Koran in his hand, swearing all the time that the land he is walking on his own. To meet the difficulty of a false oath, while he's walking over his neighbour's land, he puts a little dust from his own field into his shoes. As both sides are acquainted with the trick, the dismal farce of swearing is usually soon abandoned, in favour of an appeal to force.[1]

A Pashtun man is obliged to protect his *zan*, *zar* and *zamin* at all times. A challenge or insult to any of them is an insult to his honour. To defend them is to defend his personal honour, his family's honour and the honour of his tribe. When a tribesman's *nang* is at stake, he should stop at nothing to preserve his tribe's integrity. If he succeeds he is a *nangialay*, a man that brings honour and prestige to his tribe. If he fails, he is a *benanga*, shameless or undignified. It is among the worst of insults.[2]

If he does not act in defence against dishonour, then his social status, his membership of the tribe and even his Pashtun identity are all threatened. He can be stripped of his rights, assets and protection. He can be banished from the tribe. This is why lives are willingly laid down to defend honour and to prevent perceptions of *sharm* (shame). This 'death before dishonour' attitude was summed up by the revered Pashtun warrior-poet, Khushal Khan Khattak:

Let the head be gone, wealth be gone, but the honour must not go, because the whole of dignity of a man is due to this honour.[3]

Pashtunwali is the blueprint for leading an honourable life. While most frequently described as an 'honour code', it has also been variously called a code of conduct, a set of guidelines, tribal edicts, a moral code, social currency, an unwritten constitution, internalized social and political norms, a frame of reference, a cultural identity, a tradition, customary law or a belief system that governs behaviour.[4] It has even been described simply as collective Pashtun wisdom built up over the centuries which, in the absence or weakness of state structures, furnishes the rules and laws to live by. Some say this makes it similar to the holy Jewish Torah.[5]

'The way of the Pathans' is a term coined by a former US Ambassador who wrote a book of the same name in the 1960s.[6] Other observers simply translate *Pashtunwali* as 'doing Pashtu'.[7] The German anthropologist Willi Steul provided a particularly comprehensive definition (1981):

Pashtunwali is comprised of the sum total values and social norms which determine the way of life peculiar to the Pashtuns. It is an all-embracing regulator for the preservation and conservation of the society and for the behavior patterns of the individual. It is an emic concept which includes everything which a Pashtun should or should not do. It is thus a means of ethnic identification and differentiation in relation to other ethnic groups . . . it can be seen above all as the values forced on the individual if he is to be a respected member of society and enjoy its acceptance.[8]

The term used to describe *Pashtunwali*'s set of values or rules is *narkh*. These rules, centred around the concept of honour, have been integral to the Pashtun identity for centuries. But exactly how far they date back is unclear. There are contradictory claims in the literature and encountered when talking to Pashtuns. The common assumption is that *Pashtunwali* pre-dates Islam's arrival in Afghanistan; although there is a lack of concrete proof. Some argue that it dates back as far as 3000–2000 BC,[9] while others suggest that many of *Pashtunwali*'s principles were only fully established by the turn of second millennium AD.[10]

The main challenge in providing an exact age, definition or interpretation of *Pashtunwali* is that it is an unwritten code. It is an inherited way of life, ingrained in Pashtuns from infancy. Children are socialized into it rather than taught about it. It is a social contract passed down through example rather than in writing. *Pashtunwali* is learned by observation and osmosis, through personal conduct and behaviour, as well as through folk tales, ancestral stories and poetry.

Despite the Western fascination with it, English language accounts of *Pashtunwali* are still relatively scarce, usually written by anthropologists and often with intrigue-laden interpretation rather than the strict understanding of the tribesman. When it is written about it is generally treated as an idealized concept – this book is no exception – and the strictest form of *Pashtunwali* is usually portrayed. In real life, however, it is implemented with flexibility and creativity depending on the context. Application of its unwritten rules varies by tribe and by territory. They are open to interpretation as the needs and outlook of the tribes evolve. One expert has explained how *Pashtunwali* represents an ideal rather than an absolute, 'not dissimilar to Western concepts of chivalry . . . just like chivalry, it is subject both to personal interpretation (which can be very creative) and to common abuse.'[11]

Pashtuns themselves interpret *Pashtunwali* variously because there is no definitive manual to refer to. It does not spring from one single authority. No single text dictates what is part of *Pashtunwali* and what is not. It is dynamic, and the strength of adherence to it depends on the tribe involved. Regional nuances as well as a rural-urban dynamics have led to localized variations in the *narkh* (values/rules). Most tribes in Pakistan tend to practise something close to the so-called *Razmak Narkh*, whereas the *Ahmadzai Narkh* is more prevalent in Afghanistan.[12] Yet in 1979, when experts at Afghanistan's Academy of Sciences tried to distil *Pashtunwali* into one text called *A dictionary of the terminology of Pashtun's tribal customary law and usages*, they explained that there are so many variations in Afghanistan that many tribes have virtually an individual *narkh* of their own.[13] Before he became Prime Minister of Pakistan in 2018, Imran Khan noted these evolutions in his own book on Pashtuns, writing that 'the wilder the tribes, the more strictly they follow the code of honour',[14] and that if Pashtuns move away from their homeland, adherence to *Pashtunwali* can weaken as 'they gradually adapt to the customs of the place where they live'.[15]

Given this flexibility, it is not uncommon for tribesmen to set aside *Pashtunwali*'s basic tenets for political expediency or adapt them to match personal ambitions. This can even be the case when it comes to patrilineality. Some Pashtuns deviate from the prerequisite of being born into a tribe in order to attain membership of it, especially if the outsider adheres to honour codes and intermarries with the right families. An oft-quoted historical example is the case of the Ghilzai confederation, with their matrilineal rather than patrilineal link to Qais Abdur Rashid. There are modern examples, too, such as dynamic individuals straying from traditional tribal collectivism in order to seize the economic opportunities brought by recent foreign interventions.

Pashtunwali's increasing elasticity, along with the supposed dilution of traditional Pashtun culture in the modern era, is why some observers – including other Afghans – will dismiss parts of *Pashtunwali* as romanticized but redundant constructs of the nineteenth century that are only kept alive by those who write about them and by continued Western fascination with them.

True or not, this narrative emphasises some important points about *Pashtunwali* and Pashtun culture in general. The flexibility with which *Pashtunwali* is interpreted today highlights the fact that pragmatism is as important a value to Pashtuns as anything else. In many cases, no code will stand in the way of seizing an opportunity. Behavioural traits – and interpretation of *Pashtunwali* – vary depending on specific contexts and individual tribes.

Also clear is that, whatever its exact age or interpretation, *Pashtunwali* is not a modern invention. It has survived the different forms of chaos and change that Pashtuns have faced over the centuries. It may evolve and adapt but, like the people who practise it, it is extremely resilient. Even if it has become less strict or more subtle, it still underpins society and politics. It is still an accepted code. It still shapes Pashtun culture and identity. It still influences the behaviour of Pashtun leaders in Pashtun areas. It still provides a window into the Pashtun psyche, because honour remains as important to today's Pashtuns as any other time in history.

This makes understanding *Pashtunwali* – and its individual principles – still a prerequisite to understanding the Pashtun tribes today.

Chapter 17

The Big Three Principles of *Pashtunwali*

The concept of revenge tends to frame foreigners' thinking on *Pashtunwali,* largely because sensationalized blood feuds grab attention and are discussed so frequently that they have been described as 'the Afghan equivalent of county cricket in the English shires'.[1]

But there is much more to the honour code than reciprocal bloodshed. It is also built around hospitality, equality and respect for elders, as well as other rules aimed at resolving disputes or governing engagement with outsiders.[2] These 'softer' tenets are equally, if not more, important Pashtun values. The anthropologist Louis Dupree, in his seminal book *Afghanistan* (1973), paraphrases *Pashtunwali's* individual rules – known as *narkh* – in this list:

- To avenge blood.
- To fight to the death for a person who has taken refuge with me no matter what his lineage.
- To defend to the last any property entrusted to me.
- To be hospitable and provide for the safety of the person and property of guests.
- To refrain from killing a woman, a Hindu, a minstrel, or a boy not yet circumcised.
- To pardon an offense on the intercession of a woman of the offender's lineage, a Sayyid or a mullah.
- To punish all adulterers with death.
- To refrain from killing a man who has entered a mosque or the shrine of a holy man so long as he remains within its precincts; also to spare a man in battle who begs for quarter.[3]

While Dupree's list is useful for introductory purposes, in reality there is no agreed or widely accepted checklist of the *narkh* – largely because it is heavily based on precedent and passed on orally between *narkhi* (experts within the tribe). Trying to create a consolidated catalogue of *narkh* would risk perpetuating simple stereotypes and reducing Pashtuns to a handful of specific behaviours. It should be clear by now that little about Pashtuns or their way of life is clear-cut or black-and-white.

Narkhis rarely rule independently of one another. Their judgements are often mutually reinforcing and intertwined. They are also context-specific and character-specific. Different people place a different degree of importance on different rules. *Pashtunwali* can also be confused with customary laws of other Afghan ethnic groups which have similar practices – reciprocal vengeance is not the sole preserve of Pashtuns. But there are some commonly recognized core tenets of *Pashtunwali*, with three that always come up in discussion:

1) *Badal* – revenge or reciprocity.
2) *Melmastia* – provision of hospitality.
3) *Nanawatai* – provision of sanctuary or forgiveness.

Badal – reciprocity more than revenge

Badal is generally regarded as the main plank of *Pashtunwali*, or its 'first and greatest commandment'.[4] It receives more foreign attention than other principles because its resultant blood feuds intrigue everyone from expert anthropologists to amateur observers. But while scores may be settled with violence, this can also be achieved through exchange – which underlines that 'revenge' is an over-simplified definition of *badal*, albeit the one normally used by Westerners.

'Exchange', 'reciprocity' or 'a transaction made to settle accounts'[5] are more nuanced and accurate descriptions, reflecting the fact that *badal* is not always about violence. It can be used to regulate the level of hospitality to be offered during a visit or to ensure equivalence in gift-giving (so that nobody is shamed if one party's ability to reciprocate is exceeded).

Weddings are another example of non-violent *badal* – although not a positive one. A daughter of one family can be married to a son of another as a form of compensation. This is known as a *baad* marriage. There are also arrangements whereby families will exchange daughters, although this is often a result of poverty as much as score-settling, since it reduces wedding costs.[6] This type of marriage usually occurs when there has been a murder, sexual assault or other violent crime. The perpetrator's family can then negotiate a marriage contract between one of their daughters and a member of the aggrieved family, to avoid a vendetta and further escalation of hostilities. Although illegal under Afghan law, as well as being counter to Islamic edicts on forced marriage, the prevalence of *baad* marriage has been well documented in recent years, as have the consequences for the women involved, whose welfare is less of a concern than the prevention of further inter-family bloodshed. These women, often young teenagers, can be mistreated by their new family, given that they represent the harm done to their kin – and honour.

Whatever the context, *badal* is all about honour – and defence of it. When it does involve violence, this normally stems from a perceived insult to a tribesman's *zan*, *zar* or *zamin* (women, gold, land).[7] Whether it concerns stolen property, physical injury or damage to personal or tribal reputation, retaliation – or reciprocity – becomes a social obligation. This is because tribesmen are judged more on how honourable they are perceived to be than on how much material wealth they possess.[8]

Revenge is not the sole responsibility of the man who has suffered the indignity. It is also incumbent on his family and tribe.[9] If he or his clan fail to take revenge, they both lose face in the eyes of the wider tribe and their rivals. They risk derision or taunting, which is called *paighore* and is something that every Pashtun wants to avoid. This is why, even if an individual is unwilling to take revenge, the rest of the tribe will often do so, to prevent the entire tribe being subject to *paighore*.

The pressure of *paighore* is why *badal* often manifests itself in a blood feud, even if the initial transgression was relatively minor. 'Turn the other cheek' is not a mantra applicable to Pashtuns. *Badal* is more about 'an eye for an eye and a tooth for a tooth', although proportionality is also important. If a revenge-seeker delivers punishment disproportionate to the crime, he can lose his own tribe's support. He can dishonour himself.

Dishonour also comes from taking revenge on the wrong person. *Badal* is only directed towards men. It is cowardly and dishonourable to attack women, even if they are part of the feud.[10] Sometimes women will even be the strongest voices in demanding their men deliver revenge, since they know that their children's marriage prospects depend on how honourable their family is perceived to be.[11]

It is not uncommon for Pashtuns to see revenge as a dish best served cold. *Badal* is not time-bound. It can come years after the initial cause, with the obligation passed down the bloodline, pitting tribe against tribe in an inter-generational struggle (a *patna*).[12] If a father has been wronged, then his son and even his grandsons may take up the cause of restoring honour.[13] One case occurred within the Afridi tribe in the 1870s, when a tribesman's cousins jokingly cut the tail off a horse belonging to one of his guests. In retaliation, the tribesman shot both cousins, sparking a blood feud which a century later had claimed over a hundred lives.[14] This tendency for spats to turn into vicious, decades-long feuds is best summed up by the famous proverb, 'If a Pashtun takes revenge after a hundred years, he is still in a hurry.'

Melmastia – honour through hospitality

While *badal* attracts most attention, *melmastia* is what Pashtuns take most pride in. It is among the finest qualities a tribesman can display, and is a more defining part of Pashtun identity – at least in tribesmen's eyes. For Pashtuns, there is no honour where there is no hospitality.

The term comes from the word *melma* (guest) and, while gentler in nature than *badal*, it is no less rigorous in the obligation it imposes. It requires Pashtuns to welcome guests, feed them, protect them and provide unfettered access to any facilities, regardless of the guest's race, religion or social stature. Guests cannot be harmed or surrendered to an enemy once under the roof of a host, no matter the past relationship between host and guest.[15]

Only sinners violate *melmastia*. Those who do not offer it are shamed, shunned and said to be devoid of Pashto. Hospitality should also be provided without any expectation of remuneration. It is a moral obligation even if it is expensive. This means that hospitality is often provided to a degree that embarrasses the guest, especially if he is in no position to return it.

But there is more to *melmastia* than pure politeness or altruism. There is an ulterior motive. A guest is considered to be a blessing for a Pashtun because being able to provide hospitality presents an opportunity to enhance honour. It is a matter of personal prestige as much as charity or brotherly love – and even more important than *badal* because it allows a Pashtun to obtain and gain honour rather than simply restore it. The greater the difficulty undertaken by the host in providing hospitality, the more he and his kin will rise in the estimation of others. It is also an opportunity to build a social network and business connections, which then afford a tribesman more authority in collective tribal decision-making processes.[16]

There are arguments that *melmastia* has decayed through conflict and the process of modernization. Proponents of the idea cite Soviet-era refugee movements from Afghanistan to Pakistan as an example of *melmastia* being eroded. Afghan Pashtuns fled in droves across the border when the Soviets invaded. While they took refuge in Pashtun areas in Pakistan, they were squeezed into squalid refugee camps rather than being welcomed with hospitality by their cousins. Only tribes with blood ties across the Durand Line – like those in the Karlani branch or some Eastern Pashtuns of the Sarbani branch – were able to obtain sanctuary in their kin's territory, while others faced life in the refugee camps. The counter-argument is that such was the size of the refugee flow that Pakistan's tribes were overwhelmed and there were just too many refugees to sustain. Either way, *melmastia* was selectively offered only to members of one's own *qawm* or *khel*. Resentment still lingers about this today. Some tribes got refugee camps when they needed hospitality, sanctuary and even *nanawatai*.

Nanawatai – sanctuary even for strangers

Nanawatai is most often translated as 'sanctuary' as it comes from the Pashto verb *nanawatal*, meaning 'to enter' or 'go into'. *Nanawatai* refers to entering a

Pashtun house or community to gain sanctuary or asylum. The host is obliged to provide protection regardless of the consequences or any risk to his own life, even if the request is from a stranger or an enemy. *Nanawatai* is also used as a dispute resolution mechanism to end blood feuds, which is why it is also translated as 'forgiveness'.

Like other principles of *Pashtunwali*, *nanawatai* is underpinned by honour. It often happens when one man owes a debt to another but cannot pay, or if he has issues with another tribe that he cannot handle alone. Then he will go to seek help, via *nanawatai*, from another tribesman or tribe. *Nanawatai* is most commonly discussed in relation to murder, for example when a murderer goes to his victim's house and asks the family for forgiveness, because he wants to avoid a blood feud or retaliation. If he is invited in, then he becomes a guest and cannot be harmed. That is when he can ask for an end to the conflict. He may even slaughter a sheep or goat at the door, as a symbolic offering.[17] *Nanawatai* can also come with an offer of blood money to compensate a bereaved family, normally arranged through tribal elders.

It is rare that a perpetrator seeks *nanawatai* without being under serious duress or as a last resort. Asking another Pashtun for protection is the ultimate humiliation. It means being submissive, and it puts the supplicant in a permanently inferior position to the person he is approaching. But honour is also at stake for the host. The more difficult it is to provide asylum, the more honour is restored to those who were wronged. Yet while the potential host may gain honour, he will incur a stain if he is unwelcoming.[17] Refusing to provide sanctuary would – in the eyes of fellow Pashtuns – be cowardice, betrayal of Pashtun ideals and failure to follow *Pashtunwali*.

The exception to *nanawatai* is when a dispute relates to the honour of women. It can be refused in cases of assault, rape or adultery. But as with *badal* and *melmastia*, women are not always passive actors. They can play a role in *nanawatai* by being required to go to the house of the enemy and ask for an end to a dispute. Women can also engage in *nariqawal* (to call out). This is when a woman is being married against her wishes and instead goes to the house of the man she wants to marry and presents herself as a guest. This is not an honourable practice, but the man she asks has some obligation to marry her and negotiate terms with her father. The danger is that if the father rejects the offer, the would-be groom's honour is damaged, and this may give rise to a cycle of revenge – or *badal*.

While *badal* is still the most famous principle of *Pashtunwali*, *nanawatai* has also permeated popular culture. Much has been written about the Taliban hosting Osama bin Laden and their refusal to hand him over to the US in 2001 – which would supposedly have breached *nanawatai*. The counter-argument is that the Taliban could have handed him over without contravening *Pashtunwali*, because bin Laden was an outsider who could easily have been stigmatized as the cause of war (therefore requiring him to leave without obligation for *nanawatai*).

Pashtunwali also entered the common consciousness in 2013 via Mark Wahlberg's Hollywood blockbuster *Lone Survivor*. This movie was based on the true story of Operation Red Wings, when four US Navy SEALs sneaked into Kunar Province in 2005, only to be discovered by goat herders, who alerted the insurgents and set off a chain of events that saw three SEALs die. The lone US survivor was given sanctuary by a local Pashtun, Mohammad Gulab, until US forces extracted him. In real life, US forces subsequently provided Gulab's village with a generator, fuel and other items hard to obtain – a *badal*-esque exchange recognizing their provision of *nanawatai*. While this secured a settlement with the village, the insurgents continued to target Gulab until he was eventually given asylum in the US.

The 2015 movie *Hyena Road* also touches on *nanawatai*, telling the story of Canadian soldiers in Kandahar given shelter by a village elder, who then gets embroiled in a tribal dispute and a series of revenge killings. The 1988 film 'Beast of War' has similar themes and is based on a play called 'Nanawatai'. The plot is that a Soviet T55 tank gets lost after attacking a Pashtun village. One mujahideen leader sets out for revenge and pursues the tank (which his men call 'the beast'). While the Soviet crew searches for safety, its Afghan interpreter teaches the Soviets about *nanawatai*. The interpreter is killed by the tank commander, who alleges that he is a traitor. A Soviet crew member who befriended the Afghan is also left behind and found by the mujahideen. He pleads for *nanawatai*, which is provided. The rest of the crew are then also captured and given sanctuary. They eventually escape, but not before the Afghans have their revenge and kill the dastardly tank commander. This is a reminder that no matter what storm it has to weather, the Pashtun way tends to triumph in the end.

Chapter 18

Narkh: The Rules of Tribal Behaviour

Pashtunwali consists of much more than *badal, melmastia* and *nanawatai*. The collective *narkh* include many concepts that influence Pashtun outlook and behaviour. Some are broad beliefs, while others are specific directives. Many other *narkh* are overlapping and some even translate into the same word in English, despite being different in practice. But there is one common factor between them all – honour.

Outside of the 'Big Three' principles, one of *Pashtunwali*'s other important concepts is *musawat* (equality). This is encapsulated in the common Pashtun saying, 'Every man is a *malik.*' But rather than every tribesman being equal in terms of influence or political power, or any notion of the Western definition of equality between the sexes, *musawat* refers to equality in terms of dignity. *Musawat* means that every tribesman has the right to defend his personal honour and the honour of his clan or tribe. But this concept of equality among men has also been said to exist only as an ideal. In reality, some men are naturally senior due to age, experience, landownership, wisdom or bravery. These men are usually regarded as elders or 'whitebeards' (*spin giri*).[1]

Some tribes emphasise equality more than others. There is a story about the Safi tribe (Ghurghusti branch) which tells how a group of Safi men were sleeping one night in the local *hujra* (guest house). But there was only one bed. As they all considered themselves to be equal, regardless of age or status, none took the bed. Instead, they dragged it into the middle of the room and everyone went to sleep with one leg up on it.[2]

Pashtunwali also necessitates *imandari* (righteousness). This dictates that Pashtuns respect all creatures, including animals, and the environment. *Hamsaya* is another common principle. It describes a clan that has aligned with a tribe of a different lineage for the purposes of protection – with any attack on the *hamsaya* also representing an attack on its protector. *Hamsayagi* is similar. It refers to neighbourliness but translates as 'sharing the same shed'. *Badragah* also deals with goodwill and refers to the practice of a tribe providing an escort through their territory. In doing so, personal or tribal honour is enhanced.[3]

Other terms to recognize are *tiga*, which means 'putting down a stone' and refers to a temporary truce between warring parties. *Gundi* concerns alliances and the balance of power among tribes. *Bilga*, *bota* and *baramta* all deal with thieves and debts. *Adal-badal* (give and take) and *itbar* (trust) are also important, especially when talking about tribal economies. The point is that *Pashtunwali* is wide-ranging; it consists of much more than *badal* and other well-known principles. There is a vast repertoire of rules and terms. It would take an entire book to explain them, so this chapter focuses on five of the most prominent after the 'Big Three', all of which encapsulate what it means to be a Pashtun. A more comprehensive list of tribal terminology is included at the back of this book as Appendix B.

1) *Seyali – Competition* Competition is a constant of Pashtun life and a central aspect of *Pashtunwali*. Pashtuns are naturally competitive – and not just with their enemies. *Seyali* refers to competition within a family or a small community of relatives who compete to bring the most prosperity to their people and tribe. *Seyali* makes competition into a source of *nang* (honour). The term comes from *seyal*, which is another Pashto word for equality. This reflects the fact that *seyali* is supposed to take place only between men of equal status – otherwise it is a source of shame.[4] A tribal chief cannot engage in *seyali* with a subordinate or a *hamsaya*. He has to compete with another tribal chief.[5] The same is true of competition with cousins, which every Pashtun is obliged to engage in. This is only *seyali* if the cousins are of equal status and wealth. If not, it is *tarboorwali*.

2) *Tarboorwali – Rivalry between Cousins* *Tarboorwali* refers to the perpetual competition or animosity between cousins or other patrilineal relatives. As with other principles of *Pashtunwali*, *zan*, *zar*, or *zamin* (women, gold, land) are often at the heart of *tarboorwali*. Land rights and inheritance of land are particularly frequent drivers of intra-family conflict and blood feuds, because ownership of land is a direct reflection of a tribesman's status – and honour. Men who own part of the tribe's land are called *daftari*. Only *daftari* have an input into the processes of collective tribal decision-making. A man without land is a *faqir*, meaning 'voiceless'. As land is inherited or divided among male heirs, cousins will strategically intermarry to acquire land rather than risk dishonouring their family by becoming known as *faqirs*. The benefit of *tarboorwali* is that it 'checks political power, curbs individual ambitions and in a bloody and dramatic manner underwrites the principles of Pukhtun democracy'.[6] It is said to prevent the rise of charismatic super-leaders because they are opposed and balanced by equally exceptional cousins.[7] Paradoxically, while *tarboorwali* can lead to murder amongst relatives and fractures in families, it is still seen as a way to obtain a type of personal honour best translated as 'manliness'. The Pashto term for this is *ghairat*.

3) *Ghairat – A Different Type of Honour Ghairat* is one of the main characteristics by which *Pashtunwali* is enacted and judged every day. The literal translation is 'courage', although it is often translated as 'honour' too. But *ghairat* is a specific type of courage or honour. It is personal courage, self-honour or manliness. It has also been described as zeal, dignity, audacity or chivalry.[8] It means being an alpha male. As *ghairat* pools all core Pashtun values, a *ghairatman* embodies *Pashtunwali*. He represents the ideal Pashtun. *Ghairat* does not relate to wealth, as even the poorest Pashtun man must carry himself with dignity. Pashtuns say that 'no one is above or below us, some are just more fortunate than others'.[9] If a tribesman offends against *Pashtunwali* or brings shame on himself or the tribe, then he is branded as *beghairat*.[10] This is a serious affront to his manhood, forcing him to fight for his honour and prove his *tura*.

4) *Tura – Bravery* The direct translation of *tura* is 'the sword', but its meaning is closer to 'physical bravery'. It revolves around individual acts of aggression and the readiness to fight (symbolized by the sword). Traditionally, every Pashtun tribesman belonged to a group of fighters but he also had to prove his own *tura*. Only then did he attain the honour and dignity that come with being called a *turyalai*. When he proves his *tura*, his clan and his tribe benefit, because he has demonstrated that their men are honourable and will not back down from a challenge. The Pashtun warrior-poet Khushal Khan Khattak, whose proverbs Pashtun men often measure themselves against, encapsulated the importance of *tura* in writing, 'If you don't like weapons you should not call yourself a man.'[11] But just as tribesmen should always be ready to fight, they should also know when to should avoid it. This is the concept of *aql*.

5) *Aql – Wisdom or Responsibility Aql* translates as 'reasoning' or 'responsibility'. It refers to being socially responsible and balanced in judgement.[12] It is akin to wisdom and complementary to *tura*, in that someone with *aql* knows when aggression would be unhelpful to the individual or the tribe. *Aql* is usually associated with tribal elders, who are seen as the sensible counterbalance to reckless and impulsive younger tribesmen. These elders, or *spin giri* (whitebeards), are supposed to keep the headstrong youth in check, which is why Pashtun boys are brought up to respect their elders. The concepts of *tura* and *aql* are also useful in understanding why, as the German anthropologist Bernt Glatzer described, 'Bands of anarchic Afghan warriors were able to inflict heavy defeats on the superpowers of their time, and why most tribal warriors laid down their arms the day after their victory and went home to plough their fields – some for the first time in their life.'[13]

Understanding these five principles of *Pashtunwali*, in addition to *badal*, *melmastia* and *nanawatai*, can help to shed light on the Pashtun mindset and help build a picture of the Pashtun way of life – provided that their flexibility and variability in interpretation are recognized. It should also be recognized that *Pashtunwali* is not the *only* influence on a tribesman. Previous chapters have highlighted how Afghanistan became permeated by political and religious ideologies in the latter half of the twentieth and the early twenty-first century. Islam, in particular, is an ideology that has a complicated relationship with *Pashtunwali*.

Pashtunwali versus Islam

Afghanistan has understandably become synonymous with Islam, especially as living memory is dominated by the Islamist mujahideen's victory over communism and the post-9/11 era of perceived radical Islamic terrorism. The result is that Pashtuns, the majority of whom are Sunni, have frequently been tarred as religious extremists or Islamic fundamentalists. This has also led to questions about how Islam and *Pashtunwali* interact, given that the Pashtun way of life is supposedly dictated by *Pashtunwali*, which in its strictest sense is secular and even pre-dates Islam.

Some of *Pashtunwali*'s principles are clearly antithetical to Islamic concepts (although it is rare that Pashtuns openly admit this). Pursuing revenge is contradictory to Islam's preference for seeking justice or forgiving a wrongdoing if the perpetrator agrees to become a Muslim. The payment of blood money equally goes against Islamic practice, and ardent Islamists believe that the rule of law is established by Allah, which would seemingly make *Pashtunwali*'s laws inoperable.[14] *Pashtunwali* prioritizes an independent outlook, parochial tribalism and loyalty to the tribe. But the type of Sunni Islam (Hanafi) that most Pashtuns follow espouses Sharia principles that transcend specific kinship groups and prioritize the universality of the *umma* (the global Muslim community). These incompatibilities make it valid to ask how *Pashtunwali* and Islam can exist in harmony and, if they clash, which one prevails.

The answer is as difficult as anyone chooses to make it, because the '*Pashtunwali* vs Islam' question is so case-specific and character-specific that there is never going to be an accurate one-size-fits-all determination. It is a thought-provoking debate, but any conclusion is likely to be hypothetical. Trying to be definitive about which takes precedence is a Sisyphean task.

The simplest answer is that the Pashtun belief in Islam is equal to their acceptance of *Pashtunwali*.[15] Even if there are incompatibilities, rarely does one have to be chosen over the other. A common saying about Pashtuns, particularly among other Afghan ethnic groups, is that 'half use the Koran and half use *Pashtunwali*'.

Should there be a clash, *Pashtunwali* can override Sharia, especially where honour is at stake. The academic Tom Ginsburg, an expert in legal systems across

South Asia, neatly explained that *Pashtunwali* often takes precedence because its decisions tend to reflect the will of the collective community, whereas a sole mullah is often the repository of religious law and he is not a formal part of the tribal system.[16] A famous quote from a Pashtun politician in Pakistan also encapsulates the tribal mindset in the event of a clash. He said, 'I have been a Pakistani for thirty years, a Muslim for fourteen hundred years, and a Pashtun for five thousand years'.[17] This attitude explains why Pashtuns have been previously described as 'fundamentally Muslim, although not necessarily Islamic'.[18] They can be willing to selectively discard aspects of Islam in favour of *Pashtunwali*, because 'kinship and ethnic relations have always been more important to Pashtuns than abstract concepts based on ideologies'.[19]

But there is one area in which the tribal value system almost always takes precedence over Islamic law. In a tribal society that is undeniably male-dominated, there is one factor that shapes a Pashtun man's psyche and dictates his status more than anything else – women.

Chapter 19

The Paradox of *Pashtunwali* for Women

'She was dead within an hour.' That wasn't even the most shocking line of the news report.

Nazela's whole story is sickening. The eighteen-year-old had run away with her boyfriend to escape an arranged marriage to another man. She knew that running was a risk, so she approached the local police station and begged for protection . . . from her own family. After two days, Nazela's older brother came to collect her. He was a serving soldier in the Afghan Army and assured the police that she would be safe with him. The police handed her over, and he took her home, where he strangled her with electric cable and stabbed her until she fell limp. He then fled to Taliban-controlled territory to avoid the authorities, because this was not an accident or a heat-of-the-moment decision.[1] It was premeditated. It was calculated.

It was an honour killing.

Nazela's story is not fiction or folklore. It is not hypothetical or concocted to illustrate a point. Nor is it an incident from ancient history. She was murdered in the Baharak district of Badakhshan province in May 2020.[2] This honour killing was not a one-off either. In 2016, a former Afghan Supreme Court Justice estimated that during his career in the judiciary 80–90 per cent of the murder cases he dealt with in Pashtun areas related to *badal*. The rest were related to honour killing.[3] The United Nations documented 280 similar murders between 2015 and 2017, most going unpunished.[4] In 2019, Afghanistan's human rights body recorded 238 murders of women, 96 of them deemed to be honour killings. Many more will have gone unreported. Even as those statistics were released, a well-known Pashtun TV presenter, Mena Mangal, was gunned down in broad daylight, in public, in Kabul. The culprit was never caught, but accusations spread that her ex-husband or his family were involved.[5]

These honour killings happen across Afghanistan. They are not limited to Pashtun-only areas. This, and the fact that they are the most extreme example of *Pashtunwali*, means that using them to illustrate tribal mores risks overemphasizing the violent aspects of Pashtun life and perpetuating negative stereotypes. But they do highlight how women can be held hostage by the Pashtun concept of honour. They also hint at the lingering belief that women are the weaker sex, vulnerable to temptation and easy prey.[6] Men, as guardians of morality, must protect them. In traditional Pashtun life, women are emblematic of honour. They are 'the ultimate repositories of *nang*'.[7] The historian Nancy Dupree explained:

> In Afghanistan, women symbolize honour – of the nation and of the family. Any deviation on the part of women from honourable behaviour as it is defined by any given family or group is seen to besmirch the honour of those in authority and cannot therefore be tolerated. It is this attitude which has perpetuated overly protective institutions and customs such as the veil and seclusion.[8]

This concept, and other language often used in reference to Pashtun women, can be jarring to Westerners; it suggests that Pashtuns and other Afghans speak – and act – as if Afghanistan consists only of men, with women seen as a separate community. Whether this is reality or a misinterpretation is a debate for another book. The point is that Pashtuns and Westerners approach the protection of women in very different ways. For Pashtuns it is about tribal, family or men's honour more than chivalry, rights or equality.

Protection of *namus*

Protecting women's moral purity is known as protecting the *namus*. 'Dignity' is the literal translation, although 'gender boundaries' or 'reputation' are also used to convey its meaning in English.[9] Some Pashtuns also speak of *nang-o-namus*, given how closely the concept is tied to honour. But rather than achieving or enhancing honour, protecting the *namus* is about defending and upholding it. He who fails to protect his *namus* can be shunned or forced to take refuge as *hamsaya* with another tribe. The imperative of protecting the *namus* is encapsulated in two well-known Pashto sayings:

> He who cannot protect the integrity of his family cannot protect anything, anyone is free to snatch away from him what he wants, his possessions, his land.[10]
> I will sacrifice my wealth for my head and will sacrifice my life for my *namus*.[11]

Pashtuns will even go to war to defend their *namus*. Fighting has been known to erupt over disputes about where a woman should be buried. When a Pashtun woman dies, her paternal family will want to bury her in her home village or area. If her close paternal relatives are also dead, then more distant relatives or even local tribal elders will try to return her body to her father's family village – which can anger the family that she married into. This reflects the fact that when a woman is born she represents the *namus* (or dignity) of her father. When she is married, she is seen as the dignity of the husband and the mother of his children. But when she dies, she reverts again to being the *namus*, or the dignity, of her father.

Another example of *namus*-fuelled fighting came in the chaos of the communist era, when the anti-Soviet mujahideen did not recruit on religious or political grounds alone. They also claimed that the jihad was a defence against the threat to the common Afghan *namus*.[12] In 1978, *namus*-related narratives were used by Islamist students to spur anti-government uprisings. They spread rumours that the regime was going to force education on girls in rural areas. This perceived interference by the state in private life sparked outrage and stoked rebellion. It also led to the stricter segregation of the sexes that Afghanistan is now known for – a process called *purdah*.[13]

Purdah – segregation of the sexes

Purdah is the second most important term when it comes to understanding women and *Pashtunwali*, although it is not an exclusively Pashtun practice.[14] *Purdah* translates as 'curtain' or 'veil' and involves varying degrees of gender segregation in order to maintain the sanctity of the *namus*, especially in the eyes of competitors:

> Even more feared than the actual behaviour of women is the neighbours' gossip; that is what erodes *namus* most effectively and what is most difficult to control. Better do not let anybody see the women.[15]

While *purdah* is enforced differently depending on the tribe and locality, it usually manifests itself in restricted access to a family's women, especially by non-relatives or outsiders. This supposedly protects family and tribal honour by preventing other unmarried or unrelated men from associating with them. More extreme examples of *purdah* are women being unable to leave their homes without a male escort and restriction of their access to education or to male doctors. *Purdah* also refers to the literal veiling of women. It dictates that a woman should dress and behave modestly, on the assumption that she will not then provoke or tempt the opposite sex. The traditional belief is that the 'clothes a woman wears determine how she is treated by men, and if she wants respect, she should dress according to what her society considers respectable.'[16]

A renowned event that highlighted how traditionalists feel about *purdah* happened in 1928, when King Amanullah Khan presided over a grand assembly of tribal elders (a *Loya Jirga*). Amanullah, a reformer with a penchant for European travel, ordered all participants to wear Western business attire, something completely alien to the majority of Afghans. The tribal elders, already uncomfortably squeezed into three-piece Western business suits and feeling naked without their turbans, were astonished and angered by what came next.

Amanullah's wife, Queen Soraya, had already exasperated the tribesmen by her gender-related activism, which challenged traditional tribal custom. In the middle of the *Loya Jirga* she stood up in the audience wearing European dress and with only a small veil falling from her hat as a token concession to conservatives. The Queen also brought a throng of female aides, all of whom removed their veils in the presence of the tribal elders. This piece of theatre infuriated traditionalists, who were already concerned at Amanullah's reforms. It was another nail in Amanullah's coffin. The tribes started mobilizing against him after leaving the event, and within a year he and Soraya had been forced to flee into exile.

Events like this spotlight the sensitivities around *namus* and *purdah*. Such sensitivities emerged again after 2001, when these practices became symbolic of the Taliban's repressive rule – at least in the eyes of Western media. But this only highlights how Westerners struggle to fully grasp Afghanistan's cultural context. There is no disputing the suffering of Afghan women – nor does this chapter intend to do so – but the veil may not be the most effective litmus test of women's rights or modernity. Just as there are arguments about veiling being oppressive, there are counter-claims that some Afghan women like the protection of the veil, because it allows them mobility and ensures their security in public spaces. Others suggest that the burqa is even seen 'as something of a status symbol for upwardly mobile families, since the poor cannot afford the elaborately pleated and embroidered garment'.[17] Debating whether this is true or not is far beyond the scope of this book. These issues are mentioned to underline that *namus* and *purdah* are part of a longstanding ethical order that pre-dates the Taliban or other Islamic fundamentalists; and in spite of the obvious restrictions they bring, they do not completely limit women's participation in Pashtun life.

Women's participation in *Pashtunwali*

While women's participation in *Pashtunwali* is said to remain 'little studied and even less understood', Pashtun women are clearly on the receiving end of a bad deal.[18] There is much work to be done to provide – and sustain – more freedoms for them, while also recognizing that Western stereotyping of them as weak victims lacks cultural nuance and is guilty of perpetuating some unhelpful myths.[19] It is a mistake to say that women are completely repressed or merely passive actors in Pashtun life.

The first counter-argument is that women are often portrayed as heroes in Pashtun folklore, something that Rudyard Kipling recognized in his final verse of 'The Young British Soldier':

When you're wounded and left on Afghanistan's plains,
And the woman come out to cut up what remains,
Jest roll to your rifle and blow out your brains,
An' go to your Gawd like a soldier.

But Pashtun women are not only lionized for ferrying ammunition and water to the front lines or for tending to casualties. They have also been present at various battles to remind men of the costs of acting dishonourably. Two warrior women who live on in Pashtun minds are Nazo Tokhi and Malalai of Maiwand.[20] Nazo Tokhi, the mother of Mirwais Hotak, is still known as the Mother of the Nation for her exploits on the battlefield. Malalai of Maiwand fearlessly rallied tribesmen to victory in battle against British forces during the Second Anglo-Afghan War. Later chapters probe both women's stories in more detail, showing how they shamed their tribesmen into defending the *namus* and reflecting the fact that Pashtun women are 'considered to be an authority on *Pashtunwali* as well as its legitimate keeper'.[21]

Besides being the protagonists of folk tales, Pashtun women also have a duty to pass them on. In a largely unlettered society, they are tasked with recounting stories of valour to their children. They bring up future warriors and ensure that the honour code is ingrained in them from a young age. This role as educators is encapsulated in a proverb about a mother who tells her battle-bound son that she would 'much rather he died as a brave man than lived as a coward'. Another proverb encourages boys to accept the harsh realities of Pashtun life: 'The eyes of the dove are lovely, my son. But the hawk rules the sides, so cover your dove-like eyes and grow claws.'[22]

In day-to-day life, the prevailing view is that a women's place is the home. This is a domain into which men do not intrude, leaving women as the 'sole power in the Pathan household'.[23] They manage the food, the budget and the hired help. They are responsible for preparing burials and other ceremonies. There are also roles for the matriarch to play in giving advice and in conflict resolution. She can mediate in domestic and intra-tribal disputes. Women can also be sent to argue with tribal leaders or other officials – the idea being that an official will be publicly shamed if he does not meet her request or has to address her in public.

Women symbolize honour but also play a direct role in cultivating it. They play an important role in arranging marriages and choosing suitable partners for their children that will enhance the honour of the tribe. This means women have to work hard to cultivate contacts as their 'power' depends on how large their social network is. It is also why marriage in the Afghan context is said to be 'a public decision of two families, not a private decision of two individuals', the ideal marriage being between cousins as it keeps wealth within the lineage and family solidarity strong.[24]

The lives of Pashtun women are difficult for Westerners to understand. On the one hand, women are treated in ways that seem intolerable in Western eyes. On the other, they are glorified as 'the wombs of patrilineage', since the prestige and influence of the family, clan and tribe is directly influenced by the quantity and quality of their sons.[25] A Pashtun mother is therefore 'responsible for the building up of a nation. She can change the destiny of the society because she has the power as a mother to mould the character of the rising generation.'[26]

The paradox is that *Pashtunwali* restricts women at the same time as it respects them. This, again, serves as a reminder of the need to understand the tribes as they understand themselves, rather than following the Western tendency to define the Afghan context only in relation to the West.

Pashtunwali and other tribal tendencies should be considered with cultural relativism in mind, i.e. the idea that a person's beliefs, values, and practices should be understood in the context of that person's own culture, not judged against the criteria of another. This, of course, is not to advocate that Westerners working in Afghanistan should *act* as Pashtuns do. It is rather a reminder that cultural relativism is the key to understanding why Pashtuns act as they do, especially when it comes to the value, above all else, that continues to frame *Pashtunwali*, Pashtun thinking and tribal behaviour – honour.

PART VI
Pashtunwali in Practice

Chapter 20

The *Jirga*: Collective Tribal Decision-making

A tribesman's 'Pashtun-ness' is not only measured on the battlefield or in how he protects his *namus*. The *jirga* is also where *Pashtunwali* is performed. It is the venue where equality, judgment, responsibility and honour are acted out.[1]

The term *jirga* supposedly comes from the Pashto word *jirg*, meaning 'wrestling ring'.[2] There are also suggestions – mostly unsubstantiated – that it derives from a Mongolian term for a large assembly of men sitting in a circle, which is also how Pashtun *jirgas* are arranged.[3] In practice, a *jirga* is a meeting of tribal elders and chiefs to debate key issues and resolve disputes. Pashtuns proudly state that it is one of the oldest democratic systems known to man, although what may appear as a civilised dialogue is still beset by sub-surface competition and power struggles.[4] The veneer of consultation obscures the reality that the *jirga* is simply the arena in which tribesmen do battle by non-violent means.

A *jirga* is not to be confused with a *shura* – another format for meetings. *Shura* is actually an Arabic word for 'consultation' and refers to a consultative forum used in the Middle East,[5] while the *jirga* is native to Pashtuns, with evidence of its use dating back to 977AD.[6] *Shuras* were introduced to Afghanistan more recently, only becoming established in the 1980s, mostly as a result of multi-ethnic meetings among mujahideen.[7] A *shura* has a relatively permanent membership, meets regularly and is often influenced by religious edicts. A *jirga* is ad hoc, issue-specific and more of a secular mechanism (although blessings from mullahs are still common). *Jirga* membership changes depending on the issue at hand and focuses on collective decision-making, whereas *shura* membership is static, with participant input ultimately given to an overall leader who can take or leave decisions.[8]

Whatever its origins and evolutions, the tribal *jirga* has survived the centuries. There is an argument that its influence is being eroded by the *shura* and by recent efforts to strengthen state decision-making institutions, but many Pashtuns still see *jirgas* as a more effective way to resolve disputes, deliver justice and to keep the peace among the tribes. The *jirga* remains the primary regulator of *Pashtunwali*.[9]

Regulation of revenge

In its simplest form a *jirga* is a dispute-resolution mechanism. It is a peace-making procedure, used to avoid bloodshed. It can be convened to settle small disputes between individuals and families or for broader disputes between whole tribes. At the local level, *jirgas* traditionally involve arbitration of disputes related to the three Zs: *zan, zar, zamin* (women, gold, land). Yet they are also a forum for broader political decision-making and action on other social issues. They can be convened to fundraise for local construction or public works, e.g. to build a mosque or *hujra* (community guesthouse). Some tribes also use *jirgas* to debate criminal offences, especially where there is an absence of written or formal law and reluctance to refer local disputes to institutions associated with the central government (which is often perceived as corrupt and/or 'foreign').[10]

A *jirga* is not required for every decision – only those deemed to be issues of collective importance. The village elder or a tribal chief (*malik*) is usually approached by a complainant and might resolve the dispute himself, but if he does not, either he or the parties involved can request a *jirga* to be convened. The *malik* then determines if the issue is *jirga*-worthy and whether the dispute should be resolved with a *jirga* between small households or one between larger clans. The former, which often resolves disputes between *koranay* (families), is often called a *maraka*. The larger version of a *jirga*, because it takes place between larger clans or sub-tribes (known as *khels* or *qawms*) is sometimes differentiated as a *Qwami Jirga*.

The *malik* is also responsible for gathering participants, who are called *jirgamar* (sometimes *jirgaeez*, or *marakachians* in the case of a *maraka*). The composition of the *jirgamar* varies depending on the locality, dispute and actors involved. For example, a feud within a family requires a smaller group of *jirgamar* than a deliberation about whether an entire tribe should go to war. When a *jirga* is convened to settle a dispute, the members will usually be selected with the consent of each side. The complainants want participants regarded as honest, impartial and conversant with the customary laws (*narkh*), because once a *jirga* is underway, full authority is given to the *jirgamar* to find a settlement, whether it is declaring war or agreeing a peace deal. Their decision is binding.

Jirgas are convened with the principle of *musawat* (equality) in mind. In theory, any *jirga* is open to all adult males in the tribe, especially those whose interests are at stake. They all have the right to attend, to speak and to contribute. But particularly for larger *jirgas*, elders (*mashar*) or 'whitebeards' (*spin giri*) of prominent families usually represent their tribes. Experts in *Pashtunwali* (*narkhis*) will also be present. These men, collectively, are respected for their battlefield reputations, piety and heritage. They also tend to be the landowning elite:

> The power is entirely in the hands of the landowning Pathans. The fakir or artisan classes, cultivating tenants (kashtkars), soldiery

(mallatars), musicians (doms), etc., are without the franchise, their position being practically that of serfs.[11]

Jirgas are often held in open public spaces, and participants sit in a circle to avoid anyone having a dominant position. Some larger *jirgas* may have a chairman or moderator, but he is a first among equals rather than an outright leader. This is supposed to ensure equality, although every *jirga* still contains behind-the-scenes power struggles as tribesmen compete to out-influence each other.

Unsurprisingly, local *jirgas* are usually composed exclusively of men. They are male-dominated and male-oriented. Women's interests tend to be as absent as women themselves. A woman's fate is rarely decided at a *jirga* unless her marriage is made part of the solution to a conflict. It was not until 2013 that the first all-female Pashtun *jirga* took place, in Pakistan's Swat Valley – the place where the Taliban shot the teenager Malala Yousafzai less than a year earlier. This landmark event, dubbed '*Khwaindo jirga*' (sisters' council), brought together twenty-five women in a traditional *jirga* format. The idea was that this woman-only *jirga* could settle disputes between women without having to involve men (which would then risk perceived challenges to honour and even escalation into violence).[12] One of the cases brought to the *jirga* was the death of a sixteen-year-old girl, killed in an acid attack by her husband. The male *jirga* had advised her family to marry their son to one of the perpetrator's sisters, as recompense. The victim's mother refused and instead approached the *Khwaindo jirga*, who helped organize protests, fundraise for legal fees and push the police to file a formal case.

The sisters' council is a reminder that honour is central in *jirgas*. *Jirgamar* take care to avoid the humiliation of anyone, lest the aggrieved party be compelled to act to restore lost honour. This means the *jirgamar* do not act as a judge or jury. Facts are not up for argument. A *jirga* is about preventing or resolving conflict, it 'does not ordinarily determine the guilt or inflict punishment but seeks to achieve a settlement. Both plaintiff and defendant appear before it as equals.'[13]

The *jirgamar* also work hard to ensure that complainants comply with their decisions. The first step in doing so is to ensure both parties to grant authority (*wak*) to the village elders or *jirgamar* who will mediate the dispute. The mediators are then given a fee for their work (*khalaat*), and a *baramta* (deposit) is also collected from both parties as a sign of good faith that they will accept the mediators' decision. This improves the chances of compliance because, if either party refuses to accept the decision, they forfeit their deposit. In recent decades, Sharia law has sometimes been employed as additional justification, with some *jirgas* guided by a mullah in order to enhance credibility.[14] But there is another more longstanding method of ensuring compliance. It is a pre-requisite. A *jirga* is not a *jirga* without it – consensus.

No action without unanimity

Regardless of the issue, membership or leadership, a *jirga* makes its final decision (*prikra*) by unanimous agreement, not vote. This enables joint decision-making without compromising anyone's independence. Pashtuns also credit the consensus-based system for keeping the tribes from being conquered, because any potential conquerer does not face one individual but the entire tribe.[15] A former British official in Afghanistan wrote:

> The unwritten law is that the Jirga takes decisions which in the end overbear opposition and are accepted as unanimous . . . The essential point is that everything takes place in the open and there is nothing like secret ballot.[16]

The need for unanimity means that deliberation often takes many days. It would be quicker and easier to take a vote, but the problem with voting is that it creates winners. More importantly, it also creates losers, and losing undermines honour.

When unanimity is not achievable, a dissenter will walk out of the *jirga* in protest.[17] The *jirga* then breaks up, leaving the issue unresolved or to escalate. Another scenario is when unanimity is achieved but one party then violates the *jirga*'s *prikra* (decision). This often leads to *nagha* (compensation) being requested, or even retaliatory measures such as a collective tribal boycott of the offending family or clan. The offender can also ask for an appeal, particularly if they think the *jirga*'s judgment was based on an incorrect application of *Pashtunwali* – a circumstance known as *Kog-Narkh*. If the appeal is accepted, then another *jirga* will be held, with different participants. If the conclusion is that the first *jirga* was guilty of *Kog-Narkh*, those elders who made the initial judgement can be asked to pay compensation to the parties.

Alternatively, in the event that unanimity is not possible or one party violates the *jirga*'s decision, a recourse to Sharia law or mediation by a Sufi Pir (spiritual guide) can be sought, although the latter is rare because Sufis were systematically targeted during the mujahideen and Taliban years, when they were perceived to be 'hypocrites and false worshippers' and 'terrible sinners to current fundamentalists'.[18]

The impact of the Soviet era, in the shape of the rise of *shuras* and the trend towards stronger centralized government, underpins a perception that traditional tribal structures are crumbling. The alleged decay of the *jirga* system is cited as evidence of this erosion. But a credible counter-argument can also be made that traditional *jirgas* are alive and well and still taking precedence over state-led governance in some areas (or at least operating alongside it).

The production team of a 2018 Australian film can attest to that after witnessing the inner workings of a local *jirga* – and being lucky to escape unscathed. The movie, entitled *Jirga*, is the fictional story of an Australian former soldier, Mike, who returns to Afghanistan to track down the family of an unarmed man whom he had killed while serving there. Mike travels to Kandahar to find the family and ask for forgiveness. When he is taken to the family's village he apologizes, and the villagers decide to hold a *jirga* to debate whether to punish or forgive him. The *jirga* decides that the son of the victim will seal Mike's fate. The son forgives Mike and refuses to accept the wads of US dollars offered as blood money. After a ram is slaughtered – a ceremonial symbol of forgiving one's enemy – the victory of compassion over vengeance is encapsulated by one elder who states that 'forgiveness is mightier and [more] honourable than taking revenge'.[19]

The film was initially to be filmed in Pakistan but, after reading the screenplay, Pakistan's spy agency rejected the proposal. Unperturbed, the director decided to shoot inside Afghanistan, in Kandahar, despite it being during the most violent years of the post-9/11 era. Even more remarkable is that some of the village elders in the film were not actors. They were locals who were briefed beforehand that this was a story about a former soldier returning to apologize for killing a villager. But due to miscommunication, some of the elders were not aware that the set-up was fictional. They believed the lead actor to be a real soldier returning to confess to the killing. The *jirga* scene thus played out with the elders debating the issues as if it was real.

Reality almost hit home too hard when the crew was filming the final shots of a bus leaving the village. As they did so, a real-life US army convoy happened to be patrolling along the same road, with a drone hovering overhead as their standard aerial support. The film's director courted disaster when he panicked and ran back to the safety of his vehicle. He was quickly reminded to slow down, in case US soldiers mistook him for someone suspicious – and sought to 'neutralize' a potential threat. While the movie inevitably contains some poetic licence and deviation from strict *jirga* principles, it is still a worthwhile watch for its insight into a central part of *Pashtunwali* that most Westerners never get to experience – at least at the local level.

But there is one type of *jirga* that Westerners have been part of, particularly in the post-2001 era. It is one that traditionalists argue is now being overused, undermining its once supreme importance. It is the national-level *jirga* – the *Loya Jirga*.

Chapter 21

The *Loya Jirga*: Tribal or National Leadership?

Loya Jirga translates as 'Grand Council' or 'Grand Assembly'. It is a *jirga* that convenes all tribes in a region or the whole country, usually at times of national crisis or to settle national issues. While some claim it has historic roots in *Pashtunwali*, today's *Loya Jirgas* are national, pan-ethnic events convened by central governments rather than by any collection of Pashtun tribes.

Its origins are vague and disputed. Many Pashtuns believe it has pre-Islamic roots, despite dubious evidence for this.[1] In his book *Afghanistan: Political Frailty and External Interference* (2006), Nabi Misdaq, who founded BBC Pashto before becoming President Ghani's media adviser, talks of the *Loya Jirga* being brought to Afghanistan by ancient Indo-Iranians (colloquially referred to as 'Aryans'). They used a similar system around 5,000 years ago to select their rulers.[2] Other Afghan sources suggest that Emperor Kanishka, a Buddhist of the Kushan Dynasty 2,000 years ago, may be the originator, as he was known to hold large meetings to cultivate tribal support.[3] Another common – but equally unsubstantiated – suggestion talks of a *Loya Jirga* in Ghazni Province in 977, when a freed slave named Sabuktigin was chosen to lead the Ghaznavid Empire that ruled the region from 977 to 1186.[4]

As with many aspects of Pashtun culture, clarity only begins to emerge in the eighteenth century. Mirwais Hotak is said to have organized a *Loya Jirga* in 1709 to gain tribal approval for his rebellion against the Persians.[5] This event allegedly took place in the Kakaran village near the Panjwayi area of Kandahar Province – an area that, 300 years later, became known as the Taliban's spiritual home.[6]

Mirwais Hotak's *Loya Jirga* is less famous than the one that came after it. The 1747 *Loya Jirga*, when the tribes selected Ahmad Shah Durrani as their chief, is still held up as a model for subsequent *jirgas* that deal with national or all-tribe issues. But was it even a *Loya Jirga* at all?

One school of thought is that the *Loya Jirga* is not an ancient practice but actually a modern 'invented tradition'.[7] The argument is that twentieth-century rulers simply embellished Ahmad Shah Durrani's story to appear as traditionalists in the eyes of the tribes. The extrapolation and reproduction of village-level *jirgas* at the national level has also been a way for various Afghan leaders to demonstrate their supposed home-grown credibility to foreign backers. To foreigners, with their lack of cultural awareness, the collective nature of the *Loya Jirga* looks like a measure of indigenous legitimacy.[8] Those who buy this argument look on the 1747 event as a myth 'reproduced virtually intact by the Afghan government and by local and Western postcolonial writers interested in political processes and leadership in Afghanistan'.[9]

Further fuelling the theory that it is a modern invention is the infrequency of *Loya Jirgas* between Ahmad Shah's installation and the early twentieth century. Claims that the Emir Sher Ali held one in 1886, or that Abdur Rahman Khan convened three between 1880 and 1901, are disputed.[10] The Emir Habibullah Khan is a more credible candidate as the organizer of the first *Loya Jirga*. In 1915 he brought together around 500 delegates to ratify his decision to keep Afghanistan neutral during the First World War.

In the 1920s, *Loya Jirgas* became more regular events, being institutionalized by the Emir (and later King) Amanullah Khan. After Amanullah's accession in 1919, he repeatedly used *Loya Jirgas* to cultivate support for his modernizing reforms, organizing four in his decade-long reign. Some observers suggest that rather than adopting a centuries-old tribal tradition, he borrowed the idea of extraordinary assemblies from his ancestors, who occasionally convened *darbars* (court audiences).[11] Either way, Amanullah is the man remembered for governing by *Loya Jirga* and who is central to the narrative that the *Loya Jirga* is not an ancient tribal process but a relatively recent pan-ethnic political tool.

Amanullah Khan: leadership by *Loya Jirga*

Amanullah's first *Loya Jirga* was the 'Grand Assembly of the East' in the winter of 1922. At his winter residence in Nangarhar Province, 872 handpicked participants debated the newly-independent Afghanistan's first constitution. Despite accusations that only certain tribes were represented, Amanullah got his way and the constitution was approved, including confirmation of Islam as the official religion and Kabul as the official capital.[12]

Amanullah's second *Loya Jirga* was held in July 1924 at his residence in Paghman (on the outskirts of Kabul). By then his modernizations were frustrating traditionalists, so he used the event to defend his social reforms. Over 1,000 delegates were chosen by Amanullah, with the majority (68 per cent) being from non-Pashtun provinces.[13] This did little to convince the tribes that their fellow Pashtun was acting in their interests. In fact, few Afghans trusted Amanullah, accusing him of manipulating participants (a claim common to almost all *Loya Jirgas* organized ever since). Each attendee was received with royal pomp for a three-week stay at the Emir's estate and other royal residences and promised, among other perks, that any concerns would be dealt with personally by Amanullah.[14]

Amanullah's third and fourth *Loya Jirgas* took place in August and October 1928. The first was held in Paghman and the second in a tent outside the Foreign Ministry in Kabul. With his people tiring of his reforms, the August event saw most of his policies flatly rejected – a sign of shifting political sands. Amanullah's liberalizing policies for women caused the most dissent, particularly the suggested abolition of *purdah*, outlawing of polygamy and compulsory education for both sexes. Even before the event, anger had erupted at rumours of the announcements. It was so ferocious that one Kabuli woman, who openly supported the unveiling proposals, was murdered and her body cut up by her own husband.[15]

Amanullah tinkered with some policies and added others before organizing the October *Loya Jirga*. The historian Rhea Talley Stewart, in *Fire in Afghanistan 1914–1929* (2000), lists Amanullah's proposals, including one dictating that any man who exceeded a standard height-to-weight ratio should be discharged from military service – based on Amanullah's view that fat men are usually fat because they are lazy. He also put forward the proposal that all employees of the foreign service should divorce their wives if they were non-Afghans.

To provide a better chance of his proposals being accepted, Amanullah stacked the guest list of the October event, which has been described as a series of Amanullah lectures rather than a participatory *jirga*,[16] with loyal supporters, government officials and members of the Kabul elite – who were explicitly warned not to criticize the government.[17] There are also some suggestions that the 1928 *jirgas* were the first to include women, because Amanullah's wife, Queen Soraya, attended with her all-female entourage (although it was not until the 1964 *Loya Jirga* that women first participated actively).[18]

The October 1928 event was Amanullah's last before he was overthrown. But by then he had cemented *Loya Jirgas* as a useful political tool for rulers to build national consensus – or at least a veneer of it. Recourse to these events has persisted ever since, to the point where it is now said that whenever a crisis emerges in Afghanistan, the *Loya Jirga* is suggested as the first means to resolve it.[19]

Loya Jirgas in the later twentieth century

The first post-Amanullah *Loya Jirga* was held in Kabul in 1930. Between 280 and 500 carefully selected delegates officially anointed the new King, Nadir Shah.[20] The colours of Afghanistan's flag were also confirmed – black to represent a dark past under British influence, red to represent blood shed for independence, and green to represent hope and Islam. Most incarnations of the flag also have a drawing of a mosque – one of only six national flags to include a building. Two sheaves of wheat frame the mosque, which some say is a nod to Afghanistan's agricultural past. Others believe it represents the sheaf of wheat placed on Ahmad Shah Durrani's ear when he was anointed at the 1747 *Loya Jirga*.[21]

Ten years passed before the next event in 1941, which King Zahir Shah used to confirm Afghanistan's neutrality in the Second World War. He also organized *Loya Jirgas* in 1949 and 1955 which revolved around disputes with the newly-created neighbour, Pakistan. But their memory pales in comparison to his last *Loya Jirga*. This was held in Kabul in September 1964. It gathered 452 representatives – selected by the King – to draft and endorse a democratic constitution and is still branded 'probably the freest and most effective such body ever convened by the state'.[22]

The 1964 constitution guaranteed the right of free trial in criminal cases, freedom of speech, freedom of the press and the right to form political parties. It stipulated that no members of the royal family could become Prime Minister, hold a ministerial portfolio or become Chief Justice. This made it 'one of the finest constitutions in the Middle East, which consolidated the system of constitutional monarchy in Afghanistan and strengthened the role of elected representative bodies in the political system.'[23] It was also notable for including the term *Loya Jirga*, which no official legal text had ever done previously.

The communist era saw several *Loya Jirgas*, despite attempts by Soviet-backed regimes to undermine Afghan traditions. But against a backdrop of political turmoil and conflict, the 1977, 1985, 1987 and 1990 events remain largely forgotten. The 1977 occasion was held to legitimize President Daoud Khan's ascent to power after he overthrew Zahir Shah's monarchy. The *Loya Jirga* of April 1985 was organized by President Babrak Karmal to pacify dissent towards his social policies – not unlike Amanullah's efforts in the 1920s. Karmal's assembly has since been described only as a quasi-*Loya Jirga* because only 600 of the 1,800 invitees showed up and, as a result, it was arguably less representative than it should have been.

Two years later, President Najibullah held the first of his two *Loya Jirgas*. The 1987 event sought to ratify a new constitution, which he envisaged as the basis for reconciliation with the mujahideen. Staunch communists worried that too many concessions were made to the Islamists, but the mujahideen rejected it in any case, calling Najibullah's administration illegitimate.[24] Najibullah held another *Loya Jirga* in 1990 to amend the 1987 constitution and moderate the communist face of the Afghan government.[25] But with an emboldened mujahideen and the Soviet withdrawal complete, it was too little, too late. Chaos was coming.

Consensus-based decision-making evaporated as Afghanistan broke apart in the 1990s. Mujahideen leaders rejected calls for *Loya Jirgas*, and the Taliban's brand of authoritarianism negated the need for national consensus. It was a barren decade for participatory politics – until everything changed in 2001.

Resurgence or ruin? *Loya Jirgas* after 9/11

Any illusion that the *Loya Jirga* was a traditional, once-in-a-generation event used in times of national crisis was shattered in the post-2001 era. Between September 2001 and the collapse of the Republic in August 2021 there were seven *Loya Jirgas*. The 'Emergency *Loya Jirga*' was convened in April 2002, with around 1,600 ethnically diverse delegates (including 140 women) gathering in a giant tent at Kabul Polytechnic University to reconstitute the state apparatus after the Taliban fled. But finding a tent large enough was logistically challenging at short notice, especially in a failed state, so parts were airlifted from Germany, where large tents were commonly used . . . during *Oktoberfest* celebrations. It meant that the first post-Taliban *Loya Jirga* was organized by the UN, protected by British troops, paid for by the US and EU and held inside a German beer tent.[26]

The outcome of the Emergency *Loya Jirga* was the election of a transitional administration headed by President Hamid Karzai, who was tasked with drafting a new constitution – to be passed at another constitutional *Loya Jirga* that eventually took place over a year later, in December 2003 and January 2004. The latter event saw 102 female and 400 male delegates pass the new constitution that defined a *Loya Jirga* as 'the highest manifestation of the will of the people of Afghanistan', only convened in extraordinary circumstances, to decide 'on issues related to independence, national sovereignty, territorial integrity as well as supreme national interests'.[27]

Six years passed before Afghanistan's 'National Consultative Peace *Jirga*' was convened in June 2010. The 1,600 delegates, many handpicked by President Karzai, debated how to make peace with the Taliban. This *Loya Jirga* was criticized for its ambiguity, being marketed as 'consultative' rather than constitutional, meaning its decisions would not be legally binding and the President could still act unilaterally. But the three-day event is best remembered for its opening ceremony being attacked by the Taliban, with rockets heard exploding as Karzai gave his address, calling the *talibs* 'dear brothers'.

Similar events were held in 2011 and 2013 to deal with the signing of strategic agreements with the US. The 2013 event was the last *Loya Jirga* of the Karzai era, but the trend towards consultative rather than constitutional events continued into President Ghani's tenure.

President Ghani's first *Loya Jirga* was the 'Consultative *Loya Jirga* for Peace' in April 2019. This four-day event saw 3,200 delegates discussing potential peace talks with the Taliban. Critics alleged that Ghani manipulated the process so that friendly delegates would back him ahead of the presidential election. Major political figures boycotted the event, calling it a tactic that undermined a (supposedly) traditional institution. Ghani's second *Loya Jirga* – also consultative – took place a year later in August 2020, to decide the fate of 400 high-profile Taliban prisoners. As always, rumours emerged that the list of participants had been manipulated by the presidential palace, but criticism died away when the *jirgamar* endorsed the release of the prisoners to kickstart formal peace negotiations with the Taliban.

All these post-9/11 events were accompanied by healthy debate about whether *Loya Jirgas* promoted participation or were simply political tools used to ratify decisions that rulers had already made. The trend towards consultative, rather than constitutional, forums was often criticized for creating empty consensus and undermining any authority the *Loya Jirga* had once had.[28] International involvement was also criticized, with later *Loya Jirgas* deemed to be 'the favourite consent-producing tool of American neocolonialism in the Middle East and Central Asia', hailed in Europe and the US as triumphant exercises in democracy, or as Afghan solutions for Afghan problems. Critics claimed that Western governments were duped by 'a charade cleverly staged by the American-controlled bourgeois government of Kabul' – one that Westerners uncritically accepted because it was a useful device to 'legitimize the colonially-appointed government of Kabul'.[29]

The future of *Loya Jirgas* in Afghanistan looks uncertain after the US/NATO withdrawal, the collapse of the Republic and the return of the Taliban in 2021, especially given the Taliban's history of opposing such events when they have been in power. Yet that has not stopped other politicians seeing a *Loya Jirga* as a solution. In early 2022, former President Hamid Karzai and former Chief Executive Abdullah Abdullah both called on the Taliban to hold such an event to try to improve national consultation and foster more inclusive decision-making. Even if the Taliban were to agree, it is almost certain that the future tempo of *Loya Jirgas* will not match the frequency of the post-2001 gatherings. But this should not overshadow the importance of these events in shaping modern Afghan politics, even if they may be misrepresented as an institution that grew out of a Pashtun tribal tradition.

Nor does a likely reduction in *Loya Jirgas* mean that the local-level *jirga* will occur less frequently. It will remain a permanent feature of Pashtun life, which in turn means that the mechanisms to ensure that its decisions are implemented will still be required. That task usually falls to the fighting-age men who protect the tribe – the *lashkar* and *arbaki*.

Chapter 22

Lashkar and *Arbaki*: Pashtun Tribal Protectors

Pashtun respect for elders means that the *jirga*'s consensus-based decisions are obeyed by the entire community – in theory. In reality, unquestioning compliance is not a trait often associated with independent-minded tribes, meaning someone has to enforce the *jirga*'s decision and potentially impose penalties in the event of defiance. This is the role of the *lashkar* and *arbaki*. These tribal forces are raised along kinship lines and have operated as enforcers or guarantors of tribal security for centuries, particularly in the absence of effective state security machinery.

As the best-known tribal forces, *lashkar* and *arbaki* are the topic of this chapter. But they are not the only ones. There is also the *tsalweshtai,* which is a small force of a few dozen men from various sub-clans of a tribe. Common in north-western parts of the Pashtun Belt, it is appointed for a specific purpose, such as protecting a certain area from raiders. A *chalweshtai* is larger version of this, which can also be raised to support community projects or prevent crime (even working with official police forces). Both groups follow decisions made by local elders rather than acting independently. Another tribal force, the *chagha*, is a small group raised quickly when a village or clan is under imminent threat. *Chagha* is also the term for the drum that warns villagers of a threat. It translates as 'a call to arms'.[1] All these tribal forces normally consist of young, unmarried tribesmen not yet experienced enough to participate in *jirgas* but strong and loyal enough to implement their decisions.[2] All of these forces also tend to be branded by Westerners as *lashkars* or *arbaki*, because these two are the best-known.

Lashkars: the tribal offensive force

A *lashkar* is raised to protect a tribal area, a specific tribe or an alliance of clans. It translates as 'troops' but has been referred to as a war party, raiding party, local militia, posse, a camp or even the military quarter of a town.[3] A *lashkar* is offensive in nature, operating on the principle that the best defence is a strong attack. It is raised on the orders of a *jirga* but is an ad hoc, temporary formation that disbands once the threat is neutralized.

Like most armed forces it has standardized basic battle tactics, with Pashtuns displaying a penchant for the well-executed ambush.[4] When attacking an enemy village, the *lashkar* splits into three parts. One part, the assault team, is larger than the others. It raids the village, kills the enemy and burns his buildings – colloquially called 'pulling an enemy's beard'.[5] The attackers then withdraw, protected by one of the smaller units of the *lashkar*, which slows down the pursuit. Once the attackers pass their own first defensive positions, the defenders also pull back and join the third part of the *lashkar*, which has dug in around their home territory to repel any enemy intent on retaliation. When the assault team is back in base, the defenders also pull back, and the entire force turns 'to mock the pursuers from the vantage of the walls and turrets'.[6]

A *lashkar*'s success depends on the men and resources at its disposal. Manpower can range from dozens up to hundreds of armed men. But the commander is directly answerable to the *jirga*. The *jirgamar* decide how many men he should have, based on the issue at hand and information provided by the tribe's intelligence operatives (*kishakee*).[7] A common criticism is that tribal *lashkars* have been insufficient to confront well-equipped state armies or well-organized insurgents. After 2001, they also tended to be hijacked by strongmen who used them for their own benefit. This is a trend also seen with the *lashkar*'s counterpart – the *arbaki*.

Arbaki: the tribal police force

While the *lashkar* is offensive, *arbaki* are defensive. They do not venture out of their tribe's territory and instead operate like a local community police force.[8] The term comes from the Pashto for 'messenger',[9] and Pashtuns have described *arbaki* as

> a group of voluntary adults who are selected by a special procedure, who carry out the responsibilities to implement the Jirga's decisions, secure the territory of the tribe or the respected community and take action against those who want to perform an illegal act.[10]

Traditionally, *arbaki* are formed at a *jirga*'s request and sometimes take orders from multiple *jirgas* (at community, clan or tribe level), although higher level *jirgas* only intervene if a dispute over a decision needs to be transmitted upwards.[11] The *jirga* is responsible for providing logistical and financial support to the *arbaki*, although its members are traditionally unpaid. This is why Pashtuns deny that they are a militia.

Arbaki, in theory, have greater support than any militia because they are embedded in the community and act for the common good rather than purely for financial gain. It is an honour for a tribesman to be an *arbaki*, whereas joining a militia is more like being a mercenary, which is seen as shameful.[12] As with *lashkars*, the *jirga* determines how many men the *arbaki* commander needs and what level he operates at, i.e to protect the tribe, a *qawm* or a *khel*. The *jirga* uses a quota system whereby one of every forty *mirah* (men who embody *Pashtunwali*) in a tribe will be selected to serve as *arbaki* members.[13] While *arbaki* are often perceived to be paramilitaries, they are not always armed. Negotiation and mediation are also used, because their power is supposed to come from *Pashtunwali* rather than weapons. *Arbaki* (and other tribal forces) who are acting on a *jirga*'s mandate are generally exempt from *badal*, meaning they are not subject to reciprocal killings if they kill someone while performing their duties. But they can still become embroiled in disputes due to their own tribal affiliations, especially when they are tasked with enforcing *badal* between two other parties. This can tarnish the reputations of their members and lead to new cycles of violence to restore their honour.[14]

The Pashtun-dominated provinces of Nangarhar, Kunar and the Loya Paktia region are the ones best known for the use of *arbaki*, as these are areas where traditional tribal systems have generally survived more than in others. The region's mountainous geography has meant that tribal structures have taken precedence over state administration, and this is still the case today.[15] Its inaccessibility has also facilitated a more egalitarian approach to life and has generally kept power in the hands of tribal elders rather than prominent warlords, strongmen or ethnic entrepreneurs.[16]

Famous Pashtun *lashkars* and *arbaki*

Both *lashkars* and *arbaki* were used by Ahmad Shah Durrani in the mid-1700s. He employed *lashkars* to fight in India while 'devolving' border security to *arbaki*.[17] Sher Ali Khan of the Second Durrani Dynasty also flirted with local forces after he founded the national army, and in the late nineteenth century, Abdur Rahman Khan famously asked tribes to patrol border areas in return for exemption from military conscription.[18]

A particularly famous *lashkar* was formed in March 1860, when the Mahsud tribe (Karlani branch) reacted to British encroachment by forming a 3,000-strong *lashkar* to attack a British Indian fort at the town of Tank in the frontier area. But the commander of the 5th Punjab Cavalry garrisoned there had received advance warning and set out to intercept the tribal raiders. This commander, Risaldar Sadat Khan, deployed his infantry in a frontal assault while his cavalry swooped around the Mahsud *lashkar* and sabred them from behind. The decimated Mahsuds fled, pursued by the cavalrymen. Benefitting from flat ground, the cavalry caught the fleeing tribesmen and scythed down any survivors. This encounter was the foundation of a long-running animosity between the Mahsuds and the British and set the scene for multiple 'punitive expeditions' by British Indian forces into tribal areas.[19]

But the Mahsuds learned lessons, recognizing that to avoid defeat they needed to stay in their own mountains and adopt unconventional tactics, such as punishing the enemy with a calculated strategy of 'death by a thousand cuts' rather than reckless all-out attacks. These are the guerrilla tactics that the Mahsuds and other tribes have used against other invaders ever since.[20]

Another famous Pashtun *lashkar*, but one which did not fight inside Afghanistan, was 'The Great Kashmir *Lashkar*'. It was made up of 5,000 tribesmen from the Wazir, Mahsud, Turi, Afridi, Mohmand and Orakzai tribes (mostly of the Karlani branch). They were enlisted by the newly-created Pakistani state to fight in the 1947/8 Indo-Pakistan conflict.

On 22 October 1947, the 5,000-strong *lashkar* advanced into Kashmir from Pakistan. Buoyed by initial victories, the tribesmen looted and plundered many of the villages they had taken. Eyewitnesses said they 'shot everyone who couldn't recite the *kalima*' (a Muslim declaration). Many non-Muslim women were enslaved, while others preferred to jump into fast-flowing rivers to escape capture.[21]

After three days of mayhem, the *lashkar* moved towards the capital, Srinagar. Supported by the advance of Pakistani forces, their pressure led Kashmir's Maharaja to request Indian support to stave off imminent defeat. The Indians agreed, but only if the Marahaja promised to cede Kashmir to India. The 'Instrument of Accession' was hastily signed on 26 October, just as the Pashtuns approached Srinagar. Lord Mountbatten, Governor General of India, reacted swiftly and airlifted Indian troops into Kashmir. Despite some British bureaucratic infighting due to their partnerships with both the Indian and Pakistani militaries, Indian forces thwarted the tribal advance and repulsed other Pakistani attacks.

Within a month, when the winter snow fell, the Pashtun tribesmen started to return home. This led the Indians to halt their advance, stabilizing the line that still divides Kashmir today. The Pashtun *lashkar* was thus partly responsible for the long-running animosity that still grips Kashmir. It helped set a disastrous pattern for India-Pakistan relations, and one that backfired on the Pashtuns because it taught Pakistan the value of using non-state actors as proxy forces – a tactic Islamabad has employed ever since, including against the Afghan government and the Pashtun tribes, particularly from the 1980s onwards.

In more recent years, *arbaki* have also risen to international prominence. After the Afghan refugee exodus to Pakistan in the 1980s, *arbaki* were used to police some refugee camps (albeit sponsored by the mosques rather than *jirgas*).[22] In the post-9/11 era, a famous tribal *arbaki* was formed in Loya Pakitia in 2006 by the

Mangal tribe (Karlani branch). Their tribal *jirga* did not initially sanction action against the Taliban, mainly because it was seen as a threat to the state rather than to the tribe.[23] But eventually, the Mangals did start to banish insurgents. A Mangal *arbaki* was tasked with burning the houses of any Taliban-affiliated bomb-makers and poppy cultivators.[24]

There are plenty of other examples of the use of *arbaki* in the post-9/11 era – many of which backfired because international soldiers and diplomats were blind to aspects of tribal identity, basing the sponsorship of *arbaki* around state interests (i.e. fighting the Taliban) rather than tribal interests or *Pashtunwali*. US military officials mistakenly tried to transplant ideas about local defence forces from Iraq to Afghanistan, failing to grasp the unique tribal environment in their quest for 'Afghan solutions to Afghan problems'.[25] In many cases, the positive impacts of the modern *arbaki* were limited and temporary. More often they simply added more layers to a conflict, making it more complicated, more difficult to understand and even harder to operate in.

Some of these new groups were not even *arbaki* at all, despite being branded as such. They were private militias, guns for hire and warlords, rather than tribal protectors. There are even cases where internationally-backed groups of non-Pashtun militia were called *arbaki* and sent to 'police' Pashtun areas. They had no accountability to any *jirga* and were not accepted by local communities. This poisoned the concept of *arbaki* and reopened old wounds that the Soviets had inflicted by doing similar things two decades earlier. All of this only reinforced the idea in Pashtun minds that foreigners were intent on destroying tribal structures. The subsequent increase in militarization, feudalism and instability in tribal areas was a gift to the Taliban. This is yet another example of the need to understand the Pashtun tribes from the inside – to understand them as they understand themselves.

Whoever is to blame, *arbaki* (and *lashkars* to a lesser extent) are no longer seen strictly as protectors of Pashtun tribal areas and as implementing decisions of a local *jirga*. They have become conflated with warlordism. Rather than acting in the interests of the honour code, they are now often caught between various power brokers, outgunned by insurgents, embroiled in criminality or seen as partial due to their links with one side or the other. All of this only feeds the narrative that Afghanistan's recent conflicts have degraded the tribal system and have led to a crumbling of traditional tribal structures.

Chapter 23

Proverbs: A Window into the Pashtun Soul?

Pashto proverbs are often overlooked by Westerners, or even dismissed as trivial, partly because they can be difficult to put into context. If an Afghan visitor arrived in Europe wanting to learn about its people, who would recommend starting with a book of proverbs?

Yet for Pashtuns, oral storytelling is a crucial method of passing culture down the generations. Along with folklore, superstitions and songs, proverbs are particularly important in shaping Pashtun ideals. They are prisms through which to view the colourful spectrum of Pashtun values and beliefs. They reflect Pashtun attitudes by condensing the wisdom of many into the wit of a one-liner.[1] They are also a teaching tool and a method of establishing social norms – and of enforcing them, too. They are 'used for conformity; employed against individuals who attempt to deviate from social conventions with which they are fully familiar'.[2]

Spend any amount of time with Pashtuns and it won't be long before you hear one. These short, pithy sayings will be expertly dropped into any argument and quoted during any conversation. They are seen in newspapers and heard on the radio, in the bazaar or in the back of taxis. Rarely does a politician make a speech without using one.

Yet for foreigners it is not always easy to grasp the right meaning when a Pashtun uses a proverb in conversation. It is even more difficult to pick the right moment to use a proverb. But the value of a proverb is not always the point it makes. It can also be a cultural ice-breaker. Pashtuns, and other Afghans, recognize any attempt to learn and speak their language or understand their traditions. It is a gesture of respect, one that signifies that we understand that we are outsiders in their homeland. It helps foster trust and build relationships. This is a tactic that Indian Prime Minister Narendra Modi uses, often sprinkling proverbs into his speeches to present a friendly face. He used 'a tree with a bitter seed, fed with butter and sugar, will still bear a bitter fruit' when urging the Afghan Parliament to pursue peace in 2015. He also used the famous proverb 'May Kabul be without gold rather than snow', which underlines the importance of water to agrarian Afghans, when inaugurating the Afghanistan-India Friendship Dam in 2016.

The main contribution that proverbs make to understanding the Pashtun psyche is that they are not created by outsiders, unlike most written Pashtun history. They are *self*-criticisms and *self*-observations coined by Pashtuns themselves. They reveal tribesmen's insights and sentiments about their own society. This also means that they do not solely focus on exciting stories of battles, barbarity and other attention-grabbing scenes. Many are concerned with common but often overlooked character traits like friendship, equality and generosity.

If you want to know Pashtuns, know their proverbs.

Study of Pashto proverbs

There was almost no study of Pashto folklore and proverbs by foreigners until the mid-nineteenth century,[3] when it became a pastime for early British imperialist officers who were trying to understand the tribes.[4] The consensus is that the first formal attempt to study Pashto proverbs was made by the British officer S. S. Thorburn in his book *Bannú, Or Our Afghan Frontier* (1876). A range of similar European texts followed, before the establishment of the Pashto Academy in Peshawar formalized Pashtun paremiology (the study of proverbs) in 1955.[5] This institution started to turn an oral history into a written one. One of its most important works is Muhammad Nawaz Tair's two-volume book called *Rohi Mataluna* (1982). Containing more than 12,000 proverbs, it is as definitive as any collection and is often cited by other authors.[6] One of the best analyses of Tair's opus outlines how

> Pashto proverbs provide critical lessons about faith and honor, human nature and relationships, friends and enemies, power and revenge, in short, how to live in a society that is at once fragrant with friendship, fraught with ambiguities, and seared by treachery.[7]

But even *Rohi Mataluna* is incomplete. Pashtuns have an inexhaustible supply of proverbs – maybe hundreds of thousands. Consequently, they tend to be condensed into broad categories or themes, which often mirror *Pashtunwali*'s principles.

Common themes of Pashto proverbs

Honour is by far the most common theme of Pashto proverbs. 'A Pathan begs not; if he does, well, he'll beg from his sister' explains that begging is the opposite of honour. It also hints that the first stop for a Pashtun man in financial difficulty will be his elder sister, who will recognize the importance of patrilineage and the need to support her brother to maintain the family's reputation. A similar proverb about honourable behaviour is 'Food obtained through begging is licking the blood of the nose' (blood is perceived as unclean under Islamic guidelines). Boasting is a quick way to undermine honour, with one proverb declaring that a vainglorious soldier is inferior even to an unclean dog, which never boasts: 'Is a dog or a soldier the better? Confound the soldier who praises himself.'

Bravery is another common topic, given the importance of physical courage to Pashtun identity. 'A stone will not become soft, nor an enemy or a friend' is a reminder to be unflinching. It is similar to 'Tender-handed grasp a nettle, it will sting you for your pains; grasp it like a man of mettle, soft as silk it then remains.' 'The tiger rends his prey, the jackal, too, benefits by it' is another bravery-related proverb, conveying that a strong man takes care of himself and his dependants. It reminds a tribesman to defend his tribe bravely.

Bravery is often reinforced by warnings against cowardice. 'A dog when surrounded turns tail, a man fights' encapsulates the shame of cowardice in conflict, and 'He had burnt his mouth with the porridge, and was making death gasps' criticizes those who complain about minor afflictions.

Some proverbs reveal strategic thinking – and counter the negative stereotypes of simple tribesmen. 'Kill a snake of course through an enemy' is similar to the European proverb, 'Draw a snake from its hole by another man's hand.' Other proverbs encourage tribesmen to be ruthlessly unhurried in attack: 'Speak good words to an enemy very softly; gradually destroy him root and branch.'

There are also warnings about scheming enemies. 'He will say sweet words to you, and lead you into a pit' is a proverb heard often in reference to Pakistan's engagement with the Afghan state – which many Afghans regard as duplicitous. 'A goat with two fathers will never survive' is another old proverb still in circulation today. It was used to describe Afghanistan's predicament as the arena of a superpower proxy war in the 1980s. More recently, it was employed to characterize the policymaking stasis within the Afghan Government after 2014, due to the power struggle between President Ashraf Ghani and the Chief Executive Abdullah Abdullah.

Not all proverbs focus on enmity. Many underline the importance of generosity and hospitality. 'Let it be an onion but it should be given with love and pleasure' communicates that no matter how symbolic a gift is, it is offered with the utmost generosity in mind. It is the kind of proverb uttered by a host who is serving food to a guest, as a bashful apology for a simple meal (which is in fact generous). Pashtuns place such high value on generosity that proverbs such as 'When you eat it, it will become faeces. When you give it, it will turn into flowers' caution against greed. Yet some proverbs also warn against being over-generous: 'Whoever is too open-handed makes for himself loincloths of black blankets.'

'Though I am but a straw, I am as good as you' is one of many proverbs about equality. 'The master's food is being cooked, and the slave-girl's back aches' explains that Pashtuns should not be content enjoying anything that is not shared. Similar maxims on sharing are 'One sows it, one hundred eat it' or 'The fatter a hen grows, the tighter her anus becomes.'

Friendship, known as *andiwali*, is another common theme, with proverbs like 'Even in a gathering of guests there should be a friend' conveying that Pashtuns should always be accompanied by allies. But friends should be chosen carefully, in order to enhance perceptions of honour. This is encapsulated in the proverb 'Friendship with a low-bred man is like a ride on a donkey.' There is a similar attitude towards good manners. 'One's manners are a product of one's heritage but they are tempered by society' conveys that good manners are inherited but can be eroded by the company one keeps.

'Not just to the home but unto the grave' reminds tribesmen that friendships should be lifelong, and this view of enduring friendship is also summed up by 'The first day you meet, you are friends. The next day you meet, you are brothers.' This is a proverb that is very common across Afghanistan and one that many foreigners have heard at their farewell events or towards their end of their deployments – sometimes as a deliberate message that it takes more than a six-month tour to become a true friend of Afghanistan.

Fate is an equally frequent subject, as Pashtuns tend to believe in destiny and are encouraged to make the best of it. Besides the ubiquitous use of the term '*Inshallah*' in daily life, Pashtuns will use proverbs such as 'If retching come on you by destiny, close your teeth on it.' A similar theme is the idea that nature cannot be changed: 'The donkey will remain a donkey, no matter wherever it goes.' There is also 'The snake's baby is also a snake' and 'The thorn which is sharp is so from its youth', which make similar points, as does 'Don't expect good faith from a low-born man; Reeds will never become sugar cane.' The latter proverb suits the context of historical distrust between rival tribes or sub-tribes.

Proverbs on inter-ethnic and inter-tribal rivalries

Many Pashto proverbs have themes that transcend geographical and linguistic boundaries, while others are Pashtun-specific. The most stinging proverbs are aimed at other tribes, ethnicities and religions.

'A Shia's ablution is not nullified by his passing of wind' refers to the Islamic practice of cleansing the body before prayer. The Sunni view is that passing wind makes someone unclean, and he must therefore wash himself before praying again. Those who reject Shia doctrine, or consider it to be a misguided faith, use this proverb disparagingly. It suggests that a Shia's ablution is not nullified by flatulence because his ablution is pointless anyway (this is of course disputed by Shias). Another jibe is 'He is a Shia's tomb; white outwardly, but black inside' to suggest that someone might look handsome or intelligent but is empty on the inside.

One of the countless Pashto proverbs criticizing Hindus is 'The Pashtun eats his enemy, the Hindu his friend', which suggests that Hindus are untrustworthy. 'The Hindus' cooking circle is purified with dung' explains that an unclean man cannot cleanse himself regardless of what he tries. It refers to the belief among some Hindus that everything produced by a cow is sacred and purifying. To this day, the village of Gumatapura in southern India holds a dung-flinging festival as part of the closing of the Diwali ceremonies. Cow dung is widely used in India to heat homes and even for street vendors to cook with. In 2016, dried 'cow pies' for use as fuel even became available to order online, via Amazon.[8]

'A Sikh's origin is his hair' reflects bad blood between Pashtuns and Sikhs. It suggests that anyone is able to become a Sikh if he lets his hair grow long, whereas Pashtun genealogy is inborn. Pashtuns also have an historical antipathy towards Persians, with the proverb 'The full stomach speaks Persian' stemming from a time when Persian-speakers were seen as arrogant representatives of the ruling class.

Rival tribesmen are frequently on the receiving end of a stinging proverb. 'If a Wazir makes an attack, he will expose his naked back' stigmatizes Waziri tribesmen as cowards who fight defensively from behind walls and never in the open. 'A Khattak is a hen; if you seize him slowly he sits down, if suddenly then he clucks' paints the Khattak tribe as unintelligent and cowardly. Yet with tribal proverbs, as in many aspects of Pashtun life, there is usually some form of counter-argument or alternative narrative. For example, another proverb says that 'The Khattak would never have become old had he not been worrying about the problems of others.' It refers to the Khattak reputation for kindheartedness, conveying that Khattaks will destroy their own health by brooding over the problems of others.

The most common Pashto proverbs

The sheer volume of Pashto proverbs can be overwhelming, and there are many that even the proudest Pashtuns have never heard of. But among the thousands, there are some that are regularly used to encapsulate common tribal characteristics. Five of the most commonly heard in conversation are outlined below.

1) *I took my revenge after a hundred years, and I only regret that I acted in haste.* This is among the best-known and most quoted proverbs, sometimes articulated as 'If a Pashtun takes revenge after 100 years, he is still in a hurry.'

Any books, articles or blogs about *Pashtunwali* will be decorated with this aphorism. It reflects that time is not important in taking revenge, not unlike the English saying, 'Revenge is a dish best served cold' or another Pashtun proverb, 'A Pashtun's enmity is like a dung-fire', meaning that it smoulders for a long time and is not easily put out. The recent resolution of a 500-year-long land dispute between two clans of the Jaji tribe (Karlani branch) is an example of the Pashtun ability to maintain a grudge.[9]

2) *You can lead a Pashtun to hell with kindness but you can never force him to heaven.* Pashtuns say they have never been forced to beg for mercy or been coerced into cooperating with any attacker. This is why this proverb was routinely referenced after the US invasion in 2001 – and it is often heard in any discussion of peace negotiations. It was used as a reminder to international actors that threats in Afghanistan only fall on deaf ears.

3) *I against my brother. My brother and I against my cousin. My cousin, my brother, and I against the world.* This reflects the Pashtun tendency to be constantly at war with each other, only to unite in the face of an external challenger. But there is debate about whether this is a Pashto proverb. It is often said to have Arab origins. Similar proverbs include 'A cousin's tooth breaks on a cousin's' and 'It is better to kill a snake and humble a cousin.'

4) *You do for me. I will do for you.* This is one of many proverbs that apply not just to Pashtuns but also to other Afghans. It sums up the often transactional nature of relationships in Afghanistan. It is similar to the common adage that 'You can rent an Afghan but you cannot buy him.'

5) *Honour (*nang*) ate up the mountains, taxes (*qalang*) ate up the plains.* This proverb sums up the historical divide between tribesmen living in remote, mountainous areas and those who are settled in the fertile, lowland plains. The former tend to be independent-minded, more devoted adherents of *Pashtunwali* and less inclined to accept state governance. The latter more frequently support central governments and engagement with outsiders.

In all of these proverbs there are elements of the three themes that recur throughout this book. Proverbs are a primary tool for gaining an inside perspective on the Pashtun tribes – to understand them as they understand themselves. Rather than being overlooked as a quaint but insignificant element of Pashtun culture, proverbs should be relied upon by anyone seeking insight into the tribal psyche.

Another recurring theme that even this small snapshot of Pashto proverbs underlines is that while the traditional negative stereotypes of Pashtuns may have some truth to them, they may also be unbalanced, with the harshest aspects of tribal life often overrepresented in the literature. Of course there are proverbs that bolster the image of unforgiving and violent warriors, but there are just as many that focus on 'softer' aspects of tribal life such as peace, hospitality and friendship. This is a reminder that there is much more to the Pashtun tribes and their way of life than the longstanding stereotypes portray. They are not entirely inaccurate, but there is a tendency to condemn Pashtun tribesmen in too sweeping terms.

A third theme, one reinforced by the last proverb about the people of the mountains versus those of the plains, is that the Pashtun tribes are diverse and do not act as one homogeneous bloc. This proverb also hints at one factor that has a pronounced impact on the Pashtun mindset and still shapes tribal stereotypes to this day. Such is its importance that it is the topic of the next section of this book – geography.

PART VII

The Territory of the Tribes

Chapter 24

Tribal Stereotypes
Shaped by Geography

Stereotypes exist for a reason. This book, so far, has highlighted why there is a certain truth in the picture of the Pashtun tribesman as a burly, battle-hardened and forbidding warrior who lives *Pashtunwali* to the letter and spends his days lying in wait around the high mountain passes, where he has soaked every stone in the blood of successive invaders. Yet history also presents an equally applicable (albeit equally negative) portrait of a silky, sly, politically astute operator who plays opponents off against one another, cherry-picking parts of *Pashtunwali* but forming alliances with whomever the moment calls for, even foreigners or non-Pashtuns.

Both stereotypes give an unbalanced view of Pashtuns. They emphasise only the negative traits rather than their more honourable tendencies or 'softer' attributes. Yet they also emphasise that variety that can be found within the tribes. Underneath an overarching shared ethnic identity, the tribes are divided. They are not homogeneous. Their differences may be based on lineage, social outlook and political persuasion.

Locality is another determining factor. The terrain in which a tribesman lives sculpts his character and influences his interactions with others. Geography is one of the most important markers of tribal identity, determining whether he is a *Nang* Pashtun or a *Qalang* Pashtun.

Nang Pashtuns: reclusive highland warriors

Nang Pashtuns are mountain-men known for their pastoral and nomadic lifestyle. They tend to be concentrated in the east and south-east, in the Loya Paktia region and the highland areas that border Pakistan, particularly the Sulaiman and Spin Ghar mountain ranges.

Their description as *nang* is a clue to how these hill-dwellers live. It translates as 'honour', signalling that Nang Pashtuns traditionally prioritize the *Pashtunwali* honour code. They are egalitarians and prefer their disputes to be dealt with by *jirgas* rather than government intervention, meaning their territory tends to be less penetrated by state institutions. Their egalitarianism also means that they have been less prone than other tribes or ethnic groups to dominance by individual leaders or powerful strongmen, leading one anthropologist to describe them as 'jellyfish tribes', i.e. diffuse and without a backbone.[1]

These tendencies are influenced by the physical geography of their home territory. Living away from urban centres in thinly populated, steep mountain ranges, where the land is less irrigable or cultivable than in lowland areas, they are mostly pastoralists. This is why many nomadic clans are classed as Nang Pashtuns. Yet inhabiting these unforgiving badlands has consequences. Their pastoral way of life is less profitable than the agrarian economy of the lowland plains, meaning that Nang Pashtuns tend to have comparatively low standards of living. This, along with their perceived isolationism and fervent opposition to foreign incursion, is why many characteristics associated with Nang Pashtuns mesh neatly with the negative stereotype and imperialist picture of independent but primitive warriors.

Areas where Nang Pashtuns live generally overlap with the so-called 'Frontier' territory, where British Indian expeditions encountered resistance in the nineteenth and twentieth centuries. Many tribes classed as Nang Pashtuns are famed for having used the terrain to their advantage when resisting British incursions. Even at times of peak British presence these tribes maintained such territorial control that the British administrators' authority rarely reached more than 100 yards on either side of the main roads.[2] One British colonel wrote in the 1890s that 'it was a forbidden land, and no Englishman had ever been there before . . . it was impossible to go [inside] and if you did your bones would be left there'.[3]

To Nang Pashtuns, 'foreign' does not always mean external invaders. They have an ingrained antipathy towards the Afghan state, perceiving its jurisdiction as having been imposed on them. Their attitude is that taxes (which represent state authority) are a symbol of submission and a humiliation. Being taxed equates to being unable to defend oneself, and 'only those who refuse to be governed are themselves fit to rule'.[4] This independent outlook is encapsulated in a Pashto proverb that 'Behind every hillock, there sits an emperor.'

Suspicion of the state has meant that areas associated with Nang Pashtuns have had a much weaker central government presence and less interaction with state legal or military institutions than other parts of Afghanistan. The flip side of living by the 'code of the hills' is that their tribal culture is said to be purer and less diluted by recent conflicts and invasions, at least when compared to their tribal cousins – the *Qalang* Pashtuns.[5]

Qalang Pashtuns: leaders of the lowland plains

Qalang translates as 'taxes', hinting at how Qalang Pashtuns differ from their Nang Pashtun counterparts. They tend to be more statist, urbanites and landowners who live in flatter, fertile and irrigable lowland areas fed by big rivers. These are

The 'Nang' Category	The 'Qalang' Category
Economic	
Hill areas	Plain areas
Largely unirrigated	Largely irrigated
Pastoral tribal economy	Agricultural feudal economy
No rents or taxes	Rents and taxes
Social	
Mainly 'achieved' status of elders	Mainly 'ascribed' status of 'Khans'
Illiterate, oral tradition	Literate, orthodox, written tradition
Acephalous tribal society organised in segmentary descent groups	Autocephalous village organisation under Khan
Scarce population dispersed in 'fort-like' hamlets and nucleated settlements	Dense population in large villages and tendency to urbanisation
Emphasis on Pashtunwali (code of honour)	Emphasis on Taboorwali (agnatic rivalry)
Political	
Outside, or juxtaposed to, larger state systems	Encapsulated within larger system; members of civil service, district boards etc.
Jirga represents interests of the entire tribe (the vast majority of the population)	Jirga members represent landowners
Warriors participating in raids	Warlords organising battles
Egalitarian social organisation	Hierarchical social organisation based on autochthonic population

Figure 9: Nang vs Qalang Characteristics

southern provinces like Kandahar, Helmand and Nimruz, as well as Farah and southern Herat on the border with Iran.

More agriculture means more produce to sell and enhanced economic prosperity. This ability to amass wealth gives Qalang Pashtuns a more avaricious outlook than their Nang counterparts. It underpins their communities' tendency to be more hierarchical in structure and dominated by powerful individuals. It also influences the way honour is obtained, particularly on the battlefield. For Qalang Pashtuns, being an honourable fighter tends to be linked to socio-economic status; in other words, tribal chiefs and commanders gain reputation from battlefield victories. The more egalitarian Nang Pashtuns traditionally fight together as equals, regardless of prestige or economic status.

Different approaches to *Pashtunwali* are often cited as a main difference between Nang and Qalang Pashtuns.[6] *Pashtunwali* is still important to Qalang Pashtuns, but they generally use more flexible interpretations of it. Or, as one British orientalist wrote, they are 'are notorious for every sort of debauchery' – as opposed to Nang Pashtuns, who were described as 'remarkably sober, and free from vices'.[7]

The characteristics of both the Nang and Qalang Pashtuns have been succinctly laid out by Akhbar S. Ahmed in his book *Social and Economic Change in The Tribal Areas* (1977),[8] reproduced in Figure 9.

Why Nang vs Qalang matters in Afghanistan

As the Nang vs Qalang divide is based on geography rather than bloodlines, it does not mirror or neatly correlate with the Pashtun tribal structure – although some stereotypical characteristics may still sound familiar.

Qalang Pashtuns have been described in similar terms to some of the tribes and rulers of the Durrani Confederation. They live on the lowland plains in the south, particularly around Kandahar and Helmand, as well as in the south-west and along the western border with Iran. Inhabiting this more irrigable, fertile, arable land meant that the Durranis were able to amass wealth, which in turn facilitated the creation of patronage networks and the rise of powerful individuals who control them; in other words, they have a tendency towards hierarchy. This geographical factor aided the Durrani Dynasties in establishing their historic grip over the state institutions, as well as their more frequent engagement with other Afghan ethnic groups and foreigners.

Conversely, the tribes of the Ghilzai Confederation, along with the tribes of the Karlani branch, tend to fit better into the Nang Pashtun category. They are the tribes more associated with the isolated highlands in the east and south-east, particularly Loya Paktia and stretches of the border with Pakistan – or the 'Frontier' as British imperialists knew it. This less accessible terrain has helped foster a strong spirit of independence and scepticism towards state authority. Traditional tribal systems, revolving around *Pashtunwali*, have survived better in these areas. The result is that Nang Pashtuns have often been the basis for negative Western stereotypes about the tribes. Even their Qalang Pashtun cousins often disparage them as lower-class individuals who would benefit from accepting state authority. But the Ghilzais and other Nang Pashtuns see their Qalang Pashtun cousins as sell-outs who have compromised their freedom and true Pashtun identity by supporting the state and engaging with outsiders.

There is a danger of oversimplifying Pashtuns by squeezing an entire society into the confines of these two tight categories. But the Nang vs Qalang classification is useful because it hints again at the centrality of the 'state vs tribe' dynamic in the Pashtun story. It also underlines once more the fact that the Pashtun tribes are anything but one homogeneous group or a single entity – and it is arrogant or even wilfully ignorant to treat them as such.

With so many cultural complexities and subtleties, the reality is that an outsider, no matter how well briefed or how attuned to Afghan atmospherics, can only ever have a partial understanding of the Pashtun tribes. But even if it only helps build a partial understanding, the Nang vs Qalang classification is important. It is a useful organizational distinction that shows how terrain and topography influence tribal culture and character. It shows that *where* they live still shapes *how* they live – something to be borne in mind when looking at the traditional homeland of the tribes: the Pashtun Belt.

Chapter 25

The Pashtun Belt

The fortieth largest country in the world by area, Afghanistan ranks somewhere between France and Turkey. Geographically, it is sandwiched between some of Asia's largest economies and often called the 'Heart of Asia' or the 'Asian Roundabout'. Sir Muhammad Iqbal, an intellectual whose thinking underpinned Pakistan's creation, described Asia as 'a body of water and clay, of which the Afghan nation forms the heart'.

But Afghanistan's physical geography is a gift that has turned into a curse. Cycles of conflict have crippled its potential, leaving this strategic crossroads as an economic backwater that is now often thought of, at least in the West, as little more than a barren, dusty desert. Yet Afghanistan is actually a land of great variety and contrast – in both physical and human terms. Its rivers and mountain ranges, particularly the famed Hindu Kush, separate its various ethnic groups from one another, as if actively managing the inevitable chaos that would occur were they to clash. Afghanistan's physical geography has long dictated its ethnic geography, although the former is much easier to map than the latter.

Afghanistan is made up of a kaleidoscopic collection of communities, the composition of which is a long-term source of contention and political manipulation. A survey in the 1970s established that there are between forty and fifty languages in Afghanistan, belonging to seven separate linguistic groups.[1] Mapping this human landscape is a messy affair, because even if certain areas are dominated by one ethnicity, it's rare for any part of the country to be inhabited by a single ethnic group, with urban areas usually being particularly mixed.

Simplified, it can be said that each of the four main ethnicities – Pashtuns, Tajiks, Hazaras, Uzbeks – does occupy territory that is traditionally 'theirs'. The Tajiks broadly reside in the north-east (contiguous with Tajikistan's border), Uzbeks dominate the north-west (south of Uzbekistan and Turkmenistan), while Hazaras live in the area known as the Central Highlands in the middle of Afghanistan.[2]

To the south of all these areas are the Pashtuns, with their tribal territory stretching in an arc from the western border with Iran and along the entirety of the southern border with Pakistan, before curving north-eastwards and ending just south of the panhandle-like Wakhan corridor (a narrow strip of territory that acted as a buffer between the British and Russian Empires in the late nineteenth century). These areas of Afghanistan are broadly mirrored by the Pashtun parts of Pakistan. Collectively, this crescent is known as the Pashtun Belt (see Map 4).

The Pashtun Belt and tribal terminology

Pashtuns don't need maps to identify their traditional tribal territory. Every tribesman knows the location and extent of his *manteqa*, a term which translates as 'place' or 'area' but carries the meaning of 'homeland' and normally refers to 'a self-identified, culturally uniform, shared-geographic space, usually based around clusters of small villages'.[3] It can also describe usage arrangements between people who share common geographical features (valleys, forests or drainage basins).[4] *Manteqas* vary in size but traditionally represent an area controlled by a specific clan or tribe, generally being larger than a single village but smaller than a government-drawn administrative district.[5] A Western equivalent would be a township, although a *manteqa*'s boundaries are based on physical geography rather than population.[6]

Manteqa is often used interchangeably with *watan,* which translates as 'fatherland' or 'home area'. It signifies an area with which a tribesman has an emotional connection and which is the first place for him to defend in times of threat.[7] But the term has been bastardized by nationalist politicians who, to support their own causes, have attempted to extend its meaning to refer to all of Afghanistan.[8] A growing Afghan diaspora also dilutes it by referring to Afghanistan as their *watan* and any fellow Afghan as their *watandar*, rather than using it to reference a specific locality.[9]

Dzay is a more distinctive term, meaning 'landmark'. It is often used to identify a fixed point of importance to a particular tribe's identity. As an aid worker in Afghanistan and then as an ethnologist studying the country, Bernt Glatzer interviewed hundreds of Afghans travelling across the border with Pakistan from the early 1970s until the late 1990s. He found little variation in notions of locality between different ethnic groups, but significant variations over time. He also interviewed one Pashtun who explained the term *dzay* well:

> A nomad informant belonging to the western Pashtun tribe of Atsakzay [*sic*] told me that the dzay of the Atsakzay is a shrine (*ziyarat*) in Spin Boldak, a town between Kandahar and Quetta, 600km south of the place of the interview. The man had never been there, nor did he know any member of his tribe who had ever visited Spin Boldak, but he had a notion that this was the place his tribal

ancestor hailed from. This is the spiritual focus of all Atsakzay, an imaginary fixed point they think and talk about when tribal pride and unity is at stake.[10]

Mamlakat is another territorial term, meaning 'state territory' (although not a Pashto word, it is a Persian word that Pashtuns have adopted). It traditionally referred to the political sphere of influence around Kabul rather than the total land area governed by the state. Historically, state authority gradually weakened as distance from Kabul increased, with the peripheries operating more localized and traditional systems of governance.[11] The Pashtun periphery was the highlands where Nang Pashtuns lived, sometimes nicknamed 'Yaghistan' by Kabul elites, meaning 'land of the rebels' or 'land of the unruly'. Yaghistan's residents prefer 'land of the free'.[12]

Not all of these terms are in common usage today but they highlight the fact that, while Westerners talk and think in terms of the Pashtun Belt as one continuous tribal territory, Pashtuns do not. They place more importance on local homelands than collective tribal territory. In some areas, people who share a locality may display more solidarity with their immediate neighbours of different ethnicities than with fellow Pashtuns in a different region. Many people even use geographic surnames like 'Kandahari', 'Paktiawal' or 'Nuristani' before genealogical or tribal names.

The Pashtun Belt and the terms discussed are useful as an introduction to tribal geography, but a deeper understanding requires a more focused look, first at areas generally held by each of the four branches of the Pashtun tribal structure. Then the most important geographic unit – the territories of individual tribes – can be identified within these broader regions.

Traditional territory of the Sarbani branch

The territory of the Sarbani branch is not contiguous. Its geographical spread reflects its two main lineages. The tribes descending from Sarban's second son, Kharshbun, are nicknamed 'Eastern Pashtuns' because they live in Nangarhar, Laghman and Kunar Provinces in eastern Afghanistan (see Map 4). They also have a large presence on the Pakistani side of the border. Prominent Eastern Pashtun tribes include the Shinwari, Mohmand and Yusufzai. Yusufzai oral tradition has it that they originated in Kandahar but from the thirteenth century onwards gradually moved east to settle in modern-day Pakistan.[13] The Shinwari clans in Afghanistan are synonymous with Nangarhar Province, residing around the Torkham border crossing and the valleys near the Tora Bora caves, where Bin Laden and his colleagues holed up in 2001 before escaping into Pakistan.[14]

The other Sarbani lineage, mainly the tribes of the Durrani Confederation, traditionally reside much further south and west than the Eastern Pashtuns – some older sources actually refer to them as 'Western Pashtuns'. They dominate the plains of Helmand, Kandahar, Nimruz, Farah and Herat provinces (see Map 4). These tribes include the Popalzai, Barakzai, Alikozai and Achekzai (Zirak Division), as well as the Ishaqzai, Alizai and Noorzai (Panjpai division).

The general areas associated with the most prominent individual tribes can be seen in Map 5. The Popalzai are common in Kandahar and parts of Uruzgan province to its north. The Barakzai also live in northern Kandahar, but are more dominant in Helmand Province.[15] The Alikozai tribe are renowned as residents of the leafy Arghandab River valley in western Kandahar. It is one of Afghanistan's breadbaskets, with plentiful pomegranate harvests. But it is also a long-time refuge for insurgents. British soldiers in the nineteenth century wrote that forging a path through its thick vineyards was 'no child's play',[16] and Soviets called it the 'The Heart of Darkness'.[17] One Soviet soldier described it as a 15–20km-long, 7km-wide valley that is practically impassable for vehicles.[18] After repeatedly failing to clear it of mujahideen in the 1980s, the Soviets eventually gave up and built an expensive bypass through the adjoining desert.[19]

The Achekzai and Noorzai tribes have long contested the Spin Boldak area of Kandahar, one of the main border crossings into Pakistan. The Achekzai have tended to support the central government, while the Noorzai have often filled the ranks of the mujahideen and the Taliban.[20] Like the Noorzai tribe, the Ishaqzai have a history of being 'non-state' combatants. Their homeland is in Kandahar and Helmand, particularly around the Sangin area of Helmand, where they have historically been rivals of the Alikozai tribe.

The Alizai tribe inhabit northern Helmand, with Musa Qala being their homeland. Meaning 'Fortress of Moses', this is where the Taliban spent weeks bombarding a platoon of under-resourced British troops in 2006, with tribal elders eventually stepping in to negotiate a ceasefire. The Battle of Musa Qala was fought a year later, when the Taliban were ousted from their last stronghold in Afghanistan – then known as the place where the last Taliban District Governor could be interviewed live on TV without ordnance immediately raining down on him.[21]

Traditional territory of the Bettani branch

The tribes within the Bettani branch, namely the Ghilzai Confederation, tend to be classed as Nang Pashtuns and dominate the mountainous highlands of Loya Paktia and the stretch of land from Zabul Province to Kabul Province which is nicknamed 'the Ghilzai belt' (see Map 4).

Above left: Solomon, Third King of Israel in the tenth century BC. He is a central figure in the controversial theory that Pashtuns descend from the Lost Tribes of Israel. (©*Yitzilitt*)

Above right: Ahmad Shah Abdali, who later became known as Ahmad Shah Durrani and whose coronation in 1747 marked the de facto creation of modern Afghanistan.

Below: Habibullah Kalakani, the rebel leader who ended the Second Durrani Dynasty by overthrowing King Amanullah Khan in 1929, thus becoming the first non-Pashtun to rule the Afghan state.

Above: (L to R) The author, Sir Nicholas Kay, Dr Abdullah Abdullah, Masood Khalili. Dr Abdullah was the main challenger to the Pashtun candidates in the 2009, 2014 and 2019 Presidential elections.

Left: The author with tribal elders in Qalat city, February 2020. The capital of Zabul Province, it used to be called Qalat-i-Ghilzai, reflecting the concentration of tribes from the Ghilzai Confederation.

Afghan women in the burqa, sometimes called a *chadaree*. In May 2022, the Taliban regime decreed that all women should wear the burqa when in public. (©*Marius Arnesen*)

Amanullah Khan, who organized four *Loya Jirgas* when he ruled from 1919 to 1929, and his wife Soraya, who annoyed traditionalists at the 1928 events with her modern, Western-style dress.

The 2002 *Loya Jirga* in Kabul at which Hamid Karzai was chosen to be President of the Transitional Administration until official elections in 2004.

Above left: A US Army UH-60 Blackhawk over Paktia Province, July 2019. The mountainous terrain in this region is less suited to arable farming and therefore more associated with 'Nang' tribes.

Above right: The Kabul–Jalalabad Highway. This territory is routinely exploited to ambush invaders, from retreating British forces during the First Anglo-Afghan War to Soviet tanks in the late twentieth century. It was also the area controlled by Commander Zardad in the early 1990s.

The Khyber Pass in Pakistan, the gateway to Afghanistan. It is located in territory dominated by the Afridi tribe, nicknamed 'Guardians of the Pass'.

Above left: The 'Iron Emir' Abdur Rahman Khan, who ruled Afghanistan during the Second Durrani Dynasty. Installed in Kabul after the Second Anglo-Afghan War in 1880, he oversaw the forced resettlement of rebellious tribes and the imposition of the Durand Line.

Above right: Sir Henry Mortimer Durand, the British diplomat who negotiated the Durand Line Agreement in 1893 which created the contested boundary line between Afghanistan and Pakistan.

NATO Senior Civilian Representative Sir Nicholas Kay (centre) with Masood Akhunzada (left) in Kandahar, March 2019. Akhunzada is an Alokozai tribal leader who looks after the Khirqa-yi-Sharif cloak, which was allegedly presented by Allah to the Prophet Muhammad.

Remnants of an Army by Elizabeth Butler. The famous depiction of Dr William Brydon, the sole British soldier to reach Jalalabad after Ahmadzai-led tribal forces attacked the British column retreating from Kabul in January 1842.

The author (far left) in a meeting between Sir Nicholas Kay and Gulbuddin Hekmatyar, 2019. Hekmatyar was born into the Kharoti tribe but is better known for leading anti-state and insurgent forces under an Islamist banner.

The *Attan* folk dance, originally a war dance said to stem from the Mahsud tribe but which has become Afghanistan's de facto national dance. (©*Adilswati*)

Above left: Malala Yousafzai, the 2014 Nobel Peace Prize laureate who was shot by the Taliban in 2012. In her 2015 biographical film she describes being named after Malalai of Maiwand. (*©DFID*)

Above right: Abdul Rasoul Sayyaf during the 1980s, when he led a mujahideen group against Soviet forces. Sayyaf's men also came to Bin Laden's rescue during the Battle of Jaji in April 1987.

The author (left) in a meeting with Sir Nicholas Kay and Abdul Rasoul Sayyaf in his hilltop compound in Paghman district, Kabul Province, June 2019.

Left: One of the Buddhas of Bamiyan, destroyed by the Taliban in 2001 – a demolition overseen by Mullah Dadullah.

Below: Al Jazeera interviews the Taliban after their retaking of the Presidential Palace in Kabul, August 2021. Note the painting of Ahmad Shah Durrani's coronation in the background. (©*Frans van Huizen*)

القصر الرئاسي في كابل

الجزيرة حصلت على تصريحات هي الأولى من نوعها لسكرتير
الرئيس الأفغاني وقادة من طالبان من داخل القصر الرئاسي

عاجل

The Hotak and Tokhi tribes live at the southern end of this belt, particularly in Zabul and Uruzgan provinces, where they border Kandahar and the Durrani territory. The Sulaimankhel and Kharoti tribes have their homeland in south-east Loya Paktia, particularly the Katawaz area and the Sulaiman Mountains (see Map 5).

The Ahmadzai tribe have a presence in more northern parts of the Ghilzai belt, particularly in Paktia and Logar Provinces. This tribe's tentacles also stretch into other areas, partly because of their history as nomads. As time passed, they 'settled on their lands in the triangle formed by Kabul, Jalalabad and Gardez'.[22] One famous Ahmadzai who operated in this triangle is Zardad Faryadi, known as Commander Zardad and scorned for sullying the tribe's prestigious name. As a mujahideen commander in the 1980s, Zardad controlled a checkpoint in Surobi district of Kabul Province on behalf of the Hezbi Islami faction. Surobi sits on the Kabul–Jalalabad Highway and acts as the gateway between the non-Pashtun north and the Pashtun-dominated Loya Paktia. It was also where an al Qaeda training camp was levelled by US cruise missiles in 1998 as a response to al Qaeda's attacks on US facilities in East Africa.[23]

Zardad ruled his checkpoint ruthlessly. He famously kept a wild dog chained in a cave, bringing it out to intimidate travellers. This dog is alleged to have viciously bitten many of Zardad's prisoners, even eating one man's testicles.[24] But Zardad's dog was not actually a canine. He was human. This man, named Abdullah Shah, was later the first person executed by the new Afghan state after 2001. Zardad did not escape the law either. He fled to the UK on a false passport in 1998, after the rise of the Taliban.[25] There, he was found by the veteran BBC journalist John Simpson in 2000, living in the quiet London suburb of Streatham and running a pizza shop.[26] Investigations followed, and Zardad was charged with hostage-taking and conspiracy to torture. Witnesses testified via video-link from the British Embassy in Kabul, and the trial exposed his alleged involvement in murdering a minibus full of men, dousing one hostage in petrol and cutting the ear off another.[27] He was found guilty in 2005 and sentenced to twenty years' imprisonment, eventually being released and deported to Kabul in 2016 after a peace agreement between Zardad's former group, Hezbi Islami, and the Afghan government.

Traditional territory of the Ghurghushti branch

The tribes of the Ghurghushti branch are the least populous of the four branches in Afghanistan, being mostly concentrated in Quetta and the Balochistan region of Pakistan (see Map 4). Within Afghanistan, the Kakar and Safi are this branch's two main tribes. The Kakar are mostly found in the southern parts of Helmand and Kandahar that border Balochistan. They are disconnected from their Safi cousins who live much further north in similar territory to the Eastern Pashtuns of the Sarbani branch, i.e. Nangarhar, Kunar and Nuristan, as well as some pockets as far north as Parwan and Kapisa provinces.

Traditional territory of the Karlani branch

The tribes of the Karlani branch receive considerably less attention in discussion of Afghanistan's tribes, because the Durrani vs Ghilzai dynamic usually takes precedence. But treating them as secondary is an error. They have played key roles in the Pashtun story.

The Karlani tribes have a strong presence in both Afghanistan and Pakistan, with the border effectively splitting Karlani territory (see Map 4). In Afghanistan, Karlani tribes reside in Loya Paktia, particularly in Paktia and Khost Provinces. Prominent tribes include the Zadran, Mangal and Jaji (sometimes 'Zazi').

The Zadran tribe is well known because its most famous family, the Haqqanis, fought aggressively against the Soviets with US backing, before turning on the US and aligning with the Taliban after 2001. By 2021 the Haqqanis led the most powerful Taliban faction and used their outsized influence within the movement to secure key ministerial positions and dictate the early direction of the new Taliban regime in Kabul. But Kabul is not a homeland for the Haqqanis or their Zadran tribe. This tribe is more at home in the 'Zadran arc' – a stretch of land running across nine or ten districts in Khost, Paktia and Paktika Provinces. The tribe also has a smaller presence in Pakistan, creating a 'kinship bridge' across the mountainous borderlands which it uses to control strategic passes.

The Mangal tribe is another cross-border tribe with a strong presence in Paktia and Khost. Its members have had frequent spats with the Zadran tribe and instead tend to align with the Jaji tribe, who are also found in Paktia and Khost, where multiple districts are named after them.[28]

Because the collective Karlani territory is split by the border, its tribes in Pakistan cannot be discounted from the Afghan context. The Afridi tribe are nicknamed 'Guardians of the Pass', because they have dictated who traverses the famed Khyber Pass since the sixteenth century.[29] During the Soviet era they made pacts with the communists in Kabul to stem the flow of mujahideen fighters and weapons from Pakistan, much to the annoyance of their fellow Pashtuns in the mujahideen.[30]

The Mahsud tribe is renowned for having fought the British, and more recently, Mahsud territory in Pakistan has been a safe haven for Afghan insurgents. This is also true of the Wazir tribe, with the Waziristan region of Pakistan being described as 'the wildest part of the tribal areas'.[31] It is where al Qaeda and Taliban fighters sought refuge after 2001, with Pakistan's military alleging that Waziri tribesmen deliberately stopped them from closing the border.[32]

Chapter 26

Outside the Pashtun Belt: The Resettled Tribes

The Pashtun Belt is the tribal homeland. But it is not the only area where Pashtuns live in Afghanistan. None of Afghanistan's thirty-four provinces is without Pashtuns. Even Bamiyan Province, known as the heartland of the Hazaras, has some Sulaimankhel clans – allegedly former nomads who poached land from the Hazaras during the 1990s.[1] There are also pockets of Pashtun tribes scattered throughout territories normally dominated by Tajiks, Uzbeks or other ethnic groups. Some tribes even have clans positioned as far from the Pashtun Belt as is physically possible, dotted across Afghanistan's most northern reaches on the borders with the Central Asian states. The approximate spread of these pockets and the tribes resident in them are outlined in Map 6.

Afghanistan's north-west, which is regarded as Uzbek-dominated territory, is renowned for containing small pockets of tribes from the Durrani Confederation – particularly in Badghis, Faryab and Jowjan provinces. There are also some clans from Ghilzai tribes and the Kakar tribe of the Ghurghusht branch. Similarly, Afghanistan's north-east, which is traditionally Tajik territory, contains many clans related to the Ghilzai Confederation and also some of the Karlani branch. Kunduz Province is particularly well known for the presence of Pashtuns, who account for up to a third of the population.[2] Most tribesmen in Kunduz are from the tribes of the Ghilzai Confederation. The Kharoti tribe has a renowned population there, with the notorious mujahideen-era warlord Gulbuddin Hekmatyar born into a Kharoti clan in Kunduz.

These displaced tribal communities, known as *naqileen*, form minorities in northern areas, but it is a mistake to dismiss them as irrelevant. Their presence outside the Pashtun Belt has had a pronounced impact on Afghan politics for well over a century. It still influences events today, shaping Afghan history as it is being written.

141

Why the Pashtun pockets matter

Divide and rule has been a strategy used throughout Afghan history, by kings, emirs, international actors and – more recently – insurgents. Since the Taliban's formation in the 1990s, the movement has been driven by ideological rather than ethnic or tribal interests. But it still consists predominantly of Pashtuns. That makes the Pashtun pockets in northern Afghanistan useful weapons in the Taliban's arsenal. The Taliban use them as launch pads to expand into and exert control over the traditionally non-Pashtun north.

This tactic became obvious after the bulk of US/NATO forces withdrew from Afghanistan in the early 2010s. The drawdown permitted a growth in Taliban territorial control in southern areas and in the Pashtun Belt. But from 2015 onwards, the insurgency spread into non-Pashtun areas, sparking warnings from non-Pashtuns that the war was being moved from the south to the north. The Taliban were manipulating the populations in Pashtun pockets, fuelling grievances and playing on popular dissatisfaction with the central government. These pockets became fertile ground for recruitment, with sympathetic communities then acting as the backbone of Taliban support outside the Pashtun Belt. This trend stoked ethnic strife and sowed instability in the northern areas. It undermined non-Pashtun control, breaking up what had once been a large swathe of anti-Taliban territory. It also forced government and international forces to divert resources away from Taliban heartlands in the Pashtun Belt, thus helping the Taliban secure territory in southern areas.

It is no coincidence that from 2015 until the collapse of the Afghan Republic in 2021, Afghanistan's most intense fighting took place in Kunduz, Baghlan, Faryab and Badghis – all northern provinces with Pashtun pockets.[3] They became hotspots of political and social instability. For non-Pashtuns it was reminiscent of the 1990s, when they were gradually encircled by the Taliban and got little reliable support from a weak central government. This perceived repetition of history caused agitation within the multi-ethnic Afghan government and bolstered the Taliban's narrative about their expansion and impending victory.

Pashtun pockets had once again become a centrepiece in the wider divide and rule strategy of a group with designs on taking over the state. It was a scenario not dissimilar to the one that had caused these tribes to be moved out of tribal territory and scattered across the north in the first place. The man responsible for this was Abdur Rahman Khan, better known as 'The Iron Emir'.

The Iron Emir's transfer of the tribes

Born in the 1840s, Abdur Rahman was the grandson of Dost Mohammad Khan – founder of the Second Durrani Dynasty. He spent most of his teens and early twenties embroiled in the fratricidal power struggles that led to his being exiled to Central Asia in 1869.

It was a full decade before Abdur Rahman returned. Described as 'a tall, well-built man, with a large head, and a marked Afghan, almost Jewish, face',[4] he is celebrated in many stories as a patriot who crossed the Oxus River (now the Amu Darya) and marched on Kabul to save Afghanistan from the incompetent leaders who had led the country into the Second Anglo-Afghan War of 1878–1880.[5] But another, more accurate, narrative is that British officials had identified Abdur Rahman as a man malleable enough to be their client in Kabul.[6] They thrashed out a deal to back his claim to the throne, end the war and withdraw their troops, provided that he relinquished control of foreign policy to them.[7] Abdur Rahman agreed and was officially recognized as Emir in July 1880, starting a twenty-one-year reign that changed Afghanistan forever.

Abdur Rahman was a dynamic ruler. He modernized government and established the first official judicial system.[8] He used his new bureaucracy to hire rivals who agreed not to rebel against him, and he marginalized others whom he saw as a threat.[9] In his quest to centralize power in Kabul he also split the country's provinces into smaller units, so that they could never be large enough to serve as a base for revolt.[10] This obsession with centralizing power made Afghanistan into a nation state, but it came at the expense of the position of provincial leaders – particularly tribal chiefs.

While Abdur Rahman's predecessor, Sher Ali, is credited with creating the national army, it was Abdur Rahman who turned it into an effective force. Unlike previous Durrani leaders who relied on tribal *lashkars* to enforce authority, he used British subsidies to make the army the main instrument of state power. This also fostered resentment among tribal chiefs who perceived it as a challenge to their influence. To placate them, Abdur Rahman created a system of conscription that gave tribal leaders the authority to choose tribesmen who would serve in state forces. It was called *Hasht Nafari* and allowed village elders and *maliks* to choose one man from every eight households to serve in the army. The other seven households were taxed to provide financial support.

Yet Abdur Rahman's initial reputation as a unifier did not last long. His 'internal imperialism' and the brutal methods he used to try to consolidate his grip over all of Afghanistan soon stoked resentment.[11] Stories circulated about his men cutting off the hands of warlords and criminals, then dipping the spurting stumps into hot tar. His forces cruelly suppressed insurrections and crushed revolts with savage executions. One favourite method was to bend the tops of two young trees towards each other, fixing them to the ground. The victim was tied by one leg and one arm to each tree, then his bindings were cut and the trees sprang from the ground, tearing him apart. Others were suspended in iron cages above main roads to advertise Abdur Rahman's brand of justice. Frank Martin, Abdur Rahman's British engineer, devoted two chapters of his memoirs to the emir's various forms of torture. Some of the subheadings include:

> Hanging by hair and skinning alive
> Beating to death with sticks
> Cutting men in pieces
> Throwing down the mountain-side
> Starving to death in cages
> Boiling woman to soup and man drinking it before execution
> Punishment by exposure and starvation
> Burying alive
> Throwing into soap boilers
> Blinding
> Blowing from guns[12]

These tactics gave rise to the nickname 'Iron Emir', supposedly given to Abdur Rahman by British officials, although another claim is that the term stems from his own reported saying, 'People who do not know me call me cruel. They justly say that I rule with an iron hand. It is justified because I rule an iron people.' Either way, Abdur Rahman's efforts inevitably led to tribal rebellions throughout the Pashtun Belt. His rivals in the Ghilzai Confederation were the first to revolt in the 1880s, and rebellions continued throughout his tenure. Some Hazara communities also resisted, with Abdur Rahman declaring jihad on them and responding with ruthless campaigns of ethnic cleansing in which thousands of Hazara men, women and children were captured and sold off as slaves, or murdered in cold blood. It was not uncommon to see stacks of rebel heads placed as a warning to anyone else who might consider mounting a challenge to the Emir.[13]

Entire Hazara communities were completely wiped out. Others migrated to Pakistan, while some settled in the Fergana Valley of Central Asia, sowing the seeds of ethnic imbalance that still causes tension there today.[14] In 1895–6 Abdur Rahman also invaded the north-eastern area known as Kafiristan (Land of the Infidels), to convert its indigenous people to Islam.[15] Once he had done so, the region was renamed Nuristan (Land of Light) – a name still used today.

These internal campaigns were designed to reduce Abdur Rahman's potential challengers, particularly the insubordinate Ghilzai tribes. It has also been pointed out that Abdur Rahman, unlike his Durrani predecessors, was hemmed into his own borders by the superpowers. He could not go after the Persians or the Sikhs in India, so instead he turned his attention to conquering other Afghans, creating a centralized state and subduing tribal challengers.

Whatever his ultimate goal, Abdur Rahman employed a strategy that altered Afghan history – forcible relocation of some Pashtun tribes to areas outside of the

Pashtun Belt. He saw this as a way to weaken rebellious rivals, undermine traditional tribal systems and strengthen government control over hostile non-Pashtuns in the north. It would empty the southern cities of the poor and create a pool of Pashtuns to draw on in case forces were needed in northern areas. He also wanted the relocated tribes to act as a counterweight to external challengers. They could be his eyes, acting as an early-warning system against Russian encroachment.[16]

During his decade in exile, Abdur Rahman had admired the autocratic and centralized systems of Peter the Great and the other Tsars who had forcibly relocated communities to achieve their strategic aims. When a British colonel in Kabul suggested a policy of 'Afghanisation', whereby Pashtuns would be moved to the northern frontier to act as a buffer against Russian encroachment, Abdur Rahman was all ears.[17] Just three years later, approximately 200,000 Pashtuns had been moved north, the Pashtun proportion of the population in the north rising from 4 per cent in 1884 to more than 30 per cent by the end of 1888.[18] Abdur Rahman also issued a decree in 1885 forbidding any tribe to return to their traditional homeland.[19]

Although some tribes were given incentives to move, such as land grants and tax exemptions,[20] the resettled tribes have not forgotten how their ancestors were treated, and this is said to be a driver of anti-state and pro-Taliban attitudes among them today.[21] The paradox is that, while the resettlements created a Pashtun victim narrative, there were benefits at the same time, since the deportations led to their being given the best agricultural land. This enraged the indigenous ethnic groups, in turn fostering a siege mentality among the Pashtun colonists, driving them closer to the (Pashtun) government in Kabul and thus further cementing Abdur Rahman's and his successors' control of state institutions. His attacks on the Hazaras also permitted Pashtuns to gain control over Hazara lands, reinforcing the ethnic hierarchy in Afghanistan that still exists today, with Pashtuns at the top.

For the next century, multiple Afghan leaders tried to emulate the Iron Emir's tactics. In the 1920s, Amanullah Khan displaced certain Pashtuns and confiscated the lands of others.[22] His successor, Nadir Shah, encouraged Ghilzai tribesmen to invade Tajik-controlled territory in the early 1930s to weaken his rivals and challengers. Similar efforts continued right up until the communist coup and the Soviet invasion in the 1970s.

The result of all these efforts is not just an interesting geographical anomaly whereby some Pashtun tribes have a presence away from their traditional homeland. They have also led to generations of ethnic division, instability and even tribal decay. Afghanistan's current strife has no single cause, but it is partly a legacy of Abdur Rahman Khan's rule. By scattering individual tribes into enclaves where they were surrounded by hostile populations, he left them without defined tribal areas or strong leadership. This has stoked stand-offs, created ethnic faultlines and fuelled conflict with non-Pashtuns that continues to this day. The Taliban

145

recognized this – and wasted no time in coming to the 'rescue' of communities in the Pashtun pockets in the 2010s. Support from these Pashtun pockets helped the Taliban swiftly take major cities and overrun any non-Pashtun resistance in 2021.

These tribal resettlements were not the only way that the Iron Emir changed Pashtun tribal territory. He was also a central actor in an even more consequential event – one described as 'a dagger through the Pashtun heart'. He signed the agreement that sliced Pashtun tribal territory in two, fuelling tribal instability and fostering long-running animosity between Afghanistan and Pakistan.

This was the Durand Line.

Chapter 27

The Durand Line: An Honourless Agreement?

How the signing ceremony of this agreement played out in Kabul can be pieced together from what has been written about the events leading up to the deal and the main men involved.

Contemporary accounts make it easy to imagine the oily scent of the lamps, the smell of the dusty carpets and the mildewy musk of a rarely-used palace belonging to a temperamental and increasingly embattled Emir. The flickering lamps would have illuminated the hand-carved wooden table and single chair that formed the centrepiece of the ceremony.

But the surroundings did not matter to the visitors. After forty days of frustrating negotiations, the dozen or so British delegates just wanted the unpredictable Emir to put pen to paper before he changed his mind. It was 12 November 1893, and the British were eager to begin their journey back to India before heavy snows made the mountain passes too treacherous.

It had not been easy to get Abdur Rahman Khan to this point. While witty, humorous and often described as a genius by those who knew him, he was becoming less amenable and more mysterious as the years passed – less, it was alleged, because of the wisdom of old age and more because of mental deterioration.[1] It was hard to know which Emir would turn up on any given day. One day he would paint himself as a peasant, while the next he would talk of being crowned by the Prophet.[2]

Physically, too, he was not as impressive as he had once been, and rumours of a debilitating illness were circulating in Kabul. But he still had a presence. On meeting with the British delegation that day in 1893, without any entourage or advisers, his thick-set body was dressed in his normal grey tunic that barely contained his pot-belly. He was most likely wearing his favoured headdress – an impressive fur hat reminiscent of a Russian *ushanka*.[3]

After an exchange of pleasantries, the Emir would have slumped down onto the chair and scanned the document that his visitors had put in front of him. Peering over his shoulder was a tall, straight-backed man, balding and with a well-groomed handlebar moustache. He was the leader of the British delegation and the Government of India's Foreign Secretary – Sir Henry Mortimer Durand.

This was not Durand's first visit to Kabul or his first encounter with Abdur Rahman. He had joined the Indian Civil Service in 1873 and was Political Secretary in Kabul during the Second Anglo-Afghan War. He was a key player in the Great Game.

Throughout the second half of the nineteenth century, Russia's expansion into Central Asia had stoked British anxiety. Russia feared British raids into Central Asia, while Britain worried about Russia bringing India into its sphere of influence. This created an atmosphere of suspicion and a permanent fear of war between the two Empires, with Afghanistan sandwiched between them. The Russians never really intended to occupy Afghanistan or invade India, but the British feared that even a small encroachment into northern Afghanistan would highlight their own weaknesses and trigger internal unrest in British India. They worried that Pashtuns might be susceptible to Russian manipulation, or that the Pashtun wolves might be induced to fight on behalf of the great Russian bear.

All of this made Britain act to secure its sphere of influence. Attempts to impose direct control had led to two Anglo-Afghan wars, so the new strategy was to turn Afghanistan into a buffer state. The British supplied Abdur Rahman with weapons and equipment to help counter Russian influence in the north, and did not object when he resettled some Pashtun tribes. One British official summarized the policy by saying, 'Only the non-Pashtun tribes have any contact and interactions with the Russians, thus surrounding these tribes with Pashtuns would end [non-Pashtun] interactions with the Russians.'[4]

By the late nineteenth century, defining Afghanistan's borders had become the centrepiece of the Great Game. While the northern and western borders were clear, in the south the British wanted to maintain influence over Pashtun tribal areas – partly to be able to control them and partly to avoid the Russians recruiting there. The justification behind annexing tribal territory was expressed thus by Lord Lansdowne, the Viceroy of India between 1888 and 1893: 'In political geography nature abhors vacuum and any space left vacant upon our Indian frontiers will be filled up by others, if we do not step in ourselves.'[5]

It was Lansdowne who sent Durand to Kabul in 1893, with a small, handpicked delegation leaving Peshawar in September. They travelled into the Landi Kotal Mountains, home of the Khyber Pass, to meet Abdur Rahman Khan's Commander-in-Chief, who would escort them to Kabul. It was not a comfortable journey, both because of the harsh highland terrain and because of anxiety about the Afghan escort. Previous British parties had been slaughtered by similar escorts, despite assurances of protection. Durand and his delegation wondered if they would survive being led by men who, he said, 'appeared as awful ragamuffins'.[6]

But Durand's delegation swallowed their fears and pushed ahead. They had originally intended the mission to take place six months earlier. In fact, there had been five years of postponements by the Emir, even though he had initially written to British officials in 1888 to ask for negotiations to define the border between Afghanistan and India. Abdur Rahman claimed he had to deal with internal rebellions first, but the true story, it appears, is that he simply disliked the man originally proposed to lead the British delegation – Lord Roberts. Roberts had marched on Kandahar with 10,000 troops in 1880 to dish out retribution for the slaughter of British forces at the Battle of Maiwand during the Second Anglo-Afghan War. The Emir was reluctant to be associated with him and succeeded in delaying the British mission until Roberts left his post to return to England. Abdur Rahman then immediately invited the British delegation to Kabul.

But any delight over this minor victory was short-lived. Before travelling, British officials sent a map detailing their proposal to exclude certain tribal territories from Afghanistan. The Emir shot back a prescient warning:

> [If you] cut them out of my dominions, they will neither be of any use to you nor to me: you will always be engaged in fighting or other troubles with them, and they will always go on plundering. As long as your Government is strong and in peace, you will be able to keep them quiet by a strong hand, but if at any time a foreign enemy appears on the borders of India, these frontier tribes will be your worst enemies . . . In your cutting away from me these frontier tribes, who are people of my nationality and my religion, you will injure my prestige in the eyes of my subjects, and will make me weak, and my weakness is injurious to your Government.[7]

Against the backdrop of this withering retort, Durand's delegation arrived in Kabul in October 1893. While formal negotiations were supposed to focus on settling Afghanistan's southern border, some historical accounts suggest that the British priority was actually to remind the Emir to not cede territory to Russia in the north, with the British still seeing Russian encroachment as more of a threat than any Afghan invasion of the Punjab.[8] The Emir allegedly responded to British prodding over the Russian issue by saying:

> This is a matter between you and me and the Russians, my people will not care or know, whether I go backwards or forwards in Roshan or Shignan, but they care very much to know exactly how they stand on your side.[9]

With that, the focus moved to the southern border. The story is that Abdur Rahman started negotiations by stating that he wanted a wall around his entire country, so that it could be clear what he controlled.[10] His opening bid was that all territories which previous Afghan monarchs possessed were rightfully his, whereas the British occupation of India was temporary, if not a thing of the past. He claimed historical justification to possess Kashmir and Delhi, whereas the British could only 'talk of [their] fifty-year connection with the Waziris and Afridis and Bajauris'.[11]

But Durand and his delegation were no amateur negotiators. Over the next month they chipped away at the Emir, breaking him down until most of the areas he claimed were retained for British India. Only Kafiristan (modern-day Nuristan Province) was granted to the emir, with Durand later writing to his superiors that it was 'miserably poor' and ungovernable anyway.[12]

The Waziristan area, now part of Pakistan that borders Loya Paktia, turned out to be the main sticking point. Both sides wanted it. The British recognized the strategic importance of the Tochi and Gomal passes, which were used by thousands of Kuchis for their annual migration. The Gomal Pass was also the main commercial route between Ghazni and India. Abdur Rahman insisted that the area was poor, had no natural resources and was ultimately insignificant, leading Durand to ask him why he wanted it.[13] The Emir responded with one word: 'Honour'.

Most accounts suggest that the British were condescending in their response, failing to understand the importance of honour and its role in tribal politics. They belittled the Emir as simple and irrational. Durand wrote to his own superior that 'His jealousy as to our interference in his internal affairs amounts to insanity.'[14] But Durand eventually agreed to let the Emir retain some of Waziristan (although not the two passes), and the negotiations progressed to the drawing of a physical line on the map. A few final wobbles on the Emir's part were carefully smoothed over by Thomas Salter Pyne, an Englishman living in Kabul and a trusted adviser to Abdur Rahman – but who some say was actually a British spy.[15]

The final text of the Durand Agreement was put in front of the Emir on Sunday, 12 November 1893 (along with a second draft agreement on the Russo-Afghan border). It was a remarkably short, seven-paragraph document that outlined the intention to fix 'the limit of their respective spheres of influence, so that for the future there may be no difference of opinion on the subject between the allied Governments'. A map was also included, showing a line agreed between Durand and the Emir. It would become known as the Durand Line, and it still represents the boundary between Afghanistan and Pakistan today (as highlighted in Map 4). A British offer of annual financial and military subsidies was also written into the text, confirming that the 'Government of India will at no time exercise interference in the territories lying beyond this line on the side of Afghanistan, and His Highness the Amir will at no time exercise interference in the territories lying beyond this line on the side of India.'[16]

Not only did the Emir sign the final agreement, but the next day he hosted an event for 400 officials to announce it, at which he gave a speech that Durand described as 'exceedingly good and straightforward'.[17] Abdur Rahman allegedly told the assembly that Britain should now be considered as a friend and repeatedly thanked Durand and other British officials for settling the disputes cordially. The deal was done. The Durand Agreement was signed. The Emir was happy with what was agreed. He felt in control. He was satisfied.

Or was he?

Chapter 28

Subterfuge that Split the Pashtun Tribes?

What really happened that day? What made the Iron Emir bend to the British will? Why did he capitulate on the issue of tribal territories? Was the Durand Agreement supposed to impose a formal international frontier, or was it simply a boundary sketched to temporarily ease tensions? Was it a sneaky sleight-of-hand operation by the British? What was the mysterious Englishman Salter Pyne's real role? Did Durand deceive an ailing Emir into signing a dirty deal?

These questions underpin the ongoing controversy over the Durand Agreement. Written records of the time should be able to clear everything up, but longstanding conspiracy theories have been perpetuated because written accounts by witnesses to the events are rare, even though this was a formalized agreement between two senior state officials. As one former Indian diplomat wrote:

> The British texts of the period give copious details about the settlement of the boundary on the Russian side. But they fall strangely silent when it comes to the Agreement on the Indian side.[1]

Durand's own reporting back to his superiors is the source of most information.[2] There are no comprehensive Afghan notes available. There was not a single Afghan in attendance, other than the Emir himself. He did order a secretary – an Indian adviser named Sultan Mohammad Khan – to hide in the *purdah* room behind the ceremony and secretly document every word.[3] But the notes of this unseen scribe have never surfaced, leaving history to be shaped solely by Durand and his delegation.[4]

The only other (supposedly) pro-Emir person in the room was Thomas Salter Pyne, a name now synonymous with conspiracy. He was a street-smart, self-made English engineer who worked for a private merchant in India and then volunteered for a project in Kabul, rising to become Chief Engineer of Afghanistan in 1887. His efforts in training Afghans to manufacture ammunition led to his becoming a close confidant of Abdur Rahman, and he even acted as the Emir's personal messenger when engaging with the British Viceroy in India.[5]

One story has it that Salter Pyne was in fact working for the British Government, tasked with befriending an Emir who was not susceptible to blackmail or temptation, partly because 'his visits to the harem were generally limited to once a week'.[6] Durand himself later wrote that Pyne was 'a very useful man. It is amusing to feel that the mission is being personally conducted by a little cockney trader.'[7] Was Salter Pyne the man who massaged Abdur Rahman's ego and edged the Durand Agreement over the line?

Or was it sickness that led to the Iron Emir's submission? Abdur Rahman suffered from various illnesses during his reign, especially in later years. He eventually lost the use of his hands and feet, and in his final years was so crippled that he had to be carried everywhere on a palanquin.[8] He was susceptible to fits and fainting, deliberately remaining in seclusion to avoid appearing weak in public, and limiting his contacts to a few trusted advisers. Sultan Mohammad Khan, the adviser who hid in *purdah* as the Durand Agreement was signed, later described how the Emir's doctors diagnosed a serious case of gout to explain his immobility and the 'virtual paralysis of state business'.[9] But it was probably something worse. By the 1890s, it is said that Abdur Rahman experienced frequent 'hallucinations, paranoia, mania and other psychotic disorders which had a direct effect on Afghanistan's internal and foreign policy'.[10] This has led to questions being asked about his psychological stability when he signed Durand's document.

Or was he under duress? Why would an Emir who had tripled Afghan territory during his reign have a 'fit of generosity' and gift a large part of it to the British?[11] As a Pashtun, Abdur Rahman was well aware that he needed the support of the Pashtun population. Yet by giving away Pashtun territory he would slice off fifty per cent of his support base.[12] Was he forced to sign on the dotted line? Or did Durand threaten an economic blockade, knowing that the Emir relied on British subsidies, arms and ammunitions to maintain his government's control, especially in the early 1890s, when he was stretched by his various campaigns against his own people?[13]

Or was there some deceit by Durand? There is a suggestion that the agreement signed by Abdur Rahman Khan was in English – a language which he did not understand or speak – despite an earlier shared commitment to make the Persian texts binding.[14] Suspicions about forgery or false documentation, albeit unproven, have persisted as a result. Accusations are still current that the Emir was duped.[15]

None of these conspiracy theories can be ruled out, but there are of course counter-arguments to them all. Abdur Rahman's own memoirs are often quoted in response: he wrote that he knew that 'it was necessary to mark out the boundary lines between my dominions and those of my neighbours'.[16] It could even be a simple case of crossed wires or cultural misunderstanding. It is possible that the

Emir, wanting to influence rather than control tribal areas, saw the Durand Line as merely delimiting zones of dominion and responsibility, while Durand, raised on the ideals of strict sovereignty, wanted to establish an international frontier.[17] Whichever way it transpired, the consequences are clear. The Durand Agreement triggered a long-running diplomatic dispute that still has an impact on regional geopolitics to this day.

Continuing international controversy

Anyone with even a slight interest in foreign policy or geopolitics knows of the political tension between Afghanistan and Pakistan. The Durand Line is central – literally as well as figuratively – to this long-running regional dispute.

The Afghan view has always been that the Durand Agreement never laid down a formal frontier, but rather an agreed boundary.[18] No Afghan administration has been willing to accept the Durand Line, arguing that the border has never been formalized. Some Afghans even suggest that Afghan territory should actually extend up to the River Indus, and that those tribal areas now in Pakistan should be returned to Afghanistan. Others claim that Pashtun areas in Pakistan should either be united with Afghanistan or granted independent status as 'Pashtunistan'.

Those who agree with the Afghan view claim that Durand did not aim for a long-term international boundary, but simply wanted to define respective spheres of influence.[19] Another suggestion is that the 1893 agreement should have expired in 1994, one hundred years after it was negotiated. This is based on what happened with the British agreement on Hong Kong – although, unlike the Durand deal, that agreement had an expiry date explicitly written into the treaty.[20]

The Pakistani view has always been that the Durand Line is the internationally enforceable frontier. Its proponents claim that this line has existed for more than a century, and the lack of legal-historical claims makes it possible for Pakistan to argue, with legal force, that the Durand Line should continue into modern times, i.e. that there is no other feasible option.[21] There is also an argument that Afghanistan has reconfirmed the Durand Agreement three times: in 1905 (Anglo-Afghan pact), 1919 (Treaty of Rawalpindi) and 1921 (Anglo-Afghan Treaty). Advocates of Pakistan's position also argue that it is wrong to reason that the Durand Line was signed under duress, because annual payments and shipments of weapons by the British, which were written into the Durand Agreement, continued into the 1920s.[22]

A lesser-known narrative is the Indian one. India has a short border with Afghanistan as part of its claim to Jammu and Kashmir. This border is just over 100km long at the easternmost part of the Durand Line (in Afghanistan's Wakhan Corridor). Most analyses posit that both Afghanistan and India see this small part of the border as a means to maintain strategic leverage over Islamabad, and even as recently as 2015 India's National Security Adviser urged that the Indian claim to an Afghan border should not be overlooked.[23] Amid all these stakeholder claims and territorial disputes, the impact on the group at the heart of the issue is often forgotten: the Pashtun tribes.

A dagger through the Pashtun heart

In February 1894, three months after the signing ceremony, the physical demarcation of the Durand Line, spanning roughly 2,500km, got underway. But the lead engineer, Sir Thomas Hungerford Holdich, quickly realized how difficult it would be – and how unaware the negotiators had been of the practical realities. Holdich later wrote with frustration that most of his problems stemmed from the fact that Durand's delegation had not included a geographical expert.[24]

Holdich organized three surveying teams: one to work northwards from the Khyber Pass in the Landi Kotal Mountains (where Nangarhar's Torkham border crossing is today); another to mark the border in the Loya Pakita region; and a third to move along the southern border with Balochistan all the way over to Iran. The start of work was delayed after some Waziri tribesmen attacked the surveyors and because, instead of sending a geographical expert, the Emir sent various tribal leaders to represent him. This was a problem because various groups of tribesmen were engaged in feuds with one another and had to travel separately to the British camp to avoid incidents, forcing delays in the demarcation process.[25]

The British attitude is often cited as another limiting factor, with claims that the surveyors rarely took account of the needs of the Pashtun communities they encountered. An air of superiority supposedly led them to think that they were doing Afghanistan a great service, when in reality their lack of local awareness was destined to be damaging. They did not seek to understand the tribes on the tribes' own terms. The correspondent of the southern survey team, the Baloch-Afghan Commission, wrote of working with 'simple savages' who were almost child-like in their ambivalence about the new border.[26]

While the surveyors tried to account for some tribal tendencies, for example determining which tribes went to market on the British (later Pakistani) side and which had economic links on the Afghan side, demarcation was generally dictated by political expediency rather than social considerations. This had consequences. What was intended to be a quick fix for discord in the tribal areas soon amplified unrest, because the Durand Line split tribal territories down the middle. *Kors*, *khels* and *qawms* were bisected. Some tribesmen woke up to find their houses on one side of the line and their land on the other.[27]

The Waziri and Mohmand tribes were among the most affected. The Yusufzai and Shinwari were also impacted, as were some tribes of the Ghilzai Confederation and the Zadran and Mangal (Karlani branch). These tribes quickly came to see this boundary as a foreign imposition that threatened their nomadic, independent way of life. The erection of military posts in the midst of their traditional homeland angered them even more.

Abdur Rahman Khan had warned that splitting tribal lands with a foreign-created border was never going to be accepted by Pashtuns. He turned out to be right. It was seen as a violation of the right to Pashtun self-determination and an attempt to reduce Pashtun political power. The impression was of another attempt to divide and conquer. It was an affront to their honour.

The tribesmen soon took action, setting the border areas ablaze with uprising and insurrection.[28] They rejected the Emir's rule, and the British failed even more spectacularly in trying to pacify them, only adding fuel to the existing tribal belief that they had been victimized and marginalized. Over the next century, Pashtun disenchantment never dissipated. In fact, it stoked further episodes of strife in Afghanistan. The Third Anglo-Afghan War began in May 1919, when Afghan forces crossed the frontier and captured a strategically important town in British-controlled territory. Durand's de facto border was also central to various tribal revolts throughout the 1930s and 1940s. It was then weaponized to facilitate the political ascent of Daoud Khan in the 1970s – the man who led the coup that finally ended the Durrani Dynasties. This contentious boundary featured prominently in every subsequent phase of conflict, from the Soviet years to the mujahideen era, during Taliban rule and throughout the post-2001 decades. Even after the Afghan Republic collapsed in 2021, the returning Taliban regime immediately stoked Durand-related tension – taking issue with Pakistani attempts to demarcate the border with a fence.

All of these incidents are directly linked with the Durand Agreement, an event that wounded the Pashtun psyche and left psychological scars that are still visible today. The tribes perceive themselves as pawns in border disputes between Afghanistan and Pakistan, as well as in imposed wars between successive state regimes and foreign occupiers. This arbitrary boundary has never stopped the free movement of the tribes in practice, but it is one of many grievances that created an environment where extremism could flourish. It created conditions for the incubation of violent jihad that the tribal areas have become known for more recently.

The Durand Agreement may have led to handshakes in the corridors of Kabul, but it set the scene for generations of instability in the tribal areas (and beyond). It ensured that peace and tranquility have been elusive ever since.[29]

PART VIII
Individual Tribal Stereotypes

The following chapters outline key events, people and supposed stereotypical traits of the most prominent individual tribes in each branch of the Pashtun tribal structure. They should be read as an attempt to sketch the contours of the common stereotypes rather than a definitive portrayal of any tribe's intrinsic characteristics. Trying to capture the character of these communities in a few pages, or using a few prominent examples, risks being a reductionist betrayal of their rich histories and even richer social tapestries. It also risks perpetuating the Orientalist approach that this book tries to avoid.

Within each chapter, the tribes are categorized alphabetically, and for one tribe in each chapter, a diagram of its tribal tree depicts its structure, i.e. its *khels*, *koranay* and *kors*. Exclusion of some tribes is not a slight on them or a judgement on their importance. Some, like the Barakzai and Popalzai, have been detailed in other chapters. Others, like the Wardak,[1] Khattaks[2] or Urmars are left out as they mostly reside in Pakistan rather than Afghanistan, or because there are uncertainties over their genealogy.

۲۹

Chapter 29

Tribes of the Sarbani Branch

Achekzai

A 'predatory spirit' makes Achekzai tribesmen excellent soldiers, according to Mountstuart Elphinstone, the first British envoy to Kabul. Writing in 1815, he harshly added that even their closely related tribes are watchful around them because 'theft, and boldness and robbery, are great qualities among them'.[1]

Belonging to the Zirak division of the Durrani Confederation, some clans live in Helmand and western areas, while some were scattered outside the Pashtun Belt in the nineteenth century, particularly in Badghis Province.[2] But the Achekzai homeland is the plateau between Kandahar and Quetta, particularly the Spin Boldak border area. This is also the crucible of the Achekzai's long-running enmity with the Noorzai tribe (Panjpai Durranis). Their competition to control Spin Boldak has been an important undercurrent of Soviet and post-9/11 conflicts.

A tribesman who embodied the Achekzai's tough, unruly reputation was Ismatullah Muslim. Nicknamed 'Esmat', he was a Soviet-trained solider who defected to the mujahideen in the 1970s.[3] But he strained against Pakistani intelligence's grip on the mujahideen and switched sides again, joining the Afghan communists in 1986.[4] With state backing, he quickly fortified Spin Boldak, essentially becoming a legalized criminal with 'a tribe of brigands known to have smuggled everything from opium to English wool across the border into Pakistan'.[5] By the mid-1980s he was called 'the No. 1 rogue in Afghanistan since 1928' (a reference to the Tajik Habibullah Kalakani, who overthrew the Second Durrani Dynasty). Yet the government never acted against him, even after a shootout with security forces at the 1987 *Loya Jirga*. As one Western diplomat said, 'They have to patch it up with him or Kandahar will fall.'[6]

Only after the Soviet withdrawal from Kandahar in 1988, when Esmat's influence dwindled, did his Noorzai rivals retake Spin Boldak. When Esmat died in 1991, the Noorzai fastened their grip, forcing the Achekzai to take a back seat during the

1990s. But tribal rivalries do not end easily. After invading in 2001, US forces backed a young anti-Taliban fighter, Abdul Raziq, in attempts to deliver stability in Kandahar. As Kandahar's police chief, Raziq used US backing to cement control of Spin Boldak. The fact that Raziq was an Achekzai and Esmat's nephew only encouraged more Noorzais to gravitate to the Taliban.

The Taliban finally killed Raziq, after many attempts, in 2018. But his brother, Tadin Khan, took over and kept Spin Boldak under Achekzai control until the Taliban's all-out offensive against the Afghan Government in the summer of 2021. Unsurprisingly, Spin Boldak was a focal point in their strategy. Equally unsurprising was the bloodshed witnessed when generations-old tribal feuds once again ignited and when Taliban-aligned tribes took the chance to knock the Achekzai off their perch.

Alizai

The Alizai are synonymous with Helmand and defend it ferociously. Helmand is broadly split into three: the Alizai in the north, the Barakzai in the centre and the Ishaqzai in the south. Some Alizai clans also reside in Farah and in Pashtun pockets in northern Afghanistan, particularly in Faryab province.[1]

Belonging to the Panjpai division of the Durrani Confederation, the Alizai strongholds in northern Helmand are Musa Qala and Kajaki. These areas are particularly well known to British forces, who faced stiff resistance there after launching the Helmand Campaign in 2006. But the Alizai's battlefield credentials are not limited to the twenty-first century. They were one of the tribes forced to serve in the Persian armies that controlled Kandahar in the early eighteenth century and were rewarded by being given lands in Helmand that the Persians had confiscated from tribes of the Ghilzai Confederation, who were then pushed north into Loya Paktia.[2]

The 1840s are an important period in Alizai folklore. This was when a tribal chief named Aktur Khan led an uprising against Shah Shuja (of the First Durrani Dynasty). At the time, Alizai rivals in the Barakzai tribe controlled most of Helmand, treating the Alizai with 'viciousness in power' and creating an 'imbalance of fear, honour and interest' that still underpins ongoing inter-tribe animosity today.[3]Angered by Barakzai behaviour, an Alizai rebellion was triggered when they killed a tax collector in 1840. A British force was dispatched to ensure calm, which Alizais interpreted as a signal of British support for Shah Shuja and the Barakzais. A seething Aktur Khan called upon Alizai honour and fought back. In 1841 he marched on Gereshk (the Barakzai seat and a British garrison). He was repulsed, and the British subsequently launched a series of punitive expeditions into Alizai territory to finish him off.[4] They did so, but he remains an Alizai hero today, still held in high regard by Alizai tribesmen who have fought foreigners alongside the mujahideen and then as part of the Taliban.

Alikozai

'A very unusual Durrani tribe'[1] is how the Alikozai have been described. They belong to the Zirak division of the Durrani Confederation, but have an independent streak and even a confrontational relationship with fellow Durranis. Bucking tribal tradition, the Alikozai publicly supported the Tajik candidate in the 2004 presidential election, rather than fellow Durrani Hamid Karzai.

The tribe is renowned for being the 'Keepers of the Cloak'. For centuries the Alikozai's leading family, the Akhunzadas, have protected Afghanistan's most sacred artefact: the *Khirqa-yi Sharif*. This is the camel-wool cloak that was allegedly presented by Allah to the Prophet Muhammad. While those who have seen it cannot agree whether it is red, brown or black, many Afghans believe it can convert the faithless, terminate national disasters and cure disease. Alikozai tribesmen claim that it ended a cholera epidemic in the 1930s.[2]

Today it stays locked inside a shrine, inside a mosque in Kandahar that is adjacent to Ahmad Shah Durrani's mausoleum. It was Ahmad Shah who brought the cloak to Afghanistan after crushing a rebellion in 1768 in Bukhara, where it had been given to him as tribute by a local ruler who agreed that the area would lie within the Durrani sphere of influence. On returning to Kandahar, Ahmad Shah appointed the Akhundzada family as its guardians.

Many Afghan rulers have since tried to use the cloak to underpin their legitimacy. When Dost Mohammad Khan wanted to undertake jihad against the Sikhs in the mid-nineteenth century, he donned the cloak and declared himself 'Amir ul-Momineen' (Commander of the Faithful). Shah Shuja wrapped himself in it a few years later, in 1839, when attempting to legitimize his return to the throne. Taliban leader Mullah Omar visited the cloak in 1996, allegedly taking it to the roof of a mosque and putting his arms in its sleeves as his supporters chanted 'Amir ul-Momineen' from below. This was seen as a deliberate attempt to evoke memories of Dost Mohammad Khan, and it is a reminder of how prominent historical events still shape the contemporary Pashtun mindset.

The current keeper of the cloak is Masood Akhundzada. He inherited the guardianship in 2008 after five of his own family were assassinated, each one hunted down because of his connection to the cloak. Masood's father was killed in the Soviet era 'when militants demanded that the cloak be taken out of Afghanistan – and away from perceived anti-Islamic influence – but he refused.'[3] Massoud's brother was then killed at an airport in Pakistan, and a nephew was shot in broad daylight in 2005. Assassins killed another brother and a cousin in a market in 2008, leaving Massoud as the custodian. He has evaded multiple assassination attempts and, at the time of writing, is still the cloak's protector (although it is as alleged that he has not seen it since it was last unveiled in 2002).[4]

Barakzai

The Barakzai, a large tribe in the Zirak division of the Durrani Confederation, have been well covered in previous chapters given their leadership of the Second and Third Durrani Dynasties. This tribe is spread throughout south and western Afghanistan, where they were awarded extensive lands in Helmand and Kandahar after fighting for the Persians in the eighteenth century. They are concentrated around Ma'ruf in north-west Kandahar, but are recognized more for their presence in the Helmand River valley, particularly around Gereshk city.[1]

Some small Barakzai clans moved to Badghis Province during the Iron Emir's reign in 1886, before being expelled by locals and taking up residence in Faryab Province, where they remain today.[2] While resettled Pashtuns in northern pockets have generally acted as a support base for the Taliban, the Barakzai are notable for having been firmly on the side of the Afghan Republic and never being well represented within the Taliban.

Ishaqzai

'Estranged' and 'aggrieved' are terms used by detractors to describe the Ishaqzai, who belong to the Panjpai division of the Durrani Confederation. Ishaqzai tribesmen were respected warriors in the early eighteenth century, with their tribal chief Musa Khan attending the 1747 *jirga*. But having been sidelined and alienated by successive Kabul regimes, the tribe's prestige – in some eyes – has tumbled since then.

The Ishaqzai homeland is south-west Afghanistan, particularly Helmand and Farah. But the tribe is also synonymous with Pashtun pockets in northern Afghanistan, where they were resettled in the 1880s. The perceived atrocities of that era still dominate Ishaqzai folklore.[1] Ishaqzai resettlements happened when north-west Afghanistan was ravaged and depopulated in constant raids by Turkmen militia, who crossed the northern border into Badghis and Faryab Provinces.[2] The Iron Emir's strategy to repopulate the area and bolster the border was to use Pashtun tribesmen. The problem was that most Durrani chiefs, especially in the Zirak division, refused to move north. They already had land in the south, so saw little point in subjecting their people to an arduous and uncertain fate in non-Pashtun areas.

But not all tribal chiefs were opposed. An Ishaqzai chief, Taju Khan, sniffed an opportunity to obtain new land. The Iron Emir further sweetened the deal with the offer of a marriage alliance, whereby Taju Khan's daughter would marry Abdur Rahman's son, and future Emir, Habibullah.[3] Taju Khan was enticed. What better way to lift his tribe out of obscurity and secure a place in the circles of power? He was soon force-marching dozens of Ishaqzai and Noorzai families into Afghanistan's north-west.[4] But when drought crippled the area, the tribesmen lost many of the animals on which they relied. Some, including Taju Khan himself, decided to return south. Others moved further north into the Uzbek-dominated territories of Faryab, Jowzjan and Sari-i-Pul provinces.[5] Some decided to stick it out in Badghis.

This scattering of Ishaqzai (and Noorzai) destabilized their tribal structures. Nomadic herders were forced to settle and start farming, prompting derision from fellow Durranis, who called them 'vegetable people' (sogzai). To avoid famine they were all forced into the shame of accepting government grain – which damaged tribal honour.[6]

Conspiracy theories soon emerged. Did the Iron Emir want the migration to fail? Did he purposely destroy tribal systems to weaken his rival tribesmen?[7] The seeds of centuries-long Ishaqzai resentment had been planted. A lack of trust in central government remains strong today, highlighted by the Ishaqzais' relative under-representation in the early post-2001 state structures but their dominance of Taliban ranks.

Mohmand

The Mohmands are said to have an insatiable hunger for land.[1] Their reputation as hard-working ploughmen is encapsulated in an anecdote about a Mohmand tribal elder who was visited on his deathbed by the Angel of Death.

When the eerie messenger asked the man for his name to inscribe in the book of those who enter paradise, the tribesman glanced towards the ominous angel and asked, 'Tell me holy one, what is the land like in paradise?'

The Angel solemnly repeated his initial question, asking for the dying Mohmand's name. But the tribesman, still thinking of the soil, turned again to the Angel, asking, 'Well if there is no good land, then can I buy some poor land and improve it?'

The Angel sternly insisted on his name. Unperturbed, the old Mohmand suggested, 'If there is no land available to buy, then I am happy to rent some good land'.

The Angel, its patience wearing thin, growled menacingly, 'Your name, old man!'

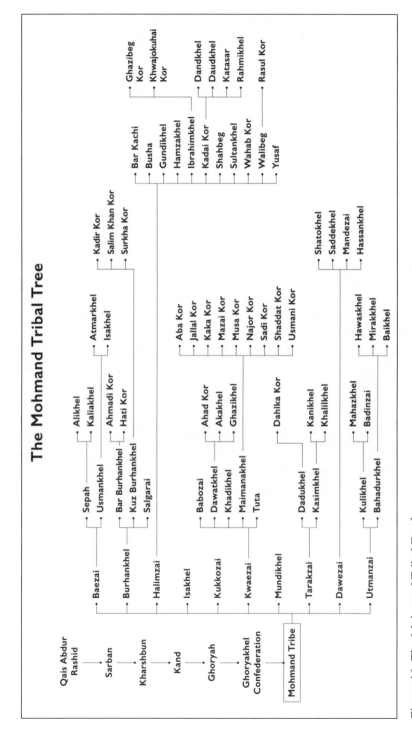

Figure 10: The Mohmand Tribal Tree[5]

The elderly tribesman peered sheepishly at his intimidating interlocutor and paused, taking a breath before proposing, 'If there is none to rent then you must at least have some I could sharecrop?'[2]

As one of the Eastern Pashtun tribes, the Mohmand have ancestral links with the Shinwari and Yusufzai, although they have better relations with the Safi tribe of the Ghurghusht branch (sometimes described as a 'vassal tribe' to the Mohmands). Mohmand territory is spread across Kunar, Nangarhar and Laghman provinces. There are also Mohmands in Kunduz, as a result of historic resettlements. The tribe is heavily concentrated in Pakistan, and when Mohmand territory was split by the Durand Line, the Iron Emir gave assurances to Mohmand clans that they would not be severed from Afghanistan. This led to their being called 'the Assured Clans'.[3]

Like most border tribes, the Mohmand are famed for fighting foreign invaders. But one Mohmand holds a special place in the history books for a different reason. Abdul Ahad Mohmand was the first Afghan, and the fourth Muslim, to reach outer space.[4] Born in 1959 in Ghazni Province, he joined the military just before the Soviet invasion in 1979 and was sent to the USSR to train as a fighter pilot. He was then selected as a cosmonaut with another Afghan, Muhammad Dauran. But Dauran got appendicitis and missed a trip to the Mir Space Station in 1988. Abdul Ahad took his place, spending nine days in space, where he was filmed reciting the Koran at the Afghan government's request, while his Commander held his legs to stop him floating away. He also called the Afghan president, and his mother, making Pashto the fifth language spoken in space.

Noorzai

The Noorzai name is often claimed to come from the Arabic word '*nur*', meaning 'light'. But this tribe has endured some dark periods. Its members have been repeatedly marginalized by their own Durrani cousins in various Kabul administrations, fuelling the sweeping stereotype of the Noorzais as being anti-state.

Belonging to the Panjpai division of the Durrani Confederation, the Noorzais' homeland is around Spin Boldak in Kandahar, where they compete for territorial control with the Achekzai. Beyond Spin Boldak, there are Noorzai clans in Helmand, Farah and Herat. Some clans reside as far east as Sind in Pakistan, where Noorzai leaders were installed as Governors after Ahmad Shah Durrani conquered the area in the mid-1700s.[1]

Today, the Noorzai are often stereotyped by their association with the Taliban. Not only did a chunk of the Noorzai gravitate to the Taliban after 2001, but the group's current leader (at the time of writing) is also a Noorzai. Mullah Haibatullah was chosen to lead the insurgency in 2016, after rising through the ranks as a Taliban religious scholar and jurist.[2] Haibatullah's accession shows that, while the Taliban maintain it is not driven by ethnic or tribal interests, tribal arithmetic is always part of its politics. Choosing Haibatullah was part of a calculation to accommodate key tribal support bases and maintain unity by rebalancing an Ishaqzai-dominated leadership.

Although Haibatullah has stayed out of the public eye, even after the Taliban took power in 2021, one common tale circulates about an incident in 2012 when an Afghan intelligence agent allegedly stood up during a Haibatullah sermon at a mosque in Quetta. He pointed a pistol directly at the cleric, but it jammed, allowing other *talibs* time to tackle the assassin. It is said that Haibatullah stood perfectly still through it all.[3] In 2017 reports also emerged that Haibatullah had sent his own son on a suicide bombing mission in Helmand Province.[4]

With anecdotes like these, the reputation of the Noorzai tribe exemplifies the way in which certain Pashtuns are negatively stereotyped or characterized by the most extreme incidents involving them. The Noorzai-Taliban correlation overshadows the fact that many Noorzais, especially in western Afghanistan, are also part of the highly educated intellectual elite. Some Noorzais were even leaders in Soviet-era communist parties, or have been notable defenders of human rights in recent years. Malalai Joya rose to fame after 2001 when, as a Member of Parliament, she campaigned energetically for women and spoke out against warlord-dominated politics. Her activism led to her inclusion on multiple 'Most Influential' lists around the world, as well as on the hit-lists of various nefarious actors inside Afghanistan.[5] Malalai's and Haibatullah's stories epitomize the Noorzai reputation for being extreme in every case; as the saying goes, 'Noorzais never learn to swim; either they become a fish or they drown.'

Popalzai

The Popalzai have been well covered in previous chapters, given their leadership of the First Durrani Dynasty and their most famous son, Ahmad Shah Durrani. Their traditional territory is among Kandahar's patchwork quilt of Pashtun tribes, particularly in northern parts of the province. Their presence also extends into Uruzgan province, which was home to another Popalzai who has had a hand in making history – Abdul Ghani Baradar.

The Popalzai, like other tribes in the Zirak division, tend to support Afghanistan's central government. But Baradar was one of the few Popalzai who joined the Taliban, rising to become Deputy to Mullah Omar in the 2000s. Baradar spent a ten-year term under house arrest in Pakistan after being apprehended in 2010 in Karachi. Rumours circulated that the Pakistani authorities chose to arrest him after finding out that he had initiated secret contact with his fellow Popalzai, President Hamid Karzai, without their knowledge and oversight.[1] Baradar was released in 2018, to become the Taliban's chief negotiator in talks with the US. He is the man who inked the US-Taliban agreement in February 2020 which started US withdrawal from Afghanistan, effectively writing himself and his tribe into the history books.

Shinwari

'Never trust these three; a snake, a whore or a Shinwari' was a British maxim describing a tribe which was notoriously troublesome to the British imperialists.[1] But 'well-educated' and 'businessmen' are also terms associated with the Shinwaris.[2] In 1885 the British orientalist Edward Balfour described them as

> continuously predatory since the British approached their borders. They are the most industrious carriers between Peshawur and the other marts on the way to Kabul, using mules and camels for carriage. They are brave, hospitable, stalwart and hardworking. They are well-educated people.[3]

As an Eastern Pashtun tribe, the Shinwaris are concentrated in eastern Nangarhar, contiguous to the Durand Line. The land on the other side, the Landi Kotal area of Pakistan, is their homeland. It is where the Khyber Pass and the Torkham border crossing are located, making the Shinwari influential on the main route into Afghanistan. They share this territory with the Afridi tribe (of the Karlani branch).

One of the most famous Shinwari feuds was with King Amanullah Khan in the 1920s. The Shinwari were the first tribe to rebel against his modernizations, attacking Jalalabad city in November 1928. Shinwari tribesmen blockaded the Kabul–Peshawar road and sent Amanullah a list of grievances – most related to his liberal policies for women.[4] They were also angered by new laws requiring them to pay taxes, which they had never previously done.[5] Amanullah responded by bombing the Shinwaris with his fledgling Air Force, before sending two government officials, including the Foreign Minister, to negotiate with Shinwari elders. The negotiations failed spectacularly, and the Shinwaris subsequently torched Amanullah's winter palace in Jalalabad.[6]

Amanullah's own brother-in-law, Ali Ahmad Khan, was then dispatched. Described as a man with an aggressive jaw and a 'moustache [that] framed his nose like parentheses',[7] he had negotiated Afghanistan's independence in 1919. His British counterpart had Ali Ahmad in mind when he said that 'Afghans are as touchy as Frenchmen, always on the look out for offence, vain as peacocks, and yet responsive to kindness and friendship to an amazing degree.'[8] Ali Ahmad eventually agreed terms with the Shinwaris in December 1928. But it was too late.

Their revolt had opened the floodgates. Other uprisings were underway, including by the Tajik Habibullah Kalakani, who seized Kabul a month later.

These events were not the last time that the Shinwari played a central role in struggles between the state and insurgents. Their territory became famous at the turn of the twenty-first century, when US Special Forces hunted bin Laden and the retreating al Qaeda in the mountains of southern Nangarhar. This was also the area where, from 2015 onwards, Da'esh made inroads in Afghanistan – although the Shinwari tribe rarely supported either the Taliban or Da'esh.

Yusufzai

This Eastern Pashtun tribe has a reputation as quintessential Pashtuns. Residing mainly in Pakistan's northern tribal areas, but with some clans in Nangarhar and Kunar in Afghanistan, it has been said:

> So pure have the Yusufzai kept their bloodlines and so rigorously have they obeyed the Pashtun code that they are universally acknowledged by the other tribes as being the most blue-blooded of all Pashtuns. This is a rare compliment, since most Pashtun spend a great deal of time impugning the Pashtunness of other Pashtuns.[1]

Pashtun origins are rarely discussed without reference to Yusufzais. Bani Israel theorists point out that their name translates as 'descendant of Joseph' and cite a long list of place names in Yusufzai territory that supposedly mirror Israelite names.[2] Yusufzai tribesmen often speak of Alexander the Great, who allegedly referred to them as 'Isapzais' around 330 BC when his forces fought in their territory.[3]

The Yusufzai were then mentioned in the *Baburnama*, the memoirs of the Mughal Emperor Babur. He captured the area around Kabul in 1504 but left Yusufzai areas to the east largely alone – at least until the Bajaur Massacre in 1519.[4] In January 1519, Babur butchered the Bajauri people who lived in the area of modern-day Pakistan that borders Kunar Province in Afghanistan. Babur's rationale was that the Bajauris were anti-Islamic rebels.[5] He allegedly sent some Bajauri heads to Kabul, Kunduz and other areas in Afghanistan to spread the news of his success.[6] Then he turned his attention to the neighbouring Yusufzai tribe.

One Yusufzai chief, who was an envoy to Babur's forces and witnessed the Bajauri bloodbath, was dispatched back to his tribe with a written warning that Babur's forces would soon march against them.[7] War was only avoided because of a marriage alliance, when Babur married Bibi Mubarika, a daughter of the Yusufzai chief. She played a key role in establishing friendly relations between Babur and the Yusufzais, especially when he went on to defeat other Pashtuns as he established his Mughal Empire.[8]

Chapter 30

Tribes of the Bettani Branch

Ahmadzai

Strong leaders. Fearsome fighters. Experts in *Pashtunwali*. This is the Ahmadzai reputation. As a large and influential tribe in the Ghilzai Confederation, the Ahmadzai are often courted by rulers and resistance leaders hoping to swing a battlefield or political balance in their favour, even though their Durrani rivals 'have never ceased to weaken them on the one hand and to conciliate them on the other'.[1]

Most Ahmadzai tribesmen reside in Loya Paktia. Some pockets also exist in Kunduz, Baghlan and Balkh due to historic deportations.[2] While they are known as nomads, the Ahmadzai character is difficult to unpick, because they have been found on both sides of any Afghan divide. In the Soviet era they had a reputation for filling the officer ranks of the army; but Ahmadzais were also the backbone of multiple mujahideen factions, demonstrating how rarely an entire tribe aligns behind a single cause.

One Ahmadzai clan, the Jabbarkhel, are among the most powerful *khels* of all the Pashtun tribes[3] and are often referred to as *Khanan*, meaning 'Lords' or 'Aristocrats'.[4] A sub-sect of the Jabbarkhel, the Arsala *khel*, is a landowning clan from the mountainous Hisarak district in Nangarhar Province who joined the mujahideen and were dubbed 'Resistance Royalty', due to their individual charm, charisma and success as battlefield commanders.[5]

But this reputation was not carved out solely in the 1980s. Arsala tribesmen were pivotal in the British retreat from Kabul in 1842, which has been called 'the worst British military disaster until the fall of Singapore exactly a century later'.[6] Arsala elders still revel in one story from this time, especially in the presence of British diplomats.[7] It concerns an incident in November 1841, when an angry mob stormed the house of the British diplomat Sir Alexander Burnes, hacking him and other officials to pieces.[8] Afghans then encircled British cantonments, and British troops decided to withdraw to Jalalabad city in Nangarhar (closer to British India). A British civil servant, Sir William Hay MacNaghten, went to negotiate safe passage with an Afghan General, Wazir Akbar Khan. But soon after arriving to

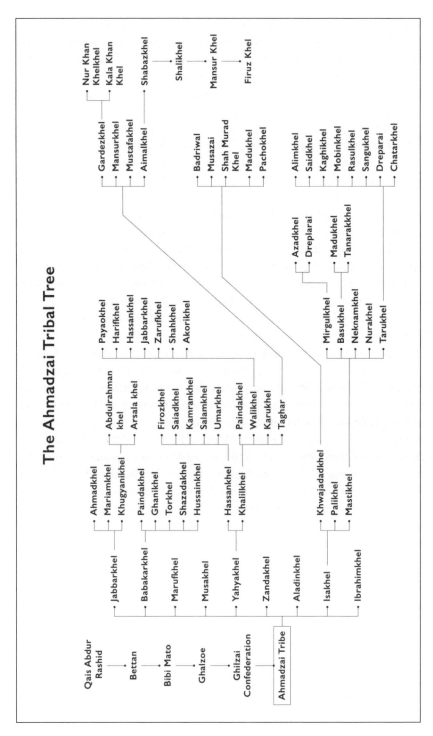

Figure 11: The Ahmadzai Tribal Tree[13]

meet the Afghans, the British delegation was slaughtered. Akbar Khan had grown tired of what he felt was British deceit and their pompous arrogance in believing they understood Afghanistan better than the Afghans. MacNaghten's mutilated body was dragged through Kabul, further galvanizing Afghan opposition.[9]

A second desperately negotiated agreement led to the Afghans allowing British forces to undertake the 90-mile journey to Jalalabad. But soon after they left Kabul's gates in sub-zero temperatures on 6 January 1842, Afghans started harassing the retreating force.[10] Wazir Akbar Khan had not kept his word. Ahmadzai tribesmen repeatedly ambushed the British column as it weaved through the narrow, snow-covered passes of the Hindu Kush. The tribesmen used the highland terrain and the cover of darkness to their advantage, massacring most of the 14–16,000-strong force. Many others succumbed to frostbite and starvation. After five days, only around sixty beleaguered Britons made their last stand at Gandamak village, 35 miles from Jalalabad. One man, Captain Souter, wrapped the regimental colours around himself in a last act of defiance. The tribesmen assumed he was important, so they took him hostage along with women and children – another humiliation for British forces, who had to surrender their women to men they saw as barbarians (although the Afghans felt they were acting with honour by protecting the women).[11]

Only one British solider made it to Jalalabad. The dishevelled Assistant-Surgeon William Brydon, hanging from his exhausted horse, is the defining image of the First Anglo-Afghan War. Brydon later wrote that the tribesmen made the journey such torture that he was frightened by every shadow. His horse suffered too – once it had brought Brydon to safety it lay down in the stable and never got up again.[12]

While the British responded with the 'Army of Retribution' that flattened Kabul, the episode is still remembered as a victory by the Ahmadzai – with the scale of the British defeat growing every time an Afghan tells the tale. The Ahmadzai tribesmen were led by Mohammad Arsala, nicknamed 'Red Beard', and his direct descendants remain influential today. A relative, Haji Din Mohammad, was a mujahideen leader in the 1980s, before becoming Governor of Nangarhar and then campaign manager for Ashraf Ghani at the 2014 presidential election. In 2020 he joined the Afghan Government's negotiating team for talks with the Taliban.

Andar

The Andar are famed for their expertise in traditional irrigation techniques and the construction of *qanat* underground aqueducts.[1] Post-2001, they have sometimes been branded as a largely pro-Taliban tribe within the Ghilzai Confederation because they dominate Ghazni Province, particularly the eponymous Andar district.[2] This is a strategic area that the Taliban used during their post-2001 campaign to gain access to Ghazni city and to attack Afghanistan's ring road, Highway 1, which passes through it (making it an ideal location to cut the main route between Kabul and Kandahar). The area is also the borderland between the Pashtun-dominated Loya Paktia and the Hazara-dominated central highlands, meaning it sees frequent ethnic conflict over land – with the Andar tribe being the Pashtun flag-bearers. Resentment lingers from the 1880s, when the Andar helped the Iron Emir crush Hazara uprisings, described as 'the most significant example of genocide in the modern history of Afghanistan'.[3] Once taken, Hazara villages were looted and their leaders executed. Land was confiscated and given to the Pashtuns – an act which underpins continuing hatred today.[4]

The Hazaras again rebelled against the state in 1892, an uprising ignited when the wife of a Hazara elder was assaulted by Afghan soldiers. This time the Iron Emir declared jihad against the Hazaras, raising an army of over 150,000 – including many Andar tribesmen – to exterminate the rebels. Another Hazara revolt in 1893 led to even more vicious retribution. Entire Hazara villages were razed, populations dispersed and lands confiscated. Hazara women committed suicide to escape slavery. In Hazara minds, this was ethnic cleansing. It laid the foundations of the ongoing animosity between Hazaras and Pashtuns, of which the Andar tribe's current struggles with Hazaras in Ghazni are the latest manifestation.

Hotak

From Mirwais Hotak to Mullah Omar, Hotak tribesmen have been historically important figures. Their traditional homeland is at the southern end of the Ghilzai areas, where they share Zabul and Uruzgan with their fellow Ghilzais in the Tokhi tribe. Territorial disputes in this area are the basis of a longstanding Hotak-Tokhi rivalry. The Hotaks also compete with the Popalzai tribe, since the southern parts of Hotak (Ghilzai) areas border the northern edge of Popalzai (Durrani) areas. But it is not just territory that these tribes fight over. The historical confrontation also has political roots, given that the Hotak Dynasty of the early eighteenth century gave way to the First Durrani Dynasty started by Ahmad Shah Durrani (a Popalzai) in the mid-eighteenth century (see Chapter 14).

After the collapse of the Hotak Dynasty, it took over 250 years for another Hotak to become any sort national figure. This was Mullah Mohammad Omar, who led the Taliban when they took control of Afghanistan in the 1990s. The majority of the Hotak tribe backed Mullah Omar, meaning that the Taliban found fertile ground in Hotak areas; they took Zabul Province in 1994 without a shot being fired and faced equally little resistance when taking control of the province after the collapse of the Republic in 2021.[1] Only a minority of Hotak clans – the Marufzai in particular[2] – did not align with the insurgents, which once again highlights how even cohesive tribes rarely display complete political harmony.

Kharoti

Kharoti folklore starts with the story of Sulaiman, Tokhi and Hotak, who were travelling together when they saw an overloaded donkey trotting towards them. Sulaiman quickly claimed the donkey for himself, and Tokhi claimed the donkey's load, leaving Hotak with whatever was on top of the load. As the donkey came closer, the tribesmen saw that it carried a load of barley bread with a small boy perched on top. Hotak took the boy and named him 'Kharota', since *kar* means 'donkey' and *rota* means 'bread'. This boy became the progenitor of the Kharoti tribe after he grew up and married a Hotak wife, and this is cited as the reason for generally positive Kharoti-Hotak relations ever since.[1]

The traditional Kharoti homeland is on the slopes of the Sulaiman Mountains in south-east Afghanistan, particularly Paktika Province.[2] Here the Kharoti share territory with the Sulaimankhel and the Waziris, with whom they have a longstanding rivalry.[3] The Kharoti have also fought with the Zadran tribe and, due to their nomadic habits, have long-running spats with Hazaras over access to land in the central highlands.[4]

More than any other Ghilzai tribe, the Kharoti are known as residents of the Pashtun pockets in northern Afghanistan. Their strong presence in Kunduz stems from their exile from the Pashtun Belt in the nineteenth century, after the Kharotis led the Ghilzai rebellion against the Iron Emir in 1885–7. That uprising started as a protest against new taxes and was led by Alam Khan Nasher, a Kharoti elder.[5] The Iron Emir forcibly exiled the Nasher family and Kharoti tribesmen to Kunduz, where they went on to become politically powerful by taking over the cotton trade.[6] Another famous Kunduz Kharoti, born in 1948, is a man who is central to Afghanistan's recent suffering – Gulbuddin Hekmatyar.

Gulbuddin, meaning 'flower of religion', was part of the nucleus of Islamist radicals at Kabul University who went on to form the anti-Soviet mujahideen in the 1980s. His faction, Hezbi Islami-Gulbuddin, was the group which received the majority of weapons distributed by Pakistan, despite his limited battlefield success. He became notorious after the Soviet withdrawal, when he indiscriminately shelled Kabul in 1992, becoming known as 'Rocketyar' or 'the Butcher of Kabul'. He maintained links to al Qaeda and the Taliban after 2001, when his relevance waned. Eventually, in 2016, he signed an agreement with the Afghan Government that allowed him to return to Kabul and re-enter mainstream politics. While driven by Islamist rather than tribal interests, Hekmatyar's actions inevitably stain the reputation of the Kharoti tribe and reinforce the narrative that Kharotis fight 'not for power, not for glory, but for blood'.[7]

Niazi

'Eighteenth-century Scots without alcohol' is how the British expert Anatol Lieven described the Niazis and other Pashtun tribes in Pakistan.[1] This tribe is part of the

172

Bettani branch but not part of the Ghilzai Confederation. 'Niazaey' was one of the three sons of Ibrahim Lodhi, who was a son of the Persian Prince Shah Hussain and his wife Bibi Mato (Ghilzais descend from a different son of Bibi Mato).[2]

The majority of Niazis live in Pakistan, which sometimes leads to the pejorative nickname 'Punjabi Pashtuns', reflecting criticism that they have strayed from Pashtun ideals. Only small communities remain in Afghanistan's Laghman and Nangarhar provinces, as well as settlements around Ghazni Province and in the village of Qalaye Niazi (Fort of the Niazis) in Paktia Province. They are said to be remnants of Niazi clans who were pushed out of the area in the thirteenth century and moved east to settle along the Indus River in modern-day Pakistan.[3]

The limited Niazai presence in Afghanistan today does not mean they have been absent from Afghan history. They fought for the Mongol Emperor Tamurlane in the fourteenth century and then assisted in the overthrow of the Mughal Empire in the sixteenth century. Two centuries later, they fought for Ahmad Shah Durrani in India and played a key role in the Third Battle of Panipat in 1761, one of the largest and bloodiest battles of the eighteenth century, when Ahmad Shah's numerically superior Pashtuns destroyed the Indian Marathas.

A more recent Niazi who shaped Afghan history was Ghulam Mohammad Niazi. He was a Professor at Kabul University in the 1960s and 70s who had spent time studying in Egypt with the Muslim brotherhood. It was their ideology that he brought back to Afghanistan, spreading it among a generation of Muslim Youth students, including Gulbuddin Hekmatyar, who went on to form the core of the Islamist mujahideen that waged the anti-Soviet jihad in the 1980s.[4]

Another famous Niazi who grew up in that era, albeit in Pakistan, is the Pakistani Prime Minister Imran Khan. While he dropped the Niazi name to appeal to a broader base, his critics make a point of calling him Niazi, playing to ethnic prejudices in Pakistan and drawing attention to the fact that it was a fellow Niazi who signed the Pakistani Instrument of Surrender in 1971 which created Bangladesh.[5] Another nickname is 'Taliban Khan' on account of his supposed sympathies towards the Taliban and his suggestion that bin Laden was 'martyred' by the US.[6]

Tokhi

The Tokhi tribe go hand-in-hand with the Hotak. Their intra-Ghilzai rivalry is well known across Afghanistan, although disharmony has not prevented alliances from occurring when necessary. Both the Tokhi and Hotak led an uprising against the Barakzai rulers in Kabul in 1842, known as the Tokhi Rebellion.[1] The tribes have an even more important shared link in the shape of Nazo Tokhi, known more commonly as Nazo Ana, who was born around 1651 to a Tokhi tribal chief and, when she came of age, was married to a Hotak tribesman called Salim Khan Hotak.

Legend has it that Nazo Ana had a dream on the night she gave birth to a baby boy. It is said that Bettan appeared and told her to take care of the new baby because he would eventually bless the entire country. When Nazo woke she decided to name this baby Mirwais. He grew up to become the man who established the Hotak Dynasty (as detailed in Chapter 14). The story goes that Nazo Ana repeatedly recounted her dream to young Mirwais, to ensure he always acted with honour.

Nazo is also remembered for being a strong proponent of *Pashtunwali*. She allegedly arbitrated in conflicts between Ghilzai and Durrani tribes in an effort to rally them in an alliance against the Persians of the Safavid Empire.[2] She is even hailed for her own battlefield exploits. When her father was killed in battle and her brother went to avenge his death, Nazo was left in charge of the household. But instead she took a sword and defended the tribal territory alongside the men.[3] Nazo died in 1717 but has lived on in Pashtun memory, and is now known as 'The Mother of the Nation'.

Unsurprisingly, Nazo has become a common name given to Pashtun girls. It is also common to hear the proverb, 'Though you may be named Nazo, who will give birth to Mirwais Khan?', which is a reminder that having the name does not automatically mean a woman will bear a son of Mirwais' status.

Chapter 31

Tribes of the Ghurghusti Branch

Kakar

Tying any entire tribe to the Taliban is unfair, inaccurate and a distortion of reality. But it is difficult to ignore the post-2001 insurgent activities of some Kakar men.

Kakars trace their lineage to Kak, a grandson of Ghurghust, and are alleged to be of Scythian origin. The nineteenth-century British anthropologist Surgeon-Major Bellew wrote that Ghurghusht is 'an altered form of Cirghiz or Ghirghiz – "wanderer on the steppe" – and indicates the country whence the people originally came, namely northern Turkistan.'[1]

The Kakars are well known in Afghanistan, despite most Ghurghusti territory now being in the Balochistan area of Pakistan.[2] In addition to their scattering around the southern border, some pockets also exist in Faryab province. Kakars suggest that they were gifted lands in the north, although rivals claim that Kakar clans in Kandahar, outnumbered by Durranis and Ghilzais, were stripped of their possessions and over-taxed in the late nineteenth century.[3] Being belittled as peasants, or *hamsaya*, drove them to move to the north-west in search of better land.[4]

As in most tribes, Kakar history (at least in English-language sources) is bloated with battles against foreigners. In the 'Zhob Valley Expedition' of 1884 British forces sought to pacify Kakar tribesmen and seize control of a strategic pass in Balochistan that was the shortest route between the Frontier and Quetta.[5] Before then, the area was largely unknown to Europeans.[6] Termed a 'punitive expedition', it did little to convince the tribes that foreigners sought friendly relations. It seeded a xenophobic attitude in the Kakars which is still evident in those who joined the Taliban generations later.

Kakar men have held some of the highest leadership positions in the Taliban. Mullah Mohammad Rabbani was a former *mujahid* who helped found the Taliban in the early 1990s. He became Prime Minister when the Taliban took Kabul in

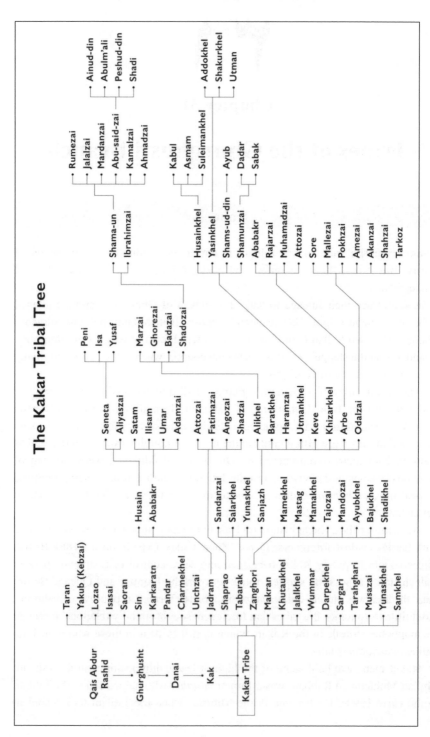

Figure 12: The Kakar Tribal Tree[12]

1996, repeatedly declaring that the Taliban would control bin Laden and that there was little evidence of his terrorist activity. But Rabbani died in a Pakistani military hospital in April 2001, before his assessment of bin Laden was proved wrong. As he was a relative moderate, conspiracy theories swirled that he was poisoned by Taliban hardliners.[7]

Another famed Kakar *talib* is Mullah Mohammad Fazl, who was Taliban Deputy Defence Minister and, soon after the US invasion in 2001, was held prisoner in the Qala-i-Jangi fortress, where Taliban detainees revolted and killed CIA officer Mike Spann – the first US casualty of the war.[8] Fazl then spent years in Guantanamo Bay, being 'too innocent to charge but too dangerous to release'.[9] He was exchanged for the US soldier Bowe Berghdahl in 2014 and later joined the Taliban negotiating team for talks between the US and the Afghan government. When the Taliban retook Kabul in August 2021, Fazl was almost immediately re-appointed Deputy Defence Minister (although he was replaced by another hardliner a few months later).

Yet of all the *talibs* with Kakar heritage, Mullah Dadullah is the most famous – so brutal that he even repulsed some Taliban colleagues.[10] In the 1990s and 2000s he was the Taliban's most feared commander and a primary contact with al Qaeda. While he was a *talib* more than a Kakar, his story still tarnishes the tribe's reputation. It will be described in more detail in Chapter 35.

Safi

The Safis have three main *khels*. Of these, the Massouds have a reputation as warriors, the Gurbaz are said to be hospitable and the Wadir are mediators. All three suffered the division of their communities when the Durand Line was imposed, and this, along with their proximity to non-Pashtun areas, has been used to explain why the Safis are said to be so fiercely tribalized.[1]

Another theory is that the Safis were not originally Pashtuns but were either from the Pashai minority or Tajiks who became Pashtunized.[2] This would explain why they live further north than other Ghurghushti tribes. Some Safis believe that their ancestry dates back to the ancient kingdom of Gandhara, which ruled Safi areas around 500 BC.[3] Today, that territory corresponds to the Peshawar basin in Pakistan and north-eastern Afghanistan, including Nuristan, Kapisa, Laghman and Parwan provinces. In Parwan there is a district named 'Kohi Safi'. The Safi are also spread across the Pech River Valley and Korangal Valley in Kunar Province. The latter is dubbed 'DaMarg Dara' (Valley of Death) by locals, due to the fierce fighting that took place there during the Soviet era.

US forces adopted this nickname after 2001, in part because the valley is where Operation Red Wings took place – made famous by Mark Wahlberg's Hollywood movie *Lone Survivor*. Also known as the Battle of Abbas Ghar, it occurred when a team of US Navy SEALs were ambushed by local insurgents. A quick reaction force sent to extract the SEALs also encountered small-arms fire, with an MH47 Chinook helicopter crashing after being hit by a rocket-propelled grenade (RPG). All sixteen of its US soldiers and airmen were killed instantly. Only one of the SEALs survived the ordeal, hence the title of the film.

Yet the Safi reputation as a thorn in the flesh of foreigners extends deeper into history. These tribesmen fought against the Mughal Emperor Aurangzeb in the seventeenth century, joining forces with Mohmands, Shinwaris and Afridi to do so. The Safis also led a famous revolt in the 1940s. Known as *Safi Kal* (Year of the Safi), this uprising was part of a period of wider tribal unrest between 1944 and 1947 called the 'Khost Disturbances'.

The Safis rebelled in early 1944, angered by the enforcement of *sekoti*, whereby farmers give a third of their harvest to the state, as well as by changes to conscription.[4] Previously, the tribes had followed the *qwami* method of conscription, allowing them to choose who was sent to the state forces. Conscripts would usually serve together, close to their tribal territory. When that system was changed to one with no tribal consultation, Safi resentment erupted, and the government sent troops to arrest three Safi tribal leaders and collect conscripts.[5]

By June 1945 tribal unrest had led to the government dispatching four Hawker Hind bi-plane bombers to blitz Safi strongholds in the Khas Kunar area of the remote Kunar Province, which sits on the Durand Line. British reports outlined that 'activities ranged from reconnaissances to the bombing and machine gunning of hostile tribal forces . . . Extensive damage is said to have been done to Safi villages by bombs and incendiaries.'[6] But it was not all one-sided. One aircraft was lost, falling into Safi hands with its three bombs, a 40mm cannon and a Lewis machine gun. The British battle report said that the Afghan pilot

> was knifed in the back and had his throat cut but lived to tell the tale through the kindness of villagers who found him unconscious with his aircraft and treated him well. The throat cutting was badly done and he recovered and is back in Kabul.[7]

In Safi eyes, the bombardment was foreign-sponsored and disproportionate. It was an affront to honour. With bodies strewn around their burning villages, the Safis formed a parallel government, appointing a King, a Prime Minister and a Minister of Defence. By August 1945 they had raised a tribal *lashkar* and besieged a government base in Kunar for two weeks, with the beleaguered garrison only surviving on air-dropped food and supplies.[8]

But Safi resistance could not be sustained, and a cessation of hostilities was negotiated in late 1945. Conscription and aerial bombardment were ended, provided that the tribesmen stopped fighting.[9] Small pockets of resistance continued, with Safi rebels taking refuge in Mohmand territory on the other side of the Durand Line, but the remaining fighters eventually agreed to a peace deal in November 1946, giving back stolen weapons in return for favourable grain prices and places for Safi students in Kabul's educational institutions.[10]

Given its timing, this Safi story is useful in countering the misperception that Afghanistan enjoyed peace and stability between the 1930s and the 1970s. There may have been no fighting with foreign invaders, but the Safi example highlights how tribal unrest has permanently challenged every Afghan government. It encapsulates the everlasting conflict between state and tribe.

Chapter 32

Tribes of the Karlani Branch

Afridi

Often described as the oldest tribe and as having links to Alexander the Great, the Afridis always appear in Pashtun origin theories. They are also known as 'Guardians of the Pass', due to their control of the famous Khyber Pass.[1] To the south-west of the Pass is the Afridi homeland, the Tirah Valley, which is on the opposite side of the Durand Line to Afghanistan's Nangarhar Province and is shared with the Orakzai tribe (Karlani Branch).[2]

Within the Afridi tribe there are eight permanently competing clans. The Adamkhel control a famous weapons bazaar,[3] while the Kukikhel are known for having made deals with Kabul's communist regime in the 1980s to disrupt the mujahideen. But the most notorious are the Zakkakhel. The former US diplomat James Spain wrote that these Afridis 'have made a fetish out of brigandage' and are so untrustworthy that other *khels* insist they swear upon the Qur'an before believing their word.[4]

Some say the Afridis' internal battles are a product of nineteenth-century British divide-and-rule tactics. Unable to defeat the Afridis, the British instead stoked inter-*khel* tension by bribing some clans while attacking others.[5] Another story revolves around the Afridi penchant for sneaking into British encampments and stealing the bolts of British rifles while their owners slept. Even when the foreigners started tucking their weapons between their legs at night they would still wake up to find the bolts missing. The Afridis became such skilful bolt-snatchers that senior British officers ordered all rifle bolts to be removed at night and locked in a steel chest watched over by a sergeant major.[6]

In 1897 Winston Churchill harshly characterized the Afridis as 'the most miserable and brutal creatures of the earth . . . more cruel, more dangerous, more destructive than wild beasts'.[7] Other British soldiers who faced the Afridi wrote that their tribesmen represented the lowest grade of civilisation and border upon the savage. Entirely illiterate, under no acknowledged control, each man his own king, the nation has dwindled down to a small community of robbers and cut throats, without principles of conduct of any kind and with nothing but the incentive of the moment as the prompter to immediate action . . . Even among Pashtuns, he is accounted as the faithless of the faithless and is held on all sides to be the most fierce and stealthy of all his enemies. He is wily, mistrusting, wolfish and wilful savage, with no other object in life but the pursuit of robbery and murder and the feuds they give rise to. His ignorance and barbarism are a bye-word among neighbour tribes.[8]

The Afridis' supposed impiety is also captured in a common anecdote about a holy man who visited Afridi territory and remarked that it did not contain a single saint's tomb. The Afridis found an easy answer to this complaint: they killed the visitor and made his tomb into a shrine.[9]

Jaji (sometimes 'Zazi')

The Jaji tribe has some clans scattered across Logar, Ghazni and Nangarhar, as well as part of the Kurram Valley in Pakistan, which they share with the Turi tribe. But their main stronghold is Khost and Paktia provinces, particularly the eponymous district of Jaji in Paktia. This area made history in the 1980s as the location of bin Laden's favourite training camp, *Al-Masada* (the Lion's Den).

This base was established in 1987 as the first al Qaeda camp solely for foreign fighters,[1] despite senior mujahideen warning that it was unsuitable for guerrilla warfare and that it was dangerous to exclude Afghans.[2] But the stubborn bin Laden pushed ahead, even inviting a prominent Saudi journalist to visit. Jamal Khashoggi (who was murdered and dismembered at the Saudi Consulate in Istanbul in 2018) spent time in the camp chronicling what was bin Laden's coming of age – the Battle of Jaji.[3] This 1987 encounter was strategically insignificant in the anti-Soviet efforts, but is still called one of the most important battles of the 1980s because it buoyed the Arab fighters in Afghanistan. Until then, they had largely been dismissed as Walter Mitty-esque fantasists by the more grizzled Afghan warriors.

The battle began with an Afghan government operation, backed by Soviet paratroops and Spetsnaz Special Forces, to cut a mujahideen supply route into Pakistan. Exact details have since become blurred, with Arabs claiming that it was their bravery and God's will that led to a resounding victory. A more likely story is that the Afghan mujahideen, including Jaji tribesmen, actually came to their rescue. Either way, Jamal Khashoggi painted bin Laden as a hero, despite heavy losses and a panicked retreat by his fighters.[4] Picturing bin Laden as a victorious field commander 'bolstered [his] hubristic belief in the superiority of his group' and 'affirmed his focus on armed jihad and separation from the Afghans'.[5] It attracted disenfranchised youths to bin Laden's ranks and meant that a pivotal historical event took place in Jaji territory, one that has unfairly tarnished the tribe ever since: the birth of al Qaeda.

Mahsud

The 'wolves of Waziristan' is how imperialists often characterized the Mahsuds. Their homeland is South Waziristan in Pakistan, with some settlements in Afghanistan's Logar, Wardak and Ghazni provinces. This tribe is also known for a practice rarely associated with ruthless warriors: dancing.

The Mahsuds created the *Attan* folk dance, which is now Afghanistan's de facto national dance. Multiple dancers equipped with scarves (or swords or rifles) form a circle and move clockwise to an increasingly rapid drumbeat, using an array of elaborate steps and swaying with outstretched arms. Originally a war dance, it is said to derive from the movements of swordsmen. Today it is part of most celebrations, even though some say that its popularity diminished towards the end of the twentieth century as religious fundamentalists condemned it.[1]

The Mahsud tribe is structured into three main clans: the Alizai, Bahlolzai and Shamankhel. The tribesmen will use the phrase *mizh dri mahsudi* (we three Mahsuds),[2] which reflects the fact that they have traditionally experienced less internal fighting than other tribes, although tensions flared after 2001, when some Mahsuds sided with the Taliban.

Mahsuds also have a reputation for strict adherence to *Pashtunwali*, including setting higher values for *badal* than other tribes.[3] Westerners tend to know Mahsuds for their historic battles with the British. Two examples are the tribal *lashkar* that was slaughtered by British forces in 1860, and the Great Kashmir *Lashkar* in 1947 (both described in Chapter 22). Both incidents are the basis for the Mahsuds being depicted as 'without doubt the wildest and fiercest of all the tribal Pashtuns'[4] who 'can never even think of submitting to a foreign power'.[5]

British historians tend to be unsympathetic to the Mahsud, mostly stereotyping them as turbulent, untrustworthy, bloodthirsty barbarians.[6] Sir Olaf Caroe, a British administrator in the tribal areas after the Second World War, was scathing about the Mahsuds and their Wazir cousins. He described them as

> aloof, and . . . continually engaged in aggressive warfare against their Wazir cousins, at whose expense they have encroached to acquire new lands. And to those who know both tribes, they present

a different appearance . . . it is not so hard to distinguish one from the other, not by his dress, for that is much the same, but by something indefinable in his air and carriage. The nearest I can get to it is to liken the Mahsud to a wolf, the Wazir to a panther. Both are splendid creatures; the panther is slier, sleeker and has more grace, the wolf-pack is more purposeful, more united and more dangerous.[7]

In the years since Caroe wrote, the Mahsud have done little to reduce foreign distrust of them. Their recent association with al Qaeda, the Taliban and various other insurgent outfits has drawn the ire of governments and bolstered their unruly, ruthless reputation – at least among outsiders.

Mangal

The Mangal reputation revolves around never having been subjugated by the state, but often being enlisted as mercenaries. Most Mangal territory is in Loya Paktia, with some clans living in the Pakistani town of Tari Mangal – a border point across which weapons and fighters flowed during the 1980s.[1] Like most border tribes, Mangals fiercely resisted nineteenth-century British forces. But their most famous clash with authority was the Mangal Uprising, or Khost Rebellion, which started in 1924 when the tribe revolted against Amanullah Khan's modernizations. His retaliation was notable as the first time that the Afghan Air Force saw combat.[2]

Mangal unrest had erupted upon publication of Amanullah's 'Nizamnama' code, which the tribesmen saw as destroying tribal and religious authority. Handing freedoms to women was interpreted as the state interfering in family affairs,[3] and further resentment was stirred by new restrictions on crossing the Durand Line, increased taxation and changes to conscription.[4] Starting in March 1924 in Khost city, clerics rallied Mangal tribesmen to protest against the supposedly anti-Islamic reforms. Official British records from 1924 capture the situation well:

With the new code in one hand and the Koran in the other, they called the tribes to choose between the word of God and that of man, and adjured them to resist demands, the acceptance of which would reduce their sons to slavery in the Afghan army and their daughters to the degrading influence of Western education.[5]

The Mangals were soon joined by other tribes, leading Amanullah to send a team to convince the rebels that modernization was not counter to Sharia or *Pashtunwali*. The negotiations failed, and Amanullah then organized the 1924 *Loya Jirga* to promote the legitimacy of his reforms and extinguish the basis for the rebellion.

This backfired when the *jirgamar* demanded that he roll back the reforms. When tribal violence escalated, the government enlisted the Shinwari and other tribes to fight the Mangal-led rebels and the Mullahs who had incited them.[6] Amanullah Khan is quoted as saying that Afghanistan teetered on the brink of chaos due to 'these so-called Mullahs from whom even Satan himself would seek protection'.[7]

By autumn 1924 government forces, including the infant Air Force, had been unleashed.[8] They beat the tribesmen back in key battles, but the conflict ebbed and flowed; at one stage it even looked as if the rebels would march on Kabul.[9] Only in late January 1925 did fighting subside, which some historians put down to the use of First World War aircraft bought from the British. They had 'a salutary effect on tribal forces when they appeared on the scene, bombing and strafing the rebels.'[10] Overall, an estimated 14,000 people were killed in the uprisings.[11] Reprisals aimed at the Mangal tribe saw another 1,500 executions and 3,000 Mangal homes incinerated.[12] But it was a pyrrhic victory for the Emir. The rebellion depleted his coffers and stoked disunity, as well as exposing the fact that the state was reliant on tribal *lashkars*. The uprising demonstrated the power of the Pashtun tribes.

Orakzai

The Orakzai tribe has been tainted in the late 2010s because of some Orakzai men who led the fledgling Da'esh presence in Afghanistan.[1] This is despite the tribe having almost no settlements in Afghanistan. Their homeland is the Orakzai Agency in Pakistan, where they share the Tirah valley with their Afridi cousins. This is one of the only Pakistani tribal areas that does not border Afghanistan, meaning it was never a substantial base for Afghan mujahideen during the 1980s.

The absence of arable land in Orakzai areas is said to be the reason for its tribesmen's tendency to take up arms.[2] Historical grievances are also blamed, as Orakzai clans in the Tirah Valley, along with theirAfridi neighbours, were frequently the target of British military campaigns in the late nineteenth century. This included the famed Tirah Expedition of 1897–8, when a British-Indian force flooded into the Valley, retaking territory that the tribesmen had captured.[3]

Among Pashtuns, the Orakzai are recognized for their willingness to take in *hamsaya* clans, i.e. those exiled from other tribes. This tendency is often linked to the tribe's own history as exiles. The story is that a tenth-century Persian prince named Sikandar Shah was exiled by his father and started using the name *Wrakzai* (lost son).[4] He travelled to what is now Pakistan and became a courtier of the king, who sent him to fight unruly tribesmen in the Tirah valley. But after receiving Pashtun hospitality, the prince chose to settle down instead, and today's Orakzai tribesmen are supposedly his descendants. Possible Persian ancestry is also used to explain why the Orakzai have one Shia clan – the Muhammadkhel. Its members have a long-running violent rivalry with the Sunni clans and also tend to be pro-state, while other Orakzai tribesmen have long-held links with insurgents.

Turi

As the only fully Shia tribe, the Turi are said to be remnants of Mongol invasions and possibly related to the Hazaras. Proponents of this theory cite the slighter and more delicate physical features of the Turi than those of most Pashtuns.[1] An alternative theory is that they descend from a Turkic community who migrated from ancient Persia.[2]

Small numbers of Turis live in Afghanistan's Paktia Province, but most reside in Pakistan's Kurram Valley. This valley was under Afghan control until the Second Anglo-Afghan War in 1878. When the war began, Turi tribesmen feared attacks from Sunni rivals and petitioned the British for help. The British sent a series of punitive expeditions into the area and annexed the valley in 1892, paying an annual allowance to the Turi in return for military service.[3] This initiated a long-running tendency on the part of the Turi to align with state forces.

But the Turis remain ideologically besieged. They have a longstanding enmity with the Mangal and the Bangash tribes which stretches back to the fifteenth and sixteenth centuries, when the Turis were semi-nomadic, migrating from the Aryob Valley in Paktia to the Kurram Valley. This meant traversing Bangash lands, which inevitably led to quarrels.[4] More recent history has been marked by Turi opposition to jihadist groups, especially during the Soviet era, when the mujahideen used the Kurram Valley to launch attacks into Afghanistan. The Turi were uncooperative and consistently fought other tribes with mujahideen or pro-Taliban tendencies.

Wazir

Foreigners have described Waziri territory as land where 'the great and proud men have tasted defeat and humiliation'.[1] Pashtuns also describe Waziri territory as 'the wildest part of the tribal areas'.[2] This is usually in reference to the Waziristan region of Pakistan, but some Waziri pockets are also found in Khost, Paktia and Paktika Provinces in Afghanistan (particularly the Bermal Valley in Paktika).[3]

Waziris pride themselves on never having paid taxes to any sovereign. While conservative, they are less strict in following Islam and *Pashtunwali* than other tribes – and are even said to be guided by their own code called *do Waziro Narkh* (customs of the Wazirs).[4] Their allegedly lax approach to *Pashtunwali* is encapsulated in an anecdote about a British political officer who travelled to Waziristan without warning. The Waziris welcomed him and his entourage with a meal, giving him the protection extended by *melmastia*. But they were suspicious that he intended to confiscate their lands, as they had not paid a fine for killing a Hindu the previous year. Taking their chance, the Wazirs massacred the visiting delegates as they ate. This sparked the tribal uprising of 1897.[5]

Within the tribe there are two main clans: the Utmanzai Wazirs and the Ahmadzai Wazirs. The most famous Utmanzai Wazir was Mirzali Khan, widely known as Faqir Ipi. He gained a reputation as a guerrilla warrior in 1936, when a British Indian court gave a ruling in a marriage dispute involving a Pashtun and a Hindu girl who had converted to Islam. After the girl's family claimed abduction and forced conversion (based on the fact that the girl was a minor), the court ruled the marriage void. The verdict enraged Pashtuns like Faqir Ipi, who began spreading anti-British sentiment and accusations that the government was interfering in a religious matter. He called a tribal *jirga* in the village of Ipi to declare war. Two large *lashkars* were raised, and anarchy ensued. The British eventually suppressed the agitation, but Faqir Ipi was never caught and went on to lead further revolts after the creation of Pakistan in 1947. He and other tribal elders organized a *jirga* in which they announced the Bannu Resolution, which demanded that the Pashtuns be given the choice to establish an independent state of 'Pashtunistan', instead of being made to join either India or Pakistan.The British refused, but by then his actions had cemented Faqir Ipi's position as a Pashtun idol.

Yet the Wazirs' reputation as wild warriors was established long before Faqir Ipi. It was built in fighting nineteenth-century British forces, who described the Waziris as panther-like and 'physically the hardest people on earth'[6] who are 'held in abomination by all their Pathan neighbours.'[7] One famed British-Waziri battle came after the Third Anglo-Afghan War in 1919, when rumours spread that Waziristan would be transferred by British India to Afghanistan. Waziri tribesmen launched guerrilla raids in an attempt to compel decision-makers to agree to the transfer. British forces fought back and defeated the tribesmen, but then made the disastrous decision to build a permanent British garrison in Waziristan, with an accompanying road network as part of a new 'Forward Policy'.

The Wazirs were not keen. When they attacked the roads, British officials tried to convince them that 'roads are the most civilising agents in the world'. The tribesmen replied that 'we have noticed that roads are always followed by guns, and according to our ideas, guns are not a civilising factor'.[8]

Zadran

Over two centuries ago, a British official warned that Zadrans are 'more like mountain bears than men . . . they are never to be met with out of their hills'.[1] Post-2001 Zadran territory, which is mostly among the mountainous border

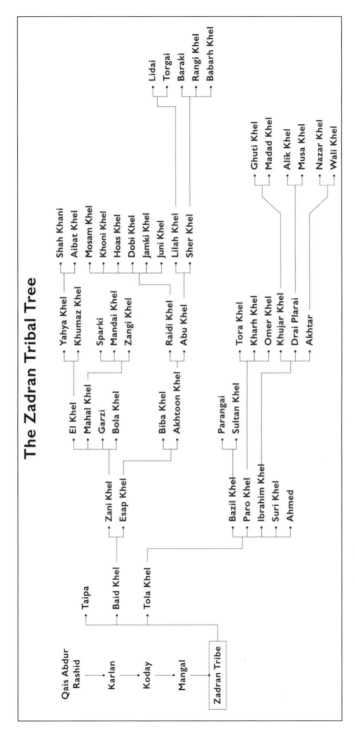

Figure 13: The Zadran Tribal Tree[13]

areas of Loya Paktia, became painted as a breeding ground of international jihad.

The Zadran tribe is also known for some famous sons. Mazrak Zadran was the tribal chief who started the Khost Disturbances in 1944 (sparking the Safi uprising mentioned in the previous chapter). Mazrak's brother, Saad Akbar Babrak, was shot dead by Pakistani police after assassinating the first Pakistani Prime Minister, Liaqat Ali Khan, in 1951. His motives remain unclear, but some speculate that he acted in accord with the USSR, which resented Liaqat's anti-communist views. Others claim that the US sponsored the hit, angry at Liaqat's calls for the US withdrawal from Pakistani airbases.[2] Either way, these brothers have been overshadowed by one Zadran who permanently altered Afghan history: Jalaluddin Haqqani.

Born into the Sultankhel sub-sect of the Zadran's Tolakhel clan,[3] Jalaluddin epitomized the dark, bearded, dead-eyed warrior who haunts the dreams of every invader. After spending the early 1970s as a madrassa student, Jalaluddin joined the mujahideen to fight the Soviets, with US backing. He was described by the CIA's lead officer in Afghanistan as 'a man of uncommon personal courage, and a deeply nuanced understanding of guerrilla tactics'. Former US Congressman Charlie Wilson, credited with sponsoring the mujahideen in the 1980s, called Haqqani 'goodness personified'.[4]

But Haqqani turned on the US after 2001, and his militants became NATO's most relentless foes. Fierce, well-disciplined fighters, they quickly became known as the Taliban's teeth. One of Haqqani's sons, Sirajuddin, became the Taliban's deputy leader and its most revered military commander in the 2010s. Another son, Anas, was released from custody in 2019 as a confidence-building measure during US-Taliban negotiations. He then joined the Taliban's negotiating team, and he and his uncle Khalid were the first senior Taliban officials to march into Kabul in August 2021. Both Serajuddin and Khalid then became prominent ministers in the new Taliban regime, highlighting the fact that the Haqqani network, and with it the Zadran tribe, will shape Afghanistan's future as much as they have influenced its past. The Haqqani story is also a reminder that pragmatism is as important as any other value to Pashtuns. No allegiance in Afghanistan is set in stone, or as the proverb says, 'You can rent an Afghan, but you cannot buy him.'

PART IX
Prominent Pashtuns

Chapter 33

The Sarbani Hero: Malalai of Maiwand

Every Afghan knows Malalai. She is an icon – particularly for Pashtuns. Many schools and hospitals now bear her name, as do many women.[1] She frequently comes up in conversation and even features prominently in the Taliban's *tarana* (chants),[2] which hints at what she is famous for.

Malalai's tale revolves around the Battle of Maiwand on 27 July 1880 – one of the last battles of the Second Anglo-Afghan War. It remains a defining victory in Afghan history and 'one of the worst ever [defeats] suffered by British arms in pitched battle'.[3] But while the battle is historical reality, the facts of Malalai's story are more fluid.

British contemporary accounts confirm that it was a searingly hot summer's day. Anyone who has been to Kandahar will know how that furnace-like air feels. It is inescapable. It leaves sweat rolling off every limb, every extremity and even places that never seem to have sweated before. The dusty air leaves a grainy taste in the mouth and smells exactly as you imagine a bone-dry desert would. Malalai would have inhaled it with every breath, as the chaos unfolded around her. Horses would have kicked up clouds of it as the cavalry wheeled around the battlefield. The dull thudding of their hooves would have mixed with booming artillery, snapping rifles and the clashing blades of the close-quarter battle.

Pashtuns recount how, amidst this bedlam, Malalai abandoned her task of ferrying ammunition and water to the front lines and instead tended to fallen comrades who were being shattered by the superior British firepower. As their courage began to fail them, the Afghans edged back from the front line. Something was needed to rally them, because being vanquished by a foreign infidel on home soil would forever stain tribal honour.

This compelled Malalai into action. She pulled off her veil, clasping it tightly in her fist. Turning towards the front line, she thrust her arm in the air, and her veil fluttered in the wind as she let out a lioness's roar.

'Young love! If you do not fall in the Battle of Maiwand, by God, someone is saving you as a symbol of shame.'[4]
Pashtuns still believe that her words injected resolve into the men around her. Their courage immediately restored, the tribesmen pressed forward as the warriors they were raised to be. When one flag-bearer was felled by a British bullet, Malalai allegedly raced forward without hesitation, picking up the flag and hoisting it skywards. This encouraged her compatriots to surge on to victory. Honour had been restored. Malalai had made sure of it.

This is the general tale that Pashtuns tell when talking about Malalai. But given their natural flair for storytelling, her heroics are often imaginatively exaggerated and elaborated. Little else is known about Malalai, either before or after the battle, that might corroborate any of these claims. All that is known is that she was born in 1861 into a shepherd's family in Khig, a village outside of Maiwand in western Kandahar which now sits on the Kandahar–Helmand highway.[5] Given Khig's location, Malalai most likely belonged to a Durrani tribe – possibly the Alizai, who have a strong presence around Maiwand.

More is known, and is verifiable, about the Battle of Maiwand itself. It occurred after the installation of the Emir Abdur Rahman Khan, with British backing, on 31 May 1880. At the same time, Ayub Khan, the previous emir and Abdur Rahman's cousin, was sulking in the western province of Herat, aggrieved at being deposed. He sought revenge. When Abdur Rahman took Kabul, Ayub immediately left Herat with his own army, heading south through Helmand to Kandahar, where he would swing north towards Ghazni and then attack Kabul.[6]

Word of his advance spread quickly, and when British officials in Kandahar heard of Ayub's plan they raced out to intercept him. They were led by Brigadier-General George Burrows, with Brigadier-General Thomas Nuttall commanding two cavalry regiments. After a few skirmishes with some tribesmen, they lay in wait for Ayub's main army halfway between Gereshk and Kandahar city.

But late on 25 July 1880, intelligence revealed that Ayub had taken a different route than expected. He had circumvented Burrows and would reach Maiwand on the 27th, from where he would move north to Ghazni. Burrows needed to move, quickly. But for some reason he waited an entire day before marching to Maiwand.

A young British officer described how the march began at 0530 hours on the 27th, after much of the night had been spent packing up. Few of the Indian sepoys had eaten breakfast or even filled their water bottles. Many were already exhausted before moving. Then came the relentless Kandahari heat which was baking even by 0900 and, as one soldier described it, 'was to become hotter still, with the temperature reaching over 120 degrees in the shade, had there been any'.[7]

Kandahar's dry, sandy scrub was so hot that when scouts finally spotted Ayub's army, they initially mistook the masses of Afghans for trees, until they started moving. When the size of the Afghan force became clear, Burrows urged his troops on to reach Maiwand first.[8] That is when they came across two villages, a kilometre apart, called Mundabad and Khig. On their other side was a ravine 100ft wide and at least 20ft deep.[9] Beyond it was an open plain, with Maiwand in the distance.

Ayub's army was now positioned at the opposite end of the plain. One British officer noted that Ayub had around 6,000 regular infantry, 4,000 cavalry and 36 guns. But 'the unknown factor was the number of tribesmen and Ghazis (religious fanatics who fought like fiends) that had joined Ayub during his march'.[10] These Afghans vastly outnumbered Burrows' three infantry regiments (roughly 1,500 men) and two cavalry regiments (350 horses). His artillery was also outmatched, and their wagon wheels were not built to negotiate ravines.

Burrows' fatal mistake was not using the ravine to his advantage. He could have dug in defensively, but instead ordered his exhausted force to haul the artillery across to the open plain. They continued forward until the Afghans were in range, igniting an artillery duel.

The problem was that the artillery advanced further than Burrows intended, leaving the rest of his men having to surge forward in haste. As Ayub's infantry massed in front of the British lines, Burrows pre-empted their charge by ordering his own infantry to advance. He then cancelled the order at the last minute, fearing that the Afghan guns would decimate his attackers. But it was too late. The troops were moving.

Burrows and other British officers also failed to notice another ravine to their right, parallel to the British line. The Afghans had cleverly filled this deep, dry watercourse with artillery and men, and only their banners and the tops of the cavalrymen's heads were visible.[11] When Burrows learned of the hordes of tribesmen advancing along the hidden ravine, he wheeled another part of his infantry to face them. This meant that by 1300 hours his force was strung out and facing three different directions in a horseshoe formation. As the enemy swarmed around them, the only escape was over the mile of undefended territory back to the ravine at the villages of Mundabad and Khig.

As Burrows' artillery ran out of ammunition and withdrew, his infantry were left exposed to Ayub's cavalry. Ayub's guns in the hidden ravine were also firing into Burrows' right flank at close range. Then Ayub unleashed his tribesmen. The inexperienced and exhausted Indian regiments melted away when faced with the charging Afghans. Burrows later wrote that 'The infantry gave way, and commencing from the left, rolled up like a wave.'[12]

Collapse was coming.

Burrows ordered Brigadier-General Nuttall to charge with his cavalry. He later blamed their half-hearted effort on the artillery fire having unnerved the horses. But other officers lamented that 'Burrows' orders were vague and half the cavalry went one way and half the other. Nuttall appears to have given no orders at all.'[13] Discipline evaporated as British soldiers flocked back to the ravine behind them. Only the remnants of the right flank stayed put, fighting until they ran out of ammunition. Exhausted, dehydrated and with empty rifles, Ayub's Afghans swept through them. None were spared. A gunner who witnessed the massacre from afar later recalled how even the 'horses were kicking and plunging in the last agonies of death'.[14]

Of the men left standing, some withdrew to Mundabad, others to Khig. Burrows gave his horse to a wounded officer but was rescued by another cavalryman. Racing along the road to Kandahar with other stragglers, he was unaware that remnants of his force were fighting to the death behind him, enabling him to escape. The escapees were also lucky that some tribesmen were distracted by the opportunity to loot abandoned British baggage.

The troops who made it to Khig wrote themselves heroically into history. Around fifty men of the 66th (Berkshire) Regiment of Foot regrouped in the village, battling on bravely against the Afghan swarm. When only two officers and nine soldiers remained, they moved further back to make their final defence – now known as 'The Last Stand of the Eleven'. A British General in Kandahar later wrote how even an officer in Ayub's army spoke with respect about the last eleven:

These eleven men charged out of the garden and died with their faces to the foe, fighting to the death . . . although the whole of the Ghazis were assembled round them, not one dared approach to cut them down. Thus standing in the open, back to back, firing steadily and truly, every shot telling, surrounded by thousands, these eleven officers and men died; and it was not until the last man had been shot down that the Ghazis dared advance upon them.[15]

This valiant effort bought time for other survivors to get a head start on the 40-mile scramble to Kandahar, which was as harrowing as the battle itself. One British officer described it vividly:

Sick men, almost naked, are astride donkeys, mules and camels . . . Guns and carriages are crowded with the helpless wounded suffering the tortures of the damned; horses are limping along with ugly wounds and men are pressing eagerly to the rear in the hope of finding water. Hordes of irregular horsemen are to be seen amongst our baggage animals, relentlessly cutting our men down and looting.[16]

The disastrous defeat suffered by Burrows was a famous victory for Ayub, but he then made the mistake of abandoning his march north, and besieged Kandahar instead. If he had gone on to Ghazni he could have ridden a groundswell of Afghan support to overall victory. But the change of plan allowed time for a British rescue mission to arrive from Kabul. This was the famed 320-mile forced march led by

General Frederick Roberts, who demolished Ayub's army on 1 September 1880, ending the Second Anglo-Afghan War.[17]

Burrows faced inevitable criticism, even though his forces achieved the initial goal of halting Ayub's advance on Kabul. It is also said that General Roberts' retribution was only possible due to the damage that Burrows had inflicted on Ayub at Maiwand. It allegedly took the Afghans a week to clear the battlefield of bodies, which included more than 5,000 of Ayub's men.[18]

Maiwand caused a sensation back in England, popularizing the phrase, 'My God, Maiwand!' The deeds of the 66th (Berkshire) Regiment of Foot were celebrated, with the 'Maiwand Lion' sculpture erected in 1886 in the city of Reading (Reading's football team still has the Maiwand Lion in its crest today). The battle hit the headlines again in 2008, when British troops in Helmand found a weapons cache including two Martini-Henry rifles that their predecessors had lost at Maiwand.[19] A wider audience is aware of Maiwand because of Rudyard Kipling's poem 'That Day', and Sherlock Holmes fans know it as the battle where Dr Watson received the wound in his leg, causing him to return to 221B Baker Street.

But one person is absent from British accounts of the battle. In Britain, Malalai is either ignored or dismissed as a quaint figure of folkore, despite Pashtun insistence that her heroics were historical reality. Without hard evidence, questions are rightly asked about her deeds that day.

Eyewitness accounts tell of a decisive victory for Ayub's army. At no point were Afghans on the brink of defeat – so when did Malalai rise up and urge the men on? Even if she did, did she really save the day? Ayub had the better terrain and battle positions. He had superior numbers and more effective artillery. He also benefited from Burrows' poor decision-making. The Afghans were not being beaten or in retreat, so was Malalai's speech really that pivotal?

Did she even exist at all? While women did act as water-carriers in battle, and a woman's body was found after a previous battle in April 1880, there are no records of one found at the Battle of Maiwand.[20] This does not necessarily confirm her absence, but it adds weight to a claim that Malalai was not associated with the battle until decades later, when her story was concocted to support the cause of Pashtun nationalism. The notable twentieth-century Afghan historian Abdul Hai Habibi is sometimes suggested as her possible creator.[21] Is Malalai's story a heavily romanticized or even a completely fabricated myth?

Regardless of its authenticity, it is easy to see why her story is still told today. It possesses many of the hallmarks of Pashtun culture, including bravery, shame and independence. Malalai personifies the Pashtun imperative to resist foreign aggressors. She epitomizes the warrior spirit. She symbolizes the *namus* that tribesmen are duty-bound to protect. Even if her story is closer to folklore than historical reality, Malalai's actions encapsulate the value that matters most to the Pashtun tribes – honour.

Chapter 34

The Bettani Mujahid: Abdul Rasoul Sayyaf

It seems like an understated approach to the house of an Afghan political heavyweight. The dirt track is in marked contrast to the high-walled compounds and teeming security personnel which guard the ostentatious homes of other warlords-cum-politicians. But the austere approach aligns with Abdul Rasoul Sayyaf's Islamist ideals and his reputation as the man who brought bin Laden to Afghanistan. It suits his nickname: 'The Man of the Mountain'.

The dirt track leads to Sayyaf's mountain-top retreat. Think of a primitive Bond villain's lair, but stripped bare and abandoned for decades. This is the impression given by Sayyaf's residence. It feels unfinished. But appearances can be deceptive in Afghanistan. The hilltop hideaway is a fortress in which Sayyaf himself stayed safe for over forty years, despite being a number one target of the Soviets, the Taliban and many others.

The site is only a 45-minute drive west of Kabul, although it feels as remote as can be after the ascent into the mountains that surround the city. Once in the Paghman Valley, there is no more city smog or multi-storey, concrete cityscape. The air among the mud-walled, shanty-like buildings is fresh, and the road narrows to accommodate only one vehicle as it weaves around the contours of the hills.

Sayyaf's turn-off is nondescript and looks like any other dirt track. The asphalt gives way to earth, and tyres settle into the ruts that previous vehicles have made in wetter weather. The track immediately climbs as it snakes its way to the hilltop. After a few hundred metres there are the first signs of security. Vehicles are brought to a stop in front of a metal barrier manned by a young Afghan. It is unclear whether he is a soldier, a militiaman or just a barrier-operator with a rifle. All tend to wear the same mismatching, untucked military garb. Bootlaces tend to be tied only to the ankles, or else old, western-style running shoes protrude from under loose-legged trousers. The only consistent feature of all combatants is the habitual AK47 rifle.

On passing this first checkpoint, vehicles throw up clouds of dust as they swoop around a tight hairpin bend and continue the ascent. Observant eyes can now see similarly shabby-looking soldiers dotted around the undulating hills, boots untied and AK47s slung over their shoulders. As the collection of buildings becomes visible on the hilltop ahead, the track becomes a steeper slope where, in winter, wheels spin as even the 4x4s slip on compacted snow. The track then turns sharply to the right, and the main gate comes into view. It is manned by more professional-looking soldiers. They have hand-held radios and look more alert than their checkpoint colleagues below, although their mismatched military fatigues still give off an amateur air.

From this small plateau on top of the hill the view stretches for miles around. Apart from the humming of the vehicle's engine, everything is quiet. One side looks over the serene Paghman valley, with its fertile, well-farmed plains rising to jagged, snow-capped mountains in the distance. On the other side, Kabul and its ceiling of smog can be discerned through a gap in the mountains.

The compound's heavy steel gate is pushed open to reveal an unpaved, uneven courtyard surrounded by single-storey buildings that look rough and not quite finished. Various men mill around. Some are dressed as soldiers, while others wear traditional shalwar kameez. Aware that a guest has arrived, a party of men emerge from one of the entrances. They spread out in a disorganized guard of honour around the doorway. These men have bigger bellies and are more neatly dressed than the guards. But they still look battle-hardened. Even the elites in Afghanistan have an edge.

Then he appears.

Ducking his head under the doorframe, for he is a giant in stature, he stands straight, towering over everyone, and scans everything in front of him. His turban is tightly wound around a skullcap that sits higher on his head than that of other Afghans. But it is his long white beard that immediately draws your eyes. It confers authority. It represents a lifetime's worth of wisdom.

His eyes are deep-set, living in the shadow of big, bushy eyebrows. He looks at you with a friendly glint in these eyes, whether it is your first meeting or not. It is a look of mischief, and even kindness – which rather contradicts the unsettling aura he otherwise gives off. He extends his hand only slightly from his body, as if trying to draw you closer. The handshake is held for longer than normal, long after your hand has gone limp and you have tried to pull away. He is making an assessment of you – as though he is staring into your soul while using your hand to read your heart.[1]

All of this gives an idea of how Sayyaf has so adeptly navigated Afghanistan's endless political turmoil, usually coming out on top. From his impenetrable hilltop fortress he has been a political shape-shifter, whose relevance has rarely waned as he has watched the rise and fall of Afghan parties and foreign empires. Even the briefest encounter makes it clear why, in 1985, a top secret CIA report concluded that Sayyaf was an 'astute and ambitious opportunist' who has been a 'central figure in most attempts to unite the splintered Afghan resistance movement' and who 'will continue to be one of the key players'.[2] It was a prescient assessment.

Born in 1946 in the Paghman Valley just outside Kabul, Sayyaf is from the Kharoti tribe of the Ghilzai Confederation (Bettani branch). But his prominence never came from tribal affiliation. Sayyaf, whose name comes from the Arabic for 'swordsman',[3] rose to fame as part of a student Islamist movement that grew into the anti-Soviet mujahideen. He was an ideologue and a religious fundamentalist more than a tribal leader.

In the 1960s Sayyaf studied at Al Azhar University in Egypt, one of the world's oldest universities and a pre-eminent centre of Islamic thought. He then became a lecturer in the Sharia Department at Kabul University in the 1970s, where he joined the young Islamists inspired by the Muslim Brotherhood in Egypt. It is claimed that he was among those who plotted the failed overthrow of President Daud Khan in 1975. He was arrested and imprisoned as a result, only to be released in 1978 by the communist leader Hafizullah Amin, who was from the same tribe and the same area (Paghman) as Sayyaf. It is also claimed that, after Amin was killed, his relatives took refuge with the exiled Sayyaf in Pakistan – highlighting the fact that 'even among the more zealous ideologues blood and honor retained some meaning'.[4]

When the Soviets invaded, Sayyaf fled to Pakistan with the other resistance leaders. From there, he formed the Ittihad-i-Islami (Islamic Union) and built links to backers in Saudi Arabia, which is why he is often blamed for internationalizing the Afghan jihad. Towards the end of the Soviet era, Sayyaf came to know Osama bin Laden, and even established some training camps with him in eastern Afghanistan. It was Sayyaf's forces who rescued bin Laden and his ineffective Arab fighters at the Battle of Jaji in 1987. Sayyaf also ran refugee camps in Pakistan which were later tied to events that changed the world.

In one refugee camp Sayyaf founded the Dawa'a al-Jihad (Call of Jihad) University, later deemed the 'pre-eminent school for terrorism'.[5] A notable alumnus was Ramzi Yousef, who organized the first World Trade Center bombing in 1993 and was planning to assassinate Pope John Paul II and fly an aircraft into the CIA headquarters.[6] Yousef's co-conspirator was his uncle and another product of Sayyaf's infrastructure, Khalid Sheikh Mohammad, who later masterminded the 9/11 attacks.[7] Sayyaf's camps are also alleged to have inspired the Filipino terror group Abu Sayyaf, which now fights for ISIS. Its founder spent time in Afghanistan in the 1980s.[8]

Sayyaf's influence did not dwindle after the Soviets withdrew in 1989. As Afghanistan descended into civil war, he was a main instigator of a 1993 incident described as one of the worst in Afghan history. The Afshar Massacre is now said to have helped set Afghanistan on a path to sectarianism,[9] with Sayyaf's forces accused of 'repeated human butchery'.[10]

Sayyaf and his Ittihad forces were nominally aligned with the mujahideen-led government that took over from the last communist president, Mohammad Najibullah, in 1992. Another prominent supporter of this government was the Tajik mujahideen leader, Ahmad Shah Massoud, who was Minister of Defence. Their combined forces fought against the former mujahideen faction led by Gulbuddin Hekmatyar (from the same Kharoti tribe as Sayyaf). Hekmatyar's Hezbi Islami group had split from the mujahideen and instead aligned with Hazara and Uzbek militias to bombard Kabul.

In early 1993 Massoud, with Sayyaf's support, planned the 'Afshar Operation' to clear Hazara-held areas of western Kabul, consolidate control of the city and weaken the rebel alliance by capturing the main Hazara leader, Abdul Ali Mazari. Prior to the operation, Massoud's men cleverly bribed Hazara commanders so that the area's defences were left exposed. This allowed artillery to be strategically inserted before the offensive was launched on 10 February 1993. Massoud, as Minister of Defence, was in overall command, but Sayyaf controlled his own Ittihad units.

The first wave of the attack on Afshar took the form of indiscriminate artillery fire. It has since been claimed that the barrage was intended to induce civilians to evacuate the area, so that they would not be caught up in the subsequent assault. But the shelling was so intense that most took shelter rather than flee. This made them vulnerable to what came next.

At 0400 hours on 11 February, Massoud's troops and Sayyaf's militia encircled Afshar. Artillery attacks continued until the middle of the day, when one of the Hazara lines collapsed. The Hazaras fled as Massoud's and Sayyaf's forces flooded into the area, capturing key buildings.[11] It is at that moment that the relatively normal battle – at least in Afghan terms – became something that Hazaras will never forget.

Sayyaf's forces ran riot. They put Hazara prisoners into shipping containers and, it is alleged, executed their family members. One fleeing witness spoke of seeing a severed head left in a window.[12] Houses were looted. Women were abducted. Multiple accusations of rape have since emerged, although these are difficult to confirm, given the stigma facing victims. But it is abundantly clear that Afshar – both physically and psychologically – was reduced to ruins.

On the second day Massoud convened a meeting at the Intercontinental Hotel to halt the abuse and looting, as well as to organize the withdrawal of attacking troops. But the damage had already been done, and violence only subsided later in the month, when the 1993 Islamabad Accord was agreed between the government and the rebel alliance.

Sayyaf remained a key actor in Afghanistan's turmoil throughout the rest of the 1990s, and has often been cited as the man who facilitated bin Laden's return to Afghanistan in 1996, after he was expelled from Sudan.[13] Sayyaf later said of bin Laden:

I did not see anything particular about him. He was not outstanding in any way, just one person among many . . . I found that he was a simple man. I don't know how the media have made such a thing out of him.[14]

At the dawn of the Taliban's era, Sayyaf became their staunchest opponent, despite holding similar Islamist views. Instead, he aligned with the Northern Alliance, claiming that he was the first Pashtun to do so.[15] Yet many of Sayyaf's commanders defected to the *talibs*, including Mohammad Abbas Stanekzai, who would later become one of the Taliban's lead negotiators in talks with the US and Deputy Foreign Minister when the Taliban took Kabul in 2021.[16]

After 2001 Sayyaf backed the Karzai government and attended the foundational *Loya Jirgas* where, it is said, he intimidated delegates to ensure that his allies gained positions in Afghanistan's new government.[17] He then became a Member of Parliament in 2005 and even stood for the position of Speaker of the House. He lost, but surprisingly gained the support of Mohammad Mohaqiq, an ethnic Hazara who had led militia that fought against Sayyaf's men in Afshar in the early 1990s.

By 2014 Sayyaf was a candidate in the presidential elections, coming fourth with seven per cent of the vote. The rehabilitation of his reputation continued, his past seemingly giving him gravitas and credibility rather than earning him disdain and condemnation. Such was his success in shaping himself as a voice of wisdom that President Ghani selected him to chair the 2019 Consultative *Loya Jirga* on Peace. Sayyaf was called upon again to mediate in the political crisis around the contested 2019 presidential elections – cementing his status as an influential 'elder'.

After the events of August 2021, when Afghanistan's Republic collapsed and the Taliban returned to power, Sayyaf was one of the elite who went into exile. He initially relocated to Delhi, but reports also spread that he had then travelled to Turkey, where other anti-Taliban politicians were considering how to form a government-in-exile or a new resistance movement. While sceptics would cite the Taliban's unassailable, vice-like grip over Kabul, as well as Sayyaf's advanced age and his health issues, history suggests that it is unwise to rule out his return to prominence.

Even this snapshot of Sayyaf's story drives home just how tumultuous recent Afghan history has been – which raises questions about how all the turmoil has affected Pashtun tribal structures. Equally important to understand will be what happens when the men who have been consistently at the forefront of the turmoil, like Sayyaf, eventually leave the scene. A power vacuum may result, and that might be the moment when the extent of any breakdown in tribal structures really becomes clear.

Sayyaf's story also provides many insights into tribal affiliation. He has always been seen as a prominent Pashtun. Yet at no point in his high-profile history has

Sayyaf been characterized as a tribal leader. There may have been specific instances, such as his release from prison in 1978, when he benefited from tribal affiliation. But Sayyaf has always been an Islamist more than a tribesman. His story is an example of how tribal ties and *Pashtunwali* can be interpreted flexibly. It shows that tribal affiliation matters, but it doesn't always matter first.

If tribal interests were the sole determinant of allegiance, then Sayyaf and his fellow Kharoti warlord Gulbuddin Hekmatyar would not have fought each other in the 1990s. His history with the Hazaras is another reminder that, while Pashtun memories are long and grudges are common, they can also be put to bed if it is opportune to do so. Sayyaf's story highlights how fluid allegiances can be in Afghanistan. It is another reminder that pragmatism can take precedence over communism, Islamism, ethnic ties and tribalism. Or as one expert noted, 'Opportunism could always be counted on to undermine any other ism.'[18]

Chapter 35

The Ghurghusti Insurgent: Mullah Dadullah

Ruthlessness ran in this man's blood. He epitomized extremism and was known for beheading disobedient disciples as readily as his enemies. Mullah Dadullah was so vicious that he acquired nicknames such as 'America's New Frankenstein' and 'the Black Mullah' – the latter referring to the darkness in his heart. Even some Taliban colleagues will not have wept when British Special Forces kicked down his door in 2007. He was responsible for some of the most heinous atrocities in modern Afghan history.

It is deeply unfair to Kakar tribesmen to suggest that Mullah Dadullah exemplifies their tribe, for that risks implying that all Ghurghustis are violent. They would certainly prefer to put forward more reputable figures, like the many Kakars who have become noted Islamic theologians, or revered historical figures like Sher Shah Suri, the sixteenth-century commander who created an empire that supplanted the Mughal dynasty in northern India and who is credited with introducing coins called 'rupees'– still the name of many currencies across South Asia today. There are also more contemporary figures who better represent the Kakars, like the singer Dr Mohammad Sadiq Fitrat, better known as 'Nashenas', who remains popular despite most of his original recordings being destroyed by the Taliban in the 1990s.

While Mullah Dadullah was born into their tribe, the Kakars are right to deny that he represents them in any way. His record tarnishes their prestige, and little in his long career of violence seems justifiable, even if the loosest definitions of honour are applied. But his abhorrent activities still merit examination. They highlight the dangers of judging entire tribes by the actions of a few individuals. Dadullah's story also hints at how the Taliban has often been the bane of Pashtuns. It gives the lie to the assumption that the Taliban and the tribes are always allied.

The details of Mullah Dadullah's early years are sketchy. Anything written about him has usually been pieced together from a variety of sources, before being regurgitated and passed on without any checking of facts. Dadullah is most often said to have been born into a Kakar family in Uruzgan province in 1966. He fought for the mujahideen in the 1980s and continued as a combatant during the civil war in the early 1990s, losing a leg after stepping on a landmine – which led to his nickname Mullah Dadullah 'Lang' (the lame).

But the injury did not slow Dadullah down. If anything, it spurred him on. Described as being exceptionally charismatic, he quickly rose to become a member of the Taliban's leadership council after it emerged in 1994, taking charge of customs control in Kandahar.[1] Later in the 1990s, he commanded a brigade of shock troops that led the the brutal repression of non-Pashtuns when the Taliban tried to consolidate their power across Afghanistan. He led the advance into Uzbek and Hazara areas, and was partly responsible for the chaos in Mazar-i-Sharif in August 1998.

Witnesses reported that, for two days *talibs* raced around the city 'killing everything that moved – shop owners, cart pullers, women and children shoppers and even goats and donkeys'.[2] Men from the Shia minority, the Hazaras, were specifically targeted in the genocidal rampage. Conservative estimates say that 2,000 were killed inside 48 hours. In blatant contravention of Islamic practice, the Taliban used loudspeakers to warn people against burying the bodies, leaving them to rot in the summer sun and be gnawed on by wild dogs.[3]

Mazar-i-Sharif was not the only massacre that Dadullah was involved in. The Taliban also besieged the Hazara homeland in Afghanistan's central highlands, known as the Hazarajat. They tried to starve the Shias out by blockading UN food supplies, forcing Harazas to eat grass to avoid starvation.[4] In September 1998 the Taliban broke through Hazara defences and took control of the Hazarajat, even killing two delegations of Hazara elders who offered to negotiate.[5] Three years of Taliban rule followed, with violent suppression at any sign of Hazara resistance. Mullah Dadullah was at the heart of this campaign, and the scorched earth policies he implemented are still regarded as genocide in Hazara eyes. Even some fellow Taliban thought he had gone too far, and he fell out of favour with more moderate Taliban leaders (although he was later reactivated to fight US forces after 9/11).[6]

One of his most infamous deeds in Hazara areas, beside the murder of civilians, was overseeing the Taliban's destruction of the UNESCO-protected Buddhas of Bamiyan in early 2001. These were two sixth-century statues in Bamiyan Province, approximately 130 miles west of Kabul. The statues, 53m and 35m tall, were carved directly out of the sandstone cliff.[7] Even before the Taliban surrounded the Hazarajat in September 1998, there had been talk that they would destroy the statues. When the *talibs* took control of the area, one commander began drilling holes in the Buddhas' heads to place explosives. His efforts were halted by a direct order in July 1999 from Mullah Omar, who decreed that because there was no longer a Buddhist population in Afghanistan, the statues were not worshipped and could be preserved.[8] Even in 2000, local Taliban authorities asked the UN for help in building drainage ditches around the Buddhas, to stop them being damaged by water running off from above.[9]

But something changed in 2001. Not long after Dadullah supervised a massacre of 300 unarmed Hazara men, women and children in Bamiyan Province, the Taliban announced their intention to destroy the Buddhas.[10] In late February 2001 Mullah Omar issued an edict against un-Islamic images, including all ancient sculptures.

A chorus of international condemnation followed. UNESCO convened ambassadors to protest against the move. The three states who officially recognized the Taliban government – Pakistan, Saudi Arabia and the UAE – joined calls to save the statues. India offered to transfer all artefacts and store them 'where they would be kept safely and preserved for all mankind'.[11] China and Japan proposed covering the Buddhas and even offered payments to halt their destruction.[12] The exiled Afghan King, Zahir Shah, made a rare public appearance to denounce the proposed demolition as 'against the national and historic interests of the Afghan people'.[13] The Taliban rejected all offers, even dismissing a Pakistani presidential envoy who travelled to Kabul to argue that the destruction would be un-Islamic.[14] Mullah Omar asked, 'What are you complaining about? We are only waging war on stones.'[15]

Over the next three weeks, the Buddhas were unceremoniously destroyed, with Dadullah supervising the vandalism. It started with an artillery bombardment and the use of anti-aircraft weapons.[16] After many days spent shooting the statues, a Taliban Minister admitted that 'This work of destruction is not as simple as people might think. You can't knock down the statues by shelling as both are carved into a cliff; they are firmly attached to the mountain.'[17]

The *talibs* then turned to anti-tank mines, placing them at the base of the Buddhas, so that falling parts would detonate them. This was equally ineffective, so eventually men were lowered from the cliff above to plant dynamite charges directly into the statues.[18] When they were finally destroyed, the Taliban treated it as a victory. Mullah Omar said that Muslims should be proud, since it was a tribute to Allah.[19] The Taliban's Foreign Minister denied that the destruction was a response to international economic sanctions, arguing that 'We are destroying the statues in accordance with Islamic law and it is purely a religious issue.'[20]

But international outrage did not subside, with many states calling the Taliban's actions a cold and calculated attack on Afghanistan. UNESCO officials branded it a 'crime against culture'.[21] Even Saudi Arabia and the UAE condemned the destruction as savage.[22] The Taliban tried to backtrack, with senior *talibs* attempting to frame the demolition as a consequence of international humanitarian inaction. One spokesman claimed that the decision was taken when foreign experts dishonoured Afghans by rejecting requests for food aid while offering money to fix statues.[23] Mullah Omar offered a similar explanation:

> I did not want to destroy the Bamiyan Buddha. In fact, some foreigners came to me and said they would like to conduct the repair work of the Bamiyan Buddha that had been slightly damaged due to rains. This shocked me. I thought, these callous people have no regard for thousands of living human beings – the Afghans who are dying of hunger, but they are so concerned about non-living objects like the Buddha. This was extremely deplorable. That is why I ordered its destruction. Had they come for humanitarian work, I would have never ordered the Buddhas' destruction.[24]

Blowing up the Buddhas would be one of the last major international outrages committed by the Taliban regime, which collapsed six months later, after 9/11. But it was not the end of Mullah Dadullah. Post-2001 he became internationally notorious for his efforts to purge foreign forces from Afghanistan.

After leading the Taliban's failed defence of Kunduz in the autumn of 2001, Dadullah paid off Northern Alliance warlords and escaped to Pakistan.[25] Over the next six years, when not enjoying sanctuary in Pakistani safe havens, he roamed around Kandahar and other southern areas like a bloodthirsty wolf. He re-established himself as one of the Taliban's most important – and most elusive – operational commanders. He coordinated militant movements, weapons distribution and finances across the entire southern zone. He also left a trail of attacks, kidnappings and assassinations wherever he went. His association with al Qaeda and his campaigns of decapitation are well documented. He is also blamed for introducing suicide bombing to Afghanistan, where this was previously unknown.[26] He was such a thorn in US flesh that he acquired the nickname 'the Taliban's al Zarqawi', after the similar savagery of the No. 1 US enemy in Iraq, Abu Musab al Zarqawi.[27]

But the 'Dark Mullah' did not only operate in the shadows. Dadullah frequently met journalists, even inviting Al-Jazeera reporters to his mountain refuge. In these interviews he would unleash extremist rhetoric that rankled with other senior Talibs, including Mullah Omar himself. He talked of his hordes of suicide bombers who would create a bloodbath and 'turn our motherland into the graveyard of the US forces'.[28] In March 2007 he kidnapped an Italian-Swiss journalist and two Afghan colleagues who were travelling to interview another Taliban commander. Dadullah's men videoed Daniele Mastrogiacomo, his driver Sayed Agha and his colleague Ajmal Naqshbandi kneeling blindfolded in front of armed *talibs*. Agha was then beheaded, before Mastrogiacomo pleaded with the Italian authorities to 'do something'.[29]

Mastrogiacomo was eventually exchanged for five Taliban prisoners. But Dadullah's men beheaded Ajmal Naqshbandi in April 2007 – an action that even repelled fellow *talibs*. It fuelled Dadullah's reputation as a terrorist and a thug, as opposed to an ideologue or any sort of tribesman. It was one of his last acts, since British Special Forces killed him a month later, having acquired intelligence of his whereabouts. There are still rumours that he may have been betrayed by fellow *talibs* who resented his growing personality cult.[30]

A wave of relief swept over Afghanistan when Dadullah's death was announced. The Governor of Kandahar, Asadullah Khalid, presented Dadullah's battered body to journalists on the veranda of his residence, stating that the backbone of the Taliban had been broken.[31] The Taliban retorted that 'The enemies will cry in exchange for slight happiness at the death of Dadullah.'[32]

Mullah Dadullah's story is rarely spoken of in tribal terms. His tribal ties tend to be mentioned only in passing or in discussion of his birthplace. This is a reminder that not everyone born into a tribe fits its stereotype. Dadullah was an anomaly. There is an argument that he embodied the Pashtun ideal of acting in daring, independent and unrelenting opposition to foreign presence. But his actions were rarely, if ever, tied to any tribal interests. Even accounting for some Western or humanitarian bias, it is hard to see Dadullah's deeds as in any way connected to a quest for honour.

Dadullah's career demonstrates that you can identify as Pashtun without obeying tribal codes or being driven by tribal motives. It highlights how adherence to *Pashtunwali* or 'doing Pashtu' does not take precedence in every situation. Nor does Islam. Dadullah, in fact, shows that some people are simply terrorists.

For anyone attempting to better understand the Pashtun tribes and their way of life, Mullah Dadullah's story also exemplifies the difficulty of trying to explain tribal character traits by using single examples or individual men. This risks tarnishing a whole tribe with the reputation of one rotten apple – as Mullah Dadullah does with the Kakar name. But Dadullah's story provides a useful insight into the nexus between the Taliban and the tribes. It demonstrates how the Taliban have tainted traditional tribesmen and distorted foreign perceptions of Pashtuns. It highlights why there is an argument that, despite their relative infancy as an organization, the Taliban have irreparably altered the tribal way of life and hastened the one thing that threatens long-term security in tribal areas – the crumbling of traditional tribal structures.

Chapter 36

The Karlani Warrior-Poet: Khushal Khan Khattak

It must have been bittersweet, stepping out of that dark, dingy fort that the Mughals used as a prison. This was in 1668 – a full decade after he had been unjustly locked away. Anger surely still surged in Khushak Khan Khattak when he thought about the indignity of it all, or when he pictured the Mughal Emperor Aurangzeb – the man he held responsible. Khushal, then in his fifties, was most likely consumed by one thought as he walked out of the prison and into the humid Indian air.

Revenge.

Khushal Khan Khattak is a man mentioned frequently in discussion of Pashtun icons. He was born around 1613 in the Akora area of the Mughal Empire, now in Pakistan's Khyber Pakhtunkhwa province (bordering Afghanistan). His father and grandfather had been chiefs of the Akorkhels, a prominent clan in the Khattak tribe (Karlani branch).[1] Khushal's grandfather had established a cordial relationship with the Mughal rulers, helping to secure the main Mughal transit routes through his tribal territory. The Mughal Emperor Shah Jahan gifted land to Khushal's grandfather as a reward, and this mutually beneficial relationship continued when Khushal's father took over as the Khattak tribal chief.[2]

Khushal's father had been a soldier in the Mughal army and had brought Khushal into skirmishes against the rival Yusufzai tribe when he was a young teenager.[3] His father was killed in one of those clashes in 1641, leaving Khushal as the tribal chief at the age of twenty-eight. He maintained the partnership between the Khattak tribe and Shah Jahan's Mughal Empire until Aurangzeb emerged as Emperor.

Aurangzeb was Shah Jahan's third son and was five years younger than Khushal. He had held various governing positions around the Mughal Empire, although his inauspicious battlefield record had meant that he was unlikely to succeed his father as Emperor.[4] Knowing this, Aurangzeb imprisoned his father and beheaded his brothers, seizing the throne by force in 1658.[5] He initially confirmed Khushal as a *mansabdar* – a high-ranking military official in the Mughal administration. But suspicion soon took hold of the insecure Emperor.

Aurangzeb was wary of powerful *mansabdars* and envious of Khushal's growing popularity, particularly among Pashtuns. In 1658 Aurangzeb ordered Khushal's arrest and imprisoned him in Gwalior Fort, now known as the 'Gibraltar of India' because it sits atop a rocky outcrop overlooking Gwalior city (some 200 miles south of Delhi).[6] His decade in captivity effectively extinguished Khushal's loyalty to the Mughals – especially since he maintained his innocence thoughout, writing that 'I am in Aurangzeb's prison undeservedly. Allah alone knows about these allegations and slander.'[7] Even after his release in 1668, Khushal repeated, 'I had done nothing wrong against the interests of the king or the empire.'[8]

Upon his release, the Mughals permitted Khushal to return to Pashtun areas, and he was even asked to accompany a Mughal expedition to quell a Yusufzai uprising – the tribe his own father had died fighting.[9] But no Mughal olive branches were going to heal wounded Pashtun pride. Khushal had been dishonoured, and that required revenge. He made this clear to the Mughals, stating that 'I served your cause to the best of my honesty, I subdued and killed my own Pashtuns to promote the Empire's interests, but my services and my loyalty did not make me a Mughal.'[10] As he continued to resist them, the Mughals demanded that Khushal decide whether he was friend or foe. It was an easy decision – foe.

Khushal returned to Pashtun territory, where he joined fellow tribesmen in inciting uprisings against Aurangzeb. Many agitators were Khattak, Mohmand, Safi and Afridi tribesmen who had previously been part of the Mughal army. They resented Aurangzeb's abolition of a toll that tribes around the Khyber Pass had relied on. Violence then spiralled when Mughal soldiers molested some Safi women in what is now Afghanistan's Kunar Province – an attack on the *namus* that could not go unchallenged.[11]

When the Safis retaliated, subsequent Mughal reprisals fuelled a much wider Pashtun revolt. Aurangzeb ordered Safi elders to hand over suspects. But the Afridi, Mohmand, Shinwari and Khattaks all united to protect the Safi men accused of *badal*.[12] To reassert imperial authority, the local Mughal governor led a large army to raze the areas around the Khyber Pass. This proved to be another miscalculation. Tribesmen emerged from the hills, surrounding the Mughals and routing them at the narrowest point of the pass. The bloodletting bolstered the tribes, and Mughal authority collapsed in Pashtun areas, humiliating Aurangzeb.[13]

By 1674 Aurangzeb himself had travelled north to personally take charge. Adopting a divide-and-rule approach to the troublesome tribes, he alternated between bribery and force. The Mughals eventually split the rebellious tribes, although they never managed to reassert total authority outside the main trade route. Aurangzeb retreated to Delhi in 1676, agreeing to pay an annual fee to the Pashtun tribes who would be loyal to him.[14]

Khushal Khan Khattak was active in all these events, but the now aging chief was not the warrior he once was, so he focused on rallying tribesmen to rebel rather than doing battle himself. He is remembered as the inspiration for the uprising, rather than the man who actually throttled the Mughals.

By the time the rebellion was suppressed, Khushal was well into his sixties, and his retirement led to a succession scramble among his alleged fifty-seven sons.[15] The Mughals bribed one son, Bahram, to kill or arrest Khushal, but Khushal learned of the plot and fled to the safety of Afridi territory. He died in 1689, leaving instructions that if any of his loyal sons should succeed in detaining their treacherous brother they should bring him to his father's grave, cut him in two and burn one part of him at the head and the other at the foot of the grave.[16]

This grave is in a village back in Khattak territory, because he had asked to be buried in a place where 'the dust of Mughal horses' hooves may not fall on his grave'.[17] Today, many Pashtuns still pay tribute at his tomb, which carries the inscription: 'I have taken up the sword to defend the pride of the Afghan, I am Khushal Khattak, the honourable man of the age.'[18]

Khushal's story is interwoven with many familiar Pashtun threads. It is a reminder that uprisings, rebellions and inter-tribal rivalries are not limited to the modern era. It shows that divide-and-rule tactics, fearless fighting against foreigners and protection of the *namus* are recurring themes of tribal history. Khushal's story also shows how Pashtun allegiances shift quickly, especially if there is a perceived injustice or challenge to honour.

Yet Khushal's incitement of revolt is not what he is most famous for. He is more greatly revered for his literary output. Today, Khushal is renowned as a warrior-poet, with the emphasis on 'poet'. Most historians suggest that Khushal penned over 200 books of poetry and more than 45,000 poems, many while he was a prisoner of the Mughals.[19] Much of his work is patriotic, focusing on motifs such as unity, war and triumphs against invaders. One of his more prominent works is *Dastarnama*, said to be one of the first written accounts of what it means to be a Pashtun. *Dastar* is a word for a turban, which itself is a symbol of Pashtun pride and courage.[20] The *Dastarnama* outlines twenty skills and twenty characteristics of the ideal Pashtun, ranging from bravery and forgiveness to agriculture and the arts – and of course, honour.

Khushal often wrote with a (Pashtun) nationalist tone, admonishing fellow tribesmen for showing divisive tendencies. This did not stop him from excoriating other tribes in one of his most famous poems, entitled 'The Pathans', which is a searing rebuke of the Mughals and any tribe loyal to them:[21]

Of the Pathans that are famed in the land of Roh,

Now-a-days are the Mohmands, the Bangash, and the Warrakzais, and Afridis.

The dogs of the Mohmands are better than the Bangash,

Though the Mohmands themselves are a thousand times worse than
the dogs.

The Warrakzais are the scavengers of the Afridis,

Though the Afridis, one and all, are but scavengers themselves.

This is the truth of the best of the dwellers in the land of Pathans,

Of those worse than these who would say that they were men?

No good qualities are there in the Pathans than are now living:

All that were of any worth are imprisoned in the grave.

This indeed is apparent to all who know them.

He of whom the Moghuls say, 'He is loyal to us',

God forbid the shame of such should be concealed!

Let the Pathans drive all thought of honour from their hearts:

For these are ensnared by the baits the Moghuls have put for them.

Not all of Khushal's writing was political. He also discussed philosophy and ethics. One observer wrote that his 'awareness of the beauties of nature and his love of gardens are typical of the Pashtun character'.[22] His book *Baznama* was on the subject of falconry, while *Tibbnama* was about home medicine. He also published a guide to writing shorthand. His later work, after his incarceration, is infused with bitterness, but his biographers reiterate that 'even in his old age he could write glowingly of the pleasures of good hunting, fine food and beautiful women'.[23] His less than strict interpretation of Islam and his penchant for wine and women have also been noted: 'His glorification of women in his love poems is rare in Pashto literature, for most Pashtuns are far more restrained and reticent in this delicate field than the great poet.'[24]

Today, Khushal's name is never far from Pashtun mouths. A small minority of Pashtuns (usually rival tribes) claim that his initial dalliance with the Mughals makes him a quisling and a traitor. But the vast majority venerate him and celebrate his 'Pashtun-ness'. His short, proverb-like quotations are often used to pad out arguments, and his thought still influences Pashtun ideological and intellectual development – especially his observations about honour:

I despise the man who does not guide his life by honour. The very word 'honour' drives me mad.[25]

The fact that his work is still quoted more than 300 years after his death is testament to his significance. He remains such an icon that a university is named after him in Pakistan, as is the Khushal Khan Khattak Express train. In 2018, a rare manuscript was found and confirmed to be his work, with a date and signature showing that it was completed five months before his death.[26]

Khushal is not the only revered Pashtun poet. Pir Roshan (Ormur tribe of the Karlani branch) was another mouthpiece of Pashtun society who lived in the sixteenth century and who is credited with creating the Pashto alphabet and writing the first Pashto book. He is often called the first Pashtun nationalist. Rahman Baba (Mohmand tribe of the Sarbani branch) was another contemporary of Khushal – he is arguably more popular for his writings which paint Pashtuns as brave and independent, while also insightful and loving. Rahman Baba's mystical verses are so highly regarded that when recited at a *jirga* they are said to be able to calm angry tribesmen and even settle arguments.[27]

There are also modern examples of great Pashtun poets, as each generation tends to have its own favoured artists. But if only one were to be picked to embody Pashtun ideals, then it is Khushal Khan Khattak who would spring to mind. His story still resonates with the tribes. Whether it was the courage to go into battle as a young teenager, the vow of revenge after being imprisoned or his rivalry with other tribes, he lived an idealized Pashtun life. His passionate struggle to repel invaders reverberates throughout Pashtun history, as does his career as a fearless fighter against injustice.

Khushal's story exemplifies the fact that there is much more to Pashtuns than barbarity or battles against the British. There are many 'softer' attributes, such as a love of poetry, literature and nature. The violent side may provide the more entertaining anecdotes and make for the most readable tales, but if it alone is allowed to characterize the tribesmen, it does them a disservice. Khushal Khan Khattak's story is a warning against perpetuating the unbalanced stereotypes that reduce Pashtuns to little more than simple, illiterate warriors or radical Islamist insurgents.

PART X

The Future of the Pashtun Tribes

Chapter 37

The Tribes and the Taliban

The Taliban walked almost unchallenged into Kabul's Presidential Palace in August 2021, their rifle-bearing militants giving a televised interview from the same desk at which President Ashraf Ghani had addressed the nation hours earlier, in his last speech before he fled the country. The symbolism of the backdrop – a large painting depicting Ahmad Shah Durrani's coronation in 1747 – was not lost on other Afghans. The image of this interview will forever be imprinted on the collective Afghan memory. It clearly signalled the Taliban's return to power.

But even though, at the time of writing, the Taliban are in firm control of the Afghan state, they still don't deserve an entire chapter in a book on the Pashtun tribes. To treat them as anything more than a side-issue risks granting them disproportionate importance. The Taliban are a tiny blip on the much wider radar of tribal and Afghan history – they are less than three decades old, while even the most cautious Pashtun origin theories talk of the tribes in terms of centuries and millennia. Compared to the tribes, the Taliban are in their infancy.

Even if the focus is limited to the modern era, the Taliban are just one of many factions, political parties and movements that have influenced Afghanistan. Why does their interaction with the tribes warrant any special attention? The simple answer is that the Taliban must be mentioned because since 9/11 the movement has framed how most outsiders – at least Westerners – view Afghanistan. While the scales of age tip heavily in favour of the tribes, the literature and headlines are decisively tipped in favour of the Taliban. Since 2001, more has been written about the Taliban than has ever been written about the tribes. The world's enemies, protagonists in a raging war and then a movement that toppled an internationally-backed Republic – this has all led to a surge in interest in the Taliban, as foreign spies, civil servants and soldiers have tried to gain an understanding of their adversary.

Yet despite their elevated importance, the Taliban's ties to the tribes are still poorly understood. Ask foreign (or Afghan) experts to answer the question of how tribal the Taliban are, and there will be a noticeable lack of coherent answers. This is partly because Western focus has been on Taliban tactics, techniques and procedures rather than tribal links. But even the more local, better-informed observers struggle to characterize the relationship, because there is no neat way to explain it.

Like the Pashtun tribes, the Taliban is not a homogeneous organization. It is a network of networks. These networks come from different regions, have different grievances, different histories and different motivations for joining the so-called jihad. Each network, and often each commander, has its own individual relationship with the tribes in the area where it operates. In general, the wider Taliban movement is *not* driven by tribal interests, even if some of its individual networks may be. If Taliban networks have any uniting factor, then it is an Islamist ideology, with the Taliban's brand of Islam being anti-modernist above all else.[1]

The confusion arises because the vast majority of Taliban members are Pashtuns. They were born in tribal territories, have tribal affiliations and maintain connections to certain clans – ones they are unlikely to turn their backs on. This presents a difficult dichotomy: how can Taliban members be both tribal and non-tribal at the same time? The answer requires a look at how the Taliban emerged and evolved.

The five phases of the Taliban

In 1898 Winston Churchill wrote of 'a host of wandering Talib-ulims', students who lived free at the expense of the people.[2] Yet only a century later did *talibs* impinge on the wider international consciousness, with 1994 usually cited as the year of the Taliban's formal establishment and introduction to the world.

The exact reasons given for the Taliban's emergence vary, but the broad narrative is that a group of madrassa students (*talibs*) in Kandahar armed themselves and rose up against the corrupt, debauched warlords who were rampaging across the country as the state fragmented in civil war. One story has it that their uprising was a response to an incident in Kandahar when two young girls were abducted by a warlord. The future Taliban leader Mullah Omar then gathered thirty *talibs*, armed with sixteen rifles, to hunt down the perpetrator. They eventually hanged him from the barrel of his own tank, and Mullah Omar was later quoted as saying, 'We were fighting against Muslims who had gone wrong.'[3]

An alternative theory is that the Taliban's first major activities were taking control of the border crossing at Spin Boldak and capturing a nearby arms dump from the rival warlord Gulbuddin Hekmatyar, before marching north to capture Kandahar. This version of events is usually offered by those who argue that the Taliban's genesis is directly tied to Pakistan. The theory is that Pakistan's military and intelligence officials had grown tired of sponsoring Hekmatyar's militants as their Afghan proxy force, due to their poor battlefield performance. Pakistani officials, in the market for a more effective movement with a better chance of becoming Pakistan's client and its 'strategic depth' in Kabul, supposedly pivoted away from Hekmatyar and started backing the upstart Taliban.[4]

Regardless of what happened in 1994, a deeper analysis traces the Taliban's roots back as far as the 1970s and 1980s, when many madrassa students joined the mujahideen. They mostly joined in groups linked to one specific madrassa, mosque or refugee camp – which became known as *talib* 'fronts'. After Soviet forces withdrew and the communist government collapsed in 1992, many of these *talib* fronts returned to their madrassas, content that the godless infidels had been defeated and believing that the mujahideen would now build an Islamic state. What happened instead was that the mujahideen turned on each other, and faction-fighting crippled efforts to form a post-communist government. Civil war erupted, and warlordism surged across the country. The *talib*s, back in their madrassas, grew angry that their Islamic state had not materialized. They felt that the mujahideen had broken their promise and so decided to remobilize and avenge the perceived betrayal of Islam. Thus the Taliban movement was born.

What these origin stories make clear is that the Taliban did not emerge as a result of any specific ethnic or tribal dynamics, or to protect any tribal interests. The *talib*s were Pashtuns, but the Taliban was not formed to represent all Pashtuns or to be 'by Pashtuns for Pashtuns'. Even as the movement repeatedly reinvented itself over the years, it kept a supra-tribal, Islamist orientation. Some analysts divide its development into four phases:

1) The Mujahideen Phase (1979–94), when various fronts made up of religious students and refugees integrated into the mujahideen, but did not form their own movement.
2) The Revolutionary Phase (1994–6), when individual *talib* fronts merged into one movement, then taking territory and capturing Kabul by 1996.
3) The Emirate Phase (1996–2001), when the popular uprising morphed into a de facto government, ruling most Afghan territory as the Islamic Emirate of Afghanistan.
4) The Insurgency Phase (post-2001), when the Taliban fled and transformed itself into an insurgency. Some leading scholars have dubbed this the 'Neo-Taliban'.

The *talib*s arguably entered a fifth phase in the 2010s, when they shaped themselves into a parallel government and even provided services like giving mining contracts or adjudicating in disputes in territory that they held (including non-Pashtun areas). A sixth phase may be said to have emerged when the Taliban started to engage in peace talks with the US and the Afghan government in the late 2010s. A final new phase undoubtedly began when the Taliban took Kabul in 2021, as the last US/NATO troops were leaving the country.

What these evolutions show is that tribalism has never been the Taliban's *raison d'être*. The Taliban leadership consistently claims to consist of supra-tribal and supra-ethnic Islamists who recruit regardless of tribal, ethnic and linguistic differences.[5] But this does not mean that *talibs* turn their back on the tribes. Like all Pashtuns, each fighter will know his particular place in the tribal structure and can recite which clan or *qawm* he was born into. All of them are aware of *Pashtunwali's* requirements and are unlikely to completely dismiss them. To enable fighters to balance their tribal backgrounds with an Islamist outlook, the Taliban leadership has shaped a dualistic structure, as explained by long-time Afghanistan expert Thomas Ruttig:

> Today's Taleban movement is dualistic in nature, both structurally and ideologically. The aspects are interdependent: A vertical organizational structure, in the form of a centralised 'shadow state', reflects its supra-tribal and supra-ethnic Islamist ideology, which appears to be 'nationalistic' – i.e., it refers to Afghanistan as a nation – at times. At the same time, the movement is characterised by horizontal, network-like structures that reflect its strong roots in the segmented Pashtun tribal society. Religious, tribal and regional components overlap even when it comes to the organizational principles of the Taleban.[6]

This overlapping structure enables the Taliban to maintain cohesion among its varied networks. With such organizational elasticity, individual commanders have the autonomy to adapt to the local conditions in which they operate, while still coming under the overarching ideological umbrella.[7] They can selectively employ or even abuse tribal connections and *Pashtunwali*. When it suits, they will couch their jihad in terms of Pashtun independence and resistance to foreign incursion. This fluidity is important, because tribal connections matter much more at the local than the national level. Individual Taliban networks and commanders must navigate local tribal issues much more carefully than the Taliban's leadership is obliged to, because their local activities, including recruitment, depend on the type of engagement they have with the local tribes. This is also why the Taliban's approach in urban areas often varies from that in rural regions – they tend to take a stricter approach to the supposedly sinful cities, while remaining more hands-off in the traditionalist countryside.

Put simply, the Taliban tend to be deeply rooted in their tribal societies as individuals, but much less so as a broader movement. They collectively identify primarily as Islamists, but tribal identity still matters to individual *talibs*. They use it to navigate the tribal arena – although this does not always manifest in a positive partnership with the tribes.

Tribal elders targeted by the Taliban

While there are examples of the Taliban negotiating buy-in from tribal elders, there are as many examples of their clashing with the tribes. One story from 2010 encapsulates how tribal elders, and thus tribal institutions, have often become victims of the Taliban.

The story centres on the Noorzai tribe in the Nad-e-Ali district of Helmand Province, a Taliban hotspot that saw many battles with British forces after 2001. Abdul Ahad Helmandwal, then in his early fifties, was a Noorzai tribal elder whose wisdom and *mashartoob* (seniority) were well-respected, as he had been an elder since his father was blown up by a Soviet mine in the 1980s.[8] But things started to change when the Taliban seeped into the area and Abdul Ahad and other tribal elders began to lose control.

To assert their authority, the Taliban started targeting tribal elders. If elders would not willingly submit to Taliban rule, they were forcibly removed, and sometimes assassinated. This posed an obvious danger to Abdul Ahad, but it also affected local tribal solidarity. Some tribesmen wanted to partner with the government and coalition forces, while others saw value in siding with the Taliban. This divided the tribes and eroded the traditional social order. Tribes started to fragment as younger men in particular were lured by the Taliban's promises of money, battlefield glory or opportunities to exact revenge for grievances.

This created a Catch-22 situation for Abdul Ahad and other elders. Siding with the Taliban meant risking the drones and night raids of government and foreign forces. But being seen to be against the Taliban – even attempting to foster some form of peace and stability – would lead to reprisals by the insurgents. Doing nothing was equally risky; it would equate to capitulation and dereliction of the elders' traditional duty of protecting the tribe and defending its honour.

Abdul Ahad was not alone in this predicament. Being caught between the Taliban, the tribe and the Afghan government is a situation many elders have faced since 2001. This trap is partly why security in Afghanistan deteriorated to the point of total collapse by 2021. Tribal leadership has always been subject to competition, but the tribal system generally provides an element of stability and resilience in times of turmoil and in the absence of state authority. It always was the 'arena in which political competition takes place',[9] rather than the object of direct attacks. This has changed over the past fifty years.

Abdul Ahad's story exemplifies how recent conflicts have damaged traditional social dynamics. It shows that when elders lose influence and when tribal systems fail to function, instability ensues – and organizations like the Taliban thrive. This is why the Taliban, despite being a relative newcomer compared to the tribes, cannot simply be treated as a side-issue. They represent a dynamic that will continually challenge Afghanistan's stability, and even threatens the future of the Pashtun tribes – the crumbling of traditional tribal structures.

Chapter 38

The Crumbling of Pashtun Tribal Structures

Pashtuns say that 'those who tie a turban are thousands, but those who understand its responsibility are only a few'. The question is, are they becoming fewer?

There now exists a theory that the world's largest tribal society is becoming increasingly detribalized because traditional tribal structures are crumbling. Its proponents cite multiple causes, some of which are as simple and inescapable as urbanization. Today, many Pashtuns who have lived for generations in multi-ethnic cities no longer speak Pashto as their first language; nor do they abide by honour codes as strictly as their rural compatriots. The argument is that urbanization separates families from traditional homelands, reducing their immersion in Pashtun culture, institutions and philosophical foundations. It dilutes tribal identity.

Recent population growth is a primary driver of urbanization (and emigration). An expanding population poses particular challenges when it comes to land. Whereas previous generations shared large plots of agricultural land among relatively few people, those plots are now becoming progressively smaller and are being shared among growing families – encouraging more migration to the cities. An expanding population can also undermine tribal traditions. As a tribe expands – numerically and geographically – *jirgas* become difficult to organize, especially those in which every tribesman participates. Even if all tribesmen could attend, various segments of the tribe would most likely struggle to stay focused on wider tribal interests and instead work to further their own clan's priorities.[1] An example of this was the 2005 parliamentary election, when Noorzai leaders convened tribal *jirgas* to pick candidates on whom the wider tribe would concentrate their votes. But since the tribe was so large and widespread, no candidate received backing from all of its members. Multiple Noorzai candidates ended up running against each other – and losing in places where concentrated votes could have won. The result was that at Afghanistan's first post-2001 parliamentary election, which established a new countrywide balance of power, Noorzais ended up – once again – under-represented in state institutions.[2]

217

The spread of modern communications is another unavoidable challenge to traditional tribalism. Whether through radio, television or the internet, the late twentieth-century Pashtun consciousness of the wider world increased markedly. With it came awareness of radical political and economic ideas, whose introduction into the tribal arena 'could hardly help but bring a whiff of the winds of change into the most remote villages in the hills'.[3] Pashtuns themselves say that alien concepts, such as materialism, have been injected into the Pashtun value system. Purdah, in particular, was challenged as women began 'to educate themselves and to ask whether their lives can be made a little bit easier'.[4]

All of these things have contributed to the destabilizing of traditional tribal structures over the past fifty years. But seldom is any of them cited as the primary reason. Most arguments tend to point to one factor above all else – conflict.

Conflict as the primary cause of tribal breakdown

The phenomenon of tribal decay is rarely discussed without it being tied to the Soviet-Afghan war or the 1973 coup, when King Zahir Shah's overthrow brought the Third Durrani Dynasty to an end. The subsequent political turmoil, Soviet invasion, multi-generational conflict and state collapse systematically eroded the traditional social order and political dynamics of Pashtun – and wider Afghan – society.[5]

The most obvious impact on the tribes was the number of deaths. The scale of casualties during the Soviet-Afghan war was staggering. For every Soviet killed, sixty Afghans died. Between 1978 and 1987 there were 876,825 unnatural deaths in Afghanistan – an average of 240 per day for an entire decade. With the fiercest fighting concentrated in the Pashtun Belt, the tribes suffered more than most, and tribal structures were inevitably eroded as a result.[6]

Tribal leadership was hit particularly hard. Tribal elders lost influence because, in the fog of war, wisdom and consensus were less in demand than fighting ability. Power shifted from dispute-settling whitebeards to jihadi commanders who could provide security, i.e. raise militias and manage armed groups.[7] These strongmen, often backed by external actors like the Soviets, Pakistan or the US, also filled the leadership vacuum left when state institutions lost control of rural areas. Pakistan was particularly culpable, as its desire to establish an indirect hegemony over Afghanistan is said to have fuelled its deliberate attempts to fragment Pashtun tribal power and undermine Afghanistan's nationalist leaders, by sponsoring pro-Pakistan, Islamist ideologues instead.[8]

The emergence of this 'commander cult' in the 1980s enabled dynamic individuals to consolidate power and resources at the expense of the collective authority of the tribes. Foreign backing meant that resource-rich warlords could then circumvent or ignore a *jirga*'s decisions – something that would have sparked retribution in the previously intact tribal society. Rather than providing security, it fuelled instability. Afghanistan still suffers from these dynamics because, unlike tribal elders, strongmen are not inclined to revert to traditional forms of leadership once conflict subsides. War is a business model they are unwilling to relinquish.

The mass migration sparked by Afghanistan's recent conflicts is also blamed for the decay of the tribal system. As fighting gripped Afghanistan in the 1980s, millions of Pashtuns left the country, mostly for refugee camps in Pakistan. At the height of the conflict more than six million Afghans fled, with millions more becoming internally displaced.[9] Repercussions on *qawm*, village and family networks were inevitable. Nomadic clans were forced to become sedentary, while influential landowning clans lost their land. The diversity of the refugee camps damaged the traditional tribal social order, as families from all tribes and ethnicities were thrown together. No longer was there the safety of a specific *manteqa* guarded by *arbaki* and *lashkars* made up of a tribe's kinsmen. No longer being in a Pashtun-only environment meant that *Pashtunwali* lost some of its authority. *Melmastia* became restricted only to small neighbourhoods and familiar acquaintances. Purdah became more stringent and shrank women's physical space. Camp life changed how men protected their *namus*.

New forms of social organization in the camps were particularly detrimental to traditional tribalism. As tribal leaders and other able-bodied men fought – and died – back in Afghanistan, a new type of elite became powerful in refugee communities. Mullahs, who had previously been kept outside the tribal system, acquired power because religion was a rallying point for Pashtun communities while outside their homelands. Religious organizations also had a hand in running the camps – meaning the mullahs controlled the resources. Exploiting their new influence, mullahs promoted stricter interpretations of Islam, including the concept of the *umma*, i.e. belonging to the wider Muslim community rather than identifying as part of a tribe or clan. They used the power of the mosque to eclipse tribal elders, khans and *maliks*.[10]

None of this damage was undone by the Soviet withdrawal in 1989 or the collapse of the communist regime three years later. Throughout the 1990s, civil war and new phases of conflict kept Pashtuns in refugee camps and continued to expose them to non-traditional world views, cultures and languages, which of course changed perceptions of tribal traditions and Pashtun life. The Taliban's rise only cemented the shift away from traditional forms of tribal leadership and towards Islamists, warlords and ethnic entrepreneurs. Many *talibs* had grown up in the refugee camps, meaning that even when they tried to respect tribal customs and traditional village values, they often adopted 'the values of the village as interpreted by refugee camp dwellers or madrassa students who typically had not known normal village life'.[11]

But everything changed in 2001. Or at least, everything might have changed. The ousting of the Taliban regime was an opportunity to undo some of the damage and revert to traditional tribalism. Yet it was an opportunity lost, because the post-2001 Kabul government and its international backers supported programmes to strengthen the central state rather than initiatives to re-establish tribal cohesion. Warlords continued to be backed in short-term efforts to secure certain territories, enabling them to reassert their influence in the new political order. This failure to empower the tribes, in favour of a state-building project, undermined tribal forces and deprived them of funding. It left them isolated and ill-equipped to fend off a resurgent Taliban.[12] Even programmes that tried to work with the tribes, like those aimed at raising *arbaki*, often failed because they were tied to the central government and reliant on state funding; they were perceived as initiatives created to satisfy international aims rather strengthen tribal authority.

Some ardent Pashtun nationalists even believe that the post-2001 decay of tribal systems was the result of a deliberate policy. Despite being headed by a Pashtun president (Hamid Karzai), many of the new state institutions – particularly the security forces and security ministries – were controlled by non-Pashtuns of the Northern Alliance who had helped US forces oust the Taliban. The dominance of the Tajik minority stoked Pashtun memories of 1929, when the Tajik rebel Habibullah Kalakani seized the throne. It fostered feelings of alienation among Pashtuns, as inter-ethnic vendettas were played out under the unwitting eye of the international coalition. For tribal traditionalists it was a lose-lose situation: they did not trust the mainly non-Pashtun security forces to protect them, but the only other options were to support strongmen-led militias or gravitate towards the Taliban – both of which were courses of action which inevitably undermined tribal norms. The emergence of a narrative about crumbling tribal structures was now inescapable.

A counter-argument to the 'crumbling' narrative?

The idea that tribal decay started with the 1973 coup and continued through subsequent conflicts is problematic, since it assumes that before then, the tribal system was fully intact and operating as it had done in previous centuries. It assumes that *Pashtunwali*, tribal territories and other customs had remained static since they first arose, i.e. had always been present in their traditional or idealized form. That assumption is incorrect. Tribalism has been repeatedly challenged throughout recorded history – as many incidents mentioned in this book exemplify.[13]

The Iron Emir's reign is one example. Abdur Rahman Khan's resettlement of tribes to northern Afghanistan or the imposition of the Durand Line are obvious developments that could be used to support the claim that there was change to tribal systems long before the 1970s – although some argue that the Durand Line actually strengthened tribalism by freeing the tribes in Afghanistan from British authority, enhancing their autonomy and keeping customary laws intact.[14]

A better example of Abdur Rahman's challenge to the tribes was his effort to centralize authority in Kabul. His reign saw the position of emir change from the head of a tribal confederation to a state authority based on Islam. His idea was that if he presented himself as a Muslim ruler he would be able to foster national unity, supersede local or tribal authorities and create one centre of power in Kabul.[15] By reforming the Afghan army and implementing conscription, he also reduced Kabul's dependency on the tribes for military support. He tried to weaken the influence of tribal *jirgas* by forming a 'National Council' and handpicking tribal elders to participate, thus isolating them from their local powerbases and changing their role from decision-makers to advisers.[16] These efforts to centralize power were clearly aimed at making the tribes dependent on the state and not vice versa.They highlight the fact that traditional tribal ways were being challenged long before the 1970s.

Nor was Abdur Rahman's reign an anomaly. Today, the Pashtun tribes are said to be in 'a state of decay under the onslaught of modernism'.[17]The man best known for modernizing Afghanistan was Amanullah Khan, who ruled from 1919 to 1929 and was constantly accused of assailing tribalism. Amanullah sought to derive his authority from the Afghan nation rather than from Islam or the tribes. He was the first Afghan leader to measure his legitimacy in terms of public acceptance rather than tribal politics or Islam.[18] His modern policies, including secular justice and education, offended traditionalists. Educational reforms challenged the informal religious education led by mullahs, who then spread dissent and stoked fears about the supposed end of tribal independence and traditions.[19] Amanullah's conscription laws caused uproar, too, as he stopped tribal elders choosing which of their kin served in the state forces, effectively making military service a lottery rather than a tribal choice.[20]

Amanullah's liberal reforms for women caused the most fury. Among other things, he banned child marriage and levirate marriage, both common tribal practices. His tenure also saw a reduction in the wearing of veils and the spread of Western dress, trends driven by his wife, Queen Soraya. To tribesmen, the reforms represented a stripping of their authority over their womenfolk. It was seen as state interference in domestic affairs, a deliberate attack on both *Pashtunwali* and Islam, and the destruction of their ability to protect their *namus*. His changes were roundly criticized, even though many of his social reforms did not spread outside Kabul and only reached rural areas by way of rumour.[21] Yet they still fuelled a sense of Pashtun alienation. They looked like deliberate detribalization. Instead of ushering in a new era of progress, Amanullah's actions actually poisoned the term 'reform' for future generations.

Both Abdur Rahman and Amanullah are now reminders of how not to navigate the tribal minefield. They are also a reminder that the perceived crumbling of traditional tribal structures is not only a mujahideen-era or twenty-first-century phenomenon.

Erosion or evolution?

Three themes consistently reappear when looking at this supposed crumbling of tribalism. First, tribal decay did not start in the 1970s and is not just a product of recent conflicts. The past fifty years may have intensified the supposed erosion, but such dynamics are not new – as the examples of the Iron Emir and Amanullah Khan show. The Pashtun way of life has in fact been continually challenged, and it is likely that the weakening of the tribal system is a narrative common to every generation. Like other social groups, Pashtuns are probably affected by what psychologists know as 'nostalgic preference patterns' or 'declinism' – where the past is viewed through rose-coloured spectacles.

The perception of tribal decay might even be the result of current conditions being compared with a time when Pashtuns were, without doubt, the leading political and social actors in Afghanistan, i.e. in 1747, when Ahmad Shah Durrani first brought all Pashtuns under the control of one political centre.[22] That period is romanticized as the time when Pashtun tribes were the backbone of the new Afghan state and received preferential treatment over other ethnic groups. If that era is the benchmark against which all others are judged, then claims about the erosion of tribalism are inevitable.

A second recurring theme suggests that, rather than eroding, tribal institutions may be better described as *evolving*. Of course, some traditional ways of life have not remained in place – this is true of any society. But overall, Pashtuns have preserved their way of life in the face of reforms, new actors or new ideologies. Even if recent conflicts have intensified change and damaged tribal traditions, tribalism has adapted rather than disappear. This points to an important conclusion. While often written about as a way of behaving, Pashtun tribalism may be better described as a way of thinking. Rather than a strict and well-defined set of rules that dictates tribal habits, it might be better understood as an instinctive mentality. This would explain why the concept of the tribe still sustains the Pashtun identity, even if traditions have faded or tribal territories have changed. What it means to be a Pashtun is still very much alive in the tribes' psyche. It still shapes how Pashtuns see themselves. No matter how their environment changes, honour still remains the primary driver of Pashtun thinking.

A third identifiable theme is one that is relevant to any discussion of the future of the Pashtun tribes in Afghanistan. It is the constant competition of tribe versus state. This book has shown how efforts to strengthen the central state – no matter which movement, faction or grouping is in control – generally mean stripping governing responsibilities from the tribes, which challenges their autonomy and is seen as an attack on their independence.[23] The state is essentially an alternative to the tribe and therefore threatens its existence – especially when it comes to state-led social change. This helps explain why post-2001, state-building efforts were not always well received in rural Pashtun areas. History has shown that as long as there is a centralized Afghan state, there will be struggle with the tribes, and hence a narrative about the crumbling of traditional tribal structures.

This tribe-versus-state dynamic also raises thought-provoking questions. If the state is the main challenger to the tribal way of life, then did tribal decay actually begin when the modern state was created in 1747? Was Ahmad Shah Durrani's coronation, which represented the pinnacle of Pashtun superiority in Afghanistan, in fact the starting point for the crumbling of the Pashtun tribes?

Chapter 39[1]

The Future of the Pashtun Tribes

'Two watermelons cannot be held in one hand.' This Pashto proverb summarizes the outlook for the Pashtun tribes. It reflects a recurring theme in this book – that traditional tribalism and the modern central state are on an unavoidable collision course. But rather than a head-on collision, they have, since the formation of the modern Afghan state, constantly rubbed up against one another, with intermittent periods of intensified friction usually damaging one or the other.

These dynamics are unlikely to change in the foreseeable future, because both sides have proved so resilient. The state has always been reconstituted – often with international investment – whenever it has collapsed. The tribes have also been reshaped by interactions with the outside world and continue to be tested by the Taliban and other conflict dynamics. But until now, Pashtun values have withstood change and the influx of new ideas. They are extremely resilient, especially when viewed over the long term. An enduring tribal identity still provides the framework for daily life – in mindset if not always in practice.

The result is that, for all the talk of external interference in the 'Graveyard of Empires', the central state will continue to constitute the existential challenge to the Pashtun tribes – regardless of who controls it. The pattern in which strengthening one means weakening the other is also likely to continue – because the two watermelons cannot be held comfortably in one hand.

This state-versus-tribe dynamic suggests that the almost unending search for stability in Afghanistan will require more than a peace agreement between warring factions or an all-out victory by one side. A peace deal or a military victory might minimize violence, but neither will fully stabilize Afghanistan, because they will not stop Pashtun tribes (or other ethnic groups) opposing or competing for control of the state institutions. At best, they may create an interlude of calm in an otherwise ongoing, multi-century struggle.

Yet the aim of this book has not been to provide prescriptions for dealing with Afghanistan's current predicament. It has deliberately steered clear of too much contemporary political analysis, and instead explored the important undercurrents and often overlooked drivers of present-day dynamics. Nor has the aim been to chart a way forward for the tribes. Rather than speculate about the future *of* the Pashtun tribes, this book is focused more on our future *with* the Pashtun tribes. The overarching intention is to help ameliorate future international engagements with Pashtuns and other Afghans, by providing an up-to-date, readable resource that goes beyond simple, superficial observations and adds depth to the snippets of common knowledge about the tribes.

Three themes have become particularly clear in trying to compile such a resource. First, that it is a mistake to treat the tribes as 'one'; second, that there is a need to understand them in the way that they understand themselves – particularly with respect to their own concept of honour; third, that the long-held stereotypes about tribesmen may not be entirely unjustified, but they are unbalanced.

The mistake of treating the tribes as 'one'

This book's clearest theme is that the Pashtun tribes are not 'one'. Thinking of the Pashtun tribes as a single bloc is a fallacy. Treating them as such is even more misguided. Shared ethnicity does not equate to unity, cohesion or a common outlook.[2] In fact, internal divisions should be seen as a core aspect of the Pashtun identity.

A better understanding of the divisions within the tribes will help to refine future international engagement with them. It will enhance our ability to understand and appreciate why certain actors think and act as they do. It will help us to read the subtext of what Afghans are telling us, and better grasp all of the shifting allegiances and subtle layers which form around people or historical incidents. While there may be new flags, new ideologies and new external backers, Afghanistan sees many of the same tribal rivalries still playing out on the same arenas and battlefields as in previous centuries. Understanding these dynamics – and what underpins them – will improve our ability to build constructive relations with Pashtuns. It will also better our ability to understand not just *what* happens in Afghanistan but *why* it is happening and what will happen next.

This is not to argue that all foreigners must spend years immersing themselves in tribal culture or become leading historians before engaging with Pashtuns or other Afghans. In fact, one of the most important realizations is that no Westerner can ever claim to have anything other than a partial understanding of the Pashtun tribes or other Afghan dynamics. Being an 'expert' simply means having more granular knowledge than others. As this book makes clear, Afghanistan always presents another layer, a counter-argument or an alternative example. No matter how many years you spend in-country, how well-read you are or how attuned to Afghan atmospherics, there will always be differences between the Western and Pashtun perspectives. This underlines the second recurring theme of this book: the importance of understanding the tribes as they understand themselves.

Understand the tribes as they understand themselves

'Difficult to understand and even harder to navigate' was a sentence used early in this book to describe the Pashtun tribes. Having probed the many paradoxes and complexities of Pashtun life, it should now be clearer why this is so. But what should also be appreciated is that Western strategic narcissism is a self-imposed obstacle to understanding and engaging with the tribes. This is the Western tendency to define the Afghan context only in relation to ourselves. We then assume that what we decide to do or not do in Afghanistan will be decisive in achieving a favourable outcome. Today, this might be partly explained as a hangover from the early years after 9/11, when the US and the wider Western coalition did determine the shape of the new state and heavily influenced other aspects of Afghan life. But it is not just a modern affliction. It is a mistake that has hampered every external actor from Alexander the Great to US/NATO Generals – and will probably afflict the diplomats of tomorrow as well. Afghanistan has become the Graveyard of Empires in part because external actors routinely dismiss the degree to which the country's inhabitants – including the Pashtun tribes – have agency, influence and authorship over Afghanistan's future.

This book has made clear that what happens to the tribes affects the entire country. It has shown how Pashtun tribal power has been the predominant political force in Afghanistan's modern history, and how it will shape Afghanistan's future, regardless of any international decisions. This underscores the importance of building more constructive relationships with Pashtuns and other Afghans, and these will be easier to build if a less narcissistic approach is adopted. Such an approach requires understanding of the Pashtun tribes as they understand themselves. It requires cultural relativism.

The necessity of employing a stance characterized by cultural relativism – judging people against the criteria of their own culture, not those of another – is particularly important when it comes to the value that, above all else, continues to frame Pashtun thinking and behaviour – honour. Many historical turning points have centred on perceived affronts to Pashtun honour, and an appreciation of the differences between Pashtun and Western concepts of honour could have avoided them. To improve future engagement with Pashtuns, they should always be approached with honour in mind – the Pashtun concept of honour.

Be wary of unbalanced stereotypes

This book ends as it started – by noting the negative stereotypes of Pashtun tribesmen as primitive, violent barbarians or fanatical semi-savages. These stereotypes can usually be traced to the biased generalizations that accompanied nineteenth-century British expeditions to the Frontier – and the various Pashtun insurgencies that (often understandably) flared in response.

Yet this book has also raised questions about whether the British should solely be blamed for these caricatures. Pashtuns have been negatively stereotyped for centuries, perhaps for millennia – the attitude is evident as far back as the time of Alexander the Great. Pashtuns themselves have arguably reinforced the stereotypes rather than offer convincing counter-narratives. Even a quick scan of their folklore and classical poets, including Khushal Khan Khattak, reveals a self-image built around courageous, confident and unforgiving warriors who will gladly sacrifice life for liberty and who devote themselves to destroying invaders. More extensive research into this topic would show that there are other perpetrators of the stereotypes, too, close to the Pashtun homeland. Pakistan's approach to Pashtun tribes in its border areas is often said to be colonialist and thus to perpetuate negative stereotyping. Recent writing on Afghanistan is also guilty of following this trend, turning descriptions of bloodthirsty barbarians into portrayals of militant sympathizers or fundamentalist extremists. These negative stereotypes are clearly cumulative.

This book did not set out on a deliberate quest to refute, debunk or even determine the origin of the stereotypes. It has been an exploration of the stereotypes, and an attempt to ascertain whether Pashtuns have been unfairly saddled with them. Many examples used in this book to explain the character of the tribes in fact do little to disprove them. Multiple incidents from Pashtun history make the negative stereotypes seem understandable, and legitimate. Even today, Afghanistan contains people and traditions that would not seem out of place in Ahmad Shah Durrani's time, or earlier. Some Pashtun customs and social values are undeniably incompatible with modern, internationally-agreed principles of human rights and equality. Rather than dispelling the stereotypes, a better question to ask is, 'Have Pashtun tribes been condemned in too sweeping terms?'

This journey into Pashtun life has shown that, while not completely incorrect, the negative stereotypes do not present a full picture. They are unbalanced. There is much more to Pashtuns than the stereotypes suggest. Important principles of Pashtun life such as peace, conciliation and protection of guests are often overlooked or misunderstood. Recognizing the Western tendency to focus only on the worst tribal tendencies, one of this book's aims has been to explore these 'softer' attributes. The intention has been to write about tribal characteristics such as courtesy, generosity or affection. The importance of friendship explains the Pashtun psyche as much as battles or barbarity do. The same can be said of folklore, fables and poetry, the latter being a field in which Pashtuns excel but which is overshadowed by the negative stereotypes – who would think to find such accomplished poetry and prose in a society of supposedly illiterate warriors?[3]

Yet if there is any way in which this book falls short, it is in the comparatively little attention devoted to 'softer' aspects of the Pashtun character. It can be accused of over-representing the worst aspects of *Pashtunwali* or perpetuating some of the tropes it set out to avoid. There is the coverage of *melmastia* and an indication of gentler qualities in the chapter on proverbs. There is also some insight into the Pashtun penchant for poetry in Khushal Khan Khattak's story. But in general, this book tends to neglect the softer tribal characteristics in favour of their more hawkish attributes.

This is an important lesson in itself, and it is one that should shape future engagements with Pashtuns. It reflects the fact that a 'trap' exists when talking about the tribes – one easy to fall into even if watching out for it. Westerners are naturally drawn to the most salacious stories and vivid anecdotes. Violence and revenge are intriguing and make the most readable examples of tribal tendencies – and these tend to dominate even the best English-language accounts as a result. Gentler traits are harder to depict than grievances and vendettas, especially in a male-dominated society where examples of love are less openly available than stories of anger. Being constantly reinforced any time the tribes are written about helps to explain why the negative stereotypes are so enduring.

In future, a more balanced view of Pashtun life could be obtained by focusing as much on the family as on tribal dynamics. It is inevitable that the history and characteristics of large tribes or even leading individuals will be dominated by collective action in key battles or in angry reactions to geopolitical events – as this book has shown. But the *Kor*, the Pashtun household, is where to gain a more accurate insight into folklore, funerals and friendship, or changing features such as dialect, decision-making, even detribalization. It is also where to find more stories about the Pashtun women, who have often been absent from, or not recorded in, wider community or national events.

Understanding the ordinary Pashtun family is one way for observers to avoid the stereotyping trap. Until we can start avoiding this, our engagements with Pashtuns will continue to be shaped by the unbalanced, and even insulting, animal-like stereotypes that the tribes have often been saddled with.

Building relationships with the Pashtun tribes in Afghanistan requires a much different mindset.

Appendix A

The Pashtun Tribal Reading List

The following is a list of books, and one or two journal articles, which focus specifically on the Pashtun tribes. More general books about Afghanistan are deliberately omitted, even if they contain sections that discuss tribal issues. The list is not exhaustive but includes a range of books that will provide as comprehensive a coverage as is available in English.

Nineteenth Century

An Account of the Kingdom of Caubul by Mountstuart Elphinstone (1819). Still seen as a definitive opus on the Pashtuns despite being written over 200 years ago. Some parts are dated, and the language is of its era, but it is still a must-read for anyone wanting an insight into the tribes.

The Races of Afghanistan by Surgeon-Major Bellew W. Bellew (1880). Easier to follow than other writers of the same era, Bellew describes the characteristics of certain tribes well, although he is as guilty as anyone of fuelling the narrative of Pashtuns as barbaric savages.

Twentieth Century

Notes on Nomad Tribes of Eastern Afghanistan by Captain J.A. Robinson (1934). A definitive book on the Kuchis and their practices although it feels dated, as nomadic lifestyles have changed since its publication. The book also provides graphic outlines of the structures of multiple tribes, but only those with nomadic tendencies.

The Pathans by Sir Olaf Caroe (1958). Universally cited as an authoritative book, but not an easy read or very accessible to the lay person. It requires some existing knowledge of Afghanistan and Pakistan. Caroe was a senior British diplomat, so there is some British bias, although less than in other texts. The book contains some of the best maps and genealogical diagrams of any published work.

'Pathan Identity and its Maintenance' by Fredrick Barth (1959). This is a single chapter in Barth's book *Ethnic Groups and Boundaries* but it is widely quoted by subsequent works on the Pashtuns. It is one of many pieces by Barth on Pashtuns that are worth reading.

The Way of the Pathans by James W. Spain (1962). An enjoyable read in which Spain mixes general detail about the tribes with anecdotes from his time as a US diplomat in Pakistan. It focuses on tribes in Pakistan rather than Afghanistan.

Social and Economic Change in the Tribal Areas by Akbar S. Ahmed (1977). An easy-to-digest book that starts with general Pashtun principles, before detailing economic aspects of tribal life. It focuses on tribes in Pakistan but is still valuable for those studying Afghanistan.

The Warrior Race by Imran Khan (1993). A coffee-table photobook more than an in-depth study of Pashtun culture. It focuses solely on the tribes in Pakistan. Very easy to read and a useful gateway book as it identifies and introduces key topics related to the tribes.

Twenty-first Century

Fire in Afghanistan 1914–1929: The First Opening to the West Undone by Tribal Ferocity Years before the Taliban by Rhea Talley Stewart (2000). This book seems largely unknown and is never mentioned in discussion of 'must-reads'. But it should be read. It is a meticulously detailed decription of Amanullah Khan's reign – and all of the ramifications of his reforms, especially in relation to the Pashtun tribes. It is packed with entertaining descriptions of events, related almost as if the author had experienced them herself. They illuminate how *and why* there was so much tribal revulsion against Amanullah's efforts.

Rohi Mataluna: Pashto Proverbs (Revised and Expanded Edition) by Mohammad Nawaz Tair and Thomas Edwards (2006). As definitive a collection of translated Pashto proverbs as exists. It includes a useful introduction, written by the book's editors Leonard Bartlotti and Raj Wali Shah Khattak, explaining why proverbs are so important to Pashtuns.

'Tribal Law of Pashtunwali and Women's Legislative Authority' by Palwasha Kakar (2006). An expertly written, well-researched journal article (*Harvard Islamic Legal*

Studies Program) that is one of the rare texts specifically on Pashtun women, despite the wealth of post-2001 literature on the oppression of women in Afghanistan in general. It focuses on *Pashtunwali* and women's role in enforcing it.

'Pushtuns, Tribalism, Leadership and Islam and Taliban: A Short View' by Vern Liebl (2007). A journal article (*Small Wars & Insurgencies*) that explains some complex trends simply, including the rise of the mullahs, *Pashtunwali* and habits of the Kuchis. Perfect for those who have a base level of knowledge on Afghan dynamics but who are looking to enhance their awareness of the specifics of Pashtun life.

Return of a King: The Battle for Afghanistan by William Dalrymple (2013). This book is a permanent feature in any discussion about the best books on Afghanistan. It is a highly readable history of the key players and events of the First Durrani Dynasty, with a particular focus on Shah Shuja and the First Anglo-Afghan War – events which have done as much as anything to shape today's Pashtun psyche, including the tribes' aversion to foreign incursion.

Fountainhead of Jihad: The Haqqani Nexus 1973–2010 by Vahid Brown and Don Rassler (2013). Focused on Jalaluddin Haqqani of the Zadran tribe and the insurgent group that takes his name, it demonstrates the flexibility of *Pashtunwali* well. It also sheds light on how Islam intertwines with tribal culture and how tribes in border areas tend to interact with the state.

The Pashtun Question: The Unresolved Key to the Future of Pakistan and Afghanistan by Abubakar Siddique (2014). One of the better modern books, although as in many of its contemporary works, the Taliban often takes precedence, which detracts from learning specifics about the tribes. Useful for showing how recent political turmoil has impacted the tribes.

Reforming the Pukhtuns and Resisting the British: An Appraisal of the Haji Sahib Turangzai's Movement by Altaf Qadir (2015). A niche book, but its opening chapters provide a good overview of the history of the tribal areas and the reasons why uprisings persisted throught the centuries. Written by a Pashtun, meaning it avoids Western bias.

Durand's Curse: A Line across the Pathan Heart by Rajiv Dogra (2017). Written by a former Indian diplomat, so some bias is evident. But an enjoyable read that details events surrounding the signing of the Durand Line, which split the Pashtuns between Pakistan and Afghanistan.

Appendix B

Tribal Terminology

Akhund/Akhundzada	Honorific title for someone who is an Islamic scholar.
Amir ul Momineen	Commander of the Faithful. A term that Taliban leaders have adopted.
Andiwali	Friendship/camaraderie.
Ansar	Translates as 'hosts' and refers to Muslims who take in refugees.
Arbab	A term similar to *malik* which means leader or landlord. Used in Persian-speaking areas as well as by Pashtuns.
Arbaki	Armed volunteers who police tribal areas. Usually defensive in nature.
Arg	Fortress. Now a common name for the Presidential Palace in Kabul.
Ashar	Voluntary or community work, often to build houses, community facilities or other collective projects.
Ashrar	A term used by Afghan communists and Soviets to refer to the mujahideen. It translates as 'people who stir up chaos'.
Atrapay	Territory associated with a tribe. Used predominantly among the tribes of the Ghilzai Confederation.
Attan	A traditional Pashtun dance. Dancers travel in a circle while clapping their hands and spinning. Often performed at celebrations and weddings.
Azan	Call to prayer.
Azizwali	Fraternity or close relations. Can also refer to ethnic support.
Baad	A traditional form of settling disputes or providing compensation by marrying a daughter or other woman from a perpetrator's family to the victim's family.

Baba	Term of endearment for an elder or father.
Badal	Reciprocity. One of the main concepts of *Pashtunwali* which can occur as both positive and negative in the context of violence. Often viewed, at least by outsiders, as being focused on violent revenge, whereas it is in fact a concept better understood in terms of rebalancing by exchange.
Badragga	A tribal escort comprised of tribesmen from an area through which travellers are passing. If a *badragga* is violated, a tribal feud will follow.
Balandra	See *Ashar.*
Baramta	Recovery of property or the resolution of a grievance. Under *baramta*, hostages or property are held until debts are paid (see also *Bota*).
Bilga	Refers to theft and stolen goods. If a man is found with stolen goods, even if he didn't steal them, he is obliged to compensate the victim. He is only absolved of *bilga* if he admits where the stolen items came from.
Bota	Retaliation against an aggressor or someone who has failed to provide the required compensation. If a debt has not been paid, a tribesman can resort to *bota* by seizing something belonging to the debtor and holding it until the debt is paid.
Burqa	The all-enveloping gown worn by women in more conservative areas. Made obligatory by the Taliban in the 1990s. Afghans call it a *chadari*.
Chalweshti (or *Tsalweshti*).	Refers to a tribal force that implements a *jirga's* decision. Derived from the word for forty, as every fortieth man in a tribe is a member. A *shalgoon* is a force derived from the number twenty.
Chegha/Chigha	A call to arms, to defend against a common enemy. Often refers to a pursuit party called together to chase a perpetrator or raider.
Darbar/Durbar	A royal assembly or ceremony.
Dob-pasbani	Protection of Pashtun culture and the defending of fellow Pashtun tribes (regardless of past enmities) if under attack by foreigners or invaders.
Emir	Head, ruler, commander. An Arabic word used to describe those in high office or other types of leaders. Often associated with Islamists.

233

Faqir (or *Dehqan*)	A person who lives simply or who cultivates someone else's land.
Ghairat	Honour in the context of male courage and dignity, i.e. self-respect.
Ghazi	An Islamic warrior. Often used interchangeably with *mujahid*. A term used to refer to Ahmad Shah Durrani's royal guard.
Ghulam	Military levies conscripted into an army. Can also mean 'slave troop'.
Gund	Party, faction, group or a bloc of people.
Gundi	Factional, tribal or personal rivalry. It revolves around alliance-building. In *Gundi*, each rival party tries to convince other clans or villages to join them. Those who do are called *Gundimar*.
Haji	A title given those who have been on the Hajj, the Islamic pilgrimage to Mecca. Sometimes used in Afghanistan as a term of respect for elders.
Hamsaya	The term for a clan or a non-Pashtun group that is protected by another tribe. The *hamsaya* do not have the same status and privileges as others in the village. The Pashtun protective group is called *anaik*. Any attack on a *hamsaya* is considered an attack on the protector.
Hamsayagi	Refers to neighbourliness and directly translates as 'sharing the same shed'.
Haq	This occurs when a *jirga* is mediating between two disputing parties. Each side can challenge the *jirga*. If one party refuses to accept the *jirga*'s decision, they can appeal by presenting a case on why the *narkh* have not been followed (see also *Waak*).
Hasht Nafari	Translates as 'one of eight' and refers to the system whereby one tribesman in eight was sent to join state military forces. Also known as *Ashna Pari*.
Hazrat	An Islamic title given to prophets, kings, Sufi *pirs* or high-ranking figures.
Hizb	Party.
Hujra	A community centre and village guesthouse. Visitors and unmarried young men are housed in the *hujra*. It also acts as an assembly hall for meetings and celebrations. It is usually exclusively for men, while women have separate meeting places such as the

	Gudar (river bank or water collection area) or *Tanur* (communal bakehouse/oven).
Imandari	Honesty. Behaving in a respectful and decent way.
Isteqamat	Steadfastness and trust in God.
Itibar	Trust or assurance. *Itibar* deals with the unwritten rules of integrity by which Pashtuns must conduct themselves. Transactions conducted with *itibar* mean that verbal agreements will not be broken.
Izzat (or *Ezzat)*	Honour, prestige, reputation.
Jagir	Land granted to military or administrative officials in lieu of a salary. Recipients (*jagirdar*) provide support and personnel to the military.
Jerib	A unit of land. A *jerib* equates to 2,000m² or 0.2 hectares.
Jihad	Struggle, to exert oneself, to strive. Derived from Arabic, it is context-dependent. Most famously known in connection with war but can also refer to a struggle to better oneself.
Jirga	A council or assembly of tribal elders gathered to resolve disputes. The main legislative authority for the tribes, which use consensus-based decision-making.
Jirgamar (or *jirgaeez*)	Members of a *jirga*.
Karez/Kareez	A subterranean irrigation system.
Khalaat	A customary fee given to *jirgamar* in return for organizing a *jirga*.
Khan	A ruler or a noble. An influential person or commander. His rights and privileges are known as *khangi*.
Khana	House.
Kharwar	A donkey-load.
Khel	A sub-tribe or clan within a larger tribe. Some *khels* have grown so large that they are now recognized as tribes in their own right. A *khel* is often based in a single village, several closely related villages or a district of a town.
Khpal	Translates as 'one's own'. It refers to one's blood relatives within a *kor* or a small village/homestead.
Killi	A village or a hamlet, usually dominated by a single *khel* or a *kor/kol*.
Kishakee	'Detection' or 'detectors' in Pashto. The intelligence branch of a tribe.

Kog-Narkh	Incorrect application of the *narkh*. Translates as 'wrong rules'.
Koh	Mountain or hill.
Kol/Kahol	The smallest group in the Pashtun tribal structure. The *kol* is the singular and denotes a small family. It can include the father, his children and even his grandchildren. The *kol* becomes a *kahol* once the third generation is born, i.e. great-grandchildren (*kawdi*).
Kor/Koranay	Translates as 'house'. Refers to a small family of blood relatives. The plural is *koranay*. Both are similar terms to *Kol* and *Kahol*.
Kuchi	Nomad. *Powinda* is the term used on the Pakistani side of the border.
Landai	A form of Pashto poetry, usually composed by women.
Lashkar	Tribal army raised to implement the *jirga*'s decision. Usually offensive.
Lewë/Lewan	Wolf/wolves
Lokhay Warkawal	Translates as 'giving of pot'. The concept that the tribe will do everything to protect an individual from an enemy.
Loya Jirga	A Grand Assembly. Larger than a normal *jirga* and inter-tribal. Recently it has been used for national decision-making and includes non-Pashtuns.
Loy Kandahar	Greater Kandahar. The region in southern Afghanistan including the provinces of Kandahar, Helmand, Farah, Uruzgan and parts of Nimruz and Zabul.
Loy Nangarhar	Greater Nangarhar. The region including Nangarhar Province and parts of neighbouring provinces in eastern Afghanistan.
Loya Paktia	Greater Paktia. The region in south-east Afghanistan centred around Paktia, Paktika and Khost provinces. But parts of Wardak, Ghazni, Logar and Zabul are sometimes included.
Madrassa	A religious school, especially in rural Pashtun areas.
Malatar	Translates as 'tying the back'. It refers to tribesmen who will join a fight on behalf of their leader.
Malik	Village leader or influential notable. Traditionally an inherited role but now charisma and resources can confer *malik* status on a man.

Mansabar	A high-ranking military or political official under the Mughals.
Manteqa	Territory controlled by a *qawm* or clan. Variable in size, it is often the basis for bazaars, schools and *lashkars*, as well as for distribution of government funding or development projects.
Maraka	A community discussion or a small *jirga* held at the family or *khel* level.
Marakachians	The participants in or members of the *maraka*.
Mashar/Mashran	Term to describe respected elders or seniors within a tribe.
Mashartoob	Seniority. Refers to respected elders or leaders.
Mateezey	Refers to a woman who dishonours the family by eloping with a lover.
Mawlawi	A title used by graduates of madrassas who have received some form of postgraduate religious education. A *mawlawi* is a member of the *Ulema*.
Meerata	Refers to the loss of all males in a household, i.e. losing the breadwinners and honour associated with them. The phrase '*meerata she!*' is an insult which translates as 'I hope you lose all the men in your house!'
Melmastia	Hospitality. Provided irrespective of race, ethnicity, religion or tribe. One of *Pashtunwali*'s core principles.
Mlatar	Refers to a tribe taking up arms and providing a group to support a fellow tribesman who has been attacked or dishonoured by an enemy.
Mujahideen	The plural version of *mujahid*, it is often translated as holy warrior. But it can also refer to spiritual inner struggle or striving to be a better person.
*Mullah*a	A cleric. Often the religious authority in a village, since they have attended a *madrassa* or can read Arabic (i.e. can read the Qur'an).
Nagha	A tribal fine imposed by tribal elders. It can be extracted by force (i.e. by a *lashkar*) and may include the perpetrator's house being burned.
Namus	Honour and respect of women. Protecting the *namus* is a prerequisite for Pashtuns. A Pashtun who cannot do so has no honour and can be shunned by the family, village or society.

Nanawati	Asylum or provision of shelter to anyone, whether friend or foe. Can also refer to forgiveness. Derives from the verb 'to go in'.
Nang	Honour. Also used to refer to bravery, courage or chivalry.
Naqileen	The term for transferees, or people resettled by the government.
Narkh	Traditional or unwritten rules that govern behaviour in tribal areas. Sometimes translated as 'price', since breaking a rule comes with a cost. *Narkhis* are people in a tribe who understand the rules well.
Nowkar	A person obliged to serve in an *arbakai* or *lashkar*.
Paighor	Ridicule, shame or taunting. It means a challenge to someone's honour. Men are *paighor* if they break the *narkh* or the codes of *Pashtunwali*.
Pashto	The language of Pashtuns. One of Afghanistan's national languages.
Pashtunwali	The Pashtun honour code or customary laws based on fundamental Pashtun values.
Patoo	Woollen blanket worn by Afghans as part of their traditional dress. Also used to sit on when outdoors and/or for daily prayers.
Pir	A Sufi leader.
Plārina	The plural of *plar*. A clan or a *khel* is further divided into *plarina*, each of which consists of several extended families. A *Plārina* is created only when the seventh child is born, meaning the father of many *kahol*.
Prikra	The final ruling made by a *jirga*.
Purdah	Gender boundaries or gender segregation. Literally means 'veiling'.
Qabeela	An Arabic word for tribe or kinship group. *Khel* or *zai* is the Afghan equivalent.
Qalang	Taxes. Refers to those Pashtuns who engage with and support the state.
Qanat	A water management system used to irrigate fields or provide water in arid regions. Also known as a *kareez*.
Qari	A title given to men who can recite the Quran.
Qawm	Generally refers to a tribe but also means a collection of people united by ethnicity, tribal affiliation or

sometimes locality, i.e. a community of common interests.

Qazi A judge. Used to denote a person who adjudicates disputes, usually someone who has studied in a madrassa or theological seminary.

Qzilbash Translates as 'redheads' and was a name given to Safavid soldiers as a result of their red caps worn under turbans. They are Shias who acted as the royal guardsmen to Durrani leaders. Now they are considered to be an independent community or ethnic group in Afghanistan.

Rahdari A payment to *nang* tribes to keep roads open and stop attacks on travellers.

Rogha A custom for settling disputes, usually between warring factions.

Sabat Loyalty to friends, family, relatives and tribe.

Saheb A term of respect used in addressing elders, the educated or those with high government positions.

Sardar A person of high rank or a military commander. Sometimes used to address high-ranking tribal leaders and members of ruling families.

Sawar/Sowar A cavalryman.

Sayyed/Sayyid Descendants of the Prophet Muhammad (PBUH). They are seen as a tribe on their own by Pashtuns. The term is sometimes used for healers or holy men in general. *Sayyeds* are highly respected in rural areas.

Saz Blood money or compensation for a killing, usually in an attempt to end enmity or prevent a long-running blood feud. Sometimes the payment can involve a marriage. *Swarah* is a similar term.

Sepoy An Indian soldier fighting for the East India Company.

Seyali Competition. But also means 'equal'. This dual meaning signifies that it is shameful to compete with those who are not equal to you in status.

Shah King, sovereign, monarch.

Shahid An Arabic word meaning 'martyred'. It carries religious connotations, fitting into the theology of jihad. Martyrs go straight to heaven and do not wait for the day of judgement. Used to describe warriors but also civilian victims of conflict.

239

Shahzada	A prince.
Shajara	The tribal structure, i.e. the tree charting patrilineal descent.
Shura	Meeting, council, assembly.
Spin giri	Whitebeards (or greybeards). It refers to respected tribal elders who represent the tribe, or parts of it, at *jirgas* and other events.
Speenpatkian	Similar to *mashar* and *spingiri* in that it refers to respected figures or elders who make up the body of a *maraka* or *jirga*. But *speenpatkian* often translates as 'people with white turbans' and thus refers to people with religious credentials, or mullahs.
Tabar	Another term for tribe, said to derive from a Turkic word for 'to be born'.
Tanzim	Organization or faction, usually referring to the mujahideen parties.
Talib	Seeker, student of Islam. *Taliban* is the plural form.
Tarr	An accord between two tribes or tribesmen over land. If one has sown a crop, the other will not allow his animals to graze there. If he does, the crop's owner does not have to pay compensation for injuring the animals.
Tiga/Teega (or *Kanrai*).	Truce, often temporary. It refers to a fixed date when hostilities between warring factions are suspended.
Tor	Translates as 'black'. It relates to cases concerned with the honour of women. *Tor* can only be converted to *spin* (white) by death.
Tura	Sword. Used to refer to a tribesman's fighting spirit or bravery in battle.
Turbor	A rival cousin.
Turboorwali	Agnatic rivalry, most often among male cousins (*turbors*).
Ulema	The Islamic clergy. A collection of Islamic scholars or religious clerics.
Umma	The global Islamic community or 'nation' of all Muslims.
Vakil/Wakil	An ambassador or representative. Modern usage is 'lawyer'.
Waak	A type of decision given at a *jirga* when the *jirgamar* have full authority to decide the case. The sentence is final, and all parties are required to abide by its stipulations. (Another type of decision is *Haq*).

Wali	A governor, senior official.
Wazir	A minister or a counsellor of the state.
Wilayat	The area or province ruled by a *wali*.
Watan	Fatherland. A term to describe a homeland. It traditionally meant a narrow area of origin (i.e. a valley or territory shared on kinship lines), but it has now become equated to the nation or entire country.
Yaghistan	Land of rebels, areas outside central government control.
-zai	A suffix attached to names of larger tribal units, e.g. Ahmadzai means 'son of Ahmad'.
Zamindar	Traditionally meaning 'landlord' and used by Persian-speaking communities, it has also come to be used interchangeably with *malik* in Pashtun areas.
Zan, Zar, Zamin	Women, Gold, Land. The resources that are the basis of many disputes or attempts to defend tribal honour.

Notes

Chapter 1: A Wolf among Men?

1. Dogra (2017:3). Whether he actually said or did this is disputed, but the stories are still told and reinforce the aura around the Pashtun tribes. For further detail on Alexander's conquests, see Pressfield (2007) or Holt (2012).
2. Lee (2018:55).
3. 'The Pashtuns of Afghanistan: Alexander the Great also got in trouble here', *New York Times* 31/4/2004 (online).
4. Excerpts from a letter written by Osama Bin Laden opining about al Qaeda remaining focused on targeting the US. See OBL (2012) *The Osama Bin Laden Files* (Delaware: Skyhorse Publishing).
5. Quote from 'The Amir's Homily' in 'Life's Handicap: Being Stories of Mine Own People' (1891). Kipling's portrayal of life under the Iron Emir is infused with all the Western stereotypes of savagery, showing how Orientalists viewed Afghans.
6. Ibid.
7. All quotes from Elphinstone (1815).
8. See p.175 of 'The Cavalry Journal Vol VIII' (1913) (online).
9. p.11 of Kaye, J. W. (1874) *History of the War in Afghanistan* Vol 1 (London: William H. Allen).
10. Holdich (1901:185).
11. Wylly (1912:9), who quotes p.94 of Enriquez, C. M. (1921) *The Pathan borderland; a consecutive account of the country and people on and beyond the Indian frontier from Chitral to Dera Ismail Khan* (Calcutta: Thacker, Spink).
12. See pp.7–8 of Tahir, M. (2017) 'The ground was always in play', *Public Culture*, Vol. 29, pp.5–16.
13. See p.98 of Kaplan, Robert D. (2001) *Soldiers of God: With Islamic Warriors in Afghanistan and Pakistan* (New York: Vintage). Also see *The Story of the Malakand Field Force* (1898), Churchill's first non-fiction book.

14. p.57 of Johansen, R. C. (1997) 'Radical Islam and nonviolence: A case study of religious empowerment and constraint among Pashtuns', *Journal of Peace Research*, Vol. 34, pp.53–71.
15. Hanifi (2016) suggests that ethnicity is the primary route to knowing Afghanistan, but there has been a fundamental voicelessness of Pashtuns in academic and international discussions.
16. Caroe (1958:25–6).
17. Khan (1993:12).
18. See Kipling, R. (1891) *Life's Handicap: Being Stories of Mine Own People* (London: Macmillan & Co.)

Chapter 2: Who are the Pashtun Tribes?

1. A panther would be a better designation to epitomize a Pashtun – and it is a term they would use to self-describe. Equally honourable is a tiger. Even a lion (*Sher*) is a better description than a wolf, and one often encountered in Afghanistan, even if it is widely considered as an Arab import.
2. The 'Pashtunistan' question is also deliberately omitted. This revolves around calls for Pashtuns on both sides of the border to unite and form an independent homeland. But it is a political issue rather than a tribal one. While interesting and relevant to relations between Afghanistan and Pakistan, it adds little insight into the tribal way of life. It is also a red herring, because unity among Pashtun tribes is a rarity, if not an impossibility – as this book will show.
3. See Spain (1962:23), who explains that 'Pathan' was a Hindi word used by Indians to designate their neighbours west of the Indus River. It was adopted by the British and corrupted to 'Paythan'. Spain also describes how many tribesmen use 'Pukhton', which is what he describes as the guttural language of the northern tribes, whereas 'Pushtun' is the softer southern dialect. Caroe (1958:xix) also mentions geographical variations of terms, saying there is a 'tribal distinction, which almost follows the line of division between Pakhtu and Pashtu in the Karlani Hill tribes. The Pakhtu-speakers wear their hair clipped short, often shaved; the Pashtu-speakers, except in the sophistication of towns, favour a chevelure falling around the ears, varying from the neatly combed and curled bob of the Khatak soldier to the ragged ringlets of the Mahsud or Wazir.'
4. p.7 of Maley, W. (2009) *The Afghanistan Wars* (London: Palgrave Macmillan).
5. Bradbury compares the Pashtun tribal structure to the Somali one: 'Kinship as a principle of social organization, nevertheless, is nothing special to the Pashtuns. Most of what is said about the Somalis would make sense for

Pashtuns as well.' pp.13–15 of Bradbury, M. (2008) *Becoming Somaliland* (UK: James Currey).

6. Gellner (1983: 483): 'A tribe is a local mutual-aid association, whose members jointly help maintain order internally and defend the unit externally. This assumption of peace-keeping and collective defence responsibility, which thus defines the tribe, is contrasted with a situation in which the maintenance of order, and defence, is assured by the central state and its specialised agencies (courts, nominated officials, police forces, army).'

7. Glatzer (2002) defines the tribe as 'a social segment based on a genealogical concept of social structure . . . in a society segmented by a principle of descent from a common ancestor or from common ancestors'. He refutes other definitions of a tribe as a political unit.

Chapter 3: Contested Origins of the Pashtun Tribes

1. See Caroe (1958:3-24) for a comprehensive analysis of Pashtun origins.

2. See p.492 of Dupree, N.H (1977) *An Historical Guide to Afghanistan* (Afghan Air Authority).

3. English translations of the *Rig Veda* are available – see Griffiths, Ralph, T. H. (2008) *Translation of Rig Veda* (London: Forgotten Books). Analyses tend to be easier to understand – see Khalil, H. & Iqbal, J (2011) 'An Analysis of the Different Theories About the Origin of the Pashtoons', *Balochistan Review*, Vol. XXIV No. 1, pp.45–54.

4. Bellow (1880:57) says that in western Afghanistan the harsh *kh* is changed into the soft *sh*, and Pukhtun becomes Pashtun. He talks of some tribes – the Afridi – pronouncing the name similarly to ancient Greek descriptions of the people in the region.

5. Excerpt from Vol I of 'History of Alexander' by Quintus Curtius (see Curtius 9146), also cited by Pressfield (2006). Curtius was a first-century Roman and, early in the reign of Claudius (41–54 CE), wrote a history of Alexander in ten books. He has been criticized for elaboration and omitting some history; nevertheless, his quote from Alexander portrays an attitude toward the Pashtuns that survived well beyond Alexander or Curtius.

6. See Holt (2012).

7. Caroe (1958:43–57) is an entire chapter dedicated to Alexander's supposed exploits in the region.

8. See pp.5–7 of Grierson, G.A (1928) *Linguistic Survey of India Volume IV* (unknown publisher).

9. See Khan (1993:10).

Chapter 4: Descendants of Jewish Kings?

1. The work of Raverty (1860), a British army officer, is a foundational contribution to the study of the languages, history and cultures of the region.

2. For an early analysis of the Bani Israel theory, on which many modern era texts are based, see Neubauer, A. (1889) 'Where Are the Ten Tribes? III. Early Translators of the Bible and Commentators: Abraham Bar Hiyya, Benjamin of Tudela, Prester John, Obadiah of Bertinoro, Abraham Levi and His Contemporaries', *The Jewish Quarterly Review* Vol. 1, No. 3, pp.185–201.

3. Ibid.

4. There is a wealth of literature on the *Makhzan-e-Afghan* being the basis of claims about Israelite origins. See p.36 of Sharma (2016) *Nation, Ethnicity and the Conflict in Afghanistan: Political Islam and the Rise of Ethno-politics 1992–1996* (London: Routledge). Or Green (2008) 'Tribe, Diaspora, and Sainthood in Afghan History', *The Journal of Asian Studies*, Vol. 61(1), pp.171–211.

5. Burnes (1834:139–41).

6. Lee (2018:40).

7. Burnes (1834: 139–41).

8. Examples include Bellow (1891), Ferrier (1858), Fraser (1834).

9. See Ben-Zvi, I. (1957) *The Exiled and the Redeemed* (Jewish Publication Society of America).

10. p.29 of Parfitt, Tudor & Fisher, Netanel (2016) *Becoming Jewish: New Jews and Emerging Jewish Communities in a Globalised World* (Cambridge Scholars Publishing). Kogan & Rozenberg (2008) also suggest that 'Names of greater Pashtun tribes include the Rubeni, Gadi, Ashuri, Efridi, Shinwari, Lewani and Yousefzai, which clearly resemble the tribes of Reuven, Gad, Asher, Ephraim, Shimon and Yosef.' See Kogan & Rozenberg (2018) 'The Afghan Pashtuns and the missing Israelite exiles', *Jerusalem Post,* 20 Feb 2018 (online).

11. p.34 of Bellew (1891) 'An Inquiry Into the Ethnography of Afghanistan' presented to the Ninth International Congress of Orientalists (London, September, 1891) (online).

12. 'Lost Ten Tribes Have Been Found and You Will Never Believe Where They Are' *Israel 365 News* 19/2/2018 (online).

13. Bellew (1880) covers physical similarities between Pashtuns and Israelites, as does Noor Dahri in 'The Lost Tribe of Israel in Pakistan and Afghanistan' (online). See also Frembgen, J. (2006) 'Honour, Shame, and Bodily Mutilation. Cutting off the Nose among Tribal Societies in Pakistan', *Journal of the Royal Asiatic Society*, Vol. 16 (3), pp.243–60.

14. See 'The 2,700 year-old Pashtun link to Israel', *Dawn Newspaper* 18 Jan 2010 (online).
15. p.43 of Abdur-Rahim, M (1961) *History of the Afghans in India, A.D. 1545–1631, with especial reference to their relations with the Mughals* (Karachi: Pakistan Publishing House).
16. Quote from Afridi (2009) 'Pashtuns and their Resemblance to Arabs', Khyber. org (online). Further analysis of ethnic mixing over history on p.100 of Crawfurd (1865) 'On the Commixture of the Races of Man as Affecting the Progress of Civilisation', *Transactions of the Ethnological Society of London, 1865,* Vol. 3, pp.98–122.
17. Discussed in Bernhard Dorn's 'History of the Afghans' (1829), which is the first history of Afghans translated into a European language. It is based on the work of the Persian scholar, Nematullah, which makes links between King Saul and the migration of his descendants to Ghor, as well as the spread of Islam and the influence of Khalid Bin-Waleed.
18. Spain (1962:28–9).

Chapter 5: The Founding Father of the Tribal Structure

1. See: Tariq, M., Malik, M.S. & Afridi, M.K. (2018) 'The Pashtun Tribal System and Issues of Security', *Global Social Sciences Review*, Vol. III, No. I (Winter 2018), pp.101–12.
2. The first chapter of Caroe (1958) details various genealogical theories. Caroe criticizes his British predecessors for pushing the Bani Israel narrative, particularly Alexander Burnes, who he says 'is not one distinguished for wisdom or judgement'. Caroe also questions Mountstuart Elphinstone but notes that Elphinstone did admit that the theories are 'clouded with many inconsistencies and contradictions'.
3. Caroe (1958:8).
4. Martin (2014:17): 'The River Helmand marks the furthest extent of the post-Mohammad Arab Islamic expansion. With Bost, modern day Lashkar Gah, being captured in 661. This accounts for the modern day Helmandi Pashtun sub-tribes who self-identify as Arabs. They trace their descent to that invasion and yet are fully incorporated into the Pashtun tribal structure, which one assumes arose beforehand. This early adoption of Islam has generated an exceptional degree of interwovenness between religion and culture, that is an enduring theme of Pashtun politics and identity. This feeds into the sense of superiority felt by the Pashtuns, particularly those who inhabit the south-west of Afghanistan.'

Chapter 6: The Segments of the Pashtun Tribal Structure

1. Rzehak (2011:8): 'Genealogical knowledge is of vital necessity in a society structured along patrilineal descent groups of different size. Ideally, a Pashtun can demonstrate his descent from Qais Abdurrashid, the common ancestor of all Pashtuns, by enumerating all linking forefathers. In reality, a Pashtun knows by heart at least all his forefathers up to the ancestor of his kahol group, i.e. for about seven or eight generations as a minimum. For genealogical knowledge which goes back deeper in history, older and experienced men who are regarded as experts in this field are contacted.'

2. See Tainter and MacGregor (2011) 'Pashtun Social Structure: Cultural Perceptions and Segmentary Lineage Organization – Understanding and Working within Pashtun Society' *SSRN* 3/8/2011 (online).

3. Rzehak (2011:8) says that some researchers believe a kinship group only becomes a *koranay* when the third offspring is born, i.e. once there is the father, a son, a grandson and a great-grandson. Other analysts use the term *plarina* (singular: *plar*) to denote the subdivisions of a *khel*. But *plarina* are supposedly created when the seventh child of a man is born. This variability in terms demonstrates the complexity of understanding the tribal structure – even Pashtun understanding is not coherent across the entirety of the tribes.

4. *Malik* is used here as it is particularly widespread and familiar to anyone who has worked in Afghanistan. But *Zamindar* and *Arbab* are similar terms that are used interchangeably with *malik* to refer to village/*khel* leaders or tribal chieftains. *Arbab* is of Persian origin and translates as 'landowner' or 'master'. It is used extensively in southern Afghanistan, particularly in areas that have non-Pashtun communities or that border non-Pashtun areas. *Zamindar* has a similar meaning but is a Pashto word. It should also be noted that there are complications, phrases and nuances in describing village-level leadership – but this chapter, with its focus on explaining the basics of the tribal structure, is not the place to delve into them. For example, a *Malik/ Zamindar/Arbab* could be a village leader, a *khel* leader, or both. Or he could be the leader of several villages but have no tribal role. Nor is he guaranteed to be the sole leader in a village. For example, a village may also have a *Mirab* (water specialist) and a *Chakbashi* (agricultural specialist), both of whom manage irrigation and farm structures. Each village can also have a *Shawunkei* (teacher), a *Qomander* (defence specialist) and a Mullah – all of whom have a leadership role to play.

5. Bellew (1880:111) also notes that -*khel* is said to be from Arabic while -*zai* comes from Persian.

6. Other useful terms are *Khpaal*, which means 'self' and is sometimes treated as the most basic unit of the structure, i.e. *Khpaal – Kor – Koranay – Khel – Qawm*. The term *Killi* means 'village' and signifies that in some areas, or in some tribes, segments are organized along geographical lines as much as genealogy. Where a *khel* has become too large to be a meaningful marker of identity, *killi* can be inserted into the segmentary line. Anderson (1979:192, 223) depicts levels of the tribal structure well, as does p.96 of Khan, M.U. (2011) 'Re-emergent Pre-State Substructures: The Case of the Pashtun Tribes', PhD Thesis, Royal Holloway, University of London Department of Politics & International Relations (online).

7. Rzehak (2011:8)

Chapter 7: The Four Branches of the Pashtun Tribal Structure

1. Spellings often vary, i.e. Bettan can be Batan or Bitan. Older British sources use Bhittani. Ghurghust can be Gharghast. Karlan is sometimes spelled Karlanri. This book's spellings are those advised by a Pashtun expert.

2. The tribes in Sharkhbun's line are sometimes known as 'Tareens'. Tareen was a son of Sharkhbun and a grandson of Qais. Tareen had four sons. One was named Bor Tareen, later called Abdal and whose offspring formed the tribes that make up the Durrani Confederation (originally called the Abdali Confederation).

3. Diagram drawn by collating input from Pashtun experts and publications such as Caroe (1958:12–13).

4. Bellew (1880:97)

5. Glatzer (2002:4–5), who quotes from Dorn (1829), details how Bibi Mato and Shah Hussain met.

6. Jamal (2008:123) covers the Lodhi Dynasty that ruled the region in the fifteenth/sixteenth centuries, as does Rasanayagam (2005) *Afghanistan: A Modern History* (Bloomsbury Academic).

7. Diagram drawn by collating input from Pashtun experts, Rose (1911:286) and Caroe (1958:19).

8. Johnson, & Mason (2008) 'No Sign until the Burst of Fire: Understanding the Pakistan-Afghanistan Frontier', *International Security*, Vol 32, pp.41-54.

9. Ibid.

10. See p.195 of Elphinstone (1815).

11. Diagram drawn by collating input from Pashtun experts, Rose (1911: 296), Caroe (1958: 15) and Robinson (1934).

12. Caroe (1958:12).

13. Noelle (2012:160).

14. Rose (1911:224), Bellew (1880:78) and Caroe (1958:11–12).
15. Diagram drawn by collating input from Pashtun experts, Caroe (1958:21) and other web-based sources.

Chapter 8: The Deadly Durrani Division

1. Barring a nine-month period in 1929 when the Tajik Habibullah Kalakani took the throne in Kabul, and a period in the early 1990s when the Tajik Burhanuddin Rabbani was President, the Afghan state has been headed continuously by Pashtuns (mostly the Durrani Confederation).
2. Martin (2014:18).
3. Elphinstone (1815:114–16).
4. Bellew (1880:112).
5. Elphinstone (1815:115).
6. They merit specific mention because, since the de facto formation of the modern Afghan state in 1747, the majority of Afghanistan's state rulers have come from these two clans.
7. See TAC (2009c) 'The Quetta Shura: A Tribal Analysis', *Tribal Analysis Center* (online) or Voskressenski, Alexei, D (eds) (2017) *Is Non-western Democracy Possible?: A Russian Perspective* (World Scientific).
8. Elphinstone (1815:154–5): 'All tribes are allied in their complaints against them, and the Douranees will hardly acknowledge them for clansmen.'
9. See Prologue in McLean, K. (2017) *Crossing the River Kabul: An Afghan Family Odyssey* (Potomac Books).
10. Two books on President Karzai that illuminate intra-Durrani dynamics and the Popalzais' prestige are Partlow (2016) and Dam, B. (2014) *A Man and a Motorcycle: How Hamid Karzai Came to Power* (Ipso Facto).
11. Elphinstone (1815:119).
12. TAC (2009d) details the Panjpai vs Zirak competition, noting that the Panjpai tribes fought for the Persian armies in the eighteenth century and were rewarded with lands formerly held by Ghilzai tribes. For detail on this land redistribution, which still underpins modern conflict, see Priestly (1999:63).

Chapter 9: Ahmad Shah Durrani: The Father of the Afghan Nation

1. Lee (2018:110) questions the location: 'Nationalist historians, as well as most European ones, claim this meeting took place in the shrine of Sher-i-Surkh. Contemporary sources, however, make no mention of this location and it

is certainly a myth invented in the late 19th or early 20th century to support the legitimacy of the Mohammadzais, for Sher-i-Surkh was the place where Haji Jamal Khan Barakzai, founder of their dynasty, was buried. Sher-I Surkh is anyway a small single domed shrine and unsuited for a gathering of such importance. More than likely, the military council met in Ahmad Shah's own tent, where secrecy was guaranteed and the ghazis were on hand in case of trouble.'

2. Most works on Afghan history recite this story. Lee (208) provides a comprehensive account.

3. It is uncertain whether the *jirga* lasted for nine days. Some accounts simply say 'several' days.

4. Lee (2018:108) says that Haji Jamal Khan Barakzai 'demanded he be acknowledged as King, for the Barakzais were the most numerous and powerful of the Abdali clans of the Helmand and Kandahar region. His status was also enhanced by his seniority of age, the fact that he was a substantial landowner and by having performed the pilgrimage to Mecca.' Ahmad was in his early twenties and a stranger to Kandahar. The confrontation was also rooted in the historic rivalry between the two clans – as the Mughals had patronized the Barakzais. As a compromise, Ahmad Shah swore on the Qur'an that Haji Jamal Khan and his heirs would hold the post of Wazir, or chief minister.

5. Lee (2018:108) wrote that in return for exemption from taxation and forcible conscription, the other chiefs agreed to supply military levies in the event of war.

6. Caroe (1958:255).

7. Khan (1900:216–17) recounts how Abdur Rahman Khan, who ruled Afghanistan in 1880–1901, shaped his own version of events at the *jirga*, suggesting that tribal chiefs also put pieces of cloth around their necks to symbolize ropes – a sign that they submitted to Ahmad Shah and gave him the powers of life and death. Lee (2018) says this is a perversion of historical events, intended to justify the absolutist monarchy that Abdur Rahman was trying to create. This narrative was an attempt to reduce all tribal leaders to slaves or defeated enemies.

8. This is a quote from Caroe (1958:255) but Lee (2018:109) writes that '[Barakzai tribe] historians in the 20th century later took up this laconic account and transformed it into an elaborate coronation myth. At least some of these Coronation myths derive from European misunderstandings of, or lack of engagement with, contemporary sources. This perversion of the historical account was designed to justify the absolutist monarchy that was the hallmark of [later leaders in Kabul].'

9. Lee (2018:112).

10. For a dedicated book on Ahmad Shah Durrani, see Singh, G. (1959) *Ahmad Shah Durrani: Father of Modern Afghanistan* (Bombay: Asia Publishing House). Lee

(2018: 113) says that the name change 'came about as a result of a dream by Sabir Shah' and was adopted by Ahmad Shah many months after his coronation. Lee cites Elpinstone's (1815) similar account of events to bolster this view.

11. The culmination of Ahmad Shah Durrani's conquests in India was the Third Battle of Panipat, just north of Delhi, in 1761. His army took on the Maratha Empire, supported by the Rohillas (ethnic Pashtuns living in India). The Rohillas were led by Najib-ud-daulah. It has been described as one of the largest battles of the eighteenth century, lasting for many days and causing (what is claimed to be) well over 100,000 casualties. Durrani's forces were victorious, but Durrani left the Mughals in control over the area, with Najib-ud-Daula staying as a regent to the Emperor.

12. p.223 of Adle, C. & Habib, I. (eds) (2008) *History of Civilizations of Central Asia: Vol. V: Development in Contrast: from the Sixteenth to the Mid-Nineteenth Century* (Motilal Banarsidass).

13. (Lee 2018:141–2).

Chapter 10: The Three Durrani Dynasties

1. Dalrymple (2013:10).
2. For further notes on the Qizilbash, see Dupree, L. (1979) 'Further Notes on Taqiyya: Afghanistan', *Journal of the American Oriental Society*, Vol. 99(4), pp.680–2. Quote on the Red Fort from Dalrymple (2013:70).
3. p.74 of Runion, M., L. (2007) *The History of Afghanistan* (Greenwood Publishing Group).
4. William Dalrymple's book *Return of a King: The Battle for Afghanistan* (2013) is an authoritative account of these events in Afghanistan in the first half of the nineteenth century.
5. Barfield (2010:7).
6. Adapted from Caroe (1958:267), with input from Pashtun experts. It is limited to only the relevant relatives.
7. Lee (2018:179).
8. During Mahmud's second reign tensions with the Barakzai started to rise, especially between Mahmud and Fateh Khan Barakzai (who had helped Mahmud secure the throne).
9. Dalrymple (2013:xvii).
10. Dalrymple (2013:64)
11. See chapters 4/5 of Lee (2018) for an account of the Durrani dynasties and their rulers. For a shorter summary see pp.72–6 of Runion, M., L. (2007) *The History of Afghanistan* (Greenwood Publishing Group).
12. Dalrymple (2013:196).

13. Dalrymple (2013:225)
14. Dalrymple (2013:xviii).
15. Lee (2018:363).
16. See Lee (2018:412–48).
17. Talley Stewart (2000:355–6).
18. Ansary (2012:124).
19. Talley Stewart (2000:480).
20. Lee (2018:502).
21. The visit to the school was on 8 November 1933. Nadir Khan was shot dead by an ethnic Hazara, Abdul Khaliq, who was immediately apprehended, tortured and executed by quartering, along with most of his male relatives.
22. See pp.167–8 of 'Afghanistan Constitution and Citizenship Law Handboook' (2016) or ICG (2003) Constitutions in 'Afghanistan's Flawed Constitutional Process', *ICG Asia Report No. 56,* 12 June 2003 (online).

Chapter 11: Ghilzai Genealogy and Geography

1. Caroe (1958:18–19): 'The Ghilzai are probably the most numerous, and possibly the most violent, of all Afghan tribes.'
2. Bellew (1880:105): 'Over the history of the Ghilji as a distinct people in Afghanistan little or nothing is known until the beginning of the last century, when they revolted against the Persian governor of Kandahar.'
3. Ibid.
4. Bellew (1880:108)
5. Elphinstone (1815:190) also described Ghilzais as 'in former times by far the most celebrated of the Afghauns. In the beginning of the last [eighteenth] century this tribe alone conquered all Persia, and routed the armies of the Ottoman Porte.' He also wrote that 'The character of the tribe is as various as the country it inhabits' (p.177).
6. Bellew (1880:100).
7. Ibid.
8. Lee (2018:52).
9. Bellew (1880:101). Ali & Elias (2013) also cover eastwards migration in *Afghanistan* (Cavendish Square Publishing).
10. Gandovsky (1964) suggested that the Huns were of Iranic or Turkic origin and the Pashtuns resulted from a union of Iranic tribes around 500 AD, which coincides with the dissolution of the Hephthalite (White Hun) confederacy in 550 AD. Another version is that the White Huns merged with the Paktha people and this is the ethnogenesis of the Pashtuns. See Gankovsky (1964) *A History of Pakistan* (Nauka Publishing House).

11. Lee (2018:52) or Caroe (1958:18). Robinson (1934:53) covers the Khalaj people and their geographical distribution, as does Minorsky, V. (1940) 'The Turkish Dialect of the Khalaj', *Bulletin of the School of Oriental Studies*, University of London, Vol. 10 (2), pp. 417–37.
12. Martin (2014:18)
13. Often called *Takht-e-Sulaiman*, meaning Throne of Solomon.

Chapter 12: The Kuchi Nomads and Other Ghilzai Tribes

1. See Tapper (2008) 'Who are the Kuchi? Nomad self-identities in Afghanistan', *The Journal of the Royal Anthropological Institute*, Vol. 14(1), pp.97–116. Ker & Locke (2010) detailed how the term '*kuchi*' conjures a romantic but ultimately anachronistic lifestyle of tattooed women in embroidered dresses, and men riding alongside flocks of goat and sheep. The reality is the Kuchis are the Afghans most affected by decades of conflict and poverty, under-represented in the Afghan state and whose culture is under threat.
2. Caroe (1958:19)
3. Ker & Locke (2010): 'The traditional kuchi lifestyle involves highly fluid units of approximately eleven households at a time, herding 450-600 sheep and/or goats [and some cattle] along migratory paths.' The 11-household figure is also quoted in Glatzer, B. & Casimir, M. J. (1983) 'Herds and Households among Pashtun Pastoral Nomads: Limits of Growth, *Ethnology*, Vol 22 (4), pp.307–25.
4. Robinson (1934:1-19). Khan (1993) also devotes an entire chapter to Kuchi tendencies (in Pakistan).
5. Khan (1993:120)
6. 'The strange story of Australia's wild camel', *BBC News* 11 April 2018 (online).
7. 'Afghanistan: Kuchi nomads seek a better deal', *Integrated Regional Information Networks* 18/02/2008 (online).
8. 'The Kuchi of Afghanistan, according to the definition used in this survey, number 2,426,304 individuals or 239,859 households. The long-range migratory Kuchi are predominant (52%), followed by the short-range migratory Kuchi (33%) and lastly the settled Kuchi (15%). The total number in settled Kuchi communities is 365,106 individuals . . . The total number of non-migrating Kuchi is 967,210 (this includes settled Kuchi in entirely settled communities and the non-migratory Kuchi in partially migratory communities).' See p.8 of De Weijer, F. with Pinney, Assil, Mehri and Kabul. (2005) 'National Multi Sectoral Assessment on Kuchi', *Afghan Government Document* (online).

9. Spain (1962: 127).
10. See p.9 of CIA (2012) 'Afghanistan-Pakistan: The Political Significance of the Durand Line', *CIA Declassified Document*, 16/11/2012 (online).
11. Ibid.
12. 'Tribal conflict in Afghanistan: Fighting for land and water', *Economist* 26/72007 (online).
13. Khan (1993:121).
14. Khan (1993:120): 'The most frequently uttered prayer of every Pathan is "God, don't make me dependent on anyone". To retain their independence and self respect, the [kuchis] lead the hardest possible life. They never have enough money to buy land and build their own homes, so they have to keep moving to wherever they can trade or find pastures to feed their animals. Yet never did once I see a [kuchi] begging. Despite their poverty they have not lost their pride and dignity, and that for me is the greatest quality.'
15. Ibid.
16. Robinson (1934) wrote extensively on the Kuchis, including a chapter on non-Ghilzai Kuchis such as clans in the Alizai, Bhittani, Daulatzai, Mohmand, Shinwari, Jaji, Mangal, Zadran and Khostwal tribes.
17. Diagram adapted from Caroe (1958:15) and other sources. Like the Zirak/Panjpai divisions of the Durrani Confederation, the Turan/Burhan terms would rarely be used as a marker of identity. Identification always begins at a lower organizational level (i.e. *qawm* or tribe).
18. Robinson (1934:55).
19. Robinson (1934:57).

Chapter 13: Recent Ghilzai Rule: Ideology over Genealogy?

1. The supposed breakdown or decay of the Pashtun tribes is covered in Chapter 39.
2. Polluda (1973:197).
3. Robinson (1934:iii)
4. There are questions about one President's tribal affiliation. Haji Mohammad Chamkani belonged to the Chamkani tribe, whose lineage is disputed. Some Pashtuns say they belong to the Sulaimankhel tribe of the Ghilzai Confederation. Others claim the Chamkanis belong to the Sarbani branch of the Pashtun tribal structure – being part of the Ghoryahkel Confederation along with the Mohmand and Daudzai tribes.
5. p.210 of Akram, A. (1996) *Histoire de la guerre d'Afghanistan* (Paris: Éditions Balland).

Chapter 14: Mirwais Hotak and the Ghilzai Golden Era

1. See Khanam, R. (2005) *Encyclopaedic Ethnography of Middle-East and Central Asia; P-Z,* Volume 3 (Global Vision Publishing House). Raza (1994) also analyses the Ghaznavid Empire and Pashtun origins, noting alleged connections to the Huns and stating that 'the Afghans are mentioned by the Chinese pilgrim Hiuen-Tsang, writing in the seventh century, as *A-po 'kien* (Avakan).' See Raza, S. J. (1994) 'The Afghans and their Relations with the Ghaznavids', *Proceedings of the Indian History Congress,* Vol. 55, pp.784–91.
2. Bellew (1880:105).
3. Foran (1992) describes the fall of the Safavids as a 'crucial turning point in Iranian history', partly blamed on 'remote causes' such as Pashtun tribal uprisings in Kandahar. See 'The Long Fall of the Safavid Dynasty: Moving beyond the Standard Views', *International Journal of Middle East Studies,* Vol. 24 (2), pp.81–304.
4. For an overview of events that led to Mirwais Hotak's revolt, see Qayum & Shah (2017) 'Afghanistan in the Historical Perspective', *Global Political Review,* Vol. II No. 1, pp.46–53.
5. Browne (1922:29).
6. p.115 of Tanner (2009) *Afghanistan:A Military History from Alexander the Great to the War Against the Taliban* (Da Capo).
7. Lee (2018:78).
8. Barfield (2010: 96): 'Once having seized power, though, the Ghilzai proved incapable of consolidating their rule. Mahmoud was mentally unbalanced, and within a year his excesses provoked a coup led by his cousin Ashraf (whose own father had been murdered earlier by Mahmoud). Although they were able to fend off an Ottoman invasion, Ghilzai authority in Iran quickly waned. As frontier feudatories, they lacked the administrative experience necessary to govern such a complex state and were Sunni rulers in a Shiite land. They were also fractured by tarburwali-style internal divisions. Their relatives in Kandahar were among the first to reject their authority).'

Chapter 15: The Durrani vs Ghilzai Rivalry

1. From: Ahmed (2017) 'The Five Wars in Afghanistan', *The Diplomat* 27 June 2017 (online).
2. For an analysis of the Safavid vs Mughal wars in the seventeenth century, see Burton, A. (1997) *The Bukharans: A Dynastic, Diplomatic, and Commercial History, 1550–1702* (Palgrave Macmillan).

3. Quote from Fida (1955:24). TAC (2009d) further details the events in 1707 and the background to the Durrani vs Ghilzai animosity. Two books by Pakistani historians Dr Sher Zaman Taizi (*Struggles for Liberation*) and Ganda Sing (*Ahmad Shah Durrani*) say that Mirwais Hotak supported Gurgin Khan in a ruthless suppression of an uprising of Abdalis [Durranis] in 1707.
4. Elphinstone (1815:152).
5. Robinson (1934:55).
6. See Liebl (2007) for coverage of Islam's interaction with *Pashtunwali* and Islam's decay of tribal structures.
7. From: Doucet, L. (2020) 'Afghan-Taliban peace talks: What's next?' *BBC News* 22 September 2020 (online).
8. See Liebl (2007).
9. Dr Abdullah's father was a Pashtun from Kandahar. His mother was Tajik. But Abdullah's political career saw him rise to the top of Tajik circles rather than present himself as a strong Pashtun – partly by virtue of his close friendship with the Tajik hero Ahmad Shah Massoud in the 1990s.
10. An overview of these post-2001 dynamics is in Mili & Townsend (2009) 'Tribal Dynamics of the Afghanistan and Pakistan Insurgencies', *CTC Sentinel* Vol. 2(8).
11. Robinson (1934:55).
12. p.13 of Tainter, J.A. & McGregor, D. (2011) 'Pashtun social structure: cultural perceptions and segmentary lineage organization', *SSRN Electronic Journal* (online).
13. See Poullada, L (1970) 'The Pashtun Role in the Afghan. Political System', *The Afghanistan Council of the Asian Society*, Occasional Paper No. I. (online).

Chapter 16: The Tribal Honour Code

1. See Chapter 1 of Churchill (1898).
2. Glatzer (1998:4).
3. Ali, Y.A. (2013) 'Understanding Pashtunwali', *The Nation* 6 August 2013 (online).
4. Raverty's Pashtu Dictionary of 1860 says it is 'the manners and customs of the Afghan tribes, the Afghan code'.
5. 'Genetic Connection: Israeli Rabbi Calls Pashtuns "my cousins" from Lost Tribe', *Express Tribune Newslab* March 2019 (online). Also see Avihail & Brin (1978) *Lost Tribes from Assyria* (Amishav): 'From their ancient customs, one can point to a connection between the Pathans and the Jewish people . . . The legal system operates according to the Pashtunwali, the Pashtun Laws, parts of which are similar to the laws of the Torah.'
6. See Spain (1962).

7. Barth (1969:119)
8. p.308 of Steul, W. (1981) *Paschtunwali: Ehrenkodex und seine rechliche Relevanz* (Wiesbaden: Steiner).
9. Ahmad (1976) quoted in Khayyam et al (2018:175): 'The reality about Pashtunwali is that it remains the cornerstone of Pashtuns' society, backed from 2000–3000 BC.'
10. See Gankovsky, Y. (1964) *A History of Pakistan* (Nauka Publishing House).
11. p.10 of Guest (2010) 'Dynamic interplay between religion and armed conflict in Afghanistan', *ICRC* (online).
12. Poett (1991) talks of Ahmadzai *narkh* and *razmak narkh* being the 'best-known' of all the variations. Other authors also point out the formation of a Waziri *narkh* specific to the Wazir tribe that dominate Pakistan's tribal areas.
13. See Atayee et al (1979).
14. Khan (1993:33).
15. See Khan (1993:36).

Chapter 17: The 'Big Three' Principles of *Pashtunwali*

1. Dalrymple (2013:3).
2. Kakar (2012) discussed the misconceptions about *Pashtunwali*. See 'The Popular Misconceptions about Pashtunwali', *Takatoo*, Vol. 4 (7).
3. Dupree (1980:126).
4. Spain (1962:46).
5. Raverty (1860:47).
6. See pp.11–13 of LandInfo (2011) Report: 'Afghanistan: Marriage', 19 May 2011 (online).
7. p.32 of Wiss, Ray (2010) *A Line in the Sand: Canadians at War in Kandahar* (Canada: Greystone Books). It should be noted that the *zar* (gold) does not just mean literally gold but anything of substance that can be valued in gold, i.e. weapons, ammunition, vehicles, etc.
8. Khan (1993:15–43).
9. 'Not seeking blood retaliation personally is deemed as a sign of moral weakness, even cowardice, not just of the individual who was wronged, but his whole kin group . . . Nor is this a task that can be shifted to the state. Reporting a murder to get action from the government officials is considered a sign of weakness, that the kin group is too weak to take revenge honourably themselves. In any event, punishment by government court does not erase the obligation to take revenge . . . People also believe that the government has no right to interfere because no crime was committed.' From p.6 of Barfield (2003) 'Afghan Customary Law and Its Relationship to Formal Judicial Institutions', USIP paper (online).

10. Khan (1993:33).
11. Kakar (2004) and Khan (1993) cover women's responsibilities in *Pashtunwali*.
12. Khan (1993:35).
13. p.4 of Miakhel, S. (2009) *Understanding Afghanistan: The Importance of Tribal Culture and Structure in Security and Governance* (Maulana Abdul Kalam Azad Institute Center for South Asian Studies).
14. Khan (1993:35).
15. Spain (1962:48).
16. Spain (1962:47).
17. The British Envoy Mountstuart Elphinstone, quoted by Shah Mahmoud Hanifi (2018:65).

Chapter 18: *Narkh*: The Rules of Tribal Behaviour

1. p.50 of Nagamine, Y. (2015) *The Legitimization Strategy of the Taliban's Code of Conduct: Through the One-Way Mirror* (USA: Palgrave Macmillan).
2. See Miakhel (2008).
3. Rzehak (2011): 'Escorting (*badraga*) is another feature of hospitality . . . A person who is travelling in a region where other tribes reside can ask for an escort. Local tribesmen will escort him and provide protection if necessary. An intelligent traveller will never cross foreign regions without seeking an escort by local people.'
4. See Miakhel (2008).
5. Ibid.
6. p.201 of Ahmed, A. (1980) *Pakhtun Economy and Society: Traditional Structure and Economic Development in a Tribal Society* (London: Routledge & Kegan Paul).
7. Ibid.
8. Ghairat is explained in Chatterjee, K. (eds) (2013) *Pakistan and Afghanistan: The (In)stability Factor in India's Neighbourhood?* (KW Publishers Ltd).
9. Khan (1993:126).
10. See Buneri, S. (2011) 'Dancing Girls of the Swat Valley', *World Policy Journal*, 28 (3), pp.73–81.
11. Rzehak (2011:10).
12. Glatzer (1997): 'A man of aql is one who reasons and acts in an integrative social way, he is hospitable and generous, he grants asylum, reaches to balanced social judgements and is able to act as a mediator in conflicts. The concept of tura and aql includes to know when to draw the sword and when to put it back to the sheath.'
13. Ibid.

14. See Liebl (2007) for a deeper analysis of the Islam/*Pashtunwali* nexus.
15. Barth (1969:123).
16. See Ginsburg, T. (2011) 'An Economic Interpretation of the Pashtunwali', University of Chicago Legal Forum, Vol 2011, Issue 1, Article 6, pp.99–114. See also Storey, P. (2015) 'The Roots of the Taliban', *The Strategy Bridge* 2 December 2015 (online) and Marsden (2002) *The Taliban: War and Religion in Afghanistan* (London: Zed Books Ltd).
17. Attributed to Abdul Wali Khan, a member of Pakistan's first directly elected parliament in the 1970s.
18. See Hopkins (2008).
19. Tainter, J.A. & McGregor, D. (2011) 'Pashtun social structure: cultural perceptions and segmentary lineage organization', *SSRN Electronic Journal* (online).

Chapter 19: The Paradox of Pashtunwali for Women

1. 'Horrific Murder of Teenage Girl Again Puts Spotlight on Afghanistan's "Honor" Killings', *Radio Free Europe/Radio Liberty* 7 May 2020 (online).
2. Badakhshan has been long-known as a Tajik-dominated province, with a smaller presence of Pashtuns, Uzbeks and other minorities. Tajiks are the dominant ethnic group in Baharak district, but it is one of the districts (along with Jurm and Warduj) where the Taliban has used madrassas to cultivate a strong presence in the 2010s. Nazela's ethnicity is not known to the author, and there is every possibility that she was not Pashtun. This further highlights the need to reiterate that honour killings are not a Pashtun-only phenomenon.
3. See paragraph 79 of Upper Tribunal (2016) 'Appeal Number: AA/05787/2012', *Immigration and Asylum Chamber* (online).
4. From 'Afghanistan: No justice for women victims of violence', *UN report* (online).
5. See Note 1 above – 'Horrific Murder of Teenage Girl Again Puts Spotlight on Afghanistan's "Honor" Killings'.
6. See Glatzer (1997): 'In general men consider young women to be less able to think and act rationally, to have less self-control and to be more inclined to sexual activity, in short they are believed to be an easy prey to any seducer who comes along. Thus men feel obliged to fight for maintaining their namus, i.e. first of all to keep the women of their families under tight control, and to protect the women from their own "weaknesses".'
7. Quote from Ahmed (2007), in the section 'Women in Conflict: Enemies and Lovers'.
8. Dupree (1984:310).
9. Raverty (1860:465).

10. See Glatzer (1997).
11. See Miakhel (2008).
12. See Glatzer (1997)
13. Khan (1993:132).
14. It is also used by other Afghan ethnic groups and other Islamic nations across South Asia, the Arab Peninsula and some African nations.
15. See Glatzer (1997).
16. Khan (1993:132).
17. Lee (2018:43)
18. See Kakar (2004).
19. This book does not intend to dismiss the abuses that Afghan women face. Afghanistan is still one of the worst places in the world to be born a woman, despite all the advocacy of the post-2001 era. Much more needs to be done to give Afghan women the rights they deserve. But this is not the focus of this chapter or this book.
20. Another famous woman is Aino Mena. Her story is recounted in Partlow (2016:67). It revolves around a man who was part of Ahmad Shah Durrani's army. Upon returning from battle, the soldiers were ordered to wait until the next day, when all duties were done, before seeing their families. One man sneaked away that night to see his wife, Aino Mena. But she refused to let him in, and when he returned to the camp he was branded as a deserter. Ahmad Shah Durrani heard what Aino Mena did and rewarded her with a large piece of land.
21. See p.19 of Jamal, A. (2015) 'Men's Perception of Women's Role and Girls' Education among Pashtun Tribes of Pakistan: A Qualitative Delphi Study', *Muslim Youth Identity in Context of Global Conflicts* (online).
22. Lindholm (2020).
23. See Chapter 5 of Khan (1993) for an introduction to some issues related to women and Pashtun tribal life.
24. Rubin (1995:23).
25. See Lindholm (2020).
26. p.315 of Alam, A. (2012) 'Women's Role and Status in Pukhtoon Society' (A Case Study of Village Sufaid Dheri, Peshawar), *International Journal of Learning & Development*, Vol. 2(3).

Chapter 20: The *Jirga*: Collective Tribal Decision-making

1. Barth (1969:108).
2. Another term sometimes used interchangeably with *jirga* (often in Pakistan) is '*maraka*'. See Karrer, L. (2012) 'Pashtun Traditions versus Western Perceptions: Cross-Cultural Negotiations in Afghanistan', *Ecahiers De L'institut 16*, Graduate Institute Publications.

3. Ibid.
4. Yousafzai & Gohar (2012:18): '[the *jirga* is] probably the closest approach to Athenian democracy that has existed since times immemorial'. Syed Abdul Qudus wrote that 'The Jirga represents the essence of democracy in operation under which every individual has a direct say in shaping the course of things around him.' See Yousufzai, H.M. & Gohar, A. (2012) *Towards Understanding Pukhtoon Jirga: An Indigenous Way of Peace-Building and More* (Sang-e-Meel Publications).
5. See Gant & McCallister (2010) 'Tribal Engagement Tutorial: The Jirga and the Shura', *Steven Pressfied Website* (online).
6. 'The first record of a *jirga* dates to 977, when one of the first Afghan heads of state in the Ghazni province was chosen. When asked about the justice delivered through *jirga* and *shura*, Afghans consistently give higher ratings to *jirga*s and *shura*s than to the state courts and consider them fair and trustworthy, effective, timely and prompt.' See Nosworthy, M. (2019) 'Jirga/ Shura (Afghanistan)', *Global Informality Project* (online).
7. They were also a way for warlords to convene congregations while still retaining overall control. See USIP (2005).
8. From: Ruttig, T. (2010b) 'Peace Jirga Blog 9: A Déjà Vu of Big Tent Democracy', *Afghanistan Analysts Network* (online).
9. See Yousaf (2019).
10. Elphinstone (1815:167).
11. p.33 of MacMahan, A. H. & Ramsay, A. D. G. (1981) *Report on the tribes of Dir, Swat and Bajure together with Uthman Khail and Sam Ranizai* (Peshawar: Saeed Book Bank).
12. 'First female jirga set up in Pakistan's Swat Valley', *UPI* 20 Aug 2013 (online).
13. Spain (1962:50).
14. For an analysis of how Islamic scholars interact with traditional tribal measures, see Khan, H.M. (2015) 'Islamic Law, Customary Law, and Afghan Informal Justice', *USIP Special Report 363*, March 2015 (online).
15. Khan (1993:32).
16. Caroe (1965:411).
17. Barth (1969:123)
18. See Liebl (2007) for the role of and perceptions towards Sufis, as well as their recent persecution.
19. 'Australian war film Jirga is a lesson in Afghan forgiveness', *The Conversation* 20 Sept 2018 (online).

Chapter 21: The *Loya Jirga*: Tribal or National Leadership

1. See Rahimi (2017): 'Hanifi, contrary to the official and semi-official narrative, asserts that one cannot find the term Loya Jirga in pre-1922 literature in

Afghanistan ... However, Afghan national writers like Mir Gholam Mohammad Ghobar and Mohammad Alam Faiz-zad insist that the Loya Jerga, as a feature of central government in Afghanistan, dates back to pre-Islamic times.'

2. See p.214 of Misdaq, N (2006) *Afghanistan: Political Failty and External Interference* (Routledge). See also Zee News (2002) 'Functioning of Loya Jirga', 10 June 2002 (online): 'The first Loya Jirga was held, according to legend, to select a king for the newly urbanised Aryan tribes some five thousand years ago.'

3. Hanifi (2004) mentions this theory but admits that 'There is no historical or archaeological evidence in support of these claims, however. There is no record of assemblies or councils or other specifically named representative bodies that the government convened or with which the rulers of Afghanistan consulted prior to 1922.'

4. Fida (1997) outlines this theory – and even refers to it in the book's title *Afghanistan: Jirgahs and Loya Jirgahs. The Afghan Tradition (977 A.D. to 1992 A.D.)*.

5. See Ruttig (2011) 'Innovative Loya Jirga-ism', *Afghanistan Analysts Network*, 13 June 2011 (online).

6. See Fraser, D. & Hanington, B. (2018) *Operation Medusa: The Furious Battle That Saved Afghanistan from the Taliban* (McClelland & Stewart).

7. See Hobsbawm, E. & Ranger, T. (ed) (1983) *The Invention of Tradition* (Cambridge).

8. See Smith (2019).

9. Hanifi (2004:305).

10. See 'Innovative Loya Jirga-ism', *Afghanistan Analysts Network*, 13 June 2011 (online).

11. See Buchholtz (2013) 'The Nation's Voice? Afghanistan's loya jirgas in the historical context' *Afghanistan Analysts Network*, 19 November 2013 (online).

12. Smith (2019): '872 representatives – likely appointed by Amanullah Khan – from the Mohmand, Bajwur, and Afridi tribes. The jirga consisted mostly of tribes from around Jalalabad because of difficulties relating to travel during the winter months.'

13. Hanifi (2004) quoted Smith (2019) writing that the delegation represented nine provinces and included: 231 delegates from the central government bureaucracy (officials chosen by Amanullah), 75 delegates from the *ulema*; 111 Sadat delegates (non-Pashtun figures who claim sacred descent); 33 *Mashayekh* delegates (non-Pashtun mystics who claim sacred descent); 240 *Khawanin* delegates (local leaders and landowners); 272 *wokala* delegates (merchants); 111 *khawanin wa wokala* (khans). Most (68 per cent) were from non-Pashtun provinces. Hanifi believes this to have been representative of the Afghan population at that time.

14. See Smith (2019) and Hanifi (2004).
15. Talley Stewart (2000:383).
16. Smith (2019:18)
17. Hanifi (2004).
18. Smith (2019:19).
19. Smith (2019:4).
20. Dupree (1980:463).
21. p.242 of Smith, H.H. (1969) *Area Handbook for Afghanistan* (Washington DC: American University).
22. Rubin (2002:73).
23. From Buchholtz, B. (2013) 'The Nation's Voice? Afghanistan's loya jirgas in the historical context' *Afghanistan Analysts Network*, 19 November 2013 (online).
24. Smith (2019:20).
25. Ibid.
26. The story of the German Oktoberfest tent is cited by many publications, although it was only some parts of the tent that were shipped from Germany – an aspect of the story often omitted from written records.
27. See Constitution (2004).
28. This event 'technically should not be considered a loya jirga because of its ambiguous intent; nonetheless, it shared many characteristics with the loya jirgas described earlier.' From: Rutting, T. (2010b) 'Peace Jirga Blog 9: A Déjà Vu of Big Tent 'Democracy', *Afghanistan Analysts Network* (online).
29. See Hanifi (2004).

Chapter 22: *Lashkar* and *Arbaki*: Pashtun Tribal Protectors

1. Liebl, V. (2018) 'Afghanistan: Informal vs Formal Governance In the land of Yaghestan', *Marine Corps University* (provided by the author).
2. Glatzer (1997:8).
3. See Spain (1962:51) or Taj, F. (2011) *Taliban and anti-Taliban* (Newcastle-upon-Tyne: Cambridge Scholars).
4. Spain (1962:51).
5. Ibid.
6. Ibid.
7. Tariq (2008:2).
8. See section 3.2.2 in Pejcinova (2007) *Afghanistan: Creation of a Warlord Democracy* (online).
9. Tariq (2008:3).
10. Ibid.

11. See p.320 of McGinnis (1999) *Polycentric Governance and Development: Readings from the Workshop in Political Theory and Policy Analysis* (Ann Arbor: University of Michigan Press).

12. Tariq (2008:3).

13. Ibid.

14. Ibid.

15. See p.3 of Trives (2006) 'Afghanistan: Tackling the Insurgency, the Case of the Southeast' (Paris: *The French Institute of International Relations*) (online).

16. p.5 of Giustozzi, A. (2004) 'Good State vs. Bad Warlords? A Critique of State-building Strategies in Afghanistan' *Working Paper No. 51*. (London School of Economics: Crisis States Program).

17. Tariq (2008:3): 'The sending of people to the central government is done through a system called *"Hasht Nafari"* or, in slang, *"Ashna Pari"*.'

18. p.275 of Harpviken, K.B (1997) 'Transcending Traditionalism: The Emergence of Non-State Military Formations in Afghanistan', *Journal of Peace Research*, Vol. 34 (3), pp.271–87.

19. See p.309 of Alikuzai, H.W. (2013) *A Concise History of Afghanistan in 25 Volumes* (Trafford Publishing).

20. Ibid.

21. 'Partition 70 years on: When tribal warriors invaded Kashmir', *BBC News* 22/10/2017 (online).

22. Tariq (2008:8–9).

23. Ibid.

24. Tariq (2008:11–12).

25. Goodhand, J. and Hakimi, A. (2014) 'Counterinsurgency, Local Militias, and Statebuilding in Afghanistan' *USIP Peaceworks Paper* (online).

Chapter 23: Proverbs: A Window into the Pashtun Soul?

1. Proverbs have been said to be particularly important for expressing the social thoughts of traditional societies. See p.173 of Webster (1982) 'Women, sex, and marriage in Moroccan proverbs', *International Journal of Middle East Studies* 14 (2): 173–84.

2. p.58 of Krikmann, A. (1985) *Some Additional Aspects of Semantic Indefiniteness of Proverbs: Proverbium 2* (Tallinn: Academy of Sciences of the Estonian SSR).

3. See p.295 of Bascom, W.R. (1965) 'Four Functions of Folklore', pp.279–91, in Dundes, Alan (ed.) *The Study of Folklore, Englewood Cliffs* (NJ: Prentice-Hall).

4. p.21 of Naeem, H. (2007) *Pashto Folklore ki Tashrihi Fehrast (Annotated Bibliography of Pashto Folklore)* [in Urdu] (Pashto Academy, University of Peshawar).

5. For an overview of the Rohi Mataluna, see Bartlotti, L. & Khattak, R.S.W. (2009) *Rohi Mataluna: Pashto Proverbs, Revised and Expanded Edition* (Resource Publications).

6. Some prominent twentieth-century texts include Cecil Boyle's 'Naqluna: Some Pushtu Proverbs and Sayings' (1926), which describes how most Pashtuns he met were illiterate villagers who relied on proverbs to pass on accumulated wisdom. In 1932, Major George Gilbertson produced a dictionary of Pashto idioms. Jens Enevoldsen's book *Sound the Bells, O Moon Arise: Pashto Proverbs and Folk Songs* (1969) is another well-known text which consists of a hundred Pashto proverbs and a hundred short songs (*tappas*).

7. See Tair (1975) *Rohi Matloona (Pashto Proverbs)* Volume I [in Pashto] (Peshawar: Pashto Academy).

8. See Singh, D. (2016) 'You've Got Dung! Amazon is Delivering Cow Pies in India', *NPR* 06/01/2016 (online). See also, AFP (2020) 'Holy dung at India cow feces festival is purifying poo', *Global Times* 19/11/2020 (online).

9. In 2012, a five-centuries-long dispute between two Jaji tribe clans, over 3,000 hectares, was resolved through the *jirga* system and with mediation by elders from the Chamkani tribe, who share similar territory. See '500 Years Old Land Dispute Resolved', *UN Assistance Mission in Afghanistan* 24 July 2012 (online).

Chapter 24: Tribal Stereotypes Shaped by Geography

1. p.36 of Tapper (2009) 'Tribe and state in Iran and Afghanistan: An Update', *Études rurales* 184, pp.33-46.

2. Barfield (2010:68).

3. See Manchanda (2017) 'The Imperial Sociology of the "Tribe" in Afghanistan', *Millenium: Journal of International Studies*, Vol. 46(2), pp.165–89.

4. Partlow (2016:125).

5. Gellner (1994:28). The term 'code of the hills' was used by Ahmed (2011) 'The Code of the Hills', *Foreign Policy* 6 May 2011 (online).

6. Manchanda (2020:105–42) writes that 'the nang Pashtuns represent tribal purity' in respect to *Pashtunwali*.

7. Elphinstone (1815:40).

8. Chart reproduced from Ahmed (1977:21) – and it should be noted that Ahmed's study almost exclusively focused on tribal areas in Pakistan rather

than Afghanistan. It should also be noted that Nang/Qalang classifications are rarely the reason for conflict between tribes, although Khan (1993) did talk of the Qalang tribes 'traditionally being constantly under pressure from those in the mountains, meaning the stronger tribes have relentlessly encroached on the land of the weaker ones'.

Chapter 25: The Pashtun Belt

1. Lee (2018:13)
2. Siddique (2012) introduces Afghanistan's 'Tapestry of Ethnicities', noting that Afghanistan's national anthem recognizes fourteen ethnic groups: Pashtuns, Tajiks, Hazaras, Uzbeks, Balochis, Turkmens, Nuristanis, Pamiris, Arabs, Gujars, Brahuis, Qizilbash, Aimaq and Pashai. See 'Afghanistan's Ethnic Divides', *CIDOB Policy Research Project* (online).
3. p.19 of Katz (2011) 'Reforming the Village War: The Afghanistan Conflict', *Middle East Quarterly*, Vol. 18(2).
4. From pp.22–3 of Katz, D. (2017) 'Community-Based Development in Rural Afghanistan: First, Assume A Community', *USIP Peaceworks Paper* (online).
5. See Glatzer (1998).
6. Ibid.
7. See Saito, M. (2007) 'Second-Generation Afghans in Neighbouring Countries: From *'Mohajer* to *Hamwatan*: Afghans return home', *Afghanistan Research and Evaluation Unit* (online).
8. See Glatzer (2001:381).
9. Ibid.
10. Ibid.
11. Glatzer (2001:380).
12. See Frembgen, J.W. (1999) 'Indus Kohistan: An Historical and Ethnographic Outline', *Central Asiatic Journal*, Vol. 43(1), pp.70–98.
13. Caroe (1958:173–5).
14. For a case study of tribes in Nangarhar Province, see Lawson, B.S., Kelly, T.K., Parker, M., Colloton, K. & Watkins, J. (2010) Chapter 4: 'Nangarhar Case Study, In: Reconstruction Under Fire: Case Studies and Further Analysis of Civil Requirements' (RAND Corporation).
15. See Martin (2014) for a detailed a study of Helmand Province. pp.20–27 cover the Barakzai.
16. See Yon, M. (2009) 'Arghandab and the Battle for Kandahar', *Michael Yon Online Magazine* 13 Dec 2009 (online). The author quotes a book called *Three Campaigns in Afghanistan*, in which a British officer writes: 'Further west,

however, there is a great gap in the hills, where the plain narrows and runs in the Arghandab Valley. To force a passage in this direction, through thickly sown villages and gardens and vineyards, was "no child's play".'

17. 'Afghans own the Arghandab', *Defence Visual Information Distribution Service* 2/5/2012 (online).

18. p.15 of Grau (1996) *The Bear Went over the Mountain: Soviet Combat Tactics In Afghanistan* (NDU Press).

19. From: 'Slow Progress in Afghanistan's Treacherous Arghandab', *The Atlantic* 3 June 2011 (online).

20. TAC (2009e) 'Putting it together in Southern Afghanistan, *Tribal Analysis Center* (online).

21. Anecdote from author's conversation with former Danish Ambassador to Afghanistan (2016).

22. Robinson (1934:57).

23. Named the 'Khalid Bin Whalid training camp'.

24. 'Afghan War Criminal Zardad Freed: No protection for witnesses', *Afghanistan Analysts Network* (online).

25. 'Landmark case involved two trials and inquiries in Afghanistan, UK', *The Irish Times* 19 July 2005 (online).

26. See Simpson, J. (2005) 'How Newsnight Found Zardad', *BBC News* 18 July 2005 (online).

27. Laville (2004) said that one of the witnesses showed his scars to the courtroom: 'Pushing back his sleeve he also showed a wound he said was caused by the ropes which had bound him as he was beaten with the butt of a Kalashnikov, after being pulled from a minibus at a checkpoint on the Jalalabad road to Kabul.' See Laville, S (2004) 'Torture scars shown to judge' *Guardian* 12 October 2004 (online).

28. Jaji district, also called Zazi, Dzadzi or Aryob, is in Paktia Province. Jaji Maidan is a district in Khost province.

29. Spain (1962:55).

30. See 'Afghan Frontier Tribe Defies Pakistani Government', *Associated Press* 3 February 1986 (online). Another resource on border dynamics during the Soviet era is Kaplan, Robert D. (2001) *Soldiers of God with Islamic Warriors in Afghanistan and Pakistan* (New York: Vintage).

31. Khan (1993:47).

32. 'The border tribes became outraged at the Pakistani government for sending troops into the area and allowing Americans to bomb their homelands in an effort to kill off al-Qaeda and root out the Afghan Taliban.' From p.349 of Atran, S. (2010) 'A Question of Honour: Why the Taliban Fight and What to Do About It', *Asian Journal of Social Science 38*, pp.341–61.

Chapter 26: Outside the Pashtun Belt: The Resettled Tribes

1. Author anecdote from conversation with former Afghan Minister of Defence Masoom Stanekzai, 2016.
2. NPS (2012) 'Kunduz Province', Program for Culture & Conflict Studies, *US Naval Postgraduate School* (online).
3. For an account of the fall of Kunduz in 2015 – the first time the Taliban had seized a major Afghan city since 2001 – see 'The Fall of Kunduz', *The Atlantic* 28 Sept 2015 (online).
4. Schuyler (1966:136).
5. See Poladi, H (1989) *The Hazaras* (Avenue Books).
6. From: Morrison (2017) 'Beyond the "Great Game": The Russian Origins of the Second Anglo–Afghan War', *Modern Asian Studies*, Vol. 51(3), pp.686–735.
7. Ibid.
8. From pp.4–5 of Malikyar & Rubin (2002) 'Center-periphery Relations in the Afghan State: Current Practices, Future Prospects', *Center on International Cooperation*, New York University December 2002 (online).
9. See Fletcher, A. (1965) *Afghanistan: Highway of Conquest* (New York: Cornell University).
10. See pp.473–86 of Mishali-Ram, M. (2008) Afghanistan: 'A Legacy of Violence? Internal and External Factors of the Enduring Violent Conflict'. *Comparative Studies of South Asia, Africa and the Middle East*, 28(3).
11. See Chapter 18 of Dupree (1980).
12. See p.57 of Martin (1907) *Under the Absolute Amir* (London: Harper & Brothers).
13. See p.90 of Bergne (2007) *The Birth of Tajikistan: National Identity and the Origins of the Republic* (I.B. Tauris).
14. Ibrahimi (2017:78–9).
15. The indigenous Nuristanis are usually described as being Hindus before their conversion to Islam, but this claim comes with some controversy. The tendency is for the English-language literature, particularly the centuries-old texts, to posit that Nuristanis were Hindus. Conversely, local sources or Russian-language literature more often suggests that Nuristanis adhered to some form of pagan religion.
16. Tomsen (2011:42).
17. Dalyrmple (2013:388).
18. Ibid.
19. See pp.69–79 of Bleuer (2012) 'State-building, migration and economic development on the frontiers of northern Afghanistan and southern Tajikistan', *Journal of Eurasian Studies*, Vol. 3.

20. Tomsen (2011:42).
21. See TAC (2009f).
22. p.4 of TAC (2010) 'Afghanistan's Development: An Instability Driver?', *Tribal Analysis Center* (online).

Chapter 27: The Durand Line: An Honourless Agreement?

1. Khan (1900) translated the 'The Life of Abdur Rahman, Amir of Afghanistan' in 1900. Khan was the Emir's former state secretary. He describes the Emir as 'a very witty and humorous genius'.
2. See Khan (1900:x): 'He says he was crowned by the prophet in his dreams; that he gained his victories by the help of an old flag which he secured from the tomb of a certain saint of Herat called Khwaja Ahrar; that he protected himself from the injuries of swords, guns, and rifles through the effect of a charm he wears round his arm; that he learned reading and writing through the love of a girl who was engaged to him. Being unable to read her letters, he remained unhappy till he was helped by the hidden mysteries of Heaven to read them.'
3. For a famous portrait of Abdur Rahman see frontispiece of Khan (1990) *The Pathans – A Sketch* (Islamabad: Pashto Adabi Society).
4. See pp.69–79 of Bleuer (2012) 'State-building, migration and economic development on the frontiers of northern Afghanistan and southern Tajikistan', *Journal of Eurasian Studies*, Vol. 3.
5. p.328 of Thornton (1895) *Colonel Sir Robert Sandeman, His Life And Work On Our Indian Frontier A Memoir, With Selections From His Correspondence And Official Writings* (Reprinted 2010 by Kessinger Legacy Reprints).
6. Other British officials described the Afghan escort as a 'parcel of ragamuffins'. See p.57 of Forbes (1892) *The Afghan Wars 1839–42 and 1878–80* (BiblioLife).
7. p.462 of Wheeler (1953) *The Cambridge History of India: The Indus Civilization* (Cambridge Univ. Press).
8. See p.11 of a report written by Durand to the Foreign Department, India in Yunas (2003) *The Durand Line Border Agreement 1893* '(Reprint by Areas Sudy Centre, University of Peshawar).
9. Misra, J.P. (1976) 'The Durand Mission And Indo-Afghan Boundary Agreement Of 1893', *Proceedings of the Indian History Congress*, Vol. 37, pp.433–40.
10. In Chapter 3 of Edwards (1996), an excerpt from Abdur Rahman's autobiography reads: 'It is easy to understand that before furnishing a house one must think of making or finding a house to furnish; and in case of building a house it must

be surrounded by walls to keep the goods safe which are put in it; and if the house is full of holes, ditches, snakes, scorpions, etc., it is necessary to get rid of these before anyone can live in it. In the same way, it was of the first and greatest importance to mark out a boundary line all around Afghanistan.'

11. p.18 of Sykes, Percy (1926) *The Right Honourable Sir Mortimer Durand: A Biography* (London: Cassell & Co).
12. From: Yaquby, S. (2019) 'The Story of the Durand Line Negotiations', *Medium* (online).
13. Ibid.
14. pp.140–1 of Loyn, D. (2008) *Butcher and Bolt: Two Hundred Years of Foreign Failure in Afghanistan* (Hutchinson).
15. See Yaquby, S. (2019) 'The Story of the Durand Line Negotiations', *Medium* (online).
16. p.574 of Alikuzai, H.W. (2013) *A Concise History of Afghanistan in 25 Volumes* (Trafford Publishing).
17. See Yaquby, S. (2019) 'The Story of the Durand Line Negotiations', *Medium* (online).

Chapter 28: Subterfuge that Split the Pashtun Tribes

1. Dogra (2017:120).
2. For Durand's own report of his mission, see Durand, H.M. (1894) 'File 26-C/94: Sir Mortimer Durand's report on his mission to Kabul', *British Library: Asian and African Studies* (online).
3. Dogra (2017:120).
4. Ibid.
5. See Misra (1976) for an overview of Salter Pyne's role with Abdur Rahman. Misra, J.P. (1976) 'The Durand Mission and Indo-Afghan Boundary Agreement Of 1893', *Proceedings of the Indian History Congress*, Vol. 37, pp.433–40.
6. Dogra (2017:124).
7. p.138 of Loyn (2008) *Butcher and Bolt: Two Hundred Years of Foreign Failure in Afghanistan* (Hutchinson).
8. Martin (1907:25).
9. See Chapter 8 of Lee (2018) for a comprehensive analysis of Abdur Rahman Khan's reign. Also see Lee, J.L. (1991) 'Abd al-Raḥmān Khān and the 'maraẓ ul-mulūk', *Journal of the Royal Asiatic Society*, Vol. 1(2), pp.209–42.
10. Ibid.
11. Dogra (2017:124).
12. Dogra (2017:125).
13. See Chapter 18 of Dupree (1980). Gartenstein-Ross & Vassefi (2012) also assert: 'Abdur Rahman was forced to agree to this border by the threat

of economic embargo. He relied on British subsidies to maintain his central government's dominance, and was in particular need of it at that time . . . because he was then engaged in warfare against the Hazaras.' See Gartenstein-Ross, D & Vassefi, T. (2012) 'The Forgotten History of Afghanistan-Pakistan Relations', *Yale Journal of International Affairs*, March 2012, p.38.

14. Dogra (2012:117).
15. Possible forgery is cited in almost all analyses of the Durand Agreement, although little evidence is provided.
16. Omrani (2009).
17. Dogra (2017:146).
18. Ibid.
19. See Giunchi, E. (2013) 'The Origins of the Dispute over the Durand Line', *Internationales Asien Forum*, Vol. 44, No. 1–2, pp.25–46.
20. Dogra (2017:186).
21. Biswas (2013:21).
22. Ibid.
23. See 'Need to factor in our 106km border with Afghanistan: NSA', *Times of India*, 23 May 2015 (online).
24. See Holdich (1901:238) for Holdich's own narrative on the demarcation process.
25. Ibid.
26. For detailed notes on the Baluch-Afghan Boundary Commission of 1896, see McMahon, A. H. & Baluch-Afghan Boundary Commission (1909) 'Letters on the Baluch-Afghan Boundary Commission of 1896', *Digitized Afghanistan Materials in English from the Arthur Paul Afghanistan Collection* (online).
27. Dogra (2017:156) or p.143 of Griffiths, J.C. (1967) *Afghanistan* (New York: Fredrick A. Praeger).
28. See Chapter 21 of Dogra (2017).
29. Dogra (2017:152) wrote that many of the individual tribes 'have not lived the life of peace and tranquility ever since that agreement was signed'. Dogra also wrote (p.129) that it is the 'real life tragedy of the Pashtun people; a tragedy that continues to draw blood a century after that line was forged through an unwilling land'.

Chapter 29: Tribes of the Sarbani Branch

1. Tribes including the Sherani, Bhittani, Chamkani and Bangash have been left out as they are generally more concentrated in Pakistan than Afghanistan. The Wardak tribe, prominent in Afghanistan, has been omitted from this section as

the author is unsure about its genealogy and does not wish to further confuse the topic by giving inaccurate information. The tribe is variously linked to both the Ghilzai Confederations (of the Bettani branch) and the Karlani branch. A Wardak friend familiar with the tribal structure posited that the Wardaks are of Karlani heritage but less directly than other tribes. He told the author that Wardak was from the same mother as Karlan.

2. The Khattak tribe (Karlani branch) has been left out of this section because it is more prevalent in Pakistan than in Afghanistan and because any overview of the tribe would likely focus on its most famous son, the seventeenth-century warrior-poet Khushal Khan Khattak. His story is dealt with in the 'Prominent Pashtuns' chapter.

Achekzai

1. Elphinstone (1815:154).
2. TAC (2009g) 'Achekzai Tribe', *Tribal Analysis Center* (online).
3. Rubin (1995:159).
4. Yousaf et al (2001:130–1).
5. See Tempest (1987) 'Regime and Violent Bandit Are Uneasy Allies in Kabul', *LA Times* 14 Dec 1987 (online).
6. Ibid.

Alizai

1. Gompelman (2011:48) wrote about Alizai in the Ghormach district of Faryab Province. See 'Winning Hearts and Minds? Examining the Relationship between Aid and Security in Afghanistan's Faryab Province', *Feinstein International Center* (online).
2. See Priestly (1999).
3. p.16 of Martin, M. (2011) 'A Brief History of Helmand', *British Army, Afghan COIN Centre* (online).
4. Ibid.

Alikozai

1. TAC (2009b) 'Alikozai Tribal Dynamics: A Very Unusual Durrani Tribe', *Tribal Analysis Center* (online).
2. 'Security Blanket: Afghanistan's most venerable relic faces its greatest challenge', *The Atlantic* Jan/Feb 2009 (online).
3. 'A fight for Afghanistan's most famous artefact', *Independent* 30 Dec 2012 (online).
4. From: 'Under the Cloak of History: The Kherqa-ye Sharif from Faizabad to Kandahar', *Afghanistan Analysts Network*, 30 Jul 2014 (online).

Barakzai

1. p.825 of Rawlinson, H.C. (1841) 'Report on the Durrani Tribes Dated 19th April 1841', in McGregor (1871) *Central Asia, pt. 2: A Contribution Towards the Better Knowledge of the Topography, Ethnology, Resources, and History of Afghanistan* (Calcutta: Office of the Superintendent of Government Printing).
2. See pp.146 and 153 of Bosworth, C.E. (1967) *The Islamic Dynasties Edinburgh* (Edinburgh University Press). See also Fofalzay (1958:9–10, 242–3).

Ishaqzai

1. Lee (1996:xxiv).
2. Tapper (1983:56).
3. Lee (1996: 485–6).
4. See TAC (2009f).
5. For the consequences of Taju Khan leading Ishaqzai to the north, see pp.68–9 of Tapper, N (1991) *Bartered Brides: Politics, Gender and Marriage in an Afghan Tribal Society* (Cambridge: Cambridge University Press).
6. TAC (2009f).
7. See TAC (2009f).

Mohmand

1. Spain (1962:82).
2. Spain (1962:81).
3. See Khan, M.F. (1977) 'The Life and Times of Haji Sahib Turangzai', *Islamic Studies*, Vol 16(1), pp.329–41.
4. 'Afghanistan's first spaceman returns home', *BBC News* 23 March 2014 (online).
5. Tribal tree built upon input from multiple sources, including in-person interviews with Afghans, as well as existing resources such as Caroe (1958:13) and Naval Postgraduate School (NPS) diagrams, see the NPS Program for Culture and Conflict Studies document 'Mohmand Tribe'.

Noorzai

1. 'New Chief Is "Ideal" Taliban Leader, Analyst Says', *Voice of America* May 25 2016 (online).
2. 'Taliban's New Leader, More Scholar than Fighter, Is Slow to Impose Himself', *New York Times* 11/7/2016 (online).
3. Ibid.
4. 'Son of Afghan Taliban leader dies carrying out suicide attack', *Reuters* 22 July 2017 (online).
5. 'The 2010 TIME 100: Malalai Joya', *Time Magazine,* 29 April 2010 (online).

Popalzai

1. Mazzetti, M. & Filkins, D. (2010) 'Secret Joint Raid Captures Taliban's Top Commander', *New York Times,* 15 Feb 2010 (online).

Shinwari

1. Talley Stewart (2000:412)
2. Balfour, E. (1885) *The cyclopaedia of India and of Eastern and Southern Asia: commercial, industrial and scientific, products of the minderal, vegetable, and animal kingdoms, useful arts and manufactures* (B. Quartich).
3. 'Eastern Pashtuns' is a term used by Glatzer (1997). 'Sarbani Pashtuns' is also common.
4. See Muhammad (1999) for an account of the events that led to the Tajik Habibullah Kalakani taking Kabul (including the Shinwari revolts).
5. Ibid.
6. See Muhammad (1999:35–7).
7. Talley Stewart (2000:81).
8. Ibid.

Yusufzai

1. Spain (1962:73)
2. Bellow (1880:67) devotes achapter to the Yusufzai. pp.74–5 deal with supposed Israelite connections.
3. Caroe (1958:37) talks of Greek influences on the Aspasii and Isapzai (Yusufzai), although he is sceptical.
4. Samrin (2006) 'Yusufzais in Mughal History', *Proceedings of the Indian History Congress,* Vol. 67, pp.292–300.
5. See p.207 of Hiro, D. (2006) *Babur Nama* (India: Penguin Random House).
6. Ibid.
7. The Yusufzai chief was Shah Mansur Yusufzai, see Beveridge, A.S. (2014) *The Babur-nama in English, Memoirs of Babur* (Project Gutenberg).
8. Page 263 of Radhey, S. (1978) *Babur* (Janaki Prakashan).

Chapter 30: Tribes of the Bettani Branch

Ahmadzai

1. Robinson (1934:57)
2. See Chapter 28 of this book, or Robinson (1934).
3. Lucy Morgan Edwards, *The Afghan Solution* details the Jabbarkhel and the Arsala family within it.

4. Unverified source.
5. Morgan Edwards, L. (2011:14).
6. 'Lessons unlearned: An unnecessary war, a bloody occupation and an ignominious retreat', *Economist* 26 Jan 2013 (online).
7. Author anecdote, based on meetings with Arsala family members, including Haji Din Mohammad.
8. For an overview of events surrounding Burnes' death, see pp.235–45 of Hopkirk, P. (2001) *The Great Game: On Secret Service in High Asia* (Oxford: Oxford University Press).
9. p.223 of Mason, P. (1986) *A Matter of Honour* (London: Penguin).
10. Dalrymple (2013:366).
11. Ibid. p.378.
12. Ibid. P.387.
13. Tribal tree built upon input from multiple sources, including in-person interviews with an Ahmadzai tribal member of the Yahyakhel, as well as existing resources such as Caroe (1958:15) and Naval Postgraduate School (NPS) diagrams, see the NPS Program for Culture and Conflict Studies document 'Ahmadzai Tribe'. In particular, Robinson (1934:55–74) provides as comprehensive a breakdown and description of each Ahmadzai *khel* as exists.

Andar

1. See Anderson (1975) 'Tribe and Community among the Ghilzai Pashtun. Preliminary Notes on Ethnographic Distribution and Variation in Eastern Afghanistan', *Anthropos,* Vol. 70(3/4), pp.575–601. Alternatively, see NPS (2017) 'Tribe, Clan, & Ethnic Genealogies', *Program for Culture and Conflict Studies*, US Naval Postgraduate School (online).
2. A famous Andar, who symbolizes the tribe's resistance to foreign occupation, was Mullah Mushk-I-Alam Akhundzada. During the Second Anglo-Afghan War he scorned Kabul's Durrani leaders as accomplices in British occupation. With other clerics, he rallied a large tribal *lashkar* to march on Kabul. His Andar tribe in Ghazni were first to stir sedition, but thousands of Pashtuns soon joined his calls to defend Islam, claiming that foreign infidels were intent on its destruction. A British soldier wrote in 1881: 'The religious reputation of the Mullah was such, that the enemy began to collect in large numbers, and so great was the gathering, that it astonished both General Roberts and all the native chiefs in his camp, none of whom seem to have expected so great a rising.' Mushk-I-Alam's story highlights how Islam can take precedence over tribal interests – and how the Taliban are not the first insurgents to manipulate Islam for legitimacy.

3. See Ibrahimi (2017:54)
4. Ibid.

Hotak
1. p.33 of Rashid, A. (2000) *Taliban* (London: Pan Macmillan).
2. See p.6 of TLO (2011) 'Mehrabad Nawa', *The Liason Office* (online).

Kharoti
1. Story recounted to the author by a Pashtun friend, 2020.
2. See Chapter 11 of Bellow (1880: 97–108).
3. See 'Tribe, Clan, & Ethnic Genealogies', *Program for Culture and Conflict Studies*, US Naval Postgraduate School (online).
4. Elphinstone (1815:192).
5. Tomsen (2011:42).
6. Wörmer, Nils (2012) 'The Networks of Kunduz: A History of Conflict and Their Actors, from 1992 to 2001', *Afghanistan Analysts Network* (online).
7. Elphinstone (1815:192).

Niazi
1. See Lieven, A. (2011) *Pakistan: A Hard Country* (Penguin). See also 'Imran Khan or Imran Niazi?', *Daily Times Pakistan,* 31/8/2018 (online).
2. Nejatie, S. (2017) 'The Pearl of Pearls: The Abdālī-Durrānī Confederacy and Its Transformation under Aḥmad Shāh, Durr-i Durrān' *PhD Thesis,* Department of Near and Middle Eastern Civilizations, Univ. of Toronto (online).
3. Chapter 5 of Elphinstone (1815) details Ghilzai lands in Afghanistan, including Niazi lands.
4. The first four chapters of Sands (2019) cover Prof. Niazi and his impact on Afghanistan during the 1970s.
5. Indian Prime Minister Narendra Modi called him 'Imran Khan Niazi' in an inauguration speech for the Kartarpur Corridor in 2019.
6. 'Imran Khan criticized after calling Osama Bin Laden a "martyr"', *BBC News* 26/6/2020 (online).

Tokhi
1. See Yapp (1964) 'The Revolutions of 1841–2 in Afghanistan', *Bulletin of the School of Oriental and African Studies*, University of London, Vol 27(2), pp.333–81.
2. See Kakar (2004).
3. Ibid.

Chapter 31: Tribes of the Ghurghusht Branch

Kakar

1. Bellew (1880:31).
2. See p.56 of Ambreen, M. & Moyuddin, A. (2013) 'Power Structure and Conflict Resolution among Pashtun Tribes (A Case Study Of Zandra Village In Balochistan)', *Asian Journal Of Management Sciences And Education*, Vol. 2. No. 1, pp.55–68.
3. Noelle (2012:161) or Dupree (1980:377–8).
4. Ibid.
5. The route is the Gomal Pass, which sits on the Durand Line and takes its name from the Gomal River. It connects Ghazni Province in Afghanistan with Tank in Pakistan. It was traditionally used by kuchi nomads.
6. See p.979 of Chisholm, H. (ed) (1911) 'Zhob', *Encyclopaedia Britannica*, (11th ed.) (Cambridge Univ. Press).
7. p.479 of Ghufran (2001) 'The Taliban And The Civil War Entanglement In Afghanistan', *Asian Survey*, 41:3.
8. 'Freed Taliban leader behind first US casualty in Afghanistan could soon return to fight US, *Global Post* 25 May 2015 (online).
9. JRTF (2013) '71 Guantanamo Detainees Determined Eligible to Receive a Periodic Review Board as of April 19, 2013' (online).
10. The nickname results from the limp he acquired after stepping on a landmine in 1995.
11. Tribal tree built mainly on input from Caroe (1958:19), and tribal diagrams from Priestly (1999:144).

Safi

1. See p.32 of Archiwal, A. (2013) *Pashtuns: The Flip Side of the Coin* (Germany: Lambert Academic Publishing).
2. See Liebl (2007).
3. The Pashai are an ethnic group in Eastern Afghanistan, sometimes called 'Kohistani'. See p.601 of Weekes, R.V. (1984) *Muslim Peoples: A World Ethnographic Survey* (Greenwoord Publishing Group).
4. pp.85–6 of Mason, W. (2011) *The Rule of Law in Afghanistan: Missing in Action* (Cambridge University Press).
5. Edwards (2002:103).
6. 'Afghan Air Force – Half Yearly Report', *India Office* (online).
7. Ibid.
8. Ibid.

9. Yapp, M., Preston, P., Patridge, M. (1999) 'British documents on foreign affairs: reports and papers from the Foreign Office confidential print. From 1946 through 1950. Near and Middle East (University Publications of America).
10. See p.136 of Yapp, M. (2001) 'British documents on foreign affairs: reports and papers from the Foreign Office confidential print. Afghanistan, Persia and Turkey, Jan 1947–Dec 1947. (University Publications of America).

Chapter 32: Tribes of the Karlani Branch

Afridi
1. See Spain's chapter 'The Guardians of the Passes' in *The Way of the Pathans* (1962).
2. See Holdich, T.H. (1898) 'Tirah', *The Geographical Journal*, Vol. 12(4), pp.337–59.
3. 'Pakistan's flourishing arms bazaar', *BBC News* 21 June 2006 (online).
4. Spain (1962:57).
5. From: Shepherd, C. (1866) 'Photo of Group of Afridis at Jamrūd, 1866', *Library of Congress Digital Project*. Available online at World Digital Library (online).
6. Spain (1962:62).
7. See p.98 of Kaplan, Robert D. (2001) *Soldiers of God with Islamic Warriors in Afghanistan and Pakistan* (New York: Vintage).
8. Bellew (1880:92).
9. Spain (1962:58–9).

Jaji
1. p.35 of Sageman, M. (2004) *Understanding Terror Networks* (Philadelphia: Univ. of Pennsylvania).
2. Farrall (2017:21).
3. Excerpt from CNN interview with Khashoggi in 2006, when he admits that 'I visited the sight of that battle with him in Jaji' and for Bin Laden the battle was 'a recruiting tool. It was the start of having an independent front, where he become the Amir, the leader of those Arab Mujahedeen who are gathered around him.' See CNN (2006), 'Profile of Osama bin Laden', *Insight* (online).
4. p.18 of Lacey, R. (2010) *Inside The Kingdom: Kings, Clerics, Modernists, Terrorists and the Struggle for Saudi Arabia* (NYC: Viking/Penguin Group).
5. Farrall (2017:24).

Mahsud

1. Khan (1993:60).
2. Spain (1962:135).
3. Spain (1962:47).
4. Khan (1993:51).
5. Caroe (1958:xvii) wrote: 'They are the tribes who never fell under the effective sway of any recorded Imperial authority and now form the backbone of the so-called tribal belt.'
6. Quotation attributed to John Ayde, but usually without a source or publication cited. It is unclear if this came from an 1867 book by a British General called John Ayde – *Sitana: a Mountain Campaign on the Borders of Afghanistan in 1863* (London: Richard Bentley).
7. Caroe (1958:393).

Mangal

1. p.194 of Lohbeck, K. (1993) *Holy War, Unholy Victory: Eyewitness to the CIA's Secret War in Afghanistan* (Regnery Publishing).
2. p.51 of Adamec, L. W. (2010) *The A to Z of Afghan Wars, Revolutions and Insurgencies* (Scarecrow Press).
3. See Muhammad (1999) for a contemporary account, particularly pp.13–14.
4. Ibid.
5. British India Office Records 'Summary of Events in Afghanistan', July 15 1923 to June 30 1924, as quoted in Nawid (1996) 'The Khost Rebellion: The Reaction of Afghan Clerical and Tribal Forces to Social Change' (online).
6. Muhammad (1999:52).
7. Poullada (1973:94) describes the battle. Dixon & Sarkees (2015:475–6) list the skirmishes of autumn 1924 in *A Guide to Intra-State Wars: An Examination of Civil, Regional, and Intercommunal Wars, 1816–2014* (CQ Press).
8. p.148 of Clements, F. (2003) *Conflict in Afghanistan: A Historical Encyclopedia* (ABC-CLIO).
9. p.190 of Johnson, R. (2011) *The Afghan Way of War: How and Why They Fight* (Oxford University Press).
10. Dupree (1980:446).
11. Muhammad (1999:13–14).
12. p.200 of Trinkler (1927) *Through the Heart of Afghanistan* (edited by B.K. Featherstone) (Faber & Gwyer).

Orakzai

1. See 'Key Daesh Member Abdullah Orakzai Killed in Govt Forces Operation', *TOLONews* 18 August 2020 (online).

2. For information on sectarian clashes within the Orakzai Agency, see pp.5-6 of Zahab, M.A (2009) 'Unholy Nexus: Talibanism and Sectarianism in Pakistan's Tribal Areas', Paris: *Sciences P. CERI, CNRS*. (online).

3. See pp.1005–6 of Blunt (1911) 'Tirah Campaign'. In Chisholm, H (ed.) (1911) *Encyclopaedia Britannica. 26* (11th ed.) (Cambridge University Press).

4. The Mishi, Sheikhan, Alikhel and Mallakhel are the *hamsaya* clans of the Orakzai. For the etymology of the name, see p.149 of Gait (1901) 'Census of India, 1901, Volume 17, Part 1', *Office of the Superintendent of Government Printing*, India, 1902.

Turi

1. Spain (1962:100).
2. Caroe (1958:124).
3. See p.66 of Khan, S. (2010) 'Special Status of Tribal Areas (FATA): An Artificial Imperial Construct Bleeding Asia' *Eurasia Border Review Part II*, vol. 1, No. 1.
4. p.56 of Al Nahyan, A. & Hussain, J. (2019) *Tribes of Pakistan* (Cambridge Scholars Publishing).

Wazir

1. Spain (1962: 129).
2. Khan (1993:47).
3. The Wazir and the Kharoti are sometimes involved in a dispute over land in the Bermal valley.
4. See Wylly (1912), although this is likely to have changed with the so-called Islamification of tribes, especially in Waziristan, in the latter half of the twentieth century.
5. See p.226 of Swinson, A. (1967) *North-West Frontier: People and Events, 1839–1947* (New York: Praeger, 1967) or pp.53–4 of Moreman, T.R. (1998) (reprint) *The Army in India and the Development of Frontier Warfare, 1849–1947* (Palgrave Macmillan).
6. Caroe (1958:393).
7. Wylly (1912:425).
8. Talley Stewart (2000:103).

Zadran

1. Elphinstone (1815:100).
2. 'Unexplained assassinations', *Express Tribune* 27 December 2010 (online).
3. p.28 of Brown, V. & Rassler, D. (2013) *Fountainhead of Jihad: The Haqqani Nexus 1973–2012* (London: Hurst).
4. Bearden, Milt (2004) 'The Pashtuns of Afghanistan: Alexander the Great also got in trouble here', *New York Times* 31 March 2004 (online).

5. Tribal tree built on information contained in Brown & Rassler (2014) *Fountainhead of Jihad: The Haqqani Nexus* 1973–2012 (Oxford University Press). Caroe (1958:21) was also used. This information was cross-referenced and amalgamated with on online source attributed to 'Wakeel Khan' and uploaded to the internet on 10 July 2020. Also used was a Naval Postgraduate School (NPS) Program for Culture and Conflict Studies document entitled 'Jadran Tribe, aka Zadran Tribe'.

Chapter 33: The Sarbani Hero: Malalai of Maiwand

1. Malala Yousafzai has narrated an animated film about her ancestor, her version stating that Malalai scrambled up a nearby hill when the tribesmen started retreating, shouting, 'It is better to live like a lion for one day than to live like a slave for 100 years!' This animation is available on YouTube by searching 'He Named Me Malala'.
2. Noorzai (2019) 'The Battle of Maiwand and the Taliban's Tarani', *Iran and the Caucasus*, Vol.23, pp.233–47.
3. p.98 of Schofield, V. (2003) *Afghan Frontier: At the Crossroads of Conflict: Feuding and Fighting in Central Asia* (New York: Tauris).
4. 'The forgotten Malalai of Maiwand', *The Daily Times* 5 August 2019 (online).
5. Lee (2018:180) or Shah (2017) *Afghan Pathan Legends* (XLIBRIS).
6. p.44 of Headlam, J. (1931) *The History of the Royal Regiment of Artillery - From the Indian Mutiny to the Great War Volume III – Campaigns (1860–1914)* (Woolwich: Royal Artillery Institution).
7. See Gore (2009).
8. Robson, B. (1973) 'Maiwand, 27th July 1880', *Journal of the Society for Army Historical Research*, Vol. 51(208), pp.194–224.
9. See Gore (2009).
10. Gore (2009:168).
11. Ibid.
12. Gore (2009:170).
13. Ibid. p.171.
14. Ibid.
15. Maxwell (1979: 177).
16. Gore (2009: 173).
17. Roberts' quest is covered in Atwood (2012) *The March to Kandahar: Roberts in Afghanistan* (Pen & Sword Military).
18. Robson (1973), as note 11 above.
19. 'Soldiers in Helmand unearth British rifles lost in 1880 massacre', *Independent* 23 Oct 2011 (online).

20. See Hensman, H. (1916) *The Afghan War Of 1879–80: Being A Complete Narrative Of The Capture Of Cabul, The Siege Of Sherpur, The Battle Of Ahmed Khel, The Brilliant March To Candahar, And The Defeat Of Ayub Khan, With The Operations On The Helmund, And The Settlement With Abdur Rahman Khan* (New Delhi: Olympia Fields).
21. Habibi was an Afghan scholar and Member of Parliament during the reign of King Zahir Shah.

Chapter 34: The Bettani Mujahid: Abdul Rasoul Sayyaf

1. Based on author's meetings with Sayyaf (2014–2020).
2. See p.5 of CIA (1985) 'Afghanistan Situation Report', *Central Intelligence Agency*, (online).
3. Other sources say Sayyaf means 'executioner' or 'bearer of the sword', coming from the Arabic word 'sayf' (swords).
4. Edwards (2002:266).
5. 'The University of Dawat and Jihad was originally formed in the early 1980s as the struggle between the mujahedin groups and Soviet forces began. It was founded in Peshawar by former faculty of Kabul University in exile in Pakistan with the support of Rasul Sayyaf . . . The teaching staff were drawn primarily from the Islamic law faculty and were generally fundamentalist in orientation . . . The university closed in 1995, reopened in Kabul and eventually closed sometime after the Taliban gained control of Kabul in 1996, with its students transferring to Kabul University.' From: Canada (2000b) 'Afghanistan/Pakistan: University of Dawat and Jihad', *Canada: Immigration and Refugee Board of Canada*, 18 December 2000 (online).
6. 'Echoes of early design to use chemicals to blow up airliners', *New York Times* 11 Aug 2006 (online).
7. 'Khalid Sheikh Mohammed and the C.I.A.', *The New Yorker* 31 December 2014 (online).
8. See 'Former Warlord Primed for Afghan Presidency', *The Diplomat* 24 September 2013 (online). It should also be made clear that, while there are common claims that the Filipino group is named after the Afghan Sayyaf, there are also suggestions that it takes its name from one of the first Filipinos to travel for jihad in Afghanistan, who is also said to have been named Sayyaf.
9. See Sands (2019:327–8).
10. HRW (2006) 'Blood-Stained Hands: Past Atrocities in Kabul and Afghanistan's Legacy of Impunity (Report)', *Human Rights Watch* (online).
11. Many sources cover the events of the Afshar Operation, including Ibrahimi (2017) and Sands (2019). The most comprehensive account is AJP (2005)

'Casting Shadows: War Crimes and Crimes against Humanity, 1978–2001', *Afghanistan Justice Project* (online).
12. Ibid.
13. Bin Laden left for Sudan in 1992, leaving only around fifty fighters in Afghanistan (Farrall 2017:28).
14. 'Former Bin Laden Mentor Warns the West', *Daily Telegraph* 3 December 2001 (online).
15. Sayyaf had little influence in the Northern Alliance, due to his ethnicity but also because many of his commanders joined the Taliban.
16. Confirmed by Sayyaf in meeting with the author, June 2019.
17. See Chapter 2 (pp.41–55) of Morgan-Edwards (2011) for insight into the 2002 *Loya Jirga*.
18. Barfield (2010: 253).

Chapter 35: The Ghurghushti Insurgent: Mullah Dadullah

1. p.73 of Van Linschoten & Kuehn (eds) (2018) *The Taliban Reader: War, Islam and Politics* (London: Hurst).
2. p.73 of Rashid, A. (2000) *Taliban* (London: Pan Macmillan).
3. See HRW (1998) 'Afghanistan: The Massacre in Mazar-I Sharif', *Human Rights Watch*, 1 November 1998, C1007 (online).
4. 'Afghans Starve in Siege from Within', *LA Times* 8 May 1998 (online).
5. Ibrahimi (2017:201).
6. 'Mullah Dadullah, Top Taliban Commander, Killed in Helmand', *Long War Journal* (online).
7. Praxenthaler & Beckh (2020) 'Safeguarding and Preservation Activities at the Giant Buddhas and Other Monuments in the Bamiyan Valley 2004–2017'. In 'The Future of the Bamiyan Buddha Statues' pp.19–30 (online).
8. See p.3 of Morgan, L. (2012) *The Buddhas of Bamiyan (Wonders of the World)* (Profile Books).
9. Semple (2011) 'Why the Buddhas of Bamian were destroyed', *Afghanistan Analysts Network* 2/3/2011 (online).
10. Van Linschoten & Kuehn (2012:276).
11. O'Keefe, R. (2004) 'World Cultural Heritage: Obligations to the International Community as a Whole?', *The International and Comparative Law Quarterly*, Vol. 53(1), pp.189–209.
12. Ibid.
13. 'An attempt to wipe out history: The destruction of the Bamian Buddha colossi in 2001', *Afghanistan Analysts Network* (online).
14. The envoy was Moinuddin Haider, a retired General and Interior Minister of Pakistan. See p.120 of Zaeef (2011) *My Life with the Taliban* (London: Hurst).

15. 'Rebuilding the Bamiyan Buddhas', *SLATE Dispatches*, 23 July 2004 (online).
16. From Bobin (2015) 'Disputes damage hopes of rebuilding Afghanistan's Bamiyan Buddhas', *Guardian* 10/1/2015 (online).
17. Taleban Information Minister Qudratullah Jamal: 'Last-ditch bid to save Buddhas dismissed', *CNN* 12 March 2001 (online).
18. 'The man who helped blow up the Bamiyan Buddhas', *BBC News* 12/3/2015 (online).
19. p.42 of Delijani, C (2017) *Watching War on the Twenty-First Century Stage: Spectacles of Conflict* (Methuen).
20. p.70 of Cayli, B. (2019) *Violence and Militants: From Ottoman Rebellions to Jihadist Organizations* (McGill-Queen's University Press).
21. 'UN Confirms Destruction of Afghan Buddhas', *ABC News* 12 March 2001 (online).
22. 'Over World Protests, Taliban Are Destroying Ancient Buddhas', *New York Times* 4 March 2001 (online).
23. 'Afghani Ambassador Speaks at USC', *Islam Online* 12 Jan 2001 (online).
24. p.70 of Cayli (2019) *Violence and Militants: From Ottoman Rebellions to Jihadist Organizations.*
25. Van Linschoten & Kuehn (2012:276).
26. This is well covered in published literature on the Taliban. See also US Senate (2011) 'Al Qaeda, The Taliban, And Other Extremists Groups in Afghanistan And Pakistan', Senate Hearing 112–70, 24 May 2011 (online).
27. Van Linschoten & Kuehn (2012:228).
28. 'Taliban deploy thousands of suicide bombers – commander', *Reuters* 2 April 2007 (online).
29. 'In Afghanistan, journalist pleads for Italian authorities to meet his kidnappers' demands', *Committee for the Protection of Journalists*, 15 March 2007 (online).
30. 'Mullah Dadullah, Top Taliban Commander, Killed in Helmand', *Long War Journal* (online).
31. p.274 of Van Linschoten & Kuehn (eds) (2018) *The Taliban Reader: War, Islam and Politics* (London: Hurst).
32. p.274 of Van Linschoten & Kuehn (eds) (2018) The Taliban Reader: War, Islam and Politics (London: Hurst).

Chapter 36: The Karlani Warrior-Poet: Khushal Khan Khattak

1. 'Remembering a revered poet: Ajmal Khattak, a proponent of peace', *Express Tribune* 13 May 2012 (online).

2. See Khan & Himayatullah (2020).
3. See Chandra (2005:267–9).
4. Ibid.
5. See Khan & Himayatullah (2020) for analysis of Khushal Khan Khattak's time in prison and subsequent conflicts with the Mughals.
6. Ibid. Some sources say the prison was Ranthambore Fort near Sawai Madhopur in Rajasthan.
7. 'Khushal Khan Khattak', *History of Pashtuns* blogpost 18 Sept 2014 (online).
8. Khan & Himayatullah (2020).
9. 'Khushal Khan Khattak', *History of Pashtuns* blogpost 18 Sept 2014 (online).
10. Mogenstierne (1960:49–57).
11. Ibid.
12. Ibid.
13. See Omrani (2009).
14. By this stage, Khushal would have been well into his sixties, if not in his seventies.
15. This is a number routinely quoted in online sources, but rarely in academic, peer-reviewed research.
16. Anecdote told to the author by an Afghan student at Kabul University, 2016.
17. See Yusufzai (2013) 'Play on Khushal Khan Khattak Provces Popular', *Dawn* 5 Feb 2013 (online).
18. Quoted frequently in various online forums.
19. See Smith (2020) *The Big Book of Khushal Khan Khattak, Afghanistan's Great Sufi/Warrior Poet Selected Poems: Translation & Introduction* (New Humanity Books).
20. See Khattak, K.K. (transl. Shaheen. & Naeem 1933) *Dastar Nama (The Pathan Pride) of Khushhal Khan Khattak* (Pashto Academy, reprinted 2007).
21. See p.10 of Guest (2010) 'Dynamic interplay between religion and armed conflict in Afghanistan', *ICRC* (online).
22. Spain (1962:109).
23. Ibid.
24. See Spain (1962:108–16) for reference to Khushal's poetry on women, love and gardens.
25. For selected poetry of Khushal Khan Khattak, see Smith (2012) *Khushal Khan Khattak: The Great Warrior-Poet of Afghanistan* (Australia: New Haven Books).
26. See 'Kabul brings out handwritten poetic works of Khushal Khan Khattak', *Dawn* 14 Oct 2018 (online).
27. Lee (2018:60).

Chapter 37: The Tribes and the Taliban

1. Antonio Giustozzi's book *Koran, Kalashnikov and Laptop* explores the 'Neo-Taliban' and different evolutions of the movement. See Giustozzi (2007).
2. Churchill (1898:7). Another narrative, recounted to the author in 2021 by Vern Liebl, a longtime intelligence analyst and former adviser to the US military on Afghan (and Pashtun) cultural affairs, is that the genesis of the Taliban was arguably the Battle of Maiwand in 1880. Thousands of tribal *lashkar* warriors participated in this battle – with Liebl reporting that they were called *talibs*.
3. From 'Mullah Omar Obituary' by Sandy Gall, *Guardian* 30 July 2015.
4. Barfield (2012:257).
5. Ruttig (2012:102).
6. Ruttig (2010:1)
7. Ruttig (2010:2).
8. See Siddique, A. (2010) 'Taliban Violence Creating Social Revolution Among Pashtuns', *Radio Free Europe/Radio Liberty* (online).
9. Quote by Bernt Glatzer but found in Ruttig (2012:134).

Chapter 38: The Crumbling of Pashtun Tribal Structures

1. Liebl (2007:492).
2. Ruttig (2012:107).
3. Spain (1962:182).
4. See Khan (1993:151).
5. Ruttig (2010:2).
6. p.128 of Maley, W. (2009) *The Afghanistan Wars* (London: Palgrave Macmillan).
7. See Giustozzi & Ullah (2006) for an overview of these dynamics.
8. Rubin (1995:xii).
9. UNHCR figures from 'Afghanistan: the unending crisis – The biggest caseload in the world', *UNHC Refugees Magazine* Issue 108 (online).
10. Liebl (2007:503).
11. Barfield (2010:186).
12. Ruttig (2012:111).
13. There are also many historical events not covered in this book which would demonstrate the resilience of the Pashtun tribes. The Mongol invasion of Khwarezmia (1219–21) saw Ghenghis Khan's armies devastate Pashtun areas and raze Kabul, Kandahar, Jalalabad and other cities now in modern-day

Afghanistan. His son Ogedei countered rebellions in 1222 by slaughtering thousands of men in Ghazni and Helmand. In the 1380s, Tamurlane wreaked similar destruction on the Pashtun people and their irrigation infrastructure while creating his Timurid Empire. Both these examples highlight the resilience of the Pashtun tribes, as well as their ability to rebound, reknit and hold fast to *Pashtunwali*.

14. p.65 of Kakar, H.K. (1979) *Government and Society in Afghanistan. The Reign of Amir 'Abd al-Rahman Khan* (Austin, TX: University of Texas Press).
15. p.35 of Saikal, A. (2004). *Modern Afghanistan* (London: Tauris).
16. p.144 of Saikal (2004).
17. Glatzer (2002:9).
18. p.61 of Saikal, A. (2004). *Modern Afghanistan* (London: Tauris).
19. For an overview of King Amanullah Khan's various reforms, including in education, see Burki, S. (2011b) 'The Politics of *Zan* from Amanullah to Karzai', in Heath, J. & Zahedi (eds) *Land of the Unconquerable: The Lives of Contemporary Afghan Women*, pp.45–57 (USA: University of California Press)
20. Ewans (2002:129).
21. Poullada (1973:145)
22. See p.621 of Ahady (1995) 'The Decline of the Pashtuns in Afghanistan', *Asian Survey*, Vol. 35 (7), pp.621–34.
23. Gellner (1983:438)

Chapter 39: The Future of the Pashtun Tribes

1. Ending a book about Afghanistan on the thirty-ninth chapter is either a recipe for ridicule, or quite fitting in a book intended to help Westerners navigate its cultural sensitivities. The number thirty-nine carries some controversy in Afghanistan, often being linked to prostitution and being a slang term for a pimp. The story is that a famous pimp in Herat drove an expensive car with the number on its licence plate, while he conducted his business in an apartment with the same number. Now it is so stigmatized that, in Kabul and some other large cities, cars with that number lose value because of it, and residents with this unfortunate house number face frequent sniggering. Some Afghans will say they are 'one less than forty' rather than admit their real age. There was even a rumour that a warlord who ran in the 2010 Presidential election sparked a shootout after a traffic accident, when bystanders taunted him for being placed thirty-ninth on the ballot. See Boone, J (2011) 'The curse of number 39 and the steps Afghans take to avoid it' *Guardian* 15 June 2011 (online).

2. Although there have been some rare occasions when Pashtuns will even put aside internal grievances and, based on shared ancestry, unite to counter a larger threat or an external challenger – the post-2001 elections are often quoted as the modern example of this.

3. Spain (1962:107) 'They have bred poets as copiously as they have bred Warriors, and often one has been identical with the other. The memory of these poets is very much alive amongst Pathans; their descendants, disciples and imitators are held in high regard. It is easy to overlook this, for the outsider does not expect to find great literary figures amongst the nation of largely illiterate warrior tribesmen . . . Yet to ignore the great literary heritage of the Pathans and the deep poetic feeling which still exists amongst them is to miss an important part of their character.'

Select Bibliography

Ahmed, A. (1976) *Millennium and Charisma among Pathans: A Critical Essay in Social Anthropology* (London: Routledge & Kegan Paul).

Ahmed, A.S. (ed) (2007) *Islam in Tribal Societies: From the Atlas to the Indus* 1st Edition (Routledge).

Ahmed, A. (1983) 'Tribes and States in Waziristan', in Tapper, *Conflict of Tribe and State in Iran and Afghanistan* (St. Martin's Press).

Anderson, J.W. (1979) *Doing Pakhtu: Social Organization of the Ghilzai Pakhtun* (University of North Carolina).

Ansary, T. (2012) *Games without Rules: The Often Interrupted History of Afghanistan* (New York: Public Affairs).

Atayee, M. I., Shinwary, A. M., & Nader, A. J. (1979) *A dictionary of the terminology of Pashtun's tribal customary law and usages.* (Kabul: International Centre for Pashto Studies, Academy of Sciences of Afghanistan).

Barfield, T. (2010) *Afghanistan: A Cultural and Political History* (New Jersey: Princeton University Press)

Barth, F. (1959) *Political Leadership among Swat Pathans* (London: The Athlone Press)

Barth, F. (1969) 'Pathan Identity and its Maintenance' in *Ethnic Groups and Boundaries. The Social Organization of Culture Difference* (Boston: Little, Brown).

Barth, F. (1981) *Features of person and society in Swat: collected essays on Pathans* (Vol. 2) (London: Routledge & Kegan Paul).

Bellew, H. W. (1880) *The Races of Afghanistan, Being a Brief Account of the Principal Nations Inhabiting That Country* (London: Thacker, Spink and Co).

Boyle, C. A (1926) *'Naqluna': Some Pushtu Proverbs and Sayings.* (Allababab: The Pioneer Press).

Brown, E. G. (1922) *An Outline of the History of Persia during the Last Two Centuries* (Packard Humanities Institute).

Burnes, A. (1834) *Travels into Bokhara* (London: John Murray, 1834; reprint OUP 1974).

Caroe, O. (1958) *The Pathans* (London: Oxford University Press).

Chandra, S. (2005) *Medieval India: From Sultanat to the Mughals* (Har-Anand Publications).

Churchill, Winston (1898) *The Story of the Malakand Field Force 1897* (London: Longman).

Constitution (2004) 'The Constitution of Afghanistan Year 1382', *ICRC* (online).

Crooke, W. (1896) *The Tribes and Castes of the North-western Provinces and Oudh* (Calcutta: Office of the Superintendent of Government Printing).

Curtius, Q. (1946) *History of Alexander,* Volume I (transl. John Carew Rolfe) (Harvard University Press).

Dalrymple, W. (2013) *Return of a King: The Battle for Afghanistan* (London: Bloomsbury Publishing).

Dogra, R. (2017) *Durand's Curse: A Line across the Pathan Heart* (India: Rupa Publications).

Dorn, B. (1829) *History of the Afghans: Translated from the Persian of Neamet Ullah* (Reprinted in 1965 by Susil Gupta: London).

Dupree, L. (1980) *Afghanistan* (New Jersey: Princeton University Press).

Dupree, N.H (1984) 'Revolutionary Rhetoric and Afghan Women,' in Shahrani, M.N. & Canfield, R.L. (eds) *Revolutions and Rebellions in Afghanistan: Anthropological Perspectives*, (Bloomington, IN: Indiana University Press, 1984).

Edwards, D.B. (1996) *Heroes of the Age: Moral Fault Lines on the Afghan Frontier* (Berkeley: University of California Press).

Edwards, D.B (2002) *Before Taliban: Genealogies of the Afghan Jihad* (University of California Press).

Elphinstone, Mountstuart (1815) *An Account of the Kingdom of Caubul, and its Dependencies in Persia, Tartary and India: Comprising a View of the Afghaun Nation, and a History of the Dooraunee Monarchy* (London: Reprinted by Oxford University Press, 1972).

Ewans, M. (2002) *Afghanistan: A Short History of its People and its Politics* (New York: HarperCollins).

Farrall, L. (2017) 'Revisiting al-Qaida's Foundation and Early History', *Perspectives on Terrorism*, Vol. 11(6).

Ferrier, J.P (1858) *History of the Afghans in 1858* (London: Murray).

Fida, Y.S. (1955) *Afghanistan: Jirga and Loya Jirga in the Afghan Tradition (577 A.D. to 1992 A.D.)* (Reprinted in 1997 by the Aays).

Fofalzay, W.A. (1958) *Dorrat al-Zaman fi Tarikh Shah Zaman* (Kabul).

Fraser, J.B. (1834) *A Historical and Descriptive Account of Persia and Afghanistan* (Harper & Brothers).

Gankovsky, Y. (1964) *The Peoples of Pakistan* (Lahore: Publishing House).

Gellner, E. (1983) *Nations and Nationalism (New Perspectives on the Past)* (New Jersey: Wiley-Blackwell).

Giustozzi, A. & Ullah, N. (2006) 'Tribes and Warlords in Southern Afghanistan, 1980–2005', *LSE Crisis States Research Centre Working Paper No.7* (online).

Giustozzi, A. (Ed.) (2009) *Decoding the New Taliban: Insights from the Afghan Field* (New York: Columbia University).

Giustozzi, A. (2007) *Koran, Kalashnikov and Laptop: The Neo-Taliban Insurgency in Afghanistan* (London: Hurst).

Glatzer, B. (1997) 'Sword and Reason among Pashtuns: Notions of Individual Honour and Social Responsibility', *Revised version of a paper presented at the 14th European Conference on Modern South Asian Studies in Copenhagen,* August 1996 (online).

Glatzer, B. (1998) 'Being Pashtun – Being Muslim: Concepts of Person and War in Afghanistan', in *Essays on South Asian Society: Culture and Politics II* (Berlin: Das Arabische Buch).

Glatzer, B. (2000) 'The Pashtun Tribal System', in Pfeffer, G & Behera, D.K. (eds.): *Contemporary Society: Tribal Studies,* Volume 5, *Concept of Tribal Society.*

Glatzer, B. (2001) 'War and Boundaries in Afghanistan: Significance and Relativity of Local and Social Boundaries', in *Weld des Islams* (Leiden).

Glatzer, Bernt (2001) 'War and Boundaries in Afghanistan: Significance and Relativity of Local and Social Boundaries', *New Series*, Vol 41:3.

Gore, D. (2009) *Soldiers, Saints and Scallywags: Stirring Tales from Family History* (David Gore: First Edition).

Hanifi, M.J. (2004) 'Editing the Past: Colonial Production of Hegemony through the 'Loya Jerga' in Afghanistan,' *Iranian Studies* 37, no. 2.

Hanifi, S. M. (2016) 'The Pashtun Counter-Narrative', *Middle East Critique,* 25:4.

Hobsbawm, E.J. (1997) *Nations and Nationalism since 1780: Programme, Myth, Reality* (Cambridge: Cambridge University Press, Cambridge).

Holdich, T. H. (1901) *The Indian Borderland 1880–1900.* (Reprinted in 2016 by Wentworth Press).

Holt, F. (2012) *Into the Land of Bones: Alexander the Great in Afghanistan* (USA: University of California Press).

Hopkins, B.D. (2012) *The Making of Modern Afghanistan* (Palgrave).

Ibbetson, D. (1916) *Punjab Castes* (Reprinted in 2001 by Sang-e-Meel Publications).

Ibrahimi, N. (2017) *The Hazaras and the Afghan State: Rebellion, Exclusion and the Struggle for Recognition* (Hurst).

IBP (2013) Afghanistan Constitution and Citizenship Law Handboook – Strategic Information and Basic Laws (USA: International Business Publications).

Johnson, R. A. (2009) 'The 1897 Revolt and Tirah Valley Operations from the Pashtun Perspective', *Tribal Analysis Centre*, Williamsburg VA.

Kakar, P. (2004) 'Tribal Law of Pashtunwali and Women's Legislative Authority', *Harvard Islamic Legal Studies Program*.

Ker, M. & Locke, J. (2010) 'Singing in the Wilderness: Kuchi Nomads in Modern Afghanistan', *Cornell Internation Affairs Review*, 3(2).

Khan, I. (1993) *Warrior Race: Journey through the Land of the Tribal Pathans* (London: Random House).

Khan, S.M. (1900) *The Life of Abdur Rahman Amir of Afghanistan* (London: John Murray).

Khan, S. & Himayatullah (2020) 'Understanding the anti-Mughal Struggle of Khushal Khan Khattak, *Pakistan Perspectives*, Vol. 25, No.1, January–June 2020.

Lee, J. L. (1996) *The Ancient Supremacy: Bukhara, Afghanistan, and the Battle for Balkh, 1731–1901* (Brill).

Lee, J. L. (2018) *Afghanistan: A History from 1260 to the Present* (Reaktion Books).

Liebl, Vern (2007) 'Pushtuns, Tribalism, Leadership, Islam and Taliban: A Short View', *Small Wars & Insurgencies*.

Lindholm, C. (1980) 'Images of the Pathan: The Usefulness of Colonial Ethnography', *European Journal of Sociology*, Vol 21.

Lindholm, C. (1982) *Generosity and Jealousy: The Swat Pukhtun of Northern Pakistan* (Columbia University Press).

Lindholm, C. [publication date unknown] 'Respect Essential for Survival in Pashtun Culture' (online).

Manchanda, N. (2020) *The Emergency Episteme of the 'Tribe' in Afghanistan* (Cambridge University Press).

Martin, M. (2014) *An Intimate War: An Oral History of the Helmand Conflict* (London: Hurst).

Miakhel, S. (2008) 'The Importance of Tribal Structures and Pakhtunwali in Afghanistan; Their role in security and governance', in Roy, A.B. (ed) (2008) *Challenges And Dilemmas Of State-Building In Afghanistan: Reports of a Study Trip To Kabul* (Delhi: Shipra Publications).

Morgan Edwards, L. (2011) *The Afghan Solution: The Inside Story of Abdul Haq, The CIA and how Western Hubris Lost Afghanistan* (UK: Bactria Press).

Muhammad, F. (1999) *Kabul under Siege: Fayz Muhammad's Account of the 1929 Uprising* (edited and translated by McChesney R.D.) (Markus Weiner Publishers).

Noelle, C. (2012) *State and Tribe in Nineteenth-Century Afghanistan: The Reign of Amir Dost Muhammad Khan (1826–1863)* (London: Routledge).

Omrani, B. (2009) 'The Durand Line: History And Problems Of The Afghan-Pakistan Border', *Asian Affairs*, Vol. 40(2).

Partlow, J. (2016) *A Kingdom of Their Own: The Family Karzai and the Afghan Disaster* (Simon & Schuster).

Poett, N. (1991). *Pure Poett: the Autobiography of General Sir Nigel Poett* (Havertown: Pen and Sword).

Poullada, L. B. (1973) *Reform and Rebellion in Afghanistan, 1919–29: King Amanullah's Failure to Modernize a Tribal Society* (Ithaca/London, Cornell University Press).

Pressfield, S. (2007) *The Afghan Campaign* (London: Transworld Publishers).

Priestly, J. (1999) *Afghanistan and Its Inhabitants: Translated from The Hayati Afghani of Muhammad Hayat Khan*, 1874 (Sang-e-Meel Publications).

Qadir, A. (2015) *Reforming the Pukhtuns and Resisting the British: An Appraisal of the Haji Sahib Turangzai's Movement* (Islamabad: Quaid-i-Azam University).

Raverty, Major H.G. (1860) *A Grammar of the Pukht', Pushto or Language of the Afghans with Remarks on the Originality of the Language* (London: Longman, Green, Longman, and Roberts).

Robinson, J.A (1934) *Notes on Nomad Tribes of Eastern Afghanistan* (Quetta: Nisa Traders).

Rose, H.A. (1911) *A Glossary of the Tribes and Castes of the Punjab and North-West Frontier Province* (Delhi: New Asia).

Rubin, B.R. (1995) *Fragmentation of Afghanistan: State Formation and Collapse in the International System* (New Haven: University of Yale Press).

Ruttig, T. (2010) 'How Tribal Are the Taliban', *Afghanistan Analysts Network* (online).

Ruttig, T. (2012) 'How Tribal are the Taliban?'. In Bashir, S. and Crews, D. (eds) (2012) *Under the Drones: Modern Lives in the Afghanistan-Pakistan Borderlands* (USA: Harvard University Press).

Rzehak, Lutz (2011) 'Doing Pashto: Pashtunwali as the ideal of honourable behaviour and tribal life among the Pashtuns', *Afghanistan Analysts Network* (online).

Sands, C. with Qazizai, F (2019) *Night Letters: Gulbuddin Hekmatyar and the Afghan Islamists Who Changed the World* (London: Hurst).

Scheuer, M. (2002) *Through Our Enemies' Eyes: Osama Bin Laden, Radical Islam, and the Future of America* (Washington D.C: Brassey's).

Sherman, W.E.B. (2020) 'The Lost Tribes of the Afghans: Religious Mobility and Entanglement in Narratives of Afghan Origins', in Ghazvinia, J. & Frass, A.M, *American and Muslim Worlds Before 1900* (USA: Bloomsbury Academic).

Siddique, A. (2014) *The Pashtun Question: The Unresolved Key to the Future of Pakistan and Afghanistan* (London: Hurst).

Smith, S. (2019) 'Loya Jirgas and Political Crisis Management in Afghanistan: Drawing on the Bank of Tradition, *USIP Special Report*, 30 September 2019 (online).

Spain, J. (1962) *The Way of the Pathans* (Karachi: Oxford University Press).

Spain, J. (1963) *The Pathan Borderland* (The Hague: Mouton).

Sykes, P. (1940) *History of Afghanistan*, (London: Oxford).

TAC (2009d) 'The Panjpai Relationship with the other Durrani', *Tribal Analysis Center* (online).

TAC (2009f) 'Ishaqzai Tribe', *Tribal Analysis Center* (online).

Tair, M.N.T with Edwards, T.C. (1982) *Rohi Mataluna* (Pashto Academy, University of Peshawar).

Talley Stewart, R. (2000) *Fire in Afghanistan 1914–1929* (USA: Doubleday & Company).

Tariq, M.O. (2008) 'Tribal Security System (Arbakai) in Southeast Afghanistan', *Occasional Paper no.7*, Crisis States Research Centre December 2008 (online).

Tomsen, P. (2011) *The Wars of Afghanistan: Messianic Terrorism, Tribal Conflicts, and the Failures of Great Powers* (Public Affairs).

Van Linschoten, A.S & Kuehn, F. (2012) *An Enemy We Created: The Myth of the Taliban/Al-Qaeda Merger in Afghanistan, 1970–2010* (London: Hurst Publishers).

Wylly, H.C. (1912) *From The Black Mountain to Waziristan: Being An Account Of The Border Countries and The More Turbulent Of The Tribes Controlled By The North-West . . . Military Relations With Them In The Past* (Reprinted by Naval and Military Press 2009).

Yousaf, F. (2019) 'Pakistan's "Tribal" Pashtuns, Their "Violent" Representation, and the Pashtun Tahafuz Movement', *SAGE Open* (online).

Index